From Dependency to Development

Also of Interest

Food, Politics, and Agricultural Development: Case Studies in the Public Policy of Rural Modernization, edited by Raymond F. Hopkins, Donald J. Puchala, and Ross B. Talbot

Appropriate Technology for Development: A Discussion and Case Histories, edited by Donald D. Evans and Laurie Nogg Adler

Governments and Mining Companies in Developing Countries, James H. Cobbe

The New Economics of the Less Developed Countries: Changing Perceptions in the North-South Dialogue, edited by Nake Kamrany

Technology and Economic Development: A Realistic Perspective, edited by Samuel M. Rosenblatt

Protein, Calories, and Development: Nutritional Variables in the Economics of Developing Countries, Bernard A. Schmitt

Economic Development, Poverty, and Income Distribution, edited by William Loehr and John P. Powelson

A Select Bibliography on Economic Development: With Annotations, John P. Powelson

Technology and Underdevelopment, Frances Stewart

Migration and the Labor Market in Developing Countries, edited by R. H. Sabot

Credit for Small Farmers in Developing Countries, Gordon Donald

Renewable Energy Resources and Rural Applications in the Developing World, edited by Norman L. Brown

Transnational Enterprises: Their Impact on Third World Societies and Cultures, edited by Krishna Kumar

*The Challenge of the New International Economic Order, edited by Edwin P. Reubens

*Available in hardcover and paperback

Westview Special Studies in Social, Political, and Economic Development

From Dependency to Development:
Strategies to Overcome Underdevelopment and Inequality
edited by Heraldo Muñoz

Although much has been written on the concept, nature, and implications of dependency in underdeveloped countries, there is a noticeable lack of comprehensive material on dependency reversal—the ways and circumstances under which dependency and underdevelopment can be overcome. Dr. Muñoz brings together in a coherent volume the alternative strategies for dependency reversal that have been posed by leading social scientists; the emphasis is on commonalities, differences, and theoretical and practical derivations.

The book outlines the basic features of the dependency literature and clarifies the emergence and development of the dependency paradigm, its meaning, and its differences from other theoretical perspectives on underdevelopment. New aspects of dependency situations are also introduced. Significant alternatives to dependency are offered, taking into account varying geographical, ideological, and functional factors. Though no claim is made that all existing answers to development are included, this is clearly the most complete work available to date.

Heraldo Muñoz is professor and research associate at the Institute of International Studies, University of Chile. He was previously a guest scholar in the foreign policy section of the Brookings Institution.

From Dependency to Development: Strategies to Overcome Underdevelopment and Inequality

edited by Heraldo Muñoz

Westview Press / Boulder, Colorado

Westview Special Studies in Social, Political, and Economic Development

Copyright © 1981 by Westview Press, Inc.

Published in 1981 in the United States of America by
 Westview Press, Inc.
 5500 Central Avenue
 Boulder, Colorado 80301
 Frederick A. Praeger, President and Publisher

Library of Congress Cataloging in Publication Data
Main entry under title:
From dependency to development.
 (A Westview special study in social, political, and economic development)
 Bibliography: p.
 Includes index.
 1. Latin America—Economic conditions—Addresses, essays, lectures. 2. Latin America—Economic policy—Addresses, essays, lectures. 3. International economic relations—Addresses, essays, lectures. 4. Economic development—Addresses, essays, lectures. I. Muñoz, Heraldo. II. Series: Westview special study in social, political, and economic development.
HC125.F74   338.98   80-19374
ISBN 0-89158-902-3
ISBN 0-86531-079-3 (pbk.)

Printed and bound in the United States of America

10   9   8   7   6   5

Contents

Part Three
Overcoming Dependency: Selected Strategies

Tables

Preface

The idea for this book emerged during a panel discussion on dependency theory at the twentieth annual convention of the International Studies Association, held in Toronto, Canada, in March 1979. That session—headed by James Caporaso and attended by Christopher Chase-Dunn, Edmundo Fuenzalida, Gary Gereffi, W. Ladd Hollist, Theodore Moran, Arturo Valenzuela, and myself—revealed that one of the critical areas of disagreement among dependency theorists was "dependency reversal," or the ways and circumstances under which dependency and underdevelopment can be overcome. It also became clear that some of the most interesting alternative strategies were not sufficiently known or understood. This book—comprising both original and reprinted pieces—is intended to further the discussion of this subject. No claim is made that all the answers to the dependency problem have been included; only the most representative and relevant have been selected.

I wish to acknowledge the encouragement and assistance provided by William Loehr, Lynne C. Rienner, Jeanne Remington, Susan McRory, Arturo Valenzuela and Pamela Quick Muñoz. Special thanks are owed to James Caporaso, Joel Edelstein, Johan Galtung, Gustavo Lagos, Rodolfo Stavenhagen, Osvaldo Sunkel, and Behrouz Zare, all of whom contributed either original papers or revised versions of previously published works, and to Byron Blake, Fernando Henrique Cardoso, Kenneth Hall, Mahbub ul Haq, Jan Tinbergen, Arturo Valenzuela, J. Samuel Valenzuela, and Immanuel Wallerstein, who gave permission for the reprinting here of their previously published work.

Heraldo Muñoz

The Contributors

Byron Blake is director of Sectoral Policy and Planning for the CARICOM (Caribbean Community) Secretariat, Georgetown, Guyana. He also worked at the National Planning Agency in Jamaica. He is a Jamaican and was educated at the University of the West Indies, where he earned an M.Sc. in economics.

James A. Caporaso is the Andrew W. Mellon Professor of International Studies at the Graduate School of International Studies, University of Denver. He is the editor of *Comparative Political Studies* and of a special issue of *International Organization* (1978) on dependency. He is the author of numerous publications on development and international relations theory.

Fernando Henrique Cardoso is the director of the Centro Brasileiro de Análise e Planejamento, São Paulo, Brazil. He has written numerous works on development problems in Latin America and is one of the principal contributors to the dependency approach. His classical study *Dependencia y Desarrollo en América Latina* (1967), coauthored with Enzo Faletto, was published in English in 1978.

Joel C. Edelstein is an associate professor of political science at the University of Colorado at Denver. He is coeditor and an author of *Latin America: The Struggle with Dependency and Beyond* and edited "Cuba: La Revolución en Marcha," a special issue of the journal *Latin American Perspectives*. He has made five visits to Cuba since 1969 and is currently completing a book on the Cuban revolution.

Johan Galtung holds the chair in Conflict and Peace Research at the University of Oslo. He was editor of the *Journal of Peace Research* and has written numerous works on imperialism, development, and social conflict. His latest book is *The True Worlds: A Transnational Perspective* (1979).

Kenneth Hall is an associate professor of African history at the State University of New York at Oswego. He served as the director of Administration and General Services in the CARICOM Secretariat, Georgetown, Guyana. He is a Jamaican and was educated at the University of the West Indies and Queen's University at Kingston, Ontario, where he received his Ph.D. in 1971.

Mahbub ul Haq is director of the Policy Planning and Program Review Department of the World Bank. He was previously chief economist of the Pakistan Planning Commission. He is author of *The Poverty Curtain: Choices for the Third World* (1976) and other publications on development problems.

Gustavo Lagos is a professor and researcher at the Institute of International Studies of the University of Chile. He was minister of justice in the administration of Eduardo Frei. He is the author of *International Stratification and Underdeveloped Countries* (1963) and the coauthor of *Revolution of Being: A Latin American View of the Future* (1977).

Heraldo Muñoz is a professor and researcher at the Institute of International Studies of the University of Chile. He holds graduate degrees from the Catholic University of Chile and the Graduate School of International Studies of the University of Denver, where he obtained his Ph.D. in 1979. He is a former guest scholar of the Brookings Institution and has published several works on dependency and foreign policy questions.

Rodolfo Stavenhagen is assistant director-general for the Social Sciences and their Applications at UNESCO. He is the former director of the Center for Sociological Studies at El Colegio de Mexico. He has published numerous studies on development problems in Latin America, with particular emphasis on agrarian issues.

Osvaldo Sunkel is coordinator of the Economic Commission for Latin America/UN Environmental Program (ECLA/UNEP) project "Styles of Development and the Environment in Latin America," based in Santiago de Chile. He is the author of many works on Latin American development and is one of the principal dependency theorists.

Jan Tinbergen is emeritus professor of development planning at Erasmus University, Rotterdam, The Netherlands. He received the Nobel Prize in Economics in 1969. He was the coordinator of the project "Reshaping the International Order" (RIO) and is the author of numerous publications on development planning and international economics.

Arturo Valenzuela is associate professor of political science and director of the Comparative Area Studies Program, Duke University. He is the associate editor of the *Latin American Research Review*. He is the author of *Political Brokers in Chile* (1977) and *The Breakdown of Democratic Regimes: Chile* (1978).

J. Samuel Valenzuela is assistant professor of sociology at Yale University. He is a coauthor and the coeditor of *Chile: Politics and Society* (1976). He has written several works on Chilean society and labor.

Immanuel Wallerstein is the director of the Fernand Braudel Center, Department of Sociology, State University of New York at Binghamton. He is the editor of the journal *Review* and the author of *The Modern World System: Capitalist Agriculture and the Origins of the European Economy in the 16th Century* (1974).

Behrouz Zare is a graduate student at the Graduate School of International Studies of the University of Denver.

Introduction:
The Various Roads to Development

Heraldo Muñoz

Until the early 1960s, the literature on underdevelopment in Latin America and other Third World regions suggested that progress in poor areas could take place only through the spread of "modernism" originating in the developed world. One predominant line of argument portrayed underdeveloped countries as "dual societies" with backward-feudal hinterlands and progressive-capitalist metropoles.[1] Since the countryside was seen as having stagnated in a state of feudalism due to isolation from the forces of capitalism, the prescription called for the capitalist penetration of the archaic hinterland. Progress was to be diffused from the United States and Europe to the national urban centers, from the metropoles to the regional trading centers, and from these centers to their corresponding peripheries. Eisenstadt, for example, viewed the phenomenon of modernization as "the process of change towards those types of social, economic and political systems that have developed in Western Europe and North America from the seventeenth century to the nineteenth and have then spread to other European countries, and in the nineteenth and twentieth centuries to the South American, Asian and African continents."[2]

Another closely related conventional line of thought on underdevelopment argued that all societies pass through a process of economic growth involving five successive historical stages, namely, "the traditional society, the pre-conditions for the take-off, the take-off, the drive to maturity, and the age of high mass consumption."[3] The process of growth was facilitated by the intrusion—usually in the form of new technology—of more advanced societies at the stage of the "pre-conditions for take-off." As a corollary, orthodox trade theorists offered the classical advice that underdeveloped nations did not need to strive for rapid industrialization, particularly in view of the "comparative advantages" that derive from producing raw materials for export.

Yet, despite the rapid scientific-technological progress that characterized the post-war period, it became increasingly clear that periphery
countries remained in a state of underdevelopment. Moreover, some
analysts held that there was a growing inequality among and within
nation-states and, therefore, questioned the conventional wisdom on
backwardness.

Raúl Prebisch, one of the pioneers of the dependency approach,
argued that long-term weaknesses in raw materials prices negated the
beneficial results that were supposed to derive from comparative advantage. After portraying the world as divided into a developed center and
an underdeveloped periphery, Prebisch stated that the centers retain the
benefits of technological progress and expropriate increases in productivity
in exporting sectors of periphery nations through the "deteriorating
terms of trade" mechanism. The negative effects of this relationship of
exchange constituted an *external dependency* that the periphery had to
overcome in order to develop. The alternative strategy recommended by
Prebisch and his associates at the UN Economic Commission for Latin
America (ECLA) involved three elements: industrialization through import substitution, the promotion of exports of manufactures, and institutional changes in favor of underdeveloped countries at the international
level.[4]

During the mid-sixties Latin America witnessed the emergence of a
wave of writings that constituted a qualitative step forward in the discussion on underdevelopment and dependency. The works of Fernando H.
Cardoso, André Gunder Frank, Theotonio dos Santos, Osvaldo Sunkel,
and others went beyond Prebisch's perspective and interpreted the
phenomenon of *dependencia* in a holistic fashion and in terms of the
capitalist mode of production. These writers saw a structural link between domestic and external factors, with transnational capitalism as the
common denominator. In their works the key unit of analysis was not the
nation-state alone, but also social groups, classes, and multinational corporations. Emphasis was placed on historically grounded studies and in-
terdisciplinary research methods.[5]

More recently, there has been a massive proliferation of dependency
writings, particularly in the United States and other developed
countries.[6] A great difference between many of these newer writings and
the older *dependencia* analyses is that the former are often, though not
always, more interested in explaining international relations while the
latter are largely interested in explaining and solving the problem of
underdevelopment. For a good number of scholars, the problem of dependency is principally an imbalance or disparity in the power relation-

ship between two or more international actors, generally nation-states.[7] According to Cardoso, this perspective implies that "what had been an endeavor to be *critical* and to maintain the *continuity* of previous historical, economic, sociological, and political studies in Latin America was transformed into an article for consumption in various versions that include references to the original myth but in large measure constitute the expression of a quite distinct intellectual universe from that which gave it birth."[8] Clearly, the literature on dependency theory is far from homogeneous. Even if we considered only works by Latin Americans, disagreement would still be a feature of the dependency approach.[9]

One of the areas of major disagreement in the dependency perspective is how to overcome or reverse dependency and underdevelopment. The problem is not only that this is a highly controversial ideological issue, but also that there are different ways of conceptualizing dependency. For example, those who view dependency essentially as a problem of unequal power relations among states might consider a strategy of negotiating with the centers to capture a larger share of the world's resources sufficient, while for those who see dependency in a transnational perspective and as a function of the capitalist mode of production usually call for abandoning the capitalist system. In short, the practical issue of overcoming dependency and underdevelopment cannot be separated from the theoretical definition of dependency.

The analysis of dependency reversal is not a simple task. Specific differences among the countries involved might entail differences in the roads to follow. There are other problems. For instance, "abandoning the capitalist system" as a general strategy does not tell us much about what is sought and how: will the objective be participatory-democratic socialism or an authoritarian-bureaucratic brand of socialism? What "style of development" will prevail once dependency is overcome? Can self-reliance be both a transition strategy and a final objective? Does an effective alternative strategy involve solely changing socio-economic structures? What is the role of the individual? This volume attempts to address some of these questions through the exploration of the following broad strategies: negotiating with the centers, establishing a new world order, self-reliance at multiple levels, socialism at the national level, socialism at the world level, and another development.

These strategies are *not mutually exclusive*. It is perfectly conceivable that negotiating with the centers might also include the establishment of a new world order, or that socialism at the national level might be combined with a strategy of self-reliance. In other words, although for analytical purposes it is advisable to distinguish clearly among these strategies, in the real world they will most often appear in a combined form.

The first two chapters in this book deal with the basic features of the dependency perspective. They clarify the meaning of the dependency paradigm, discuss its development, and compare it to other theoretical approaches to underdevelopment.

Chapter 2 distinguishes between the modernization and dependency approaches to underdevelopment. The authors, J. Samuel Valenzuela and Arturo Valenzuela, assert that modernization and dependency are two sharply different perspectives seeking to explain the same reality: "They originated in different areas, with different evaluative judgments, different assumptions, different methodologies, and different explanations." Through a comparative analysis of dependency and modernization, Samuel and Arturo Valenzuela allow us to weigh the relative utility of these competing frameworks in explaining underdevelopment in the context of Latin America. They conclude that the dependency approach concentrates on a richer body of evidence and a broader range of phenomena and that it is also methodologically more promising than modernization.

In Chapter 3 James Caporaso and Behrouz Zare provide a general assessment of dependency theory and suggest ways in which future research might be conducted in this area. They place particular emphasis on definitional and conceptual issues and on the extent to which dependency theory has served as an adequate explanation of development. Following an argument made previously by Caporaso,[10] the authors distinguish between two different intellectual traditions embodied in the terms *dependence* and *dependency*. Dependence is conceived simply as external reliance; dependency is understood as "the process by which less developed countries are incorporated into the global capitalist system." This distinction is quite critical particularly since, as has already been suggested, different interpretations of dependency entail different solutions or alternatives to the problem. Given these considerations, Caporaso and Zare offer a provisional definition of dependency as "a structural condition in which a weakly integrated system cannot complete its economic cycle except by an exclusive (or limited) reliance on an external complement."

The next two chapters discuss newer themes in dependency theory. In Chapter 4 this editor analyzes the economic relations between Latin America and the developed countries, emphasizing the phenomenon called *strategic dependency*— a dependency of the capitalist core on the low-priced strategic minerals, cheap labor, and markets of, principally, underdeveloped societies. From this perspective, the essay postulates that, contrary to what is often asserted, the economic importance of Latin America for the centers has continued or increased substantially, particularly after the oil crisis.[11] The underlying assumption is that in order to evaluate the real importance of Latin America for the developed world, it is necessary to focus attention on the structural level to verify, for example, whether a decrease in the Latin American share of center trade necessarily implies a breakdown of the critical bonds that have historically existed between core and periphery economies to the advantage of the former.

In Chapter 5 Osvaldo Sunkel treats a theme not sufficiently explored in the dependency literature — the relationship between the environment, development styles[12] and the international system. His basic assumption is that different development styles have different consequences in terms of the utilization of resources, the degree of geographical concentration, and the incidence of wastes, pollution, and contamination. In Latin America, he asserts, the development pattern has consisted basically of the incorporation of the lifestyle of the Western industrial societies, particularly the United States. In the industrial sector this imported style has meant a concentration on the production of automobiles, consumer durables, electromechanic and electronic products, pulp and paper products, and petrochemicals; the utilization of capital- and energy (oil)-intensive technologies; and a heavy reliance on imports.

Sunkel asks whether the "transnational development style" of Latin America is sustainable over the long run and whether it can significantly improve the standard of living of the masses. Given the dependent nature of the prevailing development style, he reasons that this is not likely. However, in his view, there is no need for a moratorium on economic growth; growth has to continue in Latin America but as part of an alternative, more decentralized style of development. (This is essentially the same position adopted by Fernando Cardoso in Chapter 14.)

The remaining chapters outline different strategies to overcome dependency and underdevelopment. The first strategy, negotiating with the centers, is discussed in Chapter 6 by Mahbub ul Haq. In his view, the issue of dependency is largely an external problem of nation-states — or dependence, as Caporaso would say — and, hence, his preferred solution is to seek the creation of a New International Economic Order through negotiations between developed and underdeveloped countries. The author indicates that Third World countries do not seek a massive redistribution of past income and wealth, but "a redistribution of future growth opportunities."

Three fundamental elements are emphasized in ul Haq's strategy: first, that the central objective of what he calls "the emerging trade union of the poor nations" is to negotiate a new deal — similar to that of the United States in the 1930s — with the developed world "through the instrument of collective bargaining"; second, that the demand for a new global order should be seen as a long historical process rather than as a single time-limited negotiation; and third, that the deals to be achieved "must balance the interests of both the rich and the poor nations." Finally, he outlines some specific steps that would allow the north-south dialogue to progress fruitfully and discusses critical international areas in need of reform.

The next alternative strategy involves a profound alteration of the present world order. In Chapter 7 Gustavo Lagos argues that underdevelopment can be remedied only by implementing a "revolution of being," the worldwide replacement of the "anti-values" of the capitalist and socialist (Stalinist) societies by the "values" of a humanistic society embodied in a "new person." The revolution of being would be the antithesis of the historically dominant "revolution of having." The former emphasizes "living to be," while the latter stresses "living to have" and is shaped by the "religion of the GNP."

The transition to Lagos's *relevant utopia* would involve identifying the positive trends arising from the generalized crisis of the world of having and determining in what manner the historical agents of change or prospective actors could be supported to develop these trends. Professor Lagos also discusses some specific strategies that must supplement the grand strategy of revolution of being within the Latin American context and concludes that the preferred world would be a society in a process of permanent construction and would still undergo conflicts and change.

Chapter 8 by Jan Tinbergen also stresses the urgent need for innovation in the international socioeconomic order as the way to overcome underdevelopment and other related world problems. Professor Tinbergen suggests that the world has become increasingly interdependent and that this situation requires a *management scientific approach*. Consequently, he condemns proponents of national autonomy since today nobody can be "an onlooker to the world's drama."

Tinbergen's management scientific approach has qualitative and quantitative aspects. On the qualitative side, he argues that lower-level decisions may have significant effects on other levels and that, therefore, there is a limit to decentralization. In fact, he states that "centralization even *beyond* the national level may be necessary and the optimal social order may require centralization at the *world level*." Interestingly, this conflicts with Sunkel's advocacy of greater administrative and political decentralization for Latin America and with basic propositions of the self-reliance approach. On the qualitative side, Professor Tinbergen refers to the RIO[13] project's goal of minimizing geographical differences in welfare around the second decade of the next century. He adds that there is a need for slower material growth in the rich countries—that could be offset, at least partly, by increased nonmaterial welfare — and a need to reduce income inequality *within* countries.

In Chapter 9, Johan Galtung argues that the only viable alternative to dependency is a strategy of "self-reliance." He holds that the pursuit of self-reliance is not an isolated, single-level-of-analysis question, but that it involves numerous actors and levels, including individuals, small groups, local communities, nation-states, regions, and the world as a whole. Focusing on the most essential factors, he defines a "doctrine of self-reliance" based on a combination of "the regional, national, and local levels . . . in a three-pronged approach with the development of human beings everywhere as the goal."

For Galtung the key to the strategy of self-reliance is *to regain control over resources*: "capital, raw materials, labor and the most precious of them all: human creativity." He then identifies the principal obstacles to self-reliance and argues that "self-reliance as a method is entirely compatible with self-reliance as a goal." Paraphrasing Gandhi, Galtung concludes that "there is no road to self-reliance — self-reliance is the road."

Kenneth Hall and Byron Blake explore the problems and prospects of self-reliance at the international level in Chapter 10.[14] They analyze the premises on which regional economic arrangements operate and discuss the achievements and weaknesses of the Caribbean community (CARICOM). At the same time, they propose a number of solutions to specific problems of the community. Hall and Blake conclude that CARICOM's experience "suggests the necessity for the adoption of policies of self-reliance if the region as a whole is to overcome the constraints of development."

Historically, socialism at the national level has been one of the most complex and important strategies pursued by countries seeking to overcome dependency and underdevelopment. The next two chapters discuss this alternative.

Rodolfo Stavenhagen illustrates a fundamental *dependencia* position in Chapter 11 when he postulates that underdevelopment in the periphery is the structural product of "a specific historical process." As a result, the solution can be "nothing less than a profound transformation of all social and economic relations within the nations of Latin America, as well as a qualitative change in Latin America's external relations."

Stavenhagen holds that there is a wide consensus in the region as to the necessity of implementing major structural changes, although there is no such agreement as to the specific solutions. He thinks that the current tendencies point to three future options for Latin America: first, the continuation of dependent development (governing against the people); two, the pursuit of an autonomous capitalist development (governing *without* the people); and three, revolutionary socialism. In Stavenhagen's view, revolutionary socialism (accompanied by a new morality and a new kind of human being) is the only positive alternative to dependency, since the other two options preclude structural change. He rules out a sudden overthrow of the capitalist system in Latin American countries and believes that it will be necessary to undergo a "period of transition" to socialism, with particular political and economic strategies.

In Chapter 12 Joel Edelstein describes and analyzes the evolution of development programs in Cuba, illustrating the concrete obstacles that underdeveloped countries face in attempting to overcome dependency through socialist construction. Edelstein's paper identifies five periods in the Cuban development process: revolution for reform, transition to Marxism-Leninism, independent socialist development, communist construction, and dependent socialist development. He then analyzes each of these periods, identifying elements of continuity and change and explaining the origins and context of different policy choices. He rejects the position that Cuba has simply exchanged dependency on the United States for dependency on the Soviet Union. Nevertheless, he asserts that "although many efforts continue toward economic diversification and the multilateralization of relationships, the Cuban leadership has implicitly accepted that Cuba's path to independent socialist development must include a period of dependency." His view is that Cuba's development process will have to pass through a stage of "dependence" (meaning external reliance) in the Caporaso-Zare terminology.

Chapter 13, by Immanuel Wallerstein, suggests that dependency and underdevelopment cannot be solved within a capitalist context. Unlike Stavenhagen or Edelstein, however, Wallerstein argues that capitalism is an affair of the world-economy and not of nation-states and that, consequently, a country can reverse its dependency only to the extent that socialism is established at the *world level.*

Wallerstein criticizes some dependency writings for their lack of conceptual clarity and argues against those that equate state ownership and/or self-reliance with socialism. According to Wallerstein, when a socialist government materializes, it will not look anything like the USSR, China or Tanzania today, since socialism involves the creation of a new kind of world system, one that requires a single world government. In the meantime, we shall continue to live in a capitalist world-economy, although this does not imply, in Wallerstein's view, that there will be no changes in position within the capitalist world economy—in fact, the emergence of "semi-peripheral" states represents an example of such movement within the system.

In the final chapter Fernando Henrique Cardoso outlines an alternative to dependency based on the rejection of capitalist consumption models and on a new style of development rooted in humanist values. After enumerating the principal ills of modern civilization and some standard remedies, he asserts that the problem is not industrial civilization as such but the interests of privileged minorities in different countries. In short, for Cardoso the search for another development "should focus, without disguise, on the question of power."

Cardoso pleads for a "contemporary ideology of renewal," which may serve as a basis for another development. In a proposal similar to Lagos's "education for being," Cardoso suggests that the alternative model should be based on an education "not only *for* freedom but *in* freedom" and should entail "the search for the means to a cultural revolution." Like Lagos, Cardoso emphasizes "participatory democracy" as a fundamental component of another development. Finally he recommends that indicators should be developed to measure social equality, basic liberties, and other nonmaterial factors[15] that are vital dimensions of any well-balanced, comprehensive development style.

To conclude, let us summarize the principal similarities and differences among the chapters. First, there is a general rejection of conventional capitalist development as the answer to dependency and underdevelopment. Cardoso, Lagos, Galtung, Stavenhagen, and Wallerstein are very explicit in their rejection of the fundamental assumptions and values of the capitalist option. At the same time, there is a wide condemnation of "totalitarian socialism" as the solution to underdevelopment. Cardoso, Lagos, and Galtung are particularly clear on this point and favor models of "participatory democracy" or "democratic socialism." Second, the question of overcoming dependency and underdevelopment is conceived as more than just choosing between capitalism and socialism. Cardoso, Lagos, Sunkel, and, to a lesser degree, Galtung and Stavenhagen raise the issue of "styles of development," which has to do with utilization of resources, incidence of pollution, and a host of other matters covered under the label "quality of life." Third, the alternatives envisioned by Cardoso, Lagos, Galtung, Stavenhagen, and Sunkel deal with the economic dimension of dependency as well as with sociopolitical and cultural aspects. Tinbergen and the other contributors concentrate on the economic side of the problem but also make references to noneconomic elements. In addition, most of the contributors see dependency reversal as a process involving both the domestic and the international levels. Wallerstein places great emphasis on transformation at the world level, while ul Haq, Tinbergen, and Hall and Blake focus largely, although not exclusively, on interstate relations. Regarding *concrete* transition strategies, however, there is substantially greater disagreement. In the final analysis, there is at least one fundamental point of agreement: the urgent need to introduce profound changes at different levels of the world political economy to overcome dependency and underdevelopment.

Notes

1. See J. H. Boeke, "Dualistic Economics," in Gerald M. Meier (ed.), *Leading Issues in Economic Development: Studies in International Poverty* (New York: Oxford University Press, 1970), pp. 126–128.
2. S. N. Eisenstadt, *Modernization: Protest and Change* (Englewood Cliffs, N.J.: Prentice-Hall, 1966), p. 1.
3. W. W. Rostow, *The Stages of Economic Growth* (New York: Cambridge University Press, 1960), p. 4.
4. See Raúl Prebisch, *The Economic Development of Latin America and Its Problems* (New York: United Nations, Department of Social and Economic Affairs, 1950), and *Hacia una dinámica del desarrollo latinoamericano* (México: Fondo de Cultura Económica, 1963).
5. Further discussion of these methodological issues of dependency is provided in Chapters 2 and 3. See also Heraldo Muñoz, "Cambio y continuidad en el debate sobre la dependencia y el imperialismo," *Estudios Internacionales*, vol. 11, no. 44, Octubre-Diciembre 1978, pp. 88–138.
6. For a review of this newer literature see Heraldo Muñoz, "El análisis de la teoría de la dependencia en los centros: ejemplos de EE.UU.," *Estudios Internacionales*, vol. 12, no. 45, Enero-Marzo 1979, pp. 68–76.
7. See, for example, Harry Targ, "Global Dominance and Dependence, Post-Industrialism, and International Relations Theory," *International Studies Quarterly*, vol. 20, no. 3, September 1976; Robert A. Packenham, *Latin American Dependency Theories*, mimeo, Stanford University, July 1974; David Ray, "The Dependency Model of Latin American Underdevelopment: Three Basic Fallacies," *Journal of InterAmerican Studies and World Affairs*, vol. 15, February 1973; and Kathryn Morton, *Aid and Dependence: British Aid to Malawi* (London: Croom Helm and Overseas Development Institute, 1975).
8. Fernando Henrique Cardoso, "The Consumption of Dependency Theory in the United States," *Latin American Research Review*, vol. 12, no. 3, 1977, p. 8.
9. As a mere illustration, see the recent debate between José Serra, Fernando H. Cardoso, and Ruy Mauro Marini in *Revista Mexicana de Sociología*, vol. 40, Special Issue, 1978, pp. 9–106.
10. See James A. Caporaso, "Dependence, Dependency, and Power in the Global System: A Structural and Behavioral Analysis," *International Organization*, vol. 32, no. 1, Winter 1978, pp. 13–43.
11. On the relations between developed nations and resource-rich Third World countries after the oil crisis, see Heraldo Muñoz, "Strategic Dependency: The Relations Between Core Powers and Mineral-Exporting Periphery Countries," in

Charles W. Kegley, Jr., and Patrick J. McGowan (eds.), *The Political Economy of Foreign Policy Behavior* (Beverly Hills and London: Sage Publications, forthcoming).

12. On "styles of development" see Anibal Pinto, "Styles of Development in Latin America," *CEPAL Review*, First Semester, 1976, pp. 99–130; Marshall Wolfe, "Approaches to Development: Who Is Approaching What?" *CEPAL Review*, First Semester, 1976, pp. 131–172; and Jorge Graciarena, "Power and Development Styles," *CEPAL Review*, First Semester, 1976, pp. 173–193.

13. See Jan Tinbergen (coordinator), *Reshaping the International Order (RIO): A Report to the Club of Rome* (New York: E. P. Dutton & Co., 1976).

14. This article was also published in the International Foundation for Development Alternatives (IFDA) *Dossier*, no. 7, May 1979. The IFDA is a very interesting project, based in Nyon, Switzerland, which seeks the participation of institutions, groups and individuals in the elaboration of a United Nations development strategy for the 1980s and beyond. For more detail see, "A Project Description," Nyon, Switzerland, January 1978.

15. Although not sufficient in terms of measuring nonmaterial factors of development, the relatively new Physical Quality of Life Index (PQLI) and Disparity Reduction Rate (DRR) are good complements to conventional development indicators like per capita GNP and rate of growth of GNP. For an extensive discussion of these concepts see Morris D. Morris, *Measuring the Condition of the World's Poor: The Physical Quality of Life Index* (New York: Pergamon Press for the Overseas Development Council, January 1979), and James P. Grant, *Disparity Reduction Rates in Meeting Basic Needs* (Washington, D.C.: Overseas Development Council, September 1978). On this same issue one should consider the work of the United Nations University Project, "Goals, Processes, and Indicators of Development," based in Geneva, Switzerland.

Part One
The Scope and Aim of
Dependency Theory

2
Modernization and Dependency: Alternative Perspectives in the Study of Latin American Underdevelopment

J. Samuel Valenzuela
Arturo Valenzuela

The end of World War II marked the beginning of fundamental trans-formations in world affairs. The defeat of the Axis powers and the devastating toll which the war had exacted on Britain and the European allies propelled the United States into a position of economic and military preeminence. However, the United States' power did not go un-challenged. The Soviet Union was able to influence the accession of power of socialist regimes throughout Eastern Europe and Chinese Com-munists defeated their Western-backed adversaries to gain control of the most populous nation on earth. These events called for an urgent strategy to revitalize the economies of the Western nations. With massive U.S. public and private economic investment, Western Europe and Japan soon recovered from the ravages of war.

But World War II ushered in another important change whose global implications would not be felt for some years to come. The weakening of the European powers and the logic of a war effort aimed at preserving self-determination marked the final collapse of the vast colonial empires of the nineteenth century and the establishment of a multiplicity of states each claiming sovereign and independent status. The "new nations" soon drew the attention of U.S. policymakers concerned with the claim that Marxism presented the best and most logical road to full incorporation into the modern world. They also captured the attention and imagination

Reprinted with permission of the City University of New York from *Comparative Politics*, vol. 10, no. 4, July 1978, pp. 535–557.

of U.S. scholars who, in the pursuit of knowledge, as well as the desire to influence government policy, began to produce a vast literature on the "developing" nations. For many economists the solution was another Marshall plan designed for the Third World. But other social scientists argued that fundamental differences between the developmental experience of Europe and the less-developed countries mitigated against the success of such a strategy. It was not simply a matter of reconstruction but one of development and, as such, a fundamental question needed answering before policy recommendations could be advanced: Why was there such a stark contrast in the developmental experience of a few Western countries and most of the rest of the world?

The answer to this question led to the development of the "modernization perspective." Elaborated by a few economists and by anthropologists, sociologists, and political scientists, this perspective argued that it was essential to consider the cultural characteristics of "new" nations in determining their potential for development. These "noneconomic" factors became the cornerstone of a conceptual framework which would influence the U.S. response to the Third World.[1] Though "Latin Americanists" did not write the major theoretical or conceptual works of the modernization literature, that perspective soon became the dominant approach influencing the methodology and conclusions of the most important and trend-setting studies.

U.S. scholars, however, were not the only ones preoccupied with the difficulties of applying neoclassical economic assumptions to the developmental problems of Latin America. In international agencies, notably the United Nations Economic Commission for Latin America (ECLA), and university research centers, Latin American social scientists tried to come to grips with the widespread economic stagnation which affected the region in the postwar period. Working separately, often with little communication, scholars in various disciplines soon turned to the broader and more basic question of the roots of Latin American underdevelopment. Many intellectual strands came together in the 1960s with the elaboration of a more general and comprehensive conceptual framework. The "dependency perspective" became the dominant approach in most Latin American intellectual circles by the mid to late 1960s.

It is revealing that the most important writings of the "dependency perspective" still have not been translated into English, over a decade after the first mimeographed drafts began to circulate in Santiago. Dependency analysis became known in the United States and Europe not through the writings of Latin Americans but through interpreters such as André Gunder Frank whose work differs substantially from that of important authors in the field such as F. H. Cardoso, O. Sunkel, and T. dos Santos.[2]

Modernization and dependency are two sharply different perspectives seeking to explain the same reality. They originated in different areas, with different evaluative judgments, different assumptions, different methodologies, and different explanations.[3] The purpose of this review essay is not to describe the origins of the two perspectives, their "extra scientific" elements, but to compare their conceptual approaches to the study of Latin America. As such, it will be necessary to consider the two perspectives as "ideal types," accentuating important characteristics of each framework in a manner not found in any particular author. There is a good deal of variety and several polemics (particularly in the dependency literature) stemming from disagreements over the emphasis given to key elements of the conceptual framework, the operationalization of concepts, and the way in which certain processes occur empirically. Though the essay will mention some of the controversies within each perspective, its purpose is to draw broad comparisons and to provide some judgment as to the relative unity of these competing frameworks in explaining Latin American underdevelopment.

The Modernization Perspective

This review will examine the modernization perspective's conceptual framework by drawing on the work of some of its most important authors, and then illustrate the use of that framework in the study of Latin America. This format is dictated by the fact, noted earlier, that specialists on Latin America failed to contribute important theoretical efforts to the field.[4] Though there are several explanations for this failure, one of the most compelling is that Latin America's close (particularly cultural) ties to the West made it more difficult, by contrast with Asia and Africa, to point to obvious differences with the European experience. Indeed, the early theorizing made a distinction between Western and non-Western experiences, and, as J. Martz noted, "the Latin Americanist inevitably wondered if his own region was included."[5] That fact, however, did not prevent students of Latin America from drawing extensively on the modernization literature to interpret Latin American development.

Assumptions

The basic building blocks of the modernization perspective are parallel tradition-modernity ideal types of social organization and value systems, distinctions borrowed from nineteenth-century sociology.[6] Since societies are understood to move from tradition to modernity, the ideal typical dichotomy constitutes the polar ends of an evolutionary continuum, though at some point incremental changes give way to the qualitative jump into modernity. The location of this point is unclear; and yet, Third World countries, including those of Latin America, are perceived to be below the threshold of modernity, with a preponderance of traditional features.

The specific elements included in the two polarities vary substantially in the literature. The traditional society is variously understood as having a predominance of ascriptive, particularistic, diffuse, and affective patterns of action, an extended kinship structure with a multiplicity of functions, little spatial and social mobility, a deferential stratification system, mostly primary economic activities, a tendency toward autarchy of social units, an undifferentiated political structure, with traditional elitists and hierarchical sources of authority, etc. By contrast, the modern society is characterized by a predominance of achievement; universalistic, specific, and neutral orientations and patterns of action; a nuclear family structure serving limited functions; a complex and highly differentiated occupational system; high rates of spatial and social mobility; a predominance of secondary economic activities and production for exchange; the institutionalization of change and self-sustained growth; highly differentiated political structures with rational legal sources of authority; and so on.[7]

The literature assumes that the values, institutions, and patterns of action of traditional society are both an expression and a cause of underdevelopment and constitute the main obstacles in the way of modernization. To enter the modern world, underdeveloped societies have to overcome traditional norms and structures opening the way for social, economic, and political transformation. For some authors modernization derives from a greater differentiation of societal functions, institutions, and roles and the development of new sources of integration. For others, modernization is based more on the actual transformation of individuals through their assimilation of modern values.[8] But in general, the primary source of change is discussed in terms of innovations, that is, the rejection of procedures related to traditional institutions, together with the adoption of new ideas, techniques, values, and organizations. Innovations are pursued by innovators and the group that assumes this role inevitably clashes with defenders of the old order. The struggle is over two different ways of life.[9]

In describing the assumptions of the modernization literature, it is important to note that the modern pole of the parallel ideal types is the pivotal conceptual and analytical point because it best approximates the characteristics that societies must attain in order to develop. The traditional end of the dichotomy is largely a residual category, established by logical opposition to the modern end. In turn, the basic features of the modern pole are derived from characteristics attributed to those countries already considered modern. Moreover, since in the process of modernization all societies will undergo by and large similar changes, the history of the presently modern nations is taken as the source of universally useful conceptualization. Thus, as historian C. Black notes, "Although the problems raised by generalizations from a rather narrow base (the now modern countries) must be acknowledged, the definition of modernity takes the form of a set of characteristics believed to be applicable to all societies. This conception of modernity, when thought of as a model or ideal type, may be used as a yardstick with which to measure any society."[10] G. Almond adds that to study modernization in the non-Western areas the political scientist needs to "master the model of the modern, which in turn can only be derived from the most careful empirical and formal analysis of the function of the modern Western polities."[11]

These assumptions are logically consistent with the view that the impetus to modernize in the now developed countries was the result of endogenous cultural and institutional transformations, while change in the late developers results primarily from exogenous stimuli, that is, the diffusion of modern values and institutions from the early modernizers. Modernizing Third World elites are understood to be guided by the Western model, adopting and adapting its technology; assimilating its values and patterns of action; importing its financial, industrial, and educational institutions; and so on. Western colonialism, foreign aid, foreign educational opportunities, overseas business investments, the mass media, etc., are all important channels for the transmission of modernity. For some writers this means that the world is converging toward a uniform and standardized culture resembling that of the United States and Western Europe.[12]

Though, as will be noted below, there is disagreement on the extent to which traditional features will disappear, there is broad agreement on the notion that individual developing countries must in some way replicate the path followed by the early modernizers. The principal difference between already developed countries and developing ones is not in the nature of the process, but in the speed and intensity making it possible for the late modernizers to "skip stages" or "telescope time."[13] Despite the fact that the modernization perspective stresses the importance of the worldwide context in its analysis of social change, the basic historical setting for modernization is the nation state. As Black notes, "Societies in the process of modernization must . . . be considered both as *independent* entities, the traditional institutions of which are being adapted to modern functions, and also as societies under the influence of many *outside* forces."[14] The world is fragmented, and yet bound by intersocietal communication. It is, in the words of Dankwart Rustow, a "world of nations."[15]

Finally, it is clear that the stress on the differences in values from one context to another has some important implications for the modernization perspective's concept of human nature. The characteristic of developed societies which has received the most attention in the literature is the presumed "rationality" of both leaders and followers. Indeed, W. Moore has recently argued that modernization is best understood as "the process of rationalization of social behavior and social organization." Rationalization, or the "institutionalization of rationality," is defined as the "normative expectation that objective information and rational calculus of procedures will be applied in pursuit or achievement of any utilitarian goal. . . . It is exemplified but not exhausted in the use of sophisticated technology in construction and production."[16] As such, modernization theorists agree with the assumption of economic rationality implicit in the economic growth models of traditional economic theory. But as Moore noted in a 1950s article, where they differ with traditional economics is in the assumption that rational behavior is a universal human characteristic. By contrast with the developed countries, attitudes and values in developing nations are such that individuals "behave in ways that are 'irrational' or 'non-rational' as judged on economic grounds."[17] This explains why Bolivian businessmen will not take risks with their capital, preferring to put money in Swiss banks. Or why Ecuadorians will study law rather than enter a more lucrative career in business or technology.

In concluding this section it is necessary to note that from the very outset certain elements of the modernization perspective came into criticism from scholars who shared its basic assumptions. It is revealing that much of the criticism came from researchers who were experts in many of the features of individual "traditional" societies. They were uncomfortable with the arbitrary designation of a wide variety of phenomena as "traditional," with little concern for the rich, complex, and often strikingly different characteristics subsumed under that vague concept. They argued that many belief systems and institutional arrangements with no common referent in the United States or Western Europe could indeed have modernizing functions. J. Gusfield has summarized many of the relevant arguments adding that even in modern societies certain traditional characteristics may survive or gain renewed importance.[18] These arguments do not, however, constitute a rejection of the assumptions of the modernization perspective but an illustration of their use. Despite the title of his article, Gusfield does not argue that tradition and modernity are "misplaced polarities." Gusfield simply points to a confusion in the use of terms and their misapplication in concrete situations. He continues to accept the assumptions that tradition and modernity are valid theoretical polarities and that tradition in its many ramifications is the basic obstacle to modernization. If a particular society or region experiences significant economic growth, what was thought to be an other-worldly religion undermining rational economic behavior may in fact be a creed capable of promoting instrumental values conducive to modernization. There can be a "modernity of tradition."[19]

Recent amendments to the modernization perspective are extensions of the same internal critique. Reflecting the sobering reality of the 1970s, with many studies pointing to an ever increasing gap between rich and poor nations,[20] several modernization writers have questioned the earlier belief in an inevitable and uniform process leading to the convergence of societies on economic as well as social and political grounds.[21] Others, while not questioning the inevitability of the process, point more forcefully than before to its disruptive and negative effects which affect the "latecomers" much more seriously than the "survivors."[22] It still remains the case that to modernize, however good or inevitable that process may be, it is by definition necessary to overcome traditional values and institutions and substitute for them more modern ones.

Latin America and the Modernization Perspective

Mainstream U.S. scholarship on Latin America has implicitly or explicitly drawn on the modernization perspective to explain Latin American underdevelopment. Often contrasting the Latin American experience to that of the United States or Western Europe, it has argued that traditional attitudes and institutions stemming from the colonial past have proven to be serious, if not fatal, stumbling blocks to any indigenous effort to develop economically, socially, or politically. The values of Catholicism, of large Indian populations, or of aristocratic rural elites have contributed to "irrational" patterns of behavior highly detrimental to modernization.

One of the most influential statements is S. M. Lipset's "Values, Education and Entrepreneurship," the introductory essay to the best-selling text *Elites in Latin America*. Lipset draws directly from T. Parsons and D. McClelland in arguing that:

> The relative failure of Latin American countries to develop on a scale comparable to those of North America or Australasia has been seen as, in some

part, a consequence of variations in value systems dominating these two areas. The overseas offspring of Great Britain seemingly had the advantage of values derivative in part from the Protestant Ethic and from the formation of "New Societies" in which feudal ascriptive elements were missing. Since Latin America, on the other hand is Catholic, it has been dominated for centuries by ruling elites who created a social structure congruent with feudal social values.[23]

In his article Lipset concentrates primarily on explaining economic underdevelopment as a function of the lack of adequate entrepreneurial activity. The lack of instrumental behavior, weak achievement orientations, and the disdain for the pragmatic and material have prevented the rise of a risk-taking business sector oriented toward rational competitive and bureaucratic enterprise. The educational system has only served to perpetuate the problem by continuing to socialize the population with inappropriate attitudes. "Even [in Argentina] the second most developed Latin American country . . . the traditional landed, aristocratic disdain for manual work, industry, and trading, continues to affect the educational orientations of many students."[24] Lipset cites a whole host of studies, many of which were based on survey research in Latin America, to conclude that "the comparative evidence from the various nations of the Americas sustains the generalization that cultural values are among the major factors which affect the potentiality for economic development."[25] Recent textbooks on Latin America have clearly been influenced by such observations. Thus R. Adie and G. E. Poitras note that "there is in Latin America a social climate in which the very rewards which have spurred on the entrepreneurs in, for example, North America, are consistently deemphasised . . . socioeconomic change dependent on business activities . . . cannot necessarily be expected to follow the same path as it has elsewhere."[26]

The late K. H. Silvert, one of the leading authorities on Latin America, wrote extensively on the impact of traditional values not only on Latin America's economic but also its political performance. He made it very clear that Latin America's experience had to be judged by the more advanced countries. In a recently reprinted article he asked, "What else is one to do other than define development by the selection of certain characteristics of the already developed states?" On the basis of implicit comparisons with his own society, Silvert goes on to say that "there is something in the quality of the Latin American man and his culture which has made it difficult for him to be truly modern . . . which has made this part of the Western world so prone to excesses of scoundrels, so politically irrational in seeking economic growth, and so ready to reach for gimmicks."[27] Judgments such as those led him to argue, during the heyday of the Alliance for Progress, that the United States should "tip the domestic political scales" in the direction of "modernizing groups." "Moneys spent on the kind of education, for instance, which will attract persons of a modern mentality can be confidently expected to assist the general move toward development. Moneys spent in bettering or certifying the positions of students of a traditional cast will only make more robust the anti-development sectors. . . . If help can be extended to the attitudinally developed in such countries, then it should be done. Otherwise assistance merely certifies nondevelopment or invites unpredictable revolution."[28]

Similar sentiments are expressed by R. Scott, another prominent Latin Americanist. Scott notes that the "inability of Latin America's political structures to act as efficient integrating mechanisms . . . suggests that the only real solution in the long run is to alter the value system of the people."[29] A recent text echoes that theme: "A traditional psychocultural world does indeed predominate in Latin America. . . . To depict collective attitudes and value traits as basically traditional does help to explain much of political life south of the Rio Grande. . . ."[30]

The assumption that the key to Latin American society can be found in its cultural values is not only characteristic of the literature of the 1960s and of a rash of new textbooks aimed at the college market,[31] it has also found renewed currency in the writings of a number of U.S. historians and political scientists. In what has become known as the "new corporatism," an effort is being made to explain economic, social, and especially political features of Latin American countries by stressing the durability of Catholic and "Thomistic" values. Authoritarian political patterns, corporativist economic organizations, and the disdain for democratic and liberal values are the results of a "distinct tradition." H. Wiarda, a prominent representative of this "new" trend in the literature, has argued, "largely untouched by the great revolutionary movements — social, economic, religious, political, intellectual — that we associate with the emergence of the modern order, the Iberic and Latin American nations remained locked in this traditional pattern of values and institutions that postponed and retarded development."[32]

Wiarda maintains that the focus on Latin American corporatism represents a significant departure from the modernization school. He bases his claim on the fact that he stresses the importance of studying Latin America on its "own terms," without advocating the desirability or inevitability of change along United States or Western European lines. He thus questions the convergence thesis noting that "many traditional societies, and particularly those of the Iberic Latin nations, have proved remarkably permeable and flexible, assimilating at various points more 'modern' and 'rational' elements, but without losing their characteristics."[33] But this position differs little from the well-established "modernity of tradition" argument referred to earlier. Wiarda merely provides an example of the concrete application of the tradition-modernity dichotomy to the Latin American case; he does not question the basic assumptions of the perspective. The impressive examples of economic development which have occurred from time to time in Latin America are simply due to the adaptability of some traditional values and institutions to outside influences. And yet, however remarkable the "permeability" of tradition in Latin America, it is implicit in Wiarda's argument that it has been the exception rather than the rule. Otherwise, Latin America would not have fallen behind in the road of development.

The Dependency Perspective

Like the modernization perspective, the dependency perspective resulted from the work of many different scholars in different branches of the social sciences. Much of the work proceeded in an inductive fashion. This was the case with economists working in ECLA who first sought to explain the underdevelopment of Latin America by focusing on the unequal terms of trade between exporters of raw materials and exporters of manufactured goods. ECLA "doctrine" called for a concerted effort to diversify the export base of Latin American countries and accelerate industrialization efforts through import substitution. However, the continued difficulties with that model of development soon led to a focus on the internal constraints to industrialization, with an emphasis on factors such as the distorting effects of unequal land tenure patterns and the corrosive results of an inflation best explained by structural rather than monetary variables. Soon these two trends came together when scholars, such as Osvaldo Sunkel, combined the early emphasis on external variables with the internal constraints to development.[34]

But this dependency perspective was anticipated by Latin American historians who had been working for years on various aspects of economic history. Studies such as those of Sergio Bagú stressed the close interrelation of domestic developments in Latin America and developments in metropolitan countries. And in Brazil, sociologists such as Florestan Fernandes, Octavio Ianni, Fernando Henrique Cardoso, and Theotonio dos Santos also turned to broad structural analyses of the factors of underdevelopment. The fact that many of these scholars found themselves in Santiago in the 1960s only contributed to further development of the perspective.

In its emphasis on the expansive nature of capitalism and in its structural analysis of society, the dependency literature draws on Marxist insights and is related to the Marxist theory of imperialism. However, its examination of processes in Latin America implies important revisions in classical Leninist formulations, both historically and in light of recent trends. The focus is on explaining Latin American underdevelopment, and not on the functioning of capitalism, though some authors argue that their efforts will contribute to an understanding of capitalism and its contradictions.

Assumptions

The dependency perspective rejects the assumption made by modernization writers that the unit of analysis in studying underdevelopment is the national society. The domestic cultural and institutional features of Latin America are in themselves simply not the key variables accounting for the relative backwardness of the area, though, as will be seen below, domestic structures are certainly critical intervening factors. The relative presence of traditional and modern features may, or may not, help to differentiate societies: but it does not in itself explain the origins of modernity in some contexts and the lack of modernity in others. As such, the tradition-modernity polarity is of little value as a fundamental working concept. The dependency perspective assumes that the development of a national or regional unit can only be understood in connection with its historical insertion into the worldwide political-economic system which emerged with the wave of European colonizations of the world. This global system is thought to be characterized by the unequal but combined development of its different components. As Sunkel and Paz put it:

> Both underdevelopment and development are aspects of the same phenomenon, both are historically simultaneous, both are linked functionally and, therefore, interact and condition each other mutually. This results . . . in the division of the world between industrial, advanced or "central" countries, and underdeveloped, backward or "peripheral" countries. . . .[35]

The center is viewed as capable of dynamic development responsive to internal needs, and as the main beneficiary of the global links. On the other hand, the periphery is seen as having a reflex type of development, one which is both constrained by its incorporation into the global system and which results from its adaptation to the requirements of the expansion of the center. As Theotonio dos Santos indicates:

> Dependency is a situation in which a certain number of countries have their economy conditioned by the development and expansion of another . . .

placing the dependent countries in a backward position exploited by the
dominant countries.[36]

It is important to stress that the process can be understood only by
reference to its historical dimension and by focusing on the total network
of social relations as they evolve in different contexts over time. For this
reason dependence is characterized as "structural, historical and totaliz-
ing" or an "integral analysis of development."[37] It is meaningless to
develop, as some social scientists have, a series of synchronic statistical indicators to establish relative levels of dependence or independence
among different national units to test the "validity" of the model.[38] The
unequal development of the world goes back to the sixteenth century
with the formation of a capitalist world economy in which some countries in the center were able to specialize in industrial production of
manufactured goods because the peripheral areas of the world which
they colonized provided the necessary primary goods, agricultural and
mineral, for consumption in the center. Contrary to some assumptions in
economic theory the international division of labor did not lead to
parallel development through comparative advantage. The center states
gained at the expense of the periphery. But, just as significantly, the different functions of center and peripheral societies had a profound effect
on the evolution of internal social and political structures. Those which
evolved in the periphery reinforced economies with a narrow range of
primary exports. The interdependent nature of the world capitalist
system and the qualitative transformations in that system over time make
it inconceivable to think that individual nations on the periphery could
somehow replicate the evolutionary experience of the now developed nations.[39]

It follows from an emphasis on global structural processes and variations in internal structural arrangements that contextual variables, at
least in the long run, shape and guide the behavior of groups and individuals. It is not inappropriate attitudes which contribute to the
absence of entrepreneurial behavior or to institutional arrangements
reinforcing underdevelopment. Dependent, peripheral development produces an opportunity structure such that personal gain for dominant
groups and entrepreneurial elements is not conducive to the collective
gain of balanced development. This is a fundamental difference with
much of the modernization literature. It implies that dependence
analysts, though they do not articulate the point explicitly, share the
classical economic theorists' view of human nature. They assume that individuals in widely different societies are capable of pursuing rational
patterns of behavior; able to assess information objectively in the pursuit

of utilitarian goals. What varies is not the degree of rationality, but the structural foundations of the incentive systems which, in turn, produce different forms of behavior given the same process of rational calculus. It was not attitudinal transformations which generated the rapid industrialization which developed after the Great Depression, but the need to replace imports with domestic products. Or, as Cardoso points out in his studies of entrepreneurs, it is not values which condition their behavior as much as technological dependence, state intervention in the economy, and their political weakness vis-à-vis domestic and foreign actors.[40] What appear as anomalies in the modernization literature can be accounted for by a focus on contextual processes in the dependence literature.

It is necessary to underscore the fact that dependency writers stress the importance of the "way internal and external structural components are connected" in elaborating the structural context of underdevelopment. As such, underdevelopment is not simply the result of "external constraints" on peripheral societies, nor can dependency be operationalized solely with reference to clusters of external variables.[41] Dependency in any given society is a complex set of associations in which the external dimensions are determinative in varying degrees and, indeed, internal variables may very well reinforce the pattern of external linkages. Historically it has been rare for local interests to develop on the periphery which are capable of charting a successful policy of self-sustained development. Dominant local interests, given the nature of class arrangements emerging from the characteristics of peripheral economies, have tended to favor the preservation of rearticulation of patterns of dependency in their interests.

It is also important to note that while relations of dependency viewed historically help to explain underdevelopment, it does not follow that dependent relations today necessarily perpetuate across the board underdevelopment. With the evolution of the world system, the impact of dependent relations can change in particular contexts. This is why Cardoso, in studying contemporary Brazil, stresses the possibility of "associated-dependent development," and Sunkel and Fuenzalida are able to envision sharp economic growth among countries most tied into the contemporary transnational system.[42] Because external-internal relations are complex, and because changes in the world system over time introduce new realities, it is indispensable to study comparatively concrete national and historical situations. As Aníbal Quijano says, "The relationships of dependency . . . take on many forms. The national societies in Latin America are dependent, as is the case with the majority of the Asian, African and some European countries. However, each case does not present identical dependency relations."[43] The dependency perspective has thus concentrated on a careful historical evaluation of the similarities and differences in the "situations of dependency" of the various Latin American countries over time, implying careful attention to "preexisting conditions" in different contexts.[44]

The description of various phases in the world system and differing configurations of external-internal linkages follow from this insistence on diachronic analysis and its application to concrete cases. The dependency perspective is primarily a historical model with no claim to "universal validity." This is why it has paid less attention to the formulation of precise theoretical constructs, such as those found in the modernization literature, and more attention to the specification of historical phases which are an integral part of the framework.

The dependency literature distinguishes between the "mercantilistic" colonial period (1500–1750), the period of "outward growth" dependent on primary exports (1750–1914), the period of the crisis of the "liberal model" (1914–1950), and the current period of "transnational capitalism."

As already noted, because of the need for raw materials and foodstuffs for the growing industrialization of England, Germany, the United States, and France, Latin American productive structures were aimed from the outset at the export market. During the colonial period, the economic specialization was imposed by the Iberian monarchies. As Bagú notes in his classic study, "Colonial production was not directed by the needs of national consumers, and not even by the interests of local producers. The lines of production were structured and transformed to conform to an order determined by the imperial metropolis. The colonial economy was consequently shaped by its complementary character. The products that did not compete with those of Spain or Portugal in the metropolitan, international or colonial markets, found tolerance or stimulus. . . ."[45] During the nineteenth century, exports were actively pursued by the politically dominant groups. The independence movement did not attempt to transform internal productive structures; it was aimed at eliminating Iberian interference in the commercialization of products to and from England and northern Europe. The logic of the productive system in this period of "outwardly directed development," in ECLA's terms, was not conducive to the creation of a large industrial sector. Economic rationality, not only of individual entrepreneurs but also of the system, dictated payments in kind and/or extremely low wages and/or the use of slavery, thus markedly limiting the internal market. At the same time, the accumulation of foreign exchange made relatively easy the acquisition of imported industrial products. Any expansion of exports was due more to political than economic factors and depended on a saleable export commodity, and plenty of land and labor, for its success.

There were, however, important differences between regions and countries. During the colonial period these are attributable to differences in colonial administrations, natural resources, and types of production. During the nineteenth century a key difference was the degree of local elite control over productive activities for export. Though in all countries elites controlled export production initially (external commercialization was mainly under foreign control), towards the end of the century in some countries control was largely relinquished to foreign exploitation. Where this occurred, the economic role of local elites was reduced considerably, though the importance of this reduction varied depending both on the degree to which the foreign enclave displaced the local elite from the export sector and the extent to which its economic activities were diversified. Concurrently, the state bureaucracy expanded and acquired increasing importance through regulations and taxation of the enclave sector. The state thus became the principal intermediary between the local economy and the enclave, which generally had little *direct* internal secondary impact. Other differences, especially at the turn of the century, are the varying importance of incipient industrialization, the size and importance of middle- and working-class groups, variations in export products, natural resources, and so on.[46]

The world wars and the depression produced a crisis in the export-oriented economies through the collapse of external demand, and therefore of the capacity to import. The adoption of fiscal and monetary policies aimed at supporting the internal market and avoiding the negative effects of the external disequilibrium produced a favorable climate for the growth of an industrial sector under national auspices. The available foreign exchange was employed to acquire capital goods to substitute imports of consumer articles.[47] The early successes of the transition to what ECLA calls "inwardly directed development" depended to a large extent on the different political alliances which emerged in the various national settings, and on the characteristics of the social and political structures inherited from the precrisis period.

Thus, in the enclave situations the earliest developments were attained in Mexico and Chile, where middle- and lower-class groups allied in supporting state development policies, ultimately strengthening the urban bourgeoisie. The alliance was successful in Chile because of the importance of middle-class parties which emerged during the final period of export-oriented development, and the early consolidation of a trade union movement. The antecedents of the Mexican situation are to be found in the destruction of agricultural elites during the revolution. Such structural conditions were absent in other enclave situations (Bolivia, Peru, Venezuela, and Central America) where the internal development phase began later under new conditions of dependence, though in some cases with similar political alliances (Bolivia, Venezuela, Guatemala, Costa Rica). Throughout the crisis period agrarian-based and largely nonexporting groups were able to remain in power, appealing in some cases to military governments, and preserving the political scheme that characterized the export-oriented period.

In the nonenclave situations, considerable industrial growth was attained in Argentina and Brazil. In the former, export-oriented agrarian entrepreneurs had invested considerably in production for the internal market and the contraction of the export sector only accentuated this trend. In Brazil the export-oriented agrarian groups collapsed with the crisis and the state, as in Chile and Mexico, assumed a major developmental role with the support of a complex alliance of urban entrepreneurs, nonexport agrarian elites, popular sectors, and middle-class groups. In Colombia the export-oriented agrarian elites remained in power and did not foster significant internal industrialization until the 1950s.[48]

The import substituting industrialization attained greatest growth in Argentina, Brazil, and Mexico. It soon, however, reached its limits, given the parameters under which it was realized. Since capital goods for the establishment of industrial parks were acquired in the central nations, the success of the policy ultimately depended on adequate foreign exchange supplies. After reaching maximum growth through the accumulation of foreign exchange during the Second World War, the industrialization programs could only continue — given the available political options — on the basis of an increased external debt and further reliance on foreign investments. This accumulation of foreign reserves permitted the success of the national-populist alliances in Argentina and Brazil, which gave the workers greater welfare while maintaining investments. The downfall of Perón and the suicide of Vargas symbolized the end of this easy period of import substitution.

But the final blow to "import substitution" industrialization came not from difficulties in the periphery but further transformations in the center which have led, in Sunkel's term, to the creation of a new "transnational" system. With rapid economic recovery the growing multinational corporations sought new markets and cheaper production sites for their increasingly technological manufacturing processes. Dependency consequently acquired a "new character," as dos Santos noted, which would have a profound effect on Latin America. Several processes were involved, resulting in (1) the investment of centrally based corporations in manufactures within the periphery for sales in its internal market or, as Cardoso and Faletto note, the "internationalisation of the internal market"; (2) a new international division of labor in which the periphery acquires capital goods, technology, and raw materials from the central nations, and export profits, along with its traditional raw materials and a few manufactured items produced by multinational subsidiaries; and (3) a denationalization of the older import substituting industries established originally.[49] Although the "new dependence" is in evidence throughout the continent, the process has asserted itself more clearly in the largest internal markets such as Brazil, where the weakness of the trade-union movement (the comparison with Argentina in this respect is instructive) coupled with authoritarian political structures has created a singularly favorable investment climate.

In subsequent and more recent works writers in the dependency framework have pursued different strategies of research. Generally speaking, the early phases of the historical process have received less attention, though the contribution of I. Wallerstein to an understanding of the origins of the world system is a major addition to the literature.[50] Most writers have preferred to focus on the current "new situation" of dependence. Some have devoted more attention to an effort at elaborating the place of dependent capitalism as a contribution to the Marxist analysis of capitalist society. Scholars in this vein tend to argue more forcefully than others that dependent capitalism is impossible and that socialism provides the only historically viable alternative.[51] Others have focused more on the analysis of concrete cases of dependence, elaborating in some detail the various interconnections between domestic and foreign forces, and noting the possibility of different kinds of dependent development.[52] Still others have turned their attention to characterizing the nature of the new capitalist system, with particular emphasis on the emergence of a "transnational system" which is rendering more complex and problematic the old distinctions of center and periphery.[53] Particularly for the last two tendencies, the emphasis is on the design of new empirical studies while attempting to systematize further some of the propositions implicit in the conceptual framework.

Summary and Conclusions

Modernization and dependency are two different perspectives each claiming to provide conceptual and analytical tools capable of explaining the relative underdevelopment of Latin America. The object of inquiry is practically the only thing that these two competing "visions" have in common, as they differ substantially not only on fundamental assumptions, but also on methodological implications and strategies for research.

Though there are variations in the literature, the *level of analysis* of a substantial tradition in the modernization perspective, and the one which informs most reflections on Latin America, is behavioral or microsociological. The primary focus is on individuals or aggregates of individuals, their values, attitudes, and beliefs. The dependency perspective, by contrast, is structural or macrosociological. Its focus is on the mode of production, patterns of international trade, political and economic linkages between elites in peripheral and central countries, group and class alliances and conflicts, and so on. Both perspectives are concerned with the process of development in national societies. However, for the modernization writer the national society is the basic *unit of analysis*, while the writer in a dependence framework considers the global system and its various forms of interaction with national societies as the primary object of inquiry.

For the dependency perspective, the *time dimension* is a crucial aspect of what is fundamentally a historical model. Individual societies cannot be presumed to be able to replicate the evolution of other societies because the very transformation of an interrelated world system may preclude such an option. The modernization potential of individual societies must be seen in light of changes over time in the interactions between external and internal variables. The modernization perspective is obviously concerned about the origins of traditional and modern values; but, the time dimension is not fundamental to the explanatory pretensions of a model which claims "universal validity." Without knowing the source of modernity-inhibiting characteristics, it is still possible to identify them by reference to their counterparts in developing contexts.

At the root of the differences between the two perspectives is a fundamentally different *perception of human nature*. Dependency assumes that human behavior in economic matters is a "constant." Individuals will behave differently in different contexts not because they are different but because the contexts are different. The insistence on structures and, in the final analysis, on the broadest structural category of all, the world system, follows logically from the view that opportunity structures condition human behavior. Modernizationists, on the other hand, attribute the lack of certain behavioral patterns to the "relativity" of human behavior; to the fact that cultural values and beliefs, regardless of opportunity structures, underlie the patterns of economic action. Thus, the *conception of change* in the modernization perspective is a product of innovations which result from the adoption of modern attitudes among elites, and eventually followers. Though some modernization theorists are now more pessimistic about the development potential of such changes, modernizing beliefs are a prerequisite for development. For dependency analysis the conception of change is different. Change results from the realignment of dependency relations over time. Whether or not development occurs and how it occurs is subject to controversy. Given the rapid evolution of the world system, dependent development is possible in certain contexts, not in others. Autonomy, through a break in relations of dependency, may not lead to development of the kind already arrived at in the developed countries because of the inability to recreate the same historical conditions, but it might lead to a different kind of development stressing different values. Thus, the *prescription for change* varies substantially in the dependency perspective depending on the ideological outlook of particular authors. It is not a logical consequence of the historical model. In the modernization perspective the prescription for change follows more automatically from the assumptions of the model, implying greater consensus.

From a methodological point of view the modernization perspective is much more parsimonious than its counterpart. And the focus of much of the literature on the microsociological level makes it amenable to the elaboration of precise explanatory propositions such as those of D. Mc-Clelland or E. Hagen. Dependency, by contrast, is more descriptive and its macrosociological formulations are much less subject to translation into a simple set of explanatory propositions. Many aspects of dependency, and particularly the linkages between external phenomena and internal class and power relations are unclear and need to be studied with more precision and care. For this reason the dependency perspective is an "approach" to the study of underdevelopment rather than a "theory." And yet, precisely because modernization theory relies on a simple conceptual framework and a reductionist approach, it is far less useful for the study of a complex phenomenon such as development or underdevelopment.

But the strengths of the dependency perspective lie not only in its consideration of a richer body of evidence and a broader range of phenomena, it is also more promising from a methodological point of view. The modernization perspective has fundamental flaws which make it difficult to provide for a fair test of its own assumptions. It will be recalled that the modernization perspective draws on a model with "universal validity" which assumes that traditional values are not conducive to modern behavioral patterns of action. Given that underdevelopment, on the basis of various economic and social indicators, is an objective datum, the research task becomes one of identifying modernizing values and searching for their opposites in underdeveloped contexts.

In actual research efforts, the modernity-inhibiting characteristics are often "deduced" from impressionistic observation. This is the case with much of the political science literature on Latin America. However, more "rigorous" methods, such as survey research, have also been employed, particularly in studies of entrepreneurial activity. Invariably, whether through deduction or survey research, less appropriate values for modernization such as "arielismo" (a concern for transcendental as opposed to material values) or "low-achievement" (lack of risk-taking attitudes) have been identified, thus "confirming" the hypothesis that traditional values contribute to underdevelopment. If by chance the use of control groups should establish little or no difference in attitudes in a developed and underdeveloped context, the research instrument can be considered to be either faulty or the characteristics tapped not the appropriate ones for identifying traditional attitudes. The latter alternative might lead to the "discovery" of a new "modernity of tradition" literature or of greater flexibility than anticipated in traditional norms or of traditional residuals in the developed country.

The problem with the model and its behavioral level of analysis is that the explanation for underdevelopment is part of the preestablished conceptual framework. It is already "known" that in backward areas the modernity-inhibiting characteristics play the dominant role, otherwise the areas would not be backward. As such, the test of the hypothesis involves a priori acceptance of the very hypothesis up for verification, with empirical evidence gathered solely in an illustrative manner. The focus on individuals simply does not permit consideration of a broader range of contextual variables which might lead to invalidating the assumptions. Indeed, the modernity of tradition literature, which has pointed to anomalies in the use of the tradition modernity "polarities," is evidence of how such a perspective can fall victim to the "and so" fallacy. Discrepancies are accounted for not by a reformulation, but by adding a new definition or a new corollary to the preexisting conceptual framework.

Much work needs to be done within a dependency perspective to clarify its concepts and causal interrelationships, as well as to assess its capacity to explain social processes in various parts of peripheral societies. And yet the dependency approach appears to have a fundamental advantage over the modernization perspective: It is open to historically grounded conceptualization in underdeveloped contexts, while modernization is locked into an illustrative methodological style by virtue of its very assumptions.

Acknowledgments

Arturo Valenzuela wishes to acknowledge the support of the Ford Foundation and of the Institute of Development Studies at the University of Sussex, which made the completion of this paper possible during his tenure as a Visiting Fellow at IDS.

Notes

1. See Manning Nash's foreword to the anniversary issue of *Economic Development and Cultural Change*, XXV (1977, supplement), in honor of Bert Hoselitz, one of the first economists to stress "noneconomic" factors in development. See his *Sociological Aspects of Economic Growth* (New York, 1960) which was translated into twenty-five languages by the U.S. Department of State. Myron Weiner's *Modernization: The Dynamics of Growth* (New York, 1966) is a good collection of essays by prominent modernization writers which were first prepared for the "Voice of America."

2. The principal works in the dependency perspective are Fernando Henrique Cardoso and Enzo Faletto, *Dependencia y desarrollo en América Latina* (Mexico, 1969) and Osvaldo Sunkel and Pedro Paz, *El subdesarrollo latinoamericano y la teoría del desarrollo* (Mexico, 1970). The former soon will be published in English, while the latter is not scheduled for translation despite the fact that the Spanish version is in its ninth printing. Because of the language "barrier" André Gunder Frank is often thought to be the founder of the dependency school. See for example Adrian Foster-Carter, "From Rostow to Gunder Frank: Conflicting Paradigms in the Analysis of Underdevelopment," *World Development,* IV (March 1976), 1975, where Frank is referred to as "Copernicus" of a new paradigm. In fact, Frank draws extensively on Latin American scholars in studies such as *Capitalism and Underdevelopment in Latin America* (New York, 1967). He and other "interpreters" such as Susanne Bodenheimer ("Dependency and Imperialism," *Politics and Society,* I, May 1970), present oversimplified and often distorted views of much of the Latin American contribution. On this point see Cardoso, "The Consumption of Dependency Theory in the United States," *Latin American Research Review,* XII, No. 3. Frank's work was, however, extensively read and discussed in Latin American universities.

3. Though modernization and dependence can be thought of as alternative paradigms, we prefer the term "perspective" because in Thomas Kuhn's terms the social sciences are preparadigmatic, only approximating a "normal science." See Kuhn, *The Structure of Scientific Revolutions* (Chicago, 1970).

4. This is less true for developmental economics and anthropology than for

sociology and political science. Economists like Hoselitz and Everett Hagen (*On the Theory of Social Change* [Homewood, Ill., 1962]) drew in part on Latin American field research. Robert Redfield's *The Folk Cultures of Yucatan* (Chicago, 1941) is considered one of the classics. The most important sociological work was done by Gino Germani, although his most important studies were never translated. See his *Política y sociedad en una época de transición* (Buenos Aires, 1968). For an intelligent overview of his work, as well as that of Cardoso, see Joseph A. Kahl, *Modernization, Exploitation and Dependency in Latin America* (New Brunswick, N.J., 1976).

5. John Martz, "Political Science and Latin American Studies: A Discipline in Search of a Region," *Latin American Research Review*, VI (Spring 1971), 78.

6. For antecedents of the modernization literature, see the work of scholars such as Maine, Tonnies, Durkheim, Weber and Redfield.

7. For surveys of the literature, see Frank Sutton, "Social Theory and Comparative Politics," in Harry Eckstein and David Apter, eds., *Comparative Politics* (New York, 1963), and Daniel Lerner, "Modernization: Social Aspects," *International Encyclopedia of the Social Sciences* (1968).

8. See the excellent distinction made by Alejandro Portes between "development as social differentiation" and "development as the enactment of values" in Portes, "On the Sociology of National Development: Theories and Issues," *American Journal of Sociology*, LXXXII (July 1976). Examples of the former are Neil J. Smelser, "The Modernization of Social Relations," in Weiner, *Modernization* and "Mechanisms of Change and Adjustment to Change," in Jason Finkle and Robert Gable, eds., *Political Development and Social Change* (New York, 1971); and Talcott Parsons' companion volumes, *Societies: Evolutionary and Comparative Perspectives* and *The System of Modern Societies* (Englewood Cliffs, N.J., 1966 and 1971, respectively). Examples of the latter are Hagen, *On the Theory of Social Change*; and David McClelland, *The Achieving Society* (Princeton, 1961) and "The Psychological Causes and Consequences of Modernization: An Ethiopian Case Study," *Economic Development and Cultural Change*, XXV (1977, supplement). See also Alex Inkeles and David Smith, *Becoming Modern* (Cambridge, Mass., 1974). Inkeles and Smith take particular care to point out that their study does not demonstrate a causal relationship between the emergence of modern attitudes and modernizing transformations, for which McClelland takes them to task in the above cited article. But if all they establish is that people who work in modern settings have modern values, then their laborious research effort is circular and pointless.

9. See Cyril Black, *The Dynamics of Modernization* (New York, 1966), pp. 68–75.

10. Ibid., pp. 53–54.

11. Gabriel Almond, "Introduction: A Functional Approach to Comparative Politics," in Almond and James S. Coleman, *The Politics of the Developing Areas* (Princeton, 1960), p. 64. Statements such as these have led to the criticism that modernization is an ethnocentric approach. But rather than pointing out their ethnocentricity, it is more important to indicate that they reflect an assumption which becomes a key methodological option, ethnocentric or otherwise.

12. For the view that modernization is an exogenous process leading to convergence see Lerner, *The Passing of Traditional Society* (New York, 1958) and Clark Kerr, et al., *Industrialism and Industrial Man* (Cambridge, Mass., 1960).

13. See Kalman H. Silvert, *The Conflict Society: Reaction and Revolution in Latin America* (New York, 1966), p. 261.

14. Black, p. 50 (emphasis added).

15. Dankwart A. Rustow, *A World of Nations* (Washington, D.C., 1967).

16. Wilbert Moore, "Modernization and Rationalization: Processes and Restraints," *Economic Development and Cultural Change*, XXV (1977, supplement), pp. 34-35.

17. Wilbert Moore, "Motivational Aspects of Development," in Amitai and Eva Etzioni, eds., *Social Change* (New York, 1964), p. 292. See also his "Social Change" in the *International Encyclopedia of the Social Sciences* (1968).

18. J. Gusfield, "Tradition and Modernity: Misplaced Polarities in the Study of Social Change," *American Journal of Sociology*, LXXII (January 1967).

19. Lloyd I. and Susanne H. Rudolph, *The Modernity of Traditional Development in India* (Chicago, 1967). Another work in this vein is Robert Ward and Dankwart A. Rustow, eds., *Political Modernization in Japan and Turkey* (Princeton, 1964).

20. For example see Irma Adelman and Cynthia Morris, *Economic Growth and Social Equity in Developing Countries* (Stanford, 1973).

21. S. N. Eisenstadt, *Tradition, Change and Modernity* (New York, 1973) and Moore, "Modernization and Rationalization."

22. Marion Levy, Jr., *Modernization: Latecomers and Survivors* (New York, 1972).

23. Seymour Martin Lipset, "Values, Education and Entrepreneurship," in Lipset and Aldo Solari, eds., *Elites in Latin America* (New York, 1963). For another study in which Lipset expresses similar views about Latin America, while extolling the opposite values in the United States, see his *The First New Nation* (New York, 1963).

24. Lipset, "Values, Education and Entrepreneurship," p. 19.

25. Ibid., p. 30. Some of the studies cited include T. C. Cohran, "Cultural Factors in Economic Growth," *Journal of Economic History*, XX (1974); T. R. Fillol, *Social Factors in Economic Development: The Argentine Case* (Cambridge, Mass., 1961); B. J. Siegel, "Social Structure and Economic Change in Brazil," in Simon Kuznets, et al., *Economic Growth: Brazil, India, Japan* (Durham, N.C., 1955); and W. P. Strassman, "The Industrialist," In John J. Johnson, ed., *Continuity and Change in Latin America* (Stanford, 1964).

26. R. Adie and G. E. Poitras, *Latin America: the Politics of Immobility* (Englewood Cliffs, N.J., 1974), pp. 73-75. For similar views see pp. 252-53 and W. R. Duncan, *Latin American Politics: A Developmental Approach* (New York, 1976), p. 240.

27. Silvert, "The Politics of Social and Economic Change in Latin America," in Howard J. Wiarda, ed., *Politics and Social Change in Latin America: The Distinct Tradition* (Amherst, Mass., 1974), pp. 160-62.

28. Silvert, *The Conflict Society*, p. 271. For a definition of "modern man" see

p. 265. In the preface Arthur Whitacker, a well known historian, noted that the book should be made "required reading for anyone who wishes to express an opinion" on the alliance.

29. R. Scott, "Political Elites," in Lipset and Solari, pp. 133–34.

30. Duncan, p. 240. Scott emphasizes cultural determinants in later writings. See his edited volume, *Latin American Modernization Problems* (Urbana, Ill., 1973). The role of traditional features in explaining economic and political patterns in Latin America was stressed by the best known studies of the 1960s. For a sampling see the articles in the collections edited by Johnson, *Continuity and Change*, and by D. B. Heath and R. N. Adams, *Contemporary Cultures and Societies in Latin America* (New York, 1965). See also Stanislav Andreski, *Parasitism and Subversion: The Case in Latin America* (New York, 1966); George Blanksten, "The Politics of Latin America," in Almond and Coleman, *The Politics of the Developing Areas*; J. Mander, *The Unrevolutionary Society* (New York, 1969); Luis Mercier Vega, *Roads to Power in Latin America* (New York, 1969); and Martin Needler, *Latin American Politics in Perspective* (Princeton, 1967). Crude applications of modernization concepts to particular cases include Frank Jay Moreno, *Legitimacy and Stability in Latin America: A Study of Chilean Political Culture* (New York, 1969) and James Payne, *Patterns of Conflict in Colombia* (New Haven, 1968). Some important authors, however, took different approaches, much closer to those of the dependency perspective. See Merle Kling, "Toward a Theory of Power and Political Instability in Latin America," *Western Political Quarterly,* IX (1956); Charles Anderson, *Politics and Economic Change in Latin America* (Princeton, 1967); Richard Adams, *The Second Sowing: Power and Secondary Development in Latin America* (San Francisco, 1967); and Douglas Chalmers, "Developing on the Periphery: External Factors in Latin American Politics," in James Rosenau, ed., *Linkage Politics* (New York, 1969). The reader by James Petras and Maurice Zeitlin, eds., *Latin America: Reform or Revolution*? (New York, 1968), also provided a differing perspective incorporating many writings of Latin American scholars.

31. Besides the Adie and Poitras and the Duncan works cited above, see also C. F. Denton and L. L. Preston, *Latin American Politics: A Developmental Approach* (New York, 1975); and Needler, *An Introduction to Latin American Politics: the Structure of Conflict* (Englewood Cliffs, N.J., 1977). For one of the few alternative texts see Petras, *Politics and Social Structure in Latin America* (New York, 1970).

32. Wiarda, Howard J., *Politics and Social Change in Latin America*, p. 269. Another important contribution to this literature is Fredrick Pike and T. Stritch, eds., *The New Corporatism: Social-Political Structures in the Iberian World* (South Bend, Ind., 1974). Not all writers interested in corporatism draw primarily on cultural variables. Philippe C. Schmitter explicitly rejects what he considers to be the circularity of that approach. See his essay, "The Century of Corporatism?" in Pike and Stritch.

33. Wiarda, Howard J., "Toward a Framework for the Study of Political Change in the Iberic-Latin Tradition: the Corporative Model," *World Politics*, XXV (January 1973).

34. See Osvaldo Sunkel, "Política nacional de desarrollo y dependencia externa," *Estudios Internacionales*, I (April 1967). For reviews of the dependency literature see Norman Girvan, "The Development of Dependency Economics in the Caribbean and Latin America: Review and Comparison," *Social and Economic Studies,* XXII (March 1973); Ronald H. Chilcote, "A Critical Synthesis of the Dependency Literature," *Latin American Perspectives,* I (Spring 1974); and Philip O'Brien, "A Critique of Latin American Theories of Dependence," in I. Oxaal, et al., eds., *Beyond the Sociology of Development* (London, 1975).

35. Sunkel and Paz, *El Subdesarrollo Latinoamericano*, p. 6.

36. Theotonio dos Santos, "La crisis del desarrollo y las relaciones de dependencia en América Latina," (Mexico, 1970), p. 180. See also his *Dependencia y cambio social* (Santiago, 1970) and *Socialismo o Fascismo: El nuevo carácter de la dependencia y el dilema latinoamericano* (Buenos Aires, 1972).

37. Sunkel and Paz, p. 39; Cardoso and Faletto, *Dependencia y desarrollo,* chap. 2.

38. This is the problem with the studies by Robert Kaufman, et al., "A Preliminary Test of the Theory of Dependency," *Comparative Politics*, VII (April 1975), pp. 303-30, and C. Chase-Dunn, "The Effects of International Economic Dependence on Development and Inequality: A Cross National Study," *American Sociological Review*, XL (December 1975). It is interesting to note that Marxist scholars make the same mistake. They point to features in the dependency literature such as unemployment, marginalization, etc., noting that they are not peculiar to peripheral countries but characterize capitalist countries in general. Thus "dependence" is said to have no explanatory value beyond a Marxist theory of capitalist society. See Sanjaya Lall, "Is Dependence a Useful Concept in Analyzing Underdevelopment?" *World Development*, III (November 1975) and Theodore Weisskopf, "Dependence as an Explanation of Underdevelopment: A Critique," (paper presented at the Sixth Annual Latin American Studies Association Meeting, Atlanta, Georgia, 1976). The point of dependency analysis is not the relative mix at one point in time of certain identifiable factors but the evolution over time of structural relations which help to explain the differential development of capitalism in different parts of the world. As a historical model it cannot be tested with cross national data. For an attempt to differentiate conceptually contemporary capitalism of the core and peripheral countries, and thus more amenable to such criticism, see Samir Amin, *Accumulation on a World Scale* (New York, 1974).

39. Some authors have criticized the focus of the literature on the evolution of the world capitalist system. David Ray, for example, has argued that "Soviet satellites" are also in a dependent and unequal relationship vis-à-vis the Soviet Union and that the key variable should not be capitalism but "political power." Robert Packenham has also argued that the most important critique of the dependency literature is that it does not consider the implications of "power." See Ray, "The Dependency Model of Latin American Underdevelopment: Three Basic Fallacies," *Journal of Interamerican Studies and World Affairs*, XV (February 1973) and Packenham, "Latin American Dependency Theories:

Strengths and Weaknesses," (paper presented to the Harvard-MIT Joint Seminar on Political Development, February, 1974), especially pp. 16–17, 54. This criticism misses the point completely. It is not power relations today which cause underdevelopment, but the historical evolution of a world economic system which led to economic specialization more favorable to some than others. It is precisely this concern with the evolution of world capitalism which has led to the preoccupation in the dependency literature with rejecting interpretations stressing the "feudal" rather than "capitalist" nature of colonial and post colonial Latin American agriculture. On this point see Sergio Bagú, *Economía de la sociedad colonial* (Buenos Aires, 1949); Luis Vitale, "América Latina: Feudal o Capitalista?" *Revista Estrategia*, III (1966) and *Interpretación Marxista de la historia de Chile* (Santiago, 1967); and E. Laclau, "Feudalism and Capitalism in Latin America," *New Left Review*, LXVII (May-July 1971). A brilliant recent exposition of the importance of studying the evolution of the capitalist world system in order to understand underdevelopment which focuses more on the center states than on the periphery is Immanuel Wallerstein, *The Modern World System: Capitalist Agriculture and the Origins of the European World Economy in the Sixteenth Century* (New York, 1974).

40. Fernando Henrique Cardoso, *Empresario industrial e desenvolvimento economico no Brazil* (São Paulo, 1964) and *Ideologías de la burguesía industrial en sociedades dependientes* (Mexico, 1971).

41. Cardoso and Faletto, *Dependencia y desarrollo*, p. 20. Indeed Cardoso argues that the distinction between external and internal is "metaphysical." See his "teoría de la dependencia o análisis de situaciones concretas de dependencia?" *Revista Latinoamericana de Ciencia Política*, I (December 1970), p. 404. The ontology implicit in such an analysis is the one of "internal relations." See Bertell Ollman, *Alienation: Marx's Conception of Man in Capitalist Society* (London, 1971). This point is important because both Frank and the early ECLA literature were criticized for their almost mechanistic relationship between external and internal variables. Frank acknowledges this problem and tries to answer his critics in *Lumpenbourgeoisie and Lumpendevelopment* (New York, 1967). "Tests" of dependency theory also attribute an excessively mechanical dimension to the relationship. See Kaufman, et al., "A Preliminary Test of the Theory of Dependency."

42. Fernando Henrique Cardoso, "Associated Dependent Development Theoretical Implications," in Alfred Stepan, ed., *Authoritarian Brazil* (New Haven, 1973), and Sunkel and Edmundo Fuenzalida, "Transnational Capitalism and National Development (London, forthcoming). It is thus incorrect to argue that dependency analysts ignore the evidence of certain kinds of economic growth. For fallacies in the dependency literature see Fernando Henrique Cardoso, "Las contradicciones del desarrollo asociado," *Desarrollo Económico*, IV (April-June 1974).

43. Aníbal Quijano, "Dependencia, cambio social y urbanización en América Latina," in Cardoso and F. Weffort, eds., *América Latina: Ensayos de interpretación sociológico político* (Santiago, 1970).

44. Cardoso and Faletto, *Dependencia y desarrollo,* pp. 19–20; Sunkel and

Paz, *El subdesarrollo latinoamericano*, pp. 5, 9.

45. Bagú, *Economía de la sociedad colonial*, pp. 122–23.
46. On industrialization see A. Dorfman, *La industrialización en América Latina y las políticas de fomento* (Mexico, 1967).
47. See M. de C. Tavares, "El proceso de sustitución de importaciones como modelo de desarrollo reciente en América Latina," in Andres Bianchi, ed., *América Latina: Ensayos de interpretación económica* (Santiago, 1969).
48. For detailed discussions of nonenclave versus enclave situations see Cardoso and Faletto and Sunkel and Paz.
49. Osvaldo Sunkel, "Capitalismo transnacional y desintegración nacional en América Latina," *Estudios Internacionales*, IV (January-March 1971) and "Big Business and Dependencia: A Latin American View," *Foreign Affairs,* L (April 1972); Cardoso and Faletto; dos Santos, *El nuevo carácter de la dependencia* (Santiago, 1966).
50. Wallerstein, *The Modern World System.*
51. V. Bambirra, *Capitalismo dependiente latinoamericano* (Santiago, 1973); R. M. Marini, *Subdesarrollo y revolución* (Mexico, 1969); F. Hinkelammert, *El subdesarrollo latinoamericano: un caso de desarrollo capitalista* (Santiago, 1970).
52. Cardoso, "Teoría de la dependencia." A recent trend in dependency writings attempts to explain the current wave of authoritarianism in Latin America as a result of economic difficulties created by the exhaustion of the easy import substituting industrialization. The new situation leads to a process of development led by the state and the multinational corporation, which concentrates income toward the top, increases the levels of capital accumulation and expands heavy industry; the old populist alliances can therefore no longer be maintained. See Theotonio dos Santos, *Socialismo o fascismo: el nuevo carácter de la dependencia y el dilema latinoamericano* (Buenos Aires, 1972); Guillermo O'Donnell, *Modernization and Bureaucratic Authoritarianism: Studies in Latin American Politics* (Berkeley, 1973); Atilio Borón, "El fascismo como categoría histórica: en torno al problema de las dictaduras en América Latina," *Revista Mexicana de Sociología*, XXXIV (April-June 1977); the effects of this situation on labor are explored in Kenneth P. Erickson and Patrick Peppe, "Dependent Capitalist Development, U.S. Foreign Policy, and Repression of the Working Class in Chile and Brazil," *Latin American Perspectives*, III (Winter 1976). However, in the postscript to their 1968 book, Cardoso and Faletto caution against adopting an excessively mechanistic view on this point, against letting "economism kill history"; Cardoso and Faletto, "Estado y proceso político en América Latina," *Revista Mexicana de Sociología*, XXXIV (April-June 1977), p. 383. Articles with dependency perspective appear frequently in the *Revista Mexicana de Sociología* as well as in *Latin American Perspectives.*
53. Sunkel, "Capitalismo transnacional y desintegración nacional en América Latina," and Sunkel and Fuenzalida, "Transnational Capitalism and National Development."

3
An Interpretation and
Evaluation of
Dependency Theory

James A. Caporaso
Behrouz Zare

Dependency theory has become one of the foremost interpretations of development as well as a critical challenge to conventional development theory. What we attempt in this essay is to provide our evaluation of this body of theory in terms of criteria we feel are important: definitional and conceptual clarity and the extent to which dependency theory has served as an adequate explanation of development. In short, we are interested in dependency both as a concept and as a body of knowledge contributing to our understanding of development and underdevelopment.

We will have to distinguish between dependence and dependency[1] and also between the uses of dependency as a concept and as a body of theory. The failure of many scholars to make these distinctions has had two unfortunate effects. First, it has led to classification errors concerning what is and what is not a dependent country. Second, it has led to theoretical errors concerning the relationship between dependency and development.

In this chapter we offer (1) a brief description and definitional overview of dependency theory; (2) an analysis of some of the problems with this body of theory; and (3) some suggestions about how to further the analysis of dependent development situations. Central to our analysis is the notion that the evaluation of any theory requires a clear understanding of the concepts involved. As the concepts in dependency theory are holistic, i.e., they are concepts that themselves bring together important subconcepts, we start by breaking these concepts down into their elementary parts, if only as a prelude to putting them back together into a meaningful whole.

Dependency Theory: Description and Definition

If dependency were defined in different ways, this would have implications for the theory. More explicitly, if the concept of dependency entailed different things in the world, it is likely that the various concepts would relate in different ways to other, independent concepts, the most important of which would be development. To allow definitions of the central concept to vary from use to use would create anarchy in our assessment of dependency theory since the strengths and weaknesses of this body of thought would not be stable. Therefore, any critical evaluation of dependency theory must start with a definition of the key concept.

The first distinction we must make is an important one because it rests on two very different intellectual traditions. We draw a distinction between *dependence*, conceived simply as external reliance, and *dependency*, the process by which less developed countries are incorporated into the global capitalist system. It is true that there are areas of overlap between the two approaches. Both focus on relational inequalities and the vulnerabilities that may flow from them. However, the differences outweigh these similarities. The dependence orientation seeks to probe and explore the symmetries and asymmetries among nation-states. The assumption of this approach is that any sectoral dependence, e.g., in food, textiles, or light machinery, can be added to all others within any nation-state to produce a total measure of dependence. The set of sectoral dependencies represents a pool of foreign policy levers with which to influence other countries. Thus both additivity (of sectoral dependencies) and linkage (among sectors) are critical assumptions of this approach.

The dependency orientation is quite different. It attempts to clarify the process of integration of the periphery into the international capitalist system and the developmental implications thereof. Instead of focusing on unified nation-states, the level of analysis shifts to more fluid and institutionally evasive units such as class structures, the alliance between local classes and international capital, banks, industries, and firms, and so forth. In other words, the dependency orientation explicitly rejects the unified state-as-actor of the dependence approach. Finally, the object of explanation is different. For dependence theorists the object of explanation is international influence. Dependence is interesting as a concept precisely because it promises to provide an explanation of that influence. Dependency is interested in development, in both quantitative and qualitative aspects. In the remainder of this chapter we will elaborate on the dependency framework.

We regard dependency as a structural condition in an economy with certain characteristics and dependency theory as an explanation of the existence of this condition and of its relationship to development. However, this general definition of dependency is not specific enough to tell us how to proceed either theoretically or in terms of a concrete research program. Let us turn to the definition offered by Cardoso, which is much richer in detail:

> Capitalist accumulation in dependent economies does not complete its cycle. Lacking autonomous technology, as vulgar parlance has it, and compelled therefore to utilize imported technology, dependent capitalism is crippled. . . . It is crippled because it lacks a fully developed capital goods sector. The accumulation, expansion, and self-realization of local capital requires and depends on a dynamic complement outside itself. It must insert itself into the circuit of international capitalism. (Cardoso, 1973: 163)

The important thing to note about this definition is that it captures one of the central components of the dependency situation, namely the derangement manifested in the functional incompleteness of the national economy. Dependency is now considered, and rightly so, to be something more critical and more complex than the simple reliance of one country on another. However, this definition, sound as it is, is still incomplete because it does not incorporate the internal aspects of dependency into the definition. We shall return to this point shortly.

Cardoso and Faletto (1978) emphasize the functional incompleteness of the domestic economy and the way in which domestic gaps are filled in by an external complement; other definitions of dependency emphasize other factors. An examination of the definition offered by Havelock Brewster shows this: "Economic dependency we may define as a lack of capacity to manipulate the operative elements of an economic system. Such a situation is characterized by an absence of interdependence between the economic functions of a system. This lack of interdependence implies that the system has no internal dynamic which would enable it to function as an independent autonomous entity" (Brewster, 1973: 91). In this definition, dependency is equated with a particular species of nonautonomy that arises from the absence of integration of key economic sectors. The reasons for this lack of integration lie precisely in the external component of dependency. Since the local economy is tightly integrated into the international economic system, its parts are responsive to this system and not to other sectors of the domestic economy. Dependency, then, is Janus-faced. It has an internal anatomy manifesting itself in fragmentation and an external anatomy realized through its responsiveness to foreign economic activity.

Problems with Previous Definitions of Dependency

Both definitions of dependency are perfectly sound as far as they go. The difficulty is that both leave out a crucial component of dependency. Cardoso focuses on the external reliance component of dependency, the reliance on a dynamic complement outside the national economy, and the ways in which the linkage with this dynamic complement disrupts and distorts economic and political processes within the local economy. Brewster stresses the internal side of dependency, the absence of strong forward and backward linkages in the economy. Both types of emphasis result in an incomplete version of dependency theory.

Leaving out either the internal or the external component of dependency has important consequences that range far beyond a violation of our sense of aesthetic completeness. In fact, this incompleteness bears directly on our ability to provide an explanation for the process of development. In particular, two major defects follow from these partial definitions of the dependency situation. The first problem is the simple one of identification of countries that are dependent and those which are not, or in continuous-variable language, those cases that are more dependent and those less dependent.

This point can be illustrated through an elaboration of the definition offered by Cardoso. We can restate his definition as follows: Dependency is a structural condition in which capitalist accumulation does not complete its cycle domestically but relies instead on external factors for its completion. This reliance is of course the central external component of dependency in a literal sense, namely the sense in which a country depends on another for the performance of a very basic need. As the local economy opens itself up to the international system, these external factors operate in conjunction with internal (domestic) forces to produce distortions in the domestic system. These distortions (e.g., internal inequality, either across economic sectors, between urban and rural areas, and across classes; authoritarian forms of government) are clearly not the product of either external or internal factors, but of both types of factors working together.

To understand this point, let us imagine a case in which a local economy for some reason is capable of resisting the noxious effects of involvement in the international system. This is not such an absurd assumption to make. Involvement in the international system was one of the precepts of development for the early modernizing countries (Great Britain, the United States, France), as well as for the late modernizers (Germany, Japan). Even though there are important historical differences between these countries and dependent countries today, the general theoretical point that external dependence does not automatically lead to distorted development still holds. When external reliance exists without internal disintegration, the external factors (e.g., external markets, capital, and technology) are expected to add to the existing domestic factors in promoting development. In other words, in situations of external reliance unaccompanied by domestic fragmentation, the external factors act in an additive way with domestic economic factors. In situations of this sort it is appropriate to speak, not of dependency, but of a kind of reliance that is closer to what we have called dependence.

The second problem is just as serious but, because it derives from the first problem, we can dispose of it more simply. This is the problem of testing propositions based on the concept of dependency. If we have miscategorized cases of dependency by mixing together cases that exhibit only external reliance with those that are domestically nonintegrated and those that are domestically fragmented because of their incorporation into the international system, we are not likely to discover anything systematic about the relationship of dependency to other concepts. If we cannot decide whether Canada and Switzerland and South Korea, with high levels of external reliance, are qualitatively different from Chile and Brazil, or different only in degree, we are not in a strong position to discover the laws of dependent peripheral development. The questions of identification and measurement must be answered before theoretical ones can be raised.

Summary

We have said that the concept of dependency cannot be reduced to a single component such as external reliance, internal fragmentation, or the concentration of the external linkages. All three of these components are important in understanding dependency and, indeed, all of them are used as building blocks in the overall concept of dependency. However, the presence of one or two of these components, taken individually, does not necessarily reflect even partial dependency. This a critical point that we want to emphasize, for there is considerable confusion in the United

States about it. Whether implicitly or explicitly, many scholars have operated on the assumption that dependency is a general concept with several components and that these components have an additive relationship to dependency. Therefore, translated into the language of measurement, the appropriate measurement model is an additive response model with multiple indicators. A critical property of this model is that its methodological rules allow a part of the underlying concept to exist with the presence of any of the constituent indicators. This measurement model, we think, clearly violates the underlying conceptual basis of dependency.

Suggestions for Research on Dependency

We make these suggestions modestly, and in full recognition of the rich historical-structural tradition in Latin America, which has provided many excellent case studies and interpretations of dependent development in Latin America. Our approach does not deny the value of this tradition; rather, it attempts to expand it and perhaps add to it in qualitatively different ways.

Our suggestions parallel our prior analysis of dependency theory. We noted two prime difficulties with this body of thought: uncertainty as to the definitional components of dependency as a concept and, arising from this, difficulty in relating dependency to other concepts. Thus our two suggestions concern the components of dependency and the theoretical relationship between dependency and development.

Components of the Concept of Dependency

The thrust of our argument has been that an adequate definition of dependency must be holistic, i.e., it must draw together in a coherent way the separate components of dependency: external reliance, restricted choice, and internal fragmentation. We offer the following definition in a provisional way: Dependency refers to a structural condition in which a weakly integrated system cannot complete its economic cycle except by an exclusive (or limited) reliance on an external complement. This definition offers nothing new; it simply draws together external reliance, restricted choices, and domestic fragmentation into one definition. Now let us turn to an examination of each of these components.

External Reliance. In some ways the concept of external reliance is the centerpiece of dependency theory, since it points our attention to the complicated ways in which the local economy is incorporated into the international system (Cardoso and Faletto, 1978; Sunkel, 1973). In one sense, this concept presents no special difficulties – it is easy to observe external reliance whether in trade, capital, or technology. However, the functional links between the domestic economy and the outside world may be of a qualitatively different nature, either over time or for different countries.

There are two general theoretical reasons for these qualitative differences. The first has to do with what we call the phase characteristics of international capitalism, that is, the particular characteristics of capitalism at the international level during any particular period of time. Capitalism is not a stagnant mode of economic organization but one that has its own laws of development.[2] It is constantly changing, and sometimes these changes are important enough to mark off different eras. The second theoretical reason concerns the properties of domestic societies, since these also vary widely. These two sets of factors are important because out of their intersection, or conjunction, one derives the particular characteristics of dependent societies. In this sense we agree completely with the argument of Cardoso and Faletto (1978) that the laws of motion of international capitalism are capable of providing only the grossest information about the political and economic content of domestic societies. This information can be provided only by a detailed investigation of both national and international forces.

The interaction of forces at these two levels accounts for most of the differences among dependent developing countries. Failure to take differences at either level into account has transformed the rich detail of various dependent situations into a bland, homogeneous report on the strength of the linkages between trade or capital dependence and levels of development. Obviously, if internal factors are treated as passive and if the phase properties of capitalism at the time of incorporation into the international system are ignored, a uniform, bleached version of dependency will result.

Concentration. By concentration we refer to the pattern of distribution of external reliance. Given that a country depends on the external sphere for completion of its economic cycle, we can ask whether it depends on actors in one country or several and further, how evenly its reliances are distributed among these actors. The central idea is that the more concentrated (i.e., the less uniformly distributed) the external reliances, the more severe the pattern of dependency.

Concentration of reliances is tied to two other important concepts of dependency theory – vulnerability and restricted choice.[3] The greater the concentration of reliance, the greater the vulnerability of an actor for a quite simple reason – the greater difficulty the actor would have in adjusting to a break of relations. If a dependent country has seven or eight partners, each of whom supplies a part of its needs, it can suffer a withdrawal of supply much more readily than if its needs are supplied by only one or two actors. This is partly due to the obvious fact that if one out of seven withholds supplies, only one-seventh is lost, while if one out of two withholds, one-half is lost. It is also due in part to the ease with which one can make up the lost supplies by increasing supplies from others.

Internal Fragmentation. The key idea here is that the dependent economy is internally disjointed, its parts are only weakly connected, and sectoral links are loosely established. The kinship of this idea with the older one of the dual economy is obvious, but in equally important ways the ideas are different.

The "dual economy," as that idea was developed by nondependency economists (e.g., Boeke, 1953; Higgins, 1956), refers to the existence of a modern commercial economy alongside a primitive agricultural one. Although the two economies exist side by side, there is little functional relationship between them, i.e., one part of the economy is in a predeveloped state rather than one of underdevelopment. Dependent economies differ from this model of the dual economy in two important ways. First, in a dependent economy, the poor, marginalized segments are functionally connected to the modernized parts. Indeed, the backward segments are poor precisely because of their incorporation into the economy, not because they are excluded from it. Second, most of the fragmentation is not between rich and poor, modernized and backward, but among the modernized sectors themselves. Thus, whether one is thinking in terms of Brewster's (1973) disconnected economic functions (wages, exports, output, consumption) or Sunkel's sectoral analysis (Sunkel, n.d.), the fragmentation at issue is not that between modern and backward areas of the economy.

As Norman Girvan (1973: 11) notes, this approach, focusing on the internal structure of dependency, "goes well beyond the formulations which emphasize dependence on the outside world, and makes it possible to analyze and appreciate the anatomy of dependence through its characteristics and consequences within the internal functioning of the economy in question." It allows us to see clearly how the internal anatomy of dependency is functionally related to its external aspect. Although Brewster himself does not establish this connection, Sunkel has placed it on solid theoretical footing in his article "Transnational Capitalism and National Disintegration In Latin America" (1973).

Although an understanding of the internal structure of dependency is one of the most challenging aspects of dependency theory, a great deal of progress has been made in this area (Brewster, 1973; Sunkel, n.d.). For that reason we will not make any detailed suggestions here. We do hasten to point out, however, that the fragmentation of the domestic economy has often been dealt with as an isolated phenomenon rather than as part of a more complete dependency structure. In particular, there is a disturbing theoretical gap between the ideas of functional incompleteness of the domestic economy and its fragmented nature.

By pursuing the line of argument launched by Cardoso and Faletto (1978) and incorporating at the same time some of the insights of Sunkel (1973), one can trace the relationship between functional incompleteness and internal disintegration. For instance, if an economy cannot generate indigenous technology and is thus unable to produce capital goods, it automatically becomes disintegrated in one central respect, since most domestic sectors need capital goods, which they rely on for processing. Almost all material inputs into production require complex processing before they can be transformed into intermediate goods. In short, if a society does not possess its own capital goods sector, it weakens the linkages between levels of primary, intermediate, and advanced production that would be provided if the capital goods sector were domestically owned and controlled. Because ties to the external sector develop to compensate for the domestic weakness, external responsiveness is cultivated at the same time that domestic linkages are weakened.

Theoretical Questions

Up to this point we have been concerned only with the concept of dependency itself. Now the question must be asked: What is the relationship between dependency and development? Although the question is clearly formulated, the answer is surrounded by confusion and controversy. Some of this is due to the lack of a precise definition of development itself. Development has different components, which do not necessarily move in the same direction. A better understanding would be possible if the concept were broken into basic components and each one separately examined in relation to dependency.

The overall concept of development can be divided into two basic components, one quantitative, the other qualitative. By the quantitative aspect we simply mean growth, i.e., an increase in the total output of the economy. By the qualitative aspect we mean the kind of development that accompanies economic growth, e.g., growth with increasing or decreasing inequality, more or less marginalization, or more democratic or authoritarian forms of government.

As far as growth is concerned, dependency thinkers are divided. Some argue that growth is retarded by dependency (e.g., Frank, 1968); others, that growth is possible as a response to expansion in the center; while still others go even further and argue that dependency and growth are positively related (Cardoso, 1973; Evans, 1979).

The position that dependency retards growth is controversial for both theoretical and empirical reasons. The empirical objection arises because many dependent less developed countries (LDCs) are experiencing very rapid rates of growth. The theory holds that growth is limited by decapitalization of the dependent country. Decapitalization takes place through trade (unequal exchange) and direct transfer of capital in the form of profits, royalties, and debt payments. However, both the terms of trade argument and the direct capital transfer argument lack a solid theoretical foundation. With respect to the terms of trade, the blunt fact is that despite many serious efforts, no convincing theoretical rationale has yet been provided to explain why the terms of trade should systematically and adversely affect the exports of LDCs. Indeed, to the extent that the terms of trade argument is based on the predominance of primary product exports from LDCs, it is completely off the mark, since a new international division of labor is emerging in which many LDCs are increasingly exporting manufactured goods (Fröbel, Heinrichs, and Kreye, 1977; OECD, 1979).

The capital outflow argument fares no better. Indeed, hardly any theoretical arguments exist; instead, the argument is really a summary of a theoretically misguided empirical observation of net capital inflows and outflows. Since capital outflow is greater than capital inflow, it is deduced that there is a net capital transfer from the periphery to the center. The objection raised to this argument is that the mere difference between capital outflow and inflow does not necessarily represent capital loss, because the capital inflow undoubtedly adds to the productive capacity of the economy. Therefore, capital outflow should be checked against capital inflows in the previous period plus the contribution these have made to the productive capacity of the economy. Since precise measurement of this contribution may be very difficult, the argument remains inconclusive.

There is an important variant of the "dependency retards growth" argument: Growth is limited because dependency limits and retards the development of local productive forces. Even if this were true, it would not lead to a retardation of growth so long as what is destroyed is replaced by external factors. This replacement of internal factors by external factors has many important implications for what we have called the qualitative aspect of development.

The second position concerning the link between dependency and growth accepts the possibility of dependent growth. This argument seems to rest on a more solid footing, both theoretically and empirically. On theoretical grounds it is hard to imagine that massive external inputs of capital and technology, as well as access to advanced-country markets, would not have some effect on the development of productive forces. (In saying this, we are not for the moment questioning the harmful effects of dependent development.) This theoretical expectation seems to hold up empirically, with rapid growth occurring in a number of countries that are closely integrated with the international capitalist system. Recent work by Peter Evans (1979) as well as previous important work by Cardoso and Faletto (1978) bear important testimony to this.

Next we turn our attention to the qualitative aspects of development. Quality of development refers to the kind of development that is differentiated by various properties (Evans, 1979; Cardoso and Faletto, 1978; Amin, 1976). These differentiations offer a strong contrast with the more homogeneous neoclassical theories of development. The latter do not address the externalities of developmental growth, e.g., vulnerability of the economy, marginalization of certain sectors, uneven growth, etc. Traditional neoclassical theories, which are based on the historical experience of the developed nations, assume that after countries attain a certain level of development, the gains from growth will start to spread throughout the society. In addition, as development progresses, the middle class will grow and the demand for political participation will increase. Democracy emerges out of this (see Lipset, 1959). In other words, distribution of the gain (although not equal distribution) and political participation are regarded as automatic consequences of economic growth.

Dependency theory makes its greatest contribution in this area by showing that, because of the dependency conditions, the developing countries do not move along the same development path that the developed nations did. Instead, they are experiencing a qualitatively different form of development in which growth does not lead to a wider distribution of income and political participation.

The first and the most obvious characteristic of this kind of development stems from the fact that its source and dynamics lie outside the economy. That is, the economy is distorted, on the one hand, so that internal linkages are destroyed and weakened and linkages with external sectors are established instead. The economy is then very responsive to external rather than internal changes. Now, an economy whose dynamic and source of growth lie outside itself and whose structure is so rigid that it cannot easily diversify becomes very vulnerable in two senses: in the sense that if there is disruption in the supply of what is needed, the consequences are very costly and in the sense that any economic downturns in the center (or centers) would have much greater adverse effects in the dependent country.

Another qualitative feature of dependent development is that it tends to be characterized by uneven growth and, as a further expression of this, the marginalization of some social groups. This occurs for two related reasons, one reflecting the internal and the other the external aspects of dependency. Uneven growth occurs because of unequal ties of the local economy to the foreign sector. Since much of the dynamism of the local economy is externally supplied, e.g., through inputs of capital and technology, and since these inputs are concentrated in very specific sectors, it follows that growth will also follow a sectoral pattern. Marginalization occurs for derivative reasons. Since the dependent economy is fragmented, gains generated in sectors with large external inputs will not have the customary "spread effects" whereby they transfer their benefits to other sectors. The process of concentration of production and distribution creates some groups with special advantages and others with only a marginal status.

Conclusion

In this paper we have attempted to provide a general assessment of dependency theory and to suggest ways in which we might carry out future research in this area. We found it useful to distinguish among several components of dependency and to show how these components might be combined into a useful definition of dependency, one that is still consistent with some of the original dependency literature.

After dealing with the problems of dependency as a concept we moved to a consideration of dependency theory. In doing this, we had to introduce an important distinction between quantitative and qualitative aspects of development. In offering our evaluation of dependency theory, we focused mostly on a critique of the theoretical foundations of the literature on dependency, rather than on an empirical investigation of any particular ideas. If there is any conclusion to be drawn from this investigation, it is that a great deal of dependency theory rests on uncertain theoretical grounds and that this is due, for the most part, to the inadequate attention paid to the conceptualization of dependency. If these issues could be more successfully resolved, the relationships between dependency and development could be more readily examined. As it stands now, dependency theorists, when it comes to their empirical investigations, generally look only at selected aspects of both dependency and development. Yet although the empirical investigation is partial, the conclusions are drawn in more general terms. This paper has focused its energies toward the closing of this gap.

Notes

1. This distinction was made previously by Caporaso (1978: 13–43).
2. Cardoso and Faletto (1978) do an excellent job of detailing these complex laws of motion of international capitalism and the ways in which phase characteristics of capitalism affect domestic societies at the time of incorporation.
3. This aspect of dependency is quite closely related to the concept of dependence in which vulnerability is also important. See the discussion by Keohane and Nye (1977: 11–19).

References

Amin, Samir (1976). *Unequal Development* (New York: Monthly Review Press).
Boeke, J. H. (1953). *Economics and Economic Policy of Dual Societies* (New York: International Secretariat, Institute of Pacific Relations).
Brewster, Havelock (1973). "Economic Dependence: A Quantitative Interpretation," *Social and Economic Studies*, Vol. 22, no. 1, pp. 90–95.
Caporaso, James A. (1978). "Dependence, Dependency and Power in the Global System: A Structural and Behavioral Analysis," *International Organization*, Vol. 32, no. 1, pp. 13–43.
Cardoso, Fernando Henrique (1973). "Associated Dependent Development: Theoretical and Practical Implications," in Alfred Stepan (ed.), *Authoritarian Brazil: Origins, Policies, and Futures* (New Haven, Conn.: Yale University Press), pp. 142–176.
Cardoso, Fernando Henrique, and Enzo Faletto (1978). *Dependency and Development in Latin America* (Berkeley: University of California Press).
Evans, Peter (1979). *Dependent Development: The Alliance of Multinational, State, and Local Capital in Brazil* (Princeton, N.J.: Princeton University Press).
Frank, André G. (1968). *Development and Underdevelopment In Latin America* (New York: Monthly Review Press).
Fröbel, Folker, Jürgen Heinrichs, and Otto Kreye (1977). *Die Neue Internationale Arbeitsteilung* (Hamburg: Rororo Aktyell).
Girvan, Norman (1973). "The Development of Dependency Economics in the Caribbean and Latin America: Review and Comparison," *Social and*

Economic Studies, Vol. 22, no. 1, pp. 1–33.

Higgins, Benjamin (1956). "The Dualistic Theory of Underdeveloped Areas," *Economic Development and Cultural Change,* Vol. 4, no. 2, pp. 99–112.

Keohane, Robert O., and Joseph S. Nye (1977). *Power and Interdependence: World Politics In Transition* (Boston: Little, Brown and Co.).

Lipset, Seymour Martin (1959). "Some Social Requisites of Democracy: Economic Development and Political Legitimacy," *American Political Science Review,* Vol. 53, pp. 69–105.

Organisation for Economic Co-operation in Development (1979). *The Impact of Newly Industrialising Countries on Production and Trade in Manufactures* (Paris: OECD).

Sunkel, Osvaldo (n.d.). "Development and Structural Heterogeneity," mimeo, Institute of Development Studies (Sussex, England), pp. 1–23.

Sunkel, Osvaldo (1973). "Transnational Capitalism and National Disintegration in Latin America," *Social and Economic Studies*, Vol. 22, no. 1, March, pp. 132–176.

Part Two
New Themes in
Dependency Analysis

4

The Strategic Dependency of the Centers and the Economic Importance of the Latin American Periphery

Heraldo Muñoz

In recent years it has become rather common to assert that the economic importance of Latin America to the United States has declined sharply, mainly because the region's relative position in the external trade of the United States has progressively deteriorated.[1] Although specific figures do indeed reveal that nowadays the region plays a lesser role in U.S. foreign commerce than it did some decades ago, it would be grossly misleading to assume that the overall economic importance of Latin America to the United States and other core powers has also declined.

The economic relations between the Latin American periphery and the United States should not be analyzed merely in quantitative terms, on a bilateral basis, and at certain points in time. It is necessary to shift the attention to the structural level to verify, for example, whether a decrease in the Latin American share of world trade necessarily implies a breakdown of the critical bonds that have historically existed between core and periphery economies for the advantage of the former. Specifically, more emphasis should be placed on the study of the phenomenon we call the *strategic dependency* of advanced capitalist countries. Strategic dependency is a situation in which the capitalist centers depend on foreign sources, particularly underdeveloped regions, for the supply of low-priced strategic minerals, cheap labor, and markets, all of which are essential for the continued economic growth and national defense of core countries. From this perspective, and taking into account the recent sharpening of the rivalry among center nations over access to cheap raw materials, low-priced labor, and markets overseas, this chapter argues that the economic significance of Latin America for the developed coun-

A revised version of this chapter was published in *Latin American Research Review*, Fall 1981.

tries has persisted and, in some cases, increased.

Dependency theorists have focused their analyses, with good reason, mainly on the impact of imperialism on the class structures, economies, and cultures of underdeveloped societies. By contrast, the use of the concept of strategic dependency attempts to examine what occurs in the centers as capitalism develops on a world level. In this fashion, one can study the economic relations between Latin America and the core powers from the viewpoint of the needs and interests of the centers.

The concept of strategic dependency does not denote simply state-to-state dependency. Strategic dependency characterizes, in the end, a situation in which the *international* fraction (that sector associated with multinational corporations) of the dominant structure of advanced capitalist societies depends for its continued prosperity upon the cheap natural resources and labor and the markets of, principally, the underdeveloped societies. The phenomenon of strategic dependency is also related to class questions inside the core countries in that it can affect domestic intra- and inter-class conflicts and alliances. For instance, past experience shows that the exodus of U.S. multinational corporations to the periphery in search of cheap raw materials and markets is generally backed by the government, but opposed by organized labor.

The strategic dependency of the centers materialized as an outgrowth of the historical process of capitalist expansion. As capitalism expanded worldwide, it shaped the dependency presently suffered by underdeveloped countries, but it also created a dependency of the core powers on the resources, labor, and markets of the Third World. According to Avineri, Marx observed the existence of a similar phenomenon when, writing on imperialism in China and India, he suggested that "not only is Asia becoming more dependent on Europe, Europe is also, dialectically, becoming more dependent on Asia."[2] Following the Hegelian thesis that the master-slave relationship produces a dialectical dependency of the master on the slave, one could postulate that the strategic dependency of the centers on the periphery is an unavoidable consequence of the development of capitalism at the world level. Although this may seem contradictory, strategic dependency might be considered a form of *structural dependency* since it denotes an internal structural tension in capitalism as a mode of production.

However, the two types of dependencies differ because the degrees of conditioning of the societies in which they prevail are different and because the dimensions affected are also different: *Strategic* dependency is a situation that translates principally into external vulnerability and limits to action, particularly in the economic sector of developed countries, while *structural* dependency is a transnational and comprehensive phenomenon meaning that periphery societies, in both domestic and external spheres, are shaped — economically, politically, socially, and culturally — by the structural requirements of the more dynamic centers of world capitalism.[3] Of course, within concrete national contexts there is, to a certain degree, an overlapping of both types of dependency. For example, a relatively more advanced periphery country like Brazil may experience not only structural dependency but also strategic dependency. However, despite the coexistence of two types of dependency in a given nation-state, one situation tends to dominate and to ultimately define insertion of that country in the world political economy. In Brazil, as in the case of most periphery societies, "structural" dependency dominates. It follows from this conceptualization that center countries have a greater range of options to reduce or control their dependency than do periphery nations.

The Components of Strategic Dependency

Critical Minerals

Much of the world's exportable reserves of strategic[4] minerals is located in developed countries such as Canada, Australia, and South Africa. But, interestingly, a great amount of these resources (oil, bauxite, copper, manganese, and cobalt) is found in underdeveloped areas, particularly in Latin America. The strategic dependency of any core country with respect to resources arises basically from two sources: (1) the mere physical absence of given strategic minerals and/or (2) the existence of uneconomic conditions for the exploitation of physically available materials. The latter point leads to another reason why it is important for the centers to preserve access to *cheap* foreign raw materials: The importation of low-priced materials by multinational corporations allows them to slow down investment in constant capital, which translates into higher profits for the conglomerates involved.[5] Consequently, it makes sense for multinational firms to attempt to monopolize cheap raw material sources as a way of continuously earning economic rents.

The importance of cheap basic resources for the core is further revealed by the argument that successful capitalist growth and expansion is founded upon the availability of raw materials. According to Raichur, "Capitalism needs raw materials. . . . To the extent that cheaper raw materials are available outside the jurisdiction of (national) capitalism they will be sought out and used because they stretch the ability of released capital to be employed productively."[6] Similarly, Furtado argues that "the logic of the present system of accumulation with its very short time horizon, consists of exerting increasing pressure on non-renewable resources. But since these resources are located in the periphery an entirely new *problematique* has emerged."[7]

In other words, it is not simply a matter of convenience for developed nations to import minerals from abroad; it is a matter of economic advantage and structural need. Any sudden cutoff or substantial increase in the price of supplies would affect the comfort and "consumptionist" lifestyle that the population — particularly the privileged sectors — of the core countries have enjoyed by relying on use of the periphery's cheap resources. As a technical study on U.S. use of foreign raw materials indicates: "The U.S. economy, of course, has benefited from its use of foreign minerals. Imports of most minerals came from cheaper sources of supply in foreign countries. They reduced U.S. costs for materials and facilitated U.S. exports of metals and of manufactured goods containing metal. Thus they made possible larger real incomes in the United States than would have been possible if more expensive domestic resources had been developed."[8]

The strategic dependency of the centers emerged as the historical product of world capitalist development and it is therefore not a new phenomenon. In effect, the strategic dependency of the centers with regard to the natural resources of Latin America dates back to the Iberoamerican conquest, even though it became more obvious during the early part of this century.

At that time, U.S. investment in the region was highly concentrated by country and sector. American corporations were primarily interested in areas that complemented the U.S. economy and did not compete with American firms.[9] In other words, investment centered on petroleum, industrial minerals, sugar, bananas and other tropical commodities, and railroads (to facilitate the export of raw materials). In 1914 U.S. foreign investment by sector in Latin America was as shown in Table 4.1.

During World War I, armaments production spurred a renewed need for strategic mineral commodities. New mining and oil concessions were sought in South America and the rest of the Third World. After the War, the United States preempted Great Britain as the principal source of foreign capital in Latin America. The bulk of indirect investment remained in agriculture and mining (including petroleum).

By that time the Japanese had also begun a worldwide search for raw materials and markets. Among the preferred target areas for Japanese expansion were South America and, particularly, the South Seas, regions that were not only rich in natural resources but also enjoyed open spaces for colonization.[10] Germany and other European powers, on the other

Table 4.1

U.S. Foreign Investment in Latin America
(by sectors, as percentage of total U. S. investment
in the region, 1914)

Mining	43.5 %
Agriculture	18.7 %
Railways	13.7 %
Oil	10.0 %

Source: Economic Commission for Latin America (CEPAL) data cited in North American Congress on Latin America (NACLA), **Yanqui Dollar** (Berkeley, Cal.: NACLA, 1971), p. 5.

hand, centered their attention mainly on the vast resources of Africa and Asia.

From 1929 to 1945 the inflow of "new" capital into Latin America was modest. The decline in new U.S. investment was largely due to the worldwide economic crisis and to the nationalistic policies of some Latin American republics. Nonetheless, there was an increase in U.S. investment in the mineral resources (including petroleum) of the region, from 38.3 percent of total investment in 1929 to 43.1 percent in 1950 (see Table 4.2). At the same time, the manufacturing sector gained considerable importance.

The postwar period witnessed a progressive shift in U.S. foreign investment out of the extractive sector and into manufacturing activities oriented to the supply of the Latin American market. As can be seen in Table 4.2, the relative weight of mining and petroleum as a percentage of total U.S. investment in the region dropped from 43.1 percent in 1950 to 16.4 percent in 1978, while the manufacturing sector jumped, during the same years, from 17.1 percent to 35.8 percent.

In other words, throughout the last two decades, the axis of strategic dependency — particularly for the United States — has moved away from the mineral resources dimension towards the local market and cheap labor aspects. However, this historical change in the relative weight of the different components of strategic dependency is partly offset by a renewed post-oil-crisis concern in the centers regarding access to critical minerals and by the "obsolescing bargain" phenomenon, which will be explained later.

After World War II, Latin America became Japan's favorite target area for obtaining raw materials through external investment. According to one author, Japanese investments in Latin America were made "to obtain assured sources of raw materials such as iron and copper ore, for

Table 4.2

U. S. Accumulated Investment in Latin America
(in U. S. $ millions and percentages)

Year	Total	%	Mining and Smelting	%	Petroleum	%	Manu- facturing	%	Other (a)	%
1929	3,519	100	732	20.8	617	17.5	231	6.6	1,939	55.1
1943	2,798	100	405	14.5	618	22.1	325	11.6	1,450	51.8
1950	4,576	100	666	14.6	1,303	28.5	781	17.1	1,826	39.9
1960	9,249	100	1,331	14.4	3,264	35.3	1,631	17.6	3,023	32.7
1966	11,448	100	1,565	13.7	3,425	29.9	3,318	29.0	3,090	27.0
1970	14,760	100	2,071	14.0	3,938	26.7	4,621	31.3	4,131	28.0
1977	28,110	100	1,628	5.8	3,489	12.4	10,063	35.8	12,930 (b)	46.0
1978	32,509	100	1,664	5.1	3,661	11.3	11,644	35.8	15,540 (b)	47.8

(a) Includes agriculture, commerce, public services and various other non - manufacturing activities.
(b) These figures are inflated by growing flows of financial resources to tax - havens Bahamas and Bermudas.

Source: Compiled by the author from Alfredo E. Calcagno, Informe sobre las Inversiones Directas Extranjeras en América Latina, E/CEPAL/G 1108, Enero 1980, p. 35, and Survey of Current Business, vol. 59, N° 8, August 1979, pp. 26 - 27.

Japan's industries."[11] Even though at that time Japan's trade with Latin American countries was smaller than that with South East Asia and North America, Japanese investments there were the largest of all major world areas. These investments were principally concentrated in the mining industry in the Andean region (especially in Bolivia and Chile) and in Mexico, again with an eye to securing sources of vital minerals for Japanese industries.[12]

In the aftermath of the Second World War, West Germany found itself "with the same well-rounded industrial structure that it had before the war."[13] Partition reinforced the concentration on basic and capital goods industries, as almost two-thirds of prewar capacity in heavy industry and producer (capital) goods factories remained in the western zone. The new West German economic structure meshed almost perfectly with postwar patterns of world demand, but partition had separated the industrial zones of Germany from the agricultural hinterland and from access to Eastern European sources of raw materials. West Germany desperately needed foodstuffs and minerals and thus began to show great interest in Latin America and its resources. By the end of 1965 West Germany had already invested about DM 1.6 billion in the region. Although this amount was modest in comparison to investments by other advanced powers, it was large compared to German investments in other areas. Latin America's share of total German investments was high, about 20 percent, ranking second after Europe, with 54 percent.[14]

The emergence of "resources nationalism" among resource-rich periphery nations (particularly in Latin America), a growing international concern about the deterioration and possible exhaustion of the earth's resources, and the oil embargo of 1973 brought about further complications for strategically dependent center nations. According to a recent study, the 1973 oil crisis pointed out the dangers of strategic dependency and motivated significant increases in levels of economic aid ("cooperation") on the part of the United States, West Germany, Japan, and other core countries to resource-rich nations of Latin America. Differences in degrees of cooperation were found to be dependent upon variations in the levels of strategic dependency of the center nations involved.[15]

In the case of Japan, the oil crisis caused a general slowdown in overseas investment. In effect, Japanese external investment dropped considerably (31 percent), from ¥3,497 million in fiscal year 1973 to ¥2,396 million in fiscal year 1974. However, "although investment declined in almost all sectors *those in mineral industry rose* to ¥743 million."[16] Moreover, the high degree of strategic dependency experienced by Japan has forced Japanese multinationals to offer better investment terms to resource-producing periphery countries than those offered by American or German investors. For instance, "in Peru the Japanese agreed to a time limit on their investment, worker participation in management decisions and government control of their pricing and marketing practices."[17] This is why an analyst from the U.S. State Department has asserted that "the overriding consideration for Japanese participation in the mining industry of Peru is assured access to raw materials. Profit from investment or marketing in third countries is definitively subordinated to that."[18]

Interestingly, although U.S. investment in the Andean region (which includes Peru) decreased noticeably during the early 1970s, due to expropriation and divestment, American investment expenditures in resource-rich Peru itself stayed at a high level owing to Southern Peru Copper Company's expansion of activities around the huge Cuajone mine complex. Likewise, U.S. net total flows of financial resources to the Andean country jumped—despite the nationalistic policies of Velasco Alvarado—from $15 million in 1969 to $467 million in 1975.[19]

Foreign economic assistance constitutes a vital tool of the centers to gain preferential access to the critical mineral resources of Latin America. In the words of a high-level Washington spokesman:

> Why should the United States persist with foreign assistance? . . . consider first the economy. The United States is increasingly linked to the developing countries in international trade and investment. U.S. imports of energy fuels and minerals are expected to increase from $8 billion in 1970 to more than $31 billion by 1985—a fourfold increase in the next 13 years. The known reserves of many minerals are largely located in the developing countries. . . . The United States has a fundamental interest in insuring that the developing countries are part of an international trading system in which resources are freely shared.[20]

Not surprisingly then, as a consequence of the 1973 oil embargo, Section 633 of the U.S. Foreign Assistance Act of 1974 "authorizes the President to furnish military or economic aid in exchange for 'strategic raw materials' in short supply whenever he determines it to be in the national interest."[21]

In the case of Japanese aid there has been a tendency since the 1960s "to give greater preference to countries that are relatively less developed, *but that are endowed with vital natural resources needed by Japan.*"[22] A study by Sukehiro Hasegawa showed that resource-rich nations such as Brazil and Peru scored among the top twelve out of the thirty-eight countries favored with the highest ratios of nonpayable grants to total Japanese assistance.[23] There is little doubt, therefore, that, as a U.S.

government document observed, Japanese official economic aid "is being increasingly focused on countries or regions producing minerals and agricultural commodities imported by Japan."[24]

A study on West German aid to underdeveloped countries during the early 1960s also revealed that one important reason behind the economic assistance program is West Germany's need for critical minerals that some of the recipient nations have. In the words of Jack Knusel, "Since the German economy would be greatly weakened without basic raw materials, it is in their interest that they remain on good terms with the developing countries from whom most of them are obtained. Aid in effect provides Germans with the means for maintaining and strengthening their own economic health and stability.[25] As in the case of external investment, the Latin American countries that receive the most aid from West Germany are Brazil, Peru, and Mexico.

In sum, the strategic dependency of the core on the key minerals of Latin America and other periphery regions is quite evident and, together with the catalyst of the 1973 oil crisis, has led to attitudes of "cooperation" of the centers with resource-rich periphery nations. Precisely because of this, a document from the Ministry of Foreign Relations of Japan asserts that "the importance to Japan of Central and South America which has many underdeveloped resources, increased further in 1973 as the problem of resources and energy became more serious throughout the world. . . . It is considered that Japan's relations with the Central and South American countries will become even closer with economic relations as the axis."[26]

Cheap Labor

The strategic dependency of the centers on cheap labor in the periphery represents principally a phenomenon characteristic of the postwar period and is linked to the process of transfer of infrastructures of production from the centers to places such as Brazil, Mexico, and Taiwan. In short, the world economy has witnessed the emergence of the multinational corporations' "free production zones" or "platforms of production," which can be defined as "industrial enclaves set up for world-market oriented industries at sites where cheap labor is abundant."[27]

At present, the platforms of production located in underdeveloped countries constitute a *structural need* for multinational corporations due, among other reasons, to increases in the cost of labor in the centers. The exploitation of lower wages in the periphery allows individual multinational firms to reduce costs and earn higher profits. The "structural need" feature of cheap Third World labor for core corporations has been

observed by a European scholar, who described it in the following terms:
"For the first time in world history, our capitalists have both the physical
and psychological ability to exploit the Third World's most basic
resource — its cheap labor. Increasingly, they will do so, partly from
choice *but mostly from necessity*, and this development is a rope with
which many a traditional American or European multinational will be
hanged."[28] (emphasis added)

The changes that have taken place in the nature of strategic dependency during the post-war period partly explain the emergence of a new
international division of labor. In other words, the growing interest of
the core in the markets and cheap labor of periphery countries — at the
expense of their mineral resources — has been intimately linked to the
phenomenon of redistribution or relocation of production at the world
level. Hence, it is now widely accepted that the classical international
division of labor between advanced exporters of manufactures on the
one hand and underdeveloped exporters of raw materials on the other
hand has ceased to exist.

The phenomenon of redistribution or relocation of production at the
world level implies that the old international division of labor between
advanced exporters of manufactures on the one hand and
underdeveloped exporters of raw materials on the other is being substantially modified. Consequently, the pattern of insertion of Latin America
into the world economy is also experiencing a transformation that will be
analyzed later. According to one source, the new international division
of labor is distinguished by

> a single world market for labor and a single world market in industrial sites
> [that] now, for the first time, effectively encompasses both the traditional
> industrial countries as well as the underdeveloped countries. In many cases
> industrial capital can earn extra profits through a suitable reorganization of
> production, because a suitable subdivision of the production process makes
> it possible to exploit the *world-wide* industrial reserve army with the help of
> a highly developed transport and communications system.[29]

Multinational corporations based in the centers have progressively
come to value the cheap labor of periphery nations. The explanation of
this phenomenon is simple: The salaries paid to workers in the
underdeveloped nations are merely a small fraction of the wages of
workers in the developed countries, even if one takes labor productivity
into account. A recent study examined the issue through different
methodologies that included the productivity of labor (see Table 4.3) and
concluded that the salaries paid by transnational corporations to workers

Table 4.3

Salaries of Workers and Employees (Nominal and Weighted for
Productivity) in Underdeveloped and Developed Countries
(United States = 100)

	Nominal Salary per inhabitant	Cost of Salary per unit (a) of Production	Salaries Value added	Salaries Weighted for productivity (b)	Salaries Weighted for productivity (c)
Underdeveloped nations	8.0	45.0 (d)	47.3	17.3	39.3
Developed nations	79.0	-	94.5	-	73.6
Japan	47.0	-	77.3	44.3	64.3
Federal Republic of Germany	-	-	-	99.8	-
United States	100.0	100.0	100.0	100.0	100.0

(a) only steel

(b) $$WEij = \frac{WijxPj}{Oij}$$ where
- WEij: weighted salaries, branch i country j
- Wij: total salaries of the industry's branch i in country j
- Pj: unitary price
- Oij: total production of industrial branch (in value)

(c) $$WEij = \frac{Wij}{Nij}$$ $e (Lg\ 1 - \alpha\ i\ Lg\ PBIHj - \beta\ i)$ where
- WEij: weighted salaries, branch i, country j
- Wij: total distributed salaries
- Nij: number workers and employees
- PBIHj: Gross domestic product per inhabitant

(d) Brazil

Source: Alfredo Eric Calcagno, **Informe sobre las Inversiones Directas Extranjeras en América Latina**, E/CEPAL/G. 1108, Santiago de Chile, 1980, p. 14.

in the periphery are, at official exchange rates, about 60 percent to 80 percent below the wages normally paid for the same work in the United States.

An ECLA document states that, in view of the wide differences in the cost of labor in Latin American countries and the developed nations of Europe and the United States, Latin American labor will continue to be significantly cheaper than that of the centers "even if advanced income distribution policies are applied."[30] Incidentally, there are also marked differences in the labor costs of operations of one single enterprise, depending on where it is based. For example, in the case of General Motors, by the end of 1972 the average cost of one hour of production work, compared to the cost in the United States, was 35 percent less in Mexico, 18 percent less in Brazil, and 16 percent less in Argentina.[31]

Some analysts hold that the dependency of core corporations upon the cheap labor of the periphery is affected by the kind of technology utilized by the firms, i.e., capital intensive versus labor intensive. Obviously, the more a given corporation employs labor-intensive technologies, the greater its interest in the abundant cheap labor of periphery regions.[32] Hence, many U.S. companies, for instance, transfer part of their production processes to the north of Mexico where labor is relatively cheap. A major feature of this type of transfer is that it involves small amounts of fixed capital needed for installation. Therefore, it is quite easy and inexpensive to move to a more friendly country if any labor or fiscal problems arise in the host country. The implications of this situation for the bargaining power of periphery nations will be discussed later.

In any event, available evidence suggests that it is not only enterprises that utilize labor-intensive techniques that move to low-wage regions. According to Turner, "in the past only the extremely labor-intensive industries went abroad, while today the industry that can be exported has much more 'capital-intensive' orientation. Ten years ago, the high labor content in textiles threatened the existence of the industry in the developed economies; today the labor content in small cars may be enough to force their manufacture in relatively cheap-labor areas."[33] It has seemingly become quite difficult to distinguish clearly between corporations that utilize capital-intensive techniques versus those that employ labor-intensive technologies since "there is a continuum from the labor-intensive industries like textiles to the real capital-intensive industries like nuclear power plants."[34]

Several other factors related to the cost of labor stimulate the transfer of infrastructures of production from the centers to the periphery: as a rule, the working day in the underdeveloped low-wage societies is considerably longer than it is in the developed countries; the labor force in the periphery can be hired or fired virtually without limit; and the wide availability of a reserve army allows for an "optimal" selection of the most suitable labor force according to age, sex, degree of submission, etc.[35]

With respect to the productivity of labor, one should remember that the development and refinement of technology and labor organization make it possible to break down complex production processes into elementary units "so that even an unskilled labor force can easily and quickly be trained to perform otherwise complex operations."[36] Through this "fragmentation of jobs," skilled labor receiving high wages (e.g., in the United States) can be replaced by unskilled or semiskilled labor earning lower wages (as in most countries of Latin America), particularly where trade unions are ineffective and/or the defense of workers' rights is impeded by authoritarian governments.

Data on displacement of industries from the centers to the Latin

American periphery confirm these generalizations. For instance, in recent years, U.S. corporations searching for cheap labor have created more than 50,000 jobs along the Mexican border and consequently, exports from the area back to the United States have climbed from $7 million in 1966 to $350 million in 1972.[37]

Research conducted by Fröbel, Heinrichs, and Kreye indicate that the number of employees in foreign subsidiaries of West German textile and clothing manufacturers more than doubled between 1966 and 1974-1975, whereas the number employed domestically decreased by roughly a quarter. It was estimated that in 1977, for every 100 domestic workers hired by the West German textile and clothing industry, there were well over 10 foreign workers employed in West German-owned subsidiaries abroad.[38] Similarly, Barnet and Müller write that the largest U.S. global corporations, "such as Ford, ITT, Chrysler, Kodak, and Procter & Gamble, employ more than one-third of their work force outside the United States."[39]

Foreign employment in West German subsidiaries in low-wage countries as a proportion of the total foreign labor employed by West German subsidiaries in the textile and clothing industry increased from nearly a quarter in 1966 to about half in 1974-1975. During the mid-1970s, West German manufacturing companies had subsidiaries in seventy-seven countries outside the European Economic Community (EEC). Most of them were located in Latin America, principally in Brazil, Mexico, and Argentina, and were fairly well distributed over different branches of industry.[40]

The tendency toward the displacement of industries from Europe and the United States to Latin America and other low-wage regions has evidently had an impact on employment patterns in the centers. Barnet and Müller argue that such displacement has caused many cases of unemployment in the developed countries. For example, the transfer of part of the television production process of General Instruments from New England to Portugal and Taiwan entailed the firing of 3,000 to 4,000 U.S. workers; employment losses also occurred with the transfer of Warwick Electronics from Arkansas and Illinois to Mexico; and the displacement of Zenith Radio from the United States to Taiwan caused the layoff of more than 7,000 workers.[41] Similarly, a study conducted by professors Frank and Freeman of Cornell University reached the conclusion that U.S. foreign investment had meant the loss of 1,062,577 work opportunities for Americans between 1966 and 1973.[42] However, other studies, such as the one by Robert Stobaugh and others,[43] do not agree, asserting that U.S. overseas investment has had favorable effects on both the U.S. balance of payments and the level of domestic employment.

What should be emphasized here, however, is that the cheap labor factor in strategic dependency embodied in the exodus of multinational corporations to low-wage areas like Brazil and Mexico is closely linked with class issues *within* the core countries. Apparently, organized labor in the United States was slow to perceive the implications of U.S. direct investment abroad. However, the awareness level increased sharply after 1966, when global corporations dramatically accelerated their production overseas for export to the American market.[44] The result was strong opposition to what came to be called the "export of U.S. jobs."

The antagonism between U.S. labor groups and corporate sectors over the export-of-jobs issue has not subsided. On the contrary, it has been aggravated by the relatively high unemployment rates registered in the United States in recent years. This controversy is likely to continue because of the contradictions involved: On one side are the dominant interests of the corporate sectors that seek to exploit cheap periphery labor and maximize world profits; on the other, U.S. labor groups, whose aim is to preserve or increase domestic employment and salary levels. Concentration and globalization give the business sectors a valuable advantage over national labor groups:

> Corporate organization on a global scale is a highly effective weapon for undercutting the power of organized labor everywhere. . . . The ability of corporations to open and close plants rapidly and to shift their investment from one country to another erodes the basis of organized labor's bargaining leverage, the strike. . . . A global corporation can also protect itself from a strike by establishing what is called "multiple sourcing"—i.e., different plants in different countries producing the same component. It is a strategy by which the corporation can make itself independent of the labor force in any one plant.[45]

Given this scenario, perhaps one can explain the strong political support given recently by the staunchly conservative AFL-CIO to opposition, prodemocracy labor groups in Chile[46] as an attempt on the part of the U.S. body to remove the governmental control factors that make Chilean labor cheap and therefore attractive to U.S. investors. The AFL-CIO actions in Chile would then amount to an attempt to regain jobs for American workers and to erode the bargaining advantages of global firms at the same time, and would demonstrate that the confrontation between capital and labor has indeed shifted from the national to the global stage.[47]

Third World Markets

Another dimension of strategic dependency closely linked with access to cheap labor and overseas production platforms is the access, preservation, and enlargement of periphery markets. It should be emphasized that the corporations of the advanced capitalist countries prefer to establish themselves in underdeveloped countries that have all three determinants of strategic dependency: abundant low-priced raw materials, abundant cheap labor, *and* wide markets. If a periphery nation has only one or two of these elements, it occupies a place of lesser importance in the hierarchical scale of priorities of the corporations and governments of the centers. At the same time, the more the axis of strategic dependency moves away from the natural resources element and towards the markets dimension, the greater the economic and political importance of large-market countries like Brazil and Mexico, particularly as they also possess critical raw materials and abundant cheap labor.

Fernando Henrique Cardoso holds that the phenomenon he calls "associated-dependent development," one of the most recent expressions of dependency in Latin America and more specifically in Brazil, is based precisely on the growing importance of Latin America in general, and of some countries in particular, as a market for the core economies. During the previous stages of world capitalist development

> the market for goods produced in dependent economies by foreign enterprises was mostly, if not fully, the market of the advanced economies: oil, copper, coffee, iron, bauxite, manganese, etc., were produced to be sold and consumed in the advanced capitalist countries. . . . [However] today for G.M. or Volkswagen, or General Electric, or Sears Roebuck, *the Latin American market, if not the particular market in each country where those corporations are producing in Latin America, is the immediate goal in terms of profit.* So at least to some extent, a certain type of foreign investment needs some kind of internal prosperity.[48] (emphasis added)

In Cardoso's view, the internationalization of the domestic market will create the conditions for the continued prosperity of an increasing portion of Brazilian society. But "in spite of internal economic development, countries tied to international capitalism by that type of linkage remain economically dependent, insofar as the production of the means of production (technology) are concentrated in advanced capitalist economies (mainly in the U.S.)."[49]

The establishment of platforms of production in underdeveloped countries enables multinational corporations to get around import barriers of the host nations and to enjoy the same privileged oligopolistic positions they have at home. In other words, the platforms of production give corporations a greater degree of control over the domestic markets of the periphery than they could achieve merely by exporting from the home country. This is why, for example,

in 1970 nearly 80% of the production of overseas subsidiaries of transna-
tional enterprises of the United States was channeled to the internal market
of the countries in which they were located. . . . These sales can be considered as "indirect exports," since they replace sales that previously were
made from the headquarters of the home country. It is calculated that in
1971 the "indirect exports" of subsidiaries of American firms were almost
four times larger than direct exports from the United States; in the case of
the United Kingdom the proportion was two to one; and for France, the
Federal Republic of Germany, and Japan it ranged between 37 and 95%. In
addition, through these platforms the developed countries stimulate a
significant flow of direct exports from the home country of the corporations, particularly with regard to equipment, parts, and intermediary
goods.[50]

The great significance of the Latin American market for American
manufacturing corporations producing in the region can be inferred
from the figures in Table 4.4. For instance, in 1976 local sales of U.S.
subsidiaries in the region amounted to $24,354 million, while exports to
the United States and other countries outside the area reached only $1,543
million. Between 1966 and 1976 local sales were approximately 93 percent of the total.

In U.S.-Latin American trade relations, it is not merely the Latin
American markets for manufactures that are of great significance to the
U.S. economy, but the markets for agricultural products as well. Ac-
cording to ECLA, "exports of United States farm products to Latin
America in fiscal year 1977/1978 surpassed the 1973/1974 record of 2.5
billion dollars. This took place in the context of a 26 % increase in total
United States agricultural exports in the first half of 1978 compared with
the preceding six month period."[51]

Latin America is also important for the centers as a *key market for armaments.* Although an increasing number of countries in the region are
manufacturing their own weapons (indigenously designed, under license,
or in cooperation with other states), South America's weapons purchases
jumped, in constant 1975 dollars, from $72 million in 1963 to $804
million in 1977. The principal suppliers for South America were the
United States, the United Kingdom, and France.[52]

Latin America is also a very profitable market for investment capital
of core countries. In terms of volume of earnings, Latin America is by
far the most profitable region of the underdeveloped world for the
United States. In 1977 Latin America accounted for nearly 20 percent of
all earnings of U.S. multinational firms throughout the globe ($3,988
million), equivalent to 50.2 percent of all earnings of American corporations in the Third World. In turn, the Third World accounts for about 40

Table 4.4

Sales of Subsidiaries of U.S. Multinational Corporations in Latin America: Manufacturing Sector, 1966–1976
(in millions of dollars and percentages)

	1966	1967	1968	1969	1970	1971	1972	1973	1974	1975	1976
(1) Local Sales*	2,983	3,175	3,446	3,798	4,290	5,192	5,592	15,230	19,438	22,505	24,354
- Share of total	95%	94%	94%	93%	92%	93%	90%	94%	93%	94%	94%
(2) Exports to the U. S. and countries outside the region	161	187	231	289	349	396	600	990	1,421	1,457	1,543
- Share of total	5%	6%	6%	7%	8%	7%	10%	6%	7%	6%	6%
(3) Total Sales	3,144	3,362	3,677	4,087	4,639	5,588	6,192	16,220	20,859	23,962	25,897

* Sales by subsidiaries in the host countries

Source: Compiled by the author from several issues of Survey of Current Business.

Table 4.5

Adjusted Earnings (a) of U.S. Corporations in the Third World: 1975-1977
(in millions of US $ and percentages)

	1975	%	1976	%	1977	%
LATIN AMERICA	3,321	19.4	3,400	18.0	3,988	19.9
Middle East	1,643	9.9	1,938	10.3	1,956	9.7
Africa (b)	534	3.2	607	3.2	606	3.0
Asia and Pacific (c)	1,304	7.9	1,022	5.4	1,392	6.9
All Third World	6,703	40.3	6,967	37.0	7,942	39.6
TOTAL ALL COUNTRIES	16,615	100.0	18,841	100.0	20,081	100.0

(a)   Consists of the U.S. parent's shares in the earnings (net of foreign income taxes) of its foreign affiliates, plus net interest on intercompany accounts, less foreign withholding taxes.
(b)   Excludes South Africa.
(c)   Excludes Japan, Australia, and New Zealand.

Source: Compiled by the author from several issues of **Survey of Current Business.**

percent of all foreign earnings of U.S. companies (see Table 4.5).

Interestingly, overseas income is a critical component of U.S. business. In 1974, the foreign earnings of American multinationals accounted for 26.9 percent of their total earnings, up from 8.6 percent in 1957. It is estimated that the ratios of gross foreign earnings (before foreign taxes) to gross total earnings (before U.S. taxes) are even higher. Income on foreign direct investment, plus fees and royalties from affiliated foreigners, contributed over $21 billion to the U.S. balance of payments in 1974, nearly as much as total U.S. exports of capital goods (excluding automobiles).[53]

In the financial area, a sizable share of the total earnings of the twelve largest U.S. banks comes from profits on loans made *outside* the United States, particularly in Latin America. According to Wachtel, "in 1975, 63% of total income for the 12 largest U.S. banks originated in their foreign branches, up from 23% in 1971 and 43% in 1974. For several of these large banks, nearly all of their earnings in 1975 was derived from foreign branch activity. For example, Chase Manhattan received an astounding 82% of its 1975 earnings from foreign activities; First National Bank of Chicago, 63%; and First National Bank of Boston, 80%."[54]

Not surprisingly, during the post–Second World War period there was a noticeable jump in the number of American banking subsidiaries abroad, from 95 in 1950 to 847 in 1975. A high percentage of this rapid increase corresponded to the growth of U.S. banking in Latin America

Table 4.6

U. S. Banking Subsidiaries Abroad (1914 - 1975)

	1914	1918	1926	1939	1950	1960	1969	1970	1975
Latin America	6	31	61	47	49	55	235	288	529
Europe	7	26	25	16	15	19	103	147	233
Africa	-	-	-	-	-	1	1	1	5
Middle East	-	-	-	-	-	4	6	6	14
Far East	13	-	21	18	19	23	77	54	93
Other Territories	-	4	-	8	12	22	38	-	-
Total	26	61	107	89	95	124	460	496	874

Source: Xavier Gorostiaga, **Los Banqueros del Imperio** (EDUCA, 1978)

from 49 subsidiaries in 1950 to 529 in 1975, meaning that the participation of the region as a percentage of the total, increased from 52 percent in 1950 to 62 percent in 1975. The growth of U.S. banking subsidiaries in Latin America has been faster than anywhere else in the globe, Europe included (see Table 4.6).

The importance of Latin America for private lending entities has substantially increased after the oil crisis: given the high international liquidity produced by an overabundance of petrodollars, bankers are now more than eager to lend to periphery countries. This explains, at least in part, the tendency in Latin America to borrow increasingly from private sources at the expense of bilateral and multilateral public sources.[55] In effect, in 1977 the region accounted for nearly two-thirds of the gross indebtedness of non-oil-exporting underdeveloped countries to commercial banks and almost all of the net indebtedness (see Table 4.7). The bulk of this debt is carried by Brazil and Mexico, but other countries like Peru, Chile, Argentina, and Colombia also play major roles.[56] Among the principal private lending institutions are the Morgan Guaranty Trust Co., the Bank of America, and Manufacturers Hanover Trust.

It should be noted that despite the great importance of Latin America, most of the world stock of private investment is presently concentrated in the core countries themselves. In 1967 approximately two-thirds of the investment stock of the centers was located in the developed countries; eight years later, that percentage had increased to three-fourths. During the same period the relative weight of underdeveloped nations in world investment decreased from one-third to one-fourth. In other words, between 1967 and 1975, the stock of foreign investment in the centers grew

Table 4.7

Indebtedness of Non - Oil Developing Countries to Private
Commercial Banks, End December 1977 a /
(billions of dollars)

	Latin America b /	Middle East c /	Africa	Asia d /	Total
Gross	71.1	1.9	14.0	21.6	108.6
Net	36.2	- 7.1	3.0	- 1.2	30.9

a /	Includes short term debt
b /	Excludes Caribbean area and Panama
c /	Excludes Israel and residual estimate
d /	Excludes Hong Kong and Singapore

Source: Bank for International Settlements, **Forty - Eighth Annual Report**, Basle,
                12 June 1978, pp. 94 - 95.

at an average annual rate of 12.9 percent, while the stock in the periphery
grew merely at a 9.4 percent annual rate.[57]

In addition to the general decline experienced by underdeveloped nations as a whole, Latin America suffered a relative decrease in its participation in world investment, due largely to the implementation of
policies of nationalization or expropriation on the part of some countries
of the region. In 1967 Latin America attracted 17.5 percent of all world
investment but in 1975 that share fell to 14.5 percent. The speed of
foreign investment growth (9.3 percent) in Latin America during the
same period was about half the rate registered in the Far East (16.8 percent). However, countries such as Mexico and Brazil experienced spectacular rates of foreign investment growth, particularly during the
1970s.[58]

Still, of the $58,200 million invested at the end of 1973 by the ad-
vanced capitalist countries in the periphery, 44 percent was invested in
Latin America. More importantly, data on U.S. investment indicate that
in 1975 19 percent of total U.S. investment in manufacturing throughout
the world was in underdeveloped countries. Latin America accounted for
the very high proportion of 15 percent of the world total.[59]

In line with the growing relevance of the markets dimension of
strategic dependency, most of the accumulated external investment in
Latin America is concentrated in the four countries with the largest
markets, Brazil, Mexico, Argentina, and Venezuela, which together account for more than 50 percent of foreign investment in the region. In
1975 Brazil received almost 25 percent of external investment, followed
by Mexico with nearly 13 percent, Venezuela with over 10 percent, and
Argentina with about 5 percent (representing a noticeable decrease in
comparison to 1971).

Table 4.8

U. S. Investment in Latin America as a Percentage
of Total U. S. Investment Abroad

1966	1968	1970	1972	1974	1976	1978
18.6	18.2	16.9	16.2	16.9	17.3	19.3

Source: U. S. Department of Commerce data cited in **Latin America Weekly Report**, WR - 79 - 03, November 16, 1979, p.32.

With regard to the geographical origins of foreign investment in Latin America, the United States has traditionally played the most important role. However, since 1967 the U.S. presence declined in importance, owing particularly to the fast growth of Japanese investment in the region. While in 1967 the United States accounted for 63.8 percent of external investment in Latin America, in 1974 it accounted for only 50 percent; during the same period, the relative participation of the EEC grew from 17.5 percent to 25 percent and that of Japan jumped from 2.2 percent to 22 percent.[60]

On the other hand, more recent data on total U.S. foreign investment show that Latin America has regained the importance it had for the United States during the 1960s. As can be seen in Table 4.8, towards the end of 1978 the region received 19.3 percent of all U.S. foreign investment, compared to 16.2 percent in 1972 and 18.6 percent in 1966. Apparently, a good deal of this new U.S. investment flows to tax havens like Bermuda or the Bahamas.

Latin America has also become increasingly important as an investment area for Western Europe. According to a recent study conducted by the European Center of Studies and Information on Multinational Corporations, in the decade of the 1970s Latin America became the preferred target region for European external investment, displacing the United States. The more active investors include the Federal Republic of Germany, Belgium, Switzerland, and the Netherlands. In the case of West Germany, investment in Latin America jumped from DM1,500 million in 1970 to DM8,000 million in 1979 (an 80 percent increase; comparable figures were 40 percent for Africa, 30 percent for Asia, and 20 percent for the United States and Canada). The preferred target countries for the Europeans are Brazil, Mexico, Argentina, and Chile.[61]

Lastly, as stated earlier, there have been important changes in the sectors in which foreign investment in Latin America is located. In the past foreign investment was concentrated mainly in the extractive industries and services; "today there is an absolute predominance of investment in manufacturing activities oriented to the supply of the internal markets which co-exist with the remnants of foreign investment of importance in the past, namely, public services, mining and petroleum."[62]

In sum, it would appear that Latin America represents a market of great importance to the centers and that the "access, preservation and enlargement of markets" is a critical dimension of the strategic dependency of core countries. This is particularly so if one considers the liberal trade policies of countries like Chile that have unilaterally reduced or eliminated most tariffs on foreign imports and all barriers to external investment.[63] The following paragraph from a *Business Week* article on Latin America illustrates the point:

> Multinational executives who have been watching one Latin American country after another pull back from the radicalism of the early 1970s today consider the region to be one of the world's major investment opportunities. "I can just say that the area has more growth potential than the rest of the world," says Andre van Dam, Buenos Aires based director planning for CPC Latin America. "It is all there—protein, minerals, forests, water." Adds William D. Rogers, U.S. Under Secretary of State for Economic Affairs: "The center of gravity is moving toward more effective market-mixed economies." And what Rogers and van Dam are talking about is a gigantic arena for business: a fast-expanding population of 300 million and a combined gross national product of $200 billion.[64]

The Strategic Dependency of the Core and the Bargaining Power of Latin America

The strategic dependency of the advanced capitalist nations (that is the historico-structural need of the centers to have access to low-priced strategic minerals, abundant cheap labor, and markets for underdeveloped countries) has been and continues to be a central component of the economic relations between the core and the periphery. The oil embargo of 1973, world inflation, the growing trade rivalry among developed nations, the international monetary crisis, and other problems of the present world order have sharpened the strategic dependency of the centers and, therefore, have underlined the importance of Latin America for the capitalist core. These same events increased the hopes and perceived bargaining power of Latin American countries, particularly of those possessing vast natural resources, cheap labor, and wide markets. But in order to evaluate the concrete ability of these nations to exercise pressure on the developed world, one must relate "bargaining power" to each of the three basic components of strategic dependency.

The negotiating capacity of a host nation is minimal vis-à-vis multinational corporations that seek mainly to take advantage of the low-cost local labor because, if pressured, they can easily move to another country, given that their operations involve small amounts of fixed capital. The high mobility of these firms is, therefore, their best defense against the potential bargaining power of periphery nations.

Notwithstanding the fact that, historically, the axis of strategic dependency has tended to move away from the minerals dimension, the capacity of the Latin American periphery to exercise negotiating power increases considerably when it comes to multinationals interested in external deposits of raw materials. In this instance the capital invested tends to be large, and both the corporation and the government of the core power are concerned about maintaining the flow of supplies (particularly after the 1973 oil embargo experience).

The relationship between mining corporations and Third World host countries has gone through a significant transformation in recent times. In the past, the mining companies of the developed nations were able to dictate the terms of an investment, in view of the vast size of the capital usually involved. If the host nation wanted the capital inflow, it had little choice but to accept the firms' conditions. But nowadays the high fixed costs, which gave foreign corporations such strength at the start of the investment, have become a source of vulnerability; with their capital sunk, foreign investors can be trapped into continuing production as long as they recover their variable costs. The host country's need for higher revenues, coupled with an improvement in the technical skills of periphery negotiators, produces an "obsolescing bargain"[65] between the host government and the mining corporation:

> A foreign company is enticed by terms that outweigh the drawbacks of committing large lump sums of capital under conditions of great uncertainty. Once the uncertainty is dissipated and the project is profitable, the original terms appear to be overgenerous to the company, who, because it now cannot withdraw, must accept the stricter conditions of a new bargain. This process has a cyclical character: to attract new investors or new commitments from old investors the climate might improve for a period. But the new bargains, too, obsolesce.[66]

This situation is now possible because there has emerged a new, more decentralized, international political context, in which—among other things—the United States is not the undisputed world hegemonic power. Consequently, the United States can no longer easily resort to "gunboat diplomacy" to enforce agreements between private American firms and Latin American governments as it did a few decades ago.[67]

Additionally, the relative bargaining strength of a resource-rich periphery country varies according to several other factors. The scarcer the raw material involved in the negotiation, the greater the ability of the host country to extract good conditions from the multinational; the greater the natural resource dependency of the country of origin of the corporation (as in the case of Japan), the better the negotiating position of the host nation; and the greater number of firms that possess the technology for exploitation and commercialization of the resource under discussion, the stronger the bargaining position of the host country, since it can threaten to negotiate with alternative investors.[68]

The bargaining power of the Latin American periphery is probably greatest with reference to foreign investment aimed at capturing the internal market of the recipient nations, since the capital at stake tends to be considerable and since the firm and/or its home country may rely, to varying degrees, on income obtained overseas. The international context is particularly important in this case because a situation of "oversupply" in the centers increases the urgency to sell and, consequently, strengthens the bargaining position of the more advanced countries of the periphery. In the words of Wallerstein:

> When the core producers face a situation of "over-supply," they begin to compete intensely with each other to maintain their share in a comparatively shrinking world market for their finished goods (especially machinery). At that time, semi-peripheral countries can, up to a point, pick and choose among core producers not only in terms of the sale of their commodities but also in terms both of welcoming their investment in manufactures and of purchasing their producer's goods.[69]

Large-market countries like Brazil, Mexico, Argentina, and Venezuela,[70] have a particular bargaining advantage over other Latin American states in this respect, especially considering that, as stated previously, they receive a substantial portion of the growing external investment in manufacturing activities oriented to the supply of the domestic market. Likewise, countries such as Brazil that have growing middle-income strata have a greater negotiating potential vis-à-vis foreign firms that produce consumer goods than do countries with small middle-income sectors.

Brazil, Mexico, and Argentina have been highly successful in case-by-case negotiations with foreign enterprises, especially in the automotive sector (where permission is given to produce domestically as well as to export). Fiat, for instance, had to accept an agreement to export parts and pieces as a requirement to produce within Brazil; Nissan also had to sign a similar contract to export parts and pieces to Japan in order to stay in Mexico; and the Volkswagen "bug" and the Peugeot 404 models are still being manufactured in Brazil and Argentina and sold locally as well as exported, although they are no longer produced in their countries of origin. Lastly, Mexico and Brazil have also negotiated important joint ventures with foreign corporations in the steel, mechanical, atomic, and chemical industries. The Brazilian chemical firm COPENE (Petroquímica Nordeste) is a case in point: It includes national public and private capital plus capital of several multinationals of the developed world, which also contribute the technology and the administration.

In summary, due to the economic importance of Latin America, a significance linked to the strategic dependency of the core, those countries that possess large markets, cheap critical minerals, and low-cost labor can exercise substantial bargaining power vis-à-vis corporations and governments of the centers. Nonetheless, one should consider the limits to periphery negotiating power that arise from the structural dependency experienced by underdeveloped countries. The constraints of structural dependency may signify that the use of bargaining power may be reduced to very narrow fields of application and may not translate into concrete negotiating power at the national level and as a factor of interstate relations (so as to facilitate the establishment of a New International Economic Order, for example).

In addition, the bargaining power of the Latin American periphery can be easily countered by the superior bargaining power of the developed world. Because of the significant differences between the strategic dependency of the centers and the structural dependency of the periphery, an advanced power like the United States would have multiple options open to deal with a challenge from an underdeveloped country, while the latter would have few options. If the situation required it, the United States could retaliate against the structurally dependent nation by reducing import quotas, blocking loans from international institutions, impeding the sale of needed technology, and perhaps even mobilizing groups within the periphery country against the local government.[71] Although these measures, in a dialectical fashion, might also aggravate the strategic dependency of the United States and affect the interests of particular U.S. firms adversely, the harm to the United States would probably be substantially less than the damage suffered by the periphery country. In the last analysis then, the ability of the centers to manipulate the structural dependency of the periphery is greater than the ability of the periphery to take advantage of the strategic dependency of the core.

Conclusions

This chapter has attempted to demonstrate the present economic importance of Latin America for the developed world, putting special emphasis on the permanence of key linkages between the region and the core powers. From among these linkages we have focused attention on the phenomenon of strategic dependency of the centers.

The shifts that have occurred in the nature of strategic dependency reflect the changing needs of the more dynamic centers of world capitalism and hence explain—at least in part—the emergence of a new international division of labor in which countries like Brazil are no longer mere exporters of raw materials for the factories of the developed world. Brazil and Mexico now constitute a "semiperiphery" of the global political economy; the role of the semiperiphery is to produce and export manufactures while the centers provide capital and technology.

Among the semiperipheral nations of Latin America are Brazil, Mexico, and Argentina, to which one could add Venezuela and perhaps even Colombia; the rest of the countries still have problems and needs similar to the classical case of an underdeveloped society. This distinction is important because often it is asserted that *Latin America* is passing through a period of industrialization, that *Latin America* has increased its participation in the world trade of manufactures when, in reality, the greater relative weight of countries like Brazil and Mexico distort development figures at the regional level. Brazil, Mexico,[72] Argentina, and Venezuela play a most important role in the relations between the Latin American periphery and the centers and are, undoubtedly, the regional countries of highest importance for the core.

The industrialization of the Latin American periphery has meant the emergence of new competitors for scarce raw materials and has thus aggravated the problem of strategic dependency and rivalry among core countries. Brazil, for example, has become an important investor in foreign raw materials and, through the government oil monopoly PETROBRAS, is actively seeking and/or extracting oil in the Middle East, Venezuela, Bolivia, and Peru. Brazil is also active in the exploration of foreign deposits of phosphates and other minerals.

Great stress should be placed on the *qualitative* relevance of Latin America to the centers in the face of the growing international competition for scarce strategic minerals, cheap labor, and markets. Some studies indicate that the progressively increasing needs of core countries could dangerously augment the rivalry among industrialized powers. One analyst from the U.S. State Department has specifically observed mounting friction between the United States and Japan over Latin America:

> There is a good reason to believe that *an increasing share of Japan's raw material imports will come from Latin America*. . . . Japan is thus moving into an area long regarded as our backyard while the United States becomes

more dependent on its traditional Latin American sources of raw materials and its relations with the area are bedevilled by nationalism and economic conflicts of interest. In this context, *there would seem to exist a serious possibility of conflict with Japan over access to raw materials which significantly affect the overall United States security-political-economic relationship.*[73] (emphasis added)

Another scholar agreed with the preceding assessment when he stated that

Japan and several European countries have concluded that they must fashion their own "resources diplomacy" as centerpieces of their own foreign policies, and hence *Latin America is in some senses a new battleground for competition among the industrialized countries.*[74] (emphasis added)

It would seem, therefore, that, as C. Fred Bergsten, U.S. Under Secretary of the Treasury, indicated, "the sweeping changes in world economic condition have implied a sharp increase in U.S. economic interests in Latin America," to the point that Bergsten himself has advocated that *"securing assured access to Latin American raw materials at reasonable prices should be the primary objective of U.S. economic policy toward Latin America."*[75]

Recent developments also suggest that Latin America's cheap labor is still important. For example, it has been reported that, starting in 1980, Fiat's subsidiary in Brazil will begin to export 30,000 cars annually to Western Europe. Although transportation costs of the vehicles amount to $300 per unit, they will be more than offset by the low labor costs in Brazil, which are half those in Italy, itself a relatively low-wage country within the European context.[76]

The unquestionable importance of the Latin American market for the centers is clearly revealed by the controversial decision of the Federal Republic of Germany—over the strong opposition of the U.S. government—to sell nuclear machinery and technology to Brazil, thus securing a concrete market of immense value. According to one estimate, the German-Brazilian nuclear deal represents for Germany a transaction of $30 billion (book value) over a fifteen-year period—the largest commercial operation in the nuclear field between a nuclear power and a Third World country.[77] Incidentally, the international nuclear market has become, in recent years, one of the most attractive businesses for multinational conglomerates: Calculations indicate that the U.S. nuclear industry's profits for 1985 will fluctuate between $3 and $4 billion.[78]

In view of the economic importance of the Latin American periphery, it appears then that several countries of the region could—within some limits — exercise bargaining power vis-à-vis corporations or governments of the core so as to obtain more egalitarian agreements with specific firms and/or access to the markets of the developed nations.[79] The attainment of such goals would certainly contribute to improving the position of the periphery country in question in the prevailing international division of labor, but evidently it would not suffice as an answer to structural dependency and domestic inequality.

Acknowledgments

The author wishes to thank James Caporaso, John McCamant, Satish Raichur, and Peter Van Ness for the valuable comments and criticisms they provided on this and earlier drafts.

Notes

1. See, for example, Albert Fishlow, "A Proposal for a United States Economic Policy for Latin America," in Joseph Grunwald (ed.), *Latin America and the World Economy: A Changing International Order* (Beverly Hills, Calif.: Sage Publications, 1978), pp. 37–38.

2. See Shlomo Avineri, *Marx on Colonialism and Modernization* (Garden City, N.Y.: Anchor Books, 1969), p. 16.

3. On the subject of structural dependency, see Fernando H. Cardoso and Enzo Faletto, *Dependency and Development in Latin America* (Berkeley: University of California Press, 1978); Fernando H. Cardoso, "Notas sobre el estado actual de los estudios de la dependencia," in Sergio Bagú et al., *Problemas del subdesarrollo latinoamericano* (Mexico, D. F.: Editorial Nuestro Tiempo, 1973); Octavio Ianni, "La Dependencia Estructural," in A. M. Frasinetti and G. Boils (eds.), *América Latina: Dependencia y subdesarrollo* (San José de Costa Rica: Editorial Universitaria Centroamericana, 1973); Theotonio dos Santos, *Dependencia y cambio social* (Santiago de Chile: CESO, Universidad de Chile, 1970); Theotonio dos Santos, *Imperialismo y dependencia* (Mexico, D. F.: Ediciones Era, 1978); and Osvaldo Sunkel and Pedro Paz, *El subdesarrollo latinoamericano y la teoría del desarrollo* (Mexico, D. F.: Siglo XXI Editores, 1970).

4. Operationally, we consider "strategic" any material that a) is a nonrenewable resource, b) is concentrated in relatively few hands (fifteen countries or less), and c) has recognized economic and military applications.

5. Theoretically, the importation of cheap raw materials could lead to an increase in the average rate of profit of the core country in question, but only in the case that lower-priced raw materials permit an increase in the amount of labor used, so that more surplus is created.

6. Satish Raichur, "Toward a Theory of International Exchange: Some

Preliminaries," paper presented at the Conference on International Relations and Third World Development, University of Denver, Denver, Colorado, June 20–22, 1979, mimeo, p. 17.

7. Celso Furtado, "Power Resources—The Five Controls," *IFDA Dossier*, May 1979, p. 6.

8. International Economic Studies Institute, "Dependence of the Industrialized World on Imported Materials," in *Raw Materials and Foreign Policy* (Washington, D.C.: International Economic Studies Institute, 1976), p. 12.

9. See NACLA, "U.S. Private Investment in Latin America 1880–1961," in *Yanqui Dollar: The Contribution of U.S. Private Investment to Underdevelopment in Latin America* (Berkeley, Calif.: North American Congress on Latin America, 1971), p. 5.

10. See Akira Iriye, *Pacific Estrangement: Japanese and American Expansion, 1897–1911* (Cambridge, Mass.: Harvard University Press, 1972), p. 38.

11. Yoshiro Ohara, *Japan and Latin America* (Santa Monica, Calif: Rand Corporation, 1967), pp. 42–43.

12. See Ministry of International Trade and Industry, *White Paper on Economic Cooperation* (Tokyo: MITI, 1966). In the case of Japan, detailed figures on foreign investment are rather difficult to obtain. Available data are generally on "approved" rather than "materialized" overseas investment. According to one researcher, "it is also not clear in which countries the investments were made" (Nagahide Shioda, "The Sogoshosha and its Functions on Direct Foreign Investment," *The Developing Economies*, Vol. XIV, no. 4, December 1976, p. 410). It is estimated, however, that Japanese external investment has grown very rapidly since the beginning of the 1970s and that about 40 percent of total Japanese overseas investments "are of so-called natural 'resource-oriented' types, while the remaining 60 percent are of the 'market-oriented' types" (Yoshihiro Tsurumi, "The Multinational Spread of Japanese Firms and Asian Neighbors' Reactions," in David E. Apter and Louis W. Goodman [eds.], *The Multinational Corporation and Social Change* [New York: Praeger Publishers, 1976], p. 123).

13. Henry C. Wallich, quoted by Michael Kreile, "West Germany: The Dynamics of Expansion," *International Organization*, Vol. 31, no. 4, Autumn 1977, p. 776.

14. See Albrecht von Gleich, *Germany and Latin America* (Santa Monica, Calif.: Rand Corporation, June 1968), p. 53.

15. For a detailed analysis of strategic dependency and the oil crisis and its effects on the foreign policies of the United States, Japan, and West Germany, see Heraldo Muñoz, "Strategic Dependency: The Relations Between Core Powers and Mineral-Exporting Periphery Countries," in Charles Kegley, Jr., and Patrick McGowan (eds.), *The Political Economy of Foreign Policy Behavior* (Beverly Hills, Calif., and London: Sage Publications, 1980).

16. E. Chin, "The Mineral Industry of Japan," *Bureau of Mines Minerals Yearbook* (Washington, D.C.: U.S. Department of the Interior, 1975), pp. 1–2.

17. Richard Barnet and Ronald Müller, *Global Reach: The Power of Multinational Corporations* (New York: Simon & Schuster, 1974), p. 202.

18. Wendell Woodbury, *The U.S. and Japan and Latin America's Mineral Resources,* Senior Seminar in Foreign Policy, U.S. Department of State, 16th Session 1973-1974, p. 13.

19. See Organisation for Economic Co-operation and Development, *Geographical Distribution of Financial Flows to Developing Countries: Data on Disbursements 1969 to 1975* (Paris: OECD, 1977), p. 184.

20. John A. Hannah, "New Responses to the Challenge of Development," *Department of State Bulletin,* Vol. 67, December 25, 1972, pp. 734-735.

21. See International Economic Studies Institute, "Foreign Assistance and Material Needs," in *Raw Materials and Foreign Policy,* p. 334.

22. Sukehiro Hasegawa, *Japanese Foreign Aid: Policy and Practice* (New York: Praeger Publishers, 1975), p. 66.

23. Ibid., p. 67.

24. Council on International Economic Policy, Executive Office of the President, *Special Report: Critical Imported Materials* (Washington, D.C.: U.S. Government Printing Office, December 1974), p. 48.

25. Jack L. Knusel, *West German Aid to Developing Nations* (New York: Praeger Publishers, 1968), p. 13.

26. Japanese Ministry of Foreign Affairs, "Foreign Policy" in *White Papers of Japan* (Tokyo: 1975), p. 81.

27. Folker Fröbel, Jürgen Heinrichs, and Otto Kreye, "The New Industrial Division of Labor," *Social Science Information,* Vol. 17, no. 1, 1978, p. 138.

28. Louis Turner, *Multinational Companies and the Third World* (New York: Hill & Wang, 1973), p. 175.

29. Fröbel, Heinrichs, and Kreye, "New Industrial Division of Labor," p. 130.

30. CEPAL, *El desarrollo económico y social y las relaciones económicas externas de América Latina,* E/CEPAL/1061, Vol. 2, 31 de Enero de 1979, p. 192.

31. See U.S. Senate, *Implications of Multinational Firms for World Trade and Investment and for U.S. Trade and Labor* (Washington, D.C.: U.S. Government Printing Office, February 1973), Chapter 7.

32. Studies by Louis Wells have shown that, in underdeveloped countries, foreign-owned firms that compete primarily *on the basis of price* are more likely to use labor-intensive techniques than those that compete principally on the basis of brand names. Many multinational enterprises that have established "off-shore" production facilities have been driven by price competition to locate their labor-intensive stages in the periphery. (See Theodore Moran, "Multinational Corporations and Dependency: A Dialogue for Dependentistas and Non-Dependentistas," *International Organization,* Vol. 38, no. 1, Winter 1978, p. 88).

33. Turner, *Multinational Companies,* pp. 184-185.

34. Ibid., p. 184.

35. According to this selection criteria, often the "most suitable" labor force is constituted mainly by young women. See Fröbel, Heinrichs, and Kreye, "New Industrial Division of Labor," pp. 126-127.

36. Ibid., p. 120.

37. Barnet and Müller, *Global Reach,* pp. 300-308.

38. Fröbel, Heinrichs, and Kreye, "New Industrial Division of Labor," p. 135. These figures did not take into account contract production for, for instance, large department stores.

39. Barnet and Müller, *Global Reach*, p. 303.

40. Fröbel, Heinrichs, and Kreye, "New Industrial Division of Labor," pp. 135-137. In the case of West Germany, the corporations have access to low-priced labor not only by transferring production facilities to periphery nations, but also by importing "temporary guest-workers" from European countries with relatively cheap labor, e.g., Portugal, Spain, and Greece.

41. Barnet and Müller, *Global Reach*, p. 305.

42. Robert Frank and Richard Freeman, *The Distributional Consequences of Direct Foreign Investment* (Washington, D.C.: U.S. Department of Labor, December 2-3, 1976).

43. Robert Stobaugh et al., *Nine Investments Abroad and Their Impact at Home: Case Studies on Multinational Enterprises and the U.S. Economy* (Cambridge, Mass.: Harvard University Press, 1976).

44. See Barnet and Müller, *Global Reach*, p. 304.

45. Ibid., pp. 308-309.

46. The AFL-CIO's actions in support of opposition labor groups included threats of boycott of all Chilean trade if workers' rights continued to be violated by Chile's military government. See "Washington centro de operaciones," *Hoy*, no. 86, 17-23 Enero 1979, pp. 6-9; "Qué pasó con el boicott," *Hoy*, no. 87, 24-30 Enero 1979, pp. 12-13; "Trade Union Rights in Chile," *AFL-CIO Free Trade Union News*, Vol. 33, no. 10, October 1978; "Chile moves to head off boycott," *Latin American Political Report,* Vol. 13, no. 1, January 1979, pp. 1-2.

47. From a more political viewpoint, the AFL-CIO's actions in Chile could also reflect present U.S. policy towards Chile and the effort on the part of the U.S. government (including the intelligence services) to widen its influence in the Chilean labor movement, which was traditionally controlled by the left.

48. Fernando Henrique Cardoso, "Dependency and Development in Latin America," *New Left Review*, no. 74, July-August 1973, p. 90. See also F. H. Cardoso, "Associated-Dependent Development: Theoretical and Practical Implications," in Alfred Stepan (ed.), *Authoritarian Brazil* (New Haven, Conn.: Yale University Press, 1973).

49. Cardoso, "Dependency and Development," p. 90.

50. CEPAL, *El desarrollo económico y social y las relaciónes externas de América Latina*, E/CEPAL/1023, 16 de Junio de 1977, pp. 183-184.

51. CEPAL, *El desarrollo económico* (1979), p. 138.

52. See Stockholm International Peace Research Institute, *Armaments or Disarmament? The Crucial Choice* (Stockholm: SIPRI, 1978), pp. 20-22.

53. See C. Fred Bergsten, Thomas Horst and Theodore H. Moran, *American Multinationals and American Interests* (Washington, D.C.: Brookings Institution, 1978), p. 9. According to the authors, the 1957 and 1974 figures are inflated by abnormally high profits from oil companies; but the ratio for manufacturing alone more than quadrupled in the eighteen years.

54. Howard M. Wachtel, *The New Gnomes: Multinational Banks in the Third World* (Washington, D.C.: Transnational Institute, 1977), p. 9.

55. The *private* component of Latin America's total external debt jumped from 39.4 percent in 1966 to 58.6 percent in 1976. Apparently, the Latin American countries also prefer private financing because through this alternative they can reject "tied" economic assistance like U.S. foreign aid which under the Carter Administration is denied (although with important exceptions) to countries that violate human rights.

56. See Robert Devlin, *International Commercial Bank Finance and the Economic Development of Poor Countries: Congruence and Conflict*, Working Paper, Economic Development Division of CEPAL, March 1979, pp. 1–3. According to one author, "the severity of the debt burden faced by many [Latin American] countries could propel them to action to evade it. The effects on individual financial institutions, on our overall money markets, and on the U.S. balance of payments, could all be severe" (C. Fred Bergsten, "The Threat from the Third World," *Foreign Policy*, no. 11, Summer 1973, p. 114).

57. An interesting point is that, despite the stagnation of the world economy in the last few years, the average annual increase in direct investment in Latin America was much greater in 1972–1975 than in 1968–1971, rising sharply from 6.7 percent to 12 percent. In the 1972–1975 period, the biggest increases were in Peru (18.9 percent), Mexico (18.3 percent), Brazil (15.6 percent), and the tax havens such as Panama and Bermudas (See CEPAL, *Economic Survey of Latin America: 1978*, E/CEPAL/G1103, 27 December 1979, p. 932).

58. Ibid.

59. CEPAL, *El desarrollo económico* (1979), p. 189.

60. See CEPAL, *El desarrollo económico* (1977), p. 195.

61. See summaries in "Aumentan las inversiones europeas en América Latina," *El Mercurio,* February 24, 1980, p. B2; and Oscar Palma, "Crecen las inversiones de la RFA en Latinoamérica," *El Día*, México D.F., January 14, 1980.

62. CEPAL, *El Desarrollo Económico* (1977), p. 195.

63. A recent study conducted by nine experts from the U.S. Commerce Department estimated that Chile is now a key market for the United States owing, among other things, "to Chile's liberal economic scheme." Chile's imports from the United States now reach nearly $1 billion (see *El Mercurio*, July 12, 1980, p. A1).

64. "Latin America Opens the Door to Foreign Investment," *Business Week,* August 9, 1976, p. 34.

65. The term was introduced by Raymond Vernon in his *Sovereignty at Bay: The Multinational Spread of U.S. Enterprises* (New York: Basic Books, 1971), pp. 46–59.

66. C. Fred Bergsten, Thomas Horst and Theodore H. Moran, *American Multinationals,* p. 133.

67. On this point see Abraham F. Lowenthal, "The United States and Latin America: Ending the Hegemonic Presumption," *Foreign Affairs,* Vol. 55, no. 1, October 1976, pp. 199–213.

68. For a more detailed study on the options of Third World countries regarding multinational companies in the natural resources sector see Benny Widyons, "Empresas transnacionales y productos básicos de exportación," *Revista de la CEPAL*, First Semester, 1978, especially pp. 150–169.

69. Immanuel Wallerstein, "Semi-Peripheral Countries and the Contemporary World Crisis," *Theory and Society*, no. 3, 1976, p. 464.

70. In July 1980 the British Government announced that the Foreign Minister, Lord Carrington, accompanied by twelve executives of the largest British firms, would visit Barbados, Brazil, Mexico, and Venezuela with the principal objective of negotiating agreements to increase British exports to these nations. Interestingly, the visit of Lord Carrington to Brazil, Mexico, and Venezuela will be the first ever by a British Foreign Minister and, hence, it denotes the growing economic importance of the three Latin American countries (see "Canciller británico a latinoamérica," *El Mercurio*, July 15, 1980, p. A12). Incidentally, a study indicates that over the 1966–1974 period, "investment in Latin America has apparently been more profitable than British overseas investment as a whole, and British investment in Brazil has consistently outperformed investment in the rest of the continent." Moreover, "on the average British companies may recently have secured higher rates of return on their investments in Latin America than were earned by the average U.S. company operating in the same region. It would seem that recent *British investments in Brazil have been remarkably profitable and that this has pulled up the average very sharply*" (Laurence Whitehead, "Britain's Economic Relation with Latin America," in Grunwald [ed.], *Latin America and the World Economy*, p. 94).

71. In the view of some analysts, Latin America, in recent years, has increased its "defense capacity" against such actions of major powers. According to one author concrete evidence of this improvement are the following: that Latin America – unlike most core economies – experienced high rates of growth during the 1974–1975 recession; that Latin America has slowly transformed its productive system through an increasing elaboration of intermediate and capital goods; and that the region has diversified its export structure both in terms of partners (e.g., growing role of intraregional trade) and in terms of products (increasing importance of manufactures). See Ricardo Lagos, "América Latina: Algunos hechos económicos recientes y su poder de negociación," *Estudios Internacionales*, Vol. 13, no. 51, July-September, 1980, pp. 291–308.

72. Interestingly, one of the few similarities in the positions of Republican presidential candidate Ronald Reagan and President Jimmy Carter is the recognition of the vital importance of Mexico for the United States. The Republican political platform approved in Detroit states that "the Republicans recognize the *fundamental importance of Mexico*, and, therefore, a first priority will be given to the restoration of an harmonious working relationship with that country. A new Republican administration will begin immediate wide-ranging negotiations at the highest levels to seek solutions to common problems, as on the basis of common interests, recognizing that each country has specific contributions to make in solving the practical problems" (Cited in "Enmienda a política de Carter a

América Latina," *El Mercurio,* July 17, 1980, p. A12).

73. Wendell W. Woodbury, op. cit., p. 1.

74. C. Fred Bergsten, "U.S.-Latin American Relations to 1980," in K. Silvert et al., *The Americas in a Changing World* (New York: New York Times Book Co., 1975), p. 182.

75. Ibid., pp. 181–182.

76. See "Fiat uit Brazilië komen naar Europa," *NRC Handelsblad,* Rotterdam, July 2, 1979, p. 1.

77. See *Latin America Political Report*, Vol. 13, no. 15, 13 April 1979, p. 117. Before the signing of the German-Brazilian accord, the government of Brasilia held conversations with two U.S. corporations. Hence, when the White House opposed the agreement, Helmut Schmidt replied that "part of the heated discussion could be clearly related to the concrete interest of the major U.S. [nuclear] firms" (Norman Gall, "Energía atómica para Brazil—Peligro para todos," *Estrategia*, no. 42, September-October 1976, p. 78).

78. See CIDE, "Algunos datos complementarios acerca de las relaciones Estados Unidos-Brasil bajo la administración Carter," *Cuadernos Semestrales— Estados Unidos: Perspectiva Latinoamericana,* no. 5, First Semester 1979, p. 202.

79. A recent study of twenty-five cases of trade negotiations between the United States and Latin American countries found that, often, the latter—particularly Argentina, Brazil and Mexico—achieved their objectives despite the superior overall power of the United States (see John S. Odell, "Latin American Trade Negotiations with the United States," *International Organization*, vol. 34, no. 2, Spring 1980, pp. 207–228).

5
Development Styles and the Environment: An Interpretation of the Latin American Case

Osvaldo Sunkel

The environment of Latin America, that is, its natural biophysical resource context and successive artificial transformations of that context, as well as its spatial outlay, has been one of the fundamental conditioning elements of the region's historical development. Another has been the considerable influence that a series of dominant powers — particularly Spain, Portugal, Great Britain, and the United States — have had over time on Latin American societies, their lifestyles, and their development patterns.

By the decade of the 1940s this interplay between environment, culture, and the international system had produced nation-states characterized by the exploitation of a considerable part of their natural resources — land and minerals — as a result of the industrial countries' needs for food and raw materials. Their demands, investments, and technology influenced the nature and extent of the use of those resources in which Latin America had, or had created, a comparative advantage. Over time, this process reacted upon the environment as it led in turn to the depletion of the higher-yield reserves of nonrenewable resources, the clearing of forests, the overuse of some of the better agricultural lands, and the redistribution of the population between regions and between rural and urban areas.[1]

The surplus derived from the exploitation of natural resources flowed mainly abroad, influencing the development of the metropolitan soci-

This chapter is a revised and expanded version of a paper prepared for a special issue of *Mazingira* on Environment and Development, under the guest editorship of D. Mostafa Tolba. It draws heavily on work being carried out by the CEPAL/UNEP Project on Development Styles and Development.

eties. The part that was retained went largely to finance the importation of luxury consumption items for the landowning and related urban elites, allowing them to reproduce to some extent the lifestyles of the dominant societies. It also allowed some public and private investments in the urban infrastructure and urban construction, railroads and communications, ports, and some irrigation works in the rural areas.

Manufacturing industry, which had developed in the larger and richer Latin American countries, consisted mainly of small- and medium-sized textile, footwear, food processing, soap, and furniture factories and other light industries. As all these industries were based mainly on the processing of local raw materials, and as internal freight rates were high due to the inadequate transportation infrastructure, factories were located near the sources of their inputs (mostly around the capital cities, but also in various regional centers). Because most industry was based on local resources and was relatively decentralized, industrial pollution was of no great significance.[2]

Traditional agriculture consisted mainly of a complex and interrelated mix of large land holdings and "minifundia," or uneconomically small plots of land. The former were characterized generally by the underutilization of the land, the latter by heavy overutilization and consequent erosion and desertification. This was particularly the case in those countries, such as Mexico, Guatemala, and the Andean nations, in which a large indigenous population, the remnants of the breakdown of the Aztec, Maya, and Inca Empires, remained mostly engaged in subsistence agriculture.

The conditions of life of the rural and urban poor were appalling; incomes were low and basic health, education, and housing services almost totally lacking. Correspondingly, very low life expectancy, high infant and general mortality, illiteracy, undernourishment, and overcrowding were among the main characteristics of their lifestyles.[3]

This, then, is part of the background that has to be kept in mind when studying the development of the post-war era, from around 1950 onwards. It goes without saying that this, and what follows, is a grossly simplified overview of the region's long term development trends, as there are significant differences among countries.

The Development Style of the Post-war Era

The development that has taken place in Latin America over the last three decades has consisted basically of the incorporation of the lifestyle of the Western industrial societies and particularly of the United States, the powerful northern neighbor that emerged as the hegemonic center of

the capitalist system after World War II.⁴ The minority that could afford
it adopted the consumption patterns, suburban residences, nuclear family structures, weekend habits, and the values and culture of urban-
industrial mass society, characteristic of the United States. But this process of incorporation of new lifestyles was soon extended to wider social
sectors and classes. There were three main forces at work.

First, the state became more active and influential, extending its reach
both in terms of collecting taxes and of expanding its administrative,
economic, and social activities. Revenues increased through higher taxation of the primary export-producing sectors, which were the sectors of
higher productivity and the main producers of surplus income and
foreign exchange. These larger financial resources were then used to promote economic development (infrastructural investments, industrial
projects, agricultural modernization) and social welfare (health, education, housing, social security).

Second, the industrial sector, which had enjoyed heavy protection as a
consequence of the worldwide crisis of capitalism of the 1930s and the
Second World War, gained new momentum with the additional support
received through the economic development policies of the state in the
post-war period. This industrial development, as mentioned before, had
initially taken the form of the creation and expansion of the light industries aimed at the wider middle- and lower-income markets, mainly
urban. (The higher-income groups built their new U.S.-type lifestyles on
the importation of "conspicuous consumption goods" such as automobiles and consumer durables.) In the late forties and early fifties, the
emphasis shifted to heavy industries, such as iron and steel, electricity,
oil refining, and cement, in an attempt to take advantage of existing and
largely unutilized natural resources.

Third, in the late fifties, when this newly created industrial base could
have been used to expand the industrial production aimed at satisfying
fundamental needs of the majority of the population and to diversify the
export structure in order to reduce the excessive reliance on primary exports, a dramatic reorientation of the development process took place.
Several factors were involved in this change: the influence of the local
elites and higher-income groups, who wanted to continue to improve
their new lifestyle; the demonstration effect of these local elites and of
the newly expanding mass media in impressing the new lifestyle upon the
rest of the population; and the renewed vigorous national and international expansion of U.S., Western European, and Japanese capitalism,
as evidenced by the phenomenal growth and diffusion of transnational
corporations. The emphasis in development strategies shifted to the
reproduction locally of the production patterns of the industrial coun-

tries — those production patterns that were the basis of the lifestyle of the industrial societies.[5]

Accordingly, industrial development, which was intimately associated with subsidiaries of transnational corporations, concentrated mainly on the development of the automobile and petrochemical industries and the production of consumer durables, electromechanic and electronic products, and pulp and paper products. This type of industrial development utilized the highly capital- and energy (oil)-intensive technology characteristic of the industrial societies and entailed a heavy reliance on imports.[6]

In the transportation sector, oil and electricity displaced steam in railroads. Railroads themselves, and even more so animal traction, were displaced by the private car, the bus, and the truck, and for longer distances by the airplane. A new transportation style, also highly capital-, energy (oil)-, and import-intensive, superseded the old.[7]

In agriculture, a great effort at "modernization" took place. Large dams and irrigation and drainage schemes were built, continuing a policy initiated in the 1930s. Other kinds of infrastructural projects, such as rural roads and electrification, drew much of their inspiration from the Tennessee Valley Authority in the United States. Agricultural mechanization was heavily promoted and abundantly financed, and the "green revolution" introduced new high-yield varieties of grains and massive inputs of fertilizers, pesticides, and phytoregulators. Thus, highly capital-, energy-, and import-intensive technology penetrated the rural areas.[8]

In the construction industry, highly capital-, energy-, and import-intensive methods, designs, materials, and know-how displaced the existing building industry, even the traditional customs, local materials, and skills which most of the population used to build their own dwellings.

The reader can apply this line of reasoning to other sectors of the economy like fishery,[9] forestry,[10] trade, finance, health,[11] or education. In every case, to a greater or lesser degree, the new, imported, highly capital- and energy (oil)-intensive methods, patterns, designs, technologies, machinery, and forms of organization are replacing existing patterns.[12] The corresponding shift in energy consumption by sources is shown in Table 5.1. The adoption of the new lifestyle by the well-off and the relatively well-off has brought about a massive restructuring of the productive system. This has meant the partial creation of a development pattern that corresponds adequately to the new lifestyle and the displacement and disorganization of existing development patterns and lifestyles.[13] The result is a highly heterogeneous economic and social structure and complex interrelations among its parts. This, then, is the

TABLE 5.1

Consumption of Energy by Sources in Selected Countries of Latin America, 1950 and 1976
(Thousands of tons of oil equivalent of 10700 Kcal / Kg)

1950

Coal	%	Oil Derivatives	%	Gas	%	Hydroelectricity (a)	%	Vegetable fuels	%	Total	%	Country
1,250	11.84	7,307	69.23	464	4.40	77	0.73	1,457	13.80	10,555	100	Argentina
1,340	7.29	4,316	23.49	-	-	3,030	16.49	9,687	52.72	18,373	100	Brazil
710	15.84	931	20.77	180	4.02	362	8.08	2,299	51.29	4,482	100	Colombia
36	0.72	1,720	34.24	20	0.40	6	0.12	3,241	64.52	5,023	100	Cuba
1,381	34.00	1,134	27.92	-	-	694	17.09	853	21.00	4,062	100	Chile
-	-	247	30.65	-	-	35	4.34	524	65.01	806	100	Guatemala
-	-	82	18.30	-	-	21	4.69	345	77.01	448	100	Jamaica
660	4.65	7,337	51.75	1,144	8.07	821	5.79	4,217	29.74	14,179	100	Mexico
40	1.40	1,097	38.30	4	0.14	299	10.44	1,424	49.72	2,864	100	Peru
17	0.41	2,500	60.98	972	23.71	73	1.78	538	13.12	4,100	100	Venezuela
5,521	7.62	28,874	39.87	2,914	4.02	5,891	8.13	29,225	40.35	72,425	100	Total

1976

Coal	%	Oil Derivatives	%	Gas	%	Hydroelectricity (a)	%	Vegetable fuels	%	Total	%	Country
924	2.83	21,077	64.51	6,708	20.53	2,270	6.95	1,695	5.19	32,674	100	Argentina
4,336	4.92	42,327	48.07	482	0.55	24,631	27.97	16,279	18.49	88,055	100	Brazil
2,365	14.43	6,626	40.42	1,523	9.29	3,126	19.07	2,753	16.79	16,393	100	Colombia
77	0.68	7,487	65.64	18	0.16	16	0.14	3,809	33.39	11,407	100	Cuba
901	10.53	4,114	48.07	1,114	13.02	1,864	21.78	565	6.60	8,558	100	Chile
-	-	929	42.42	-	-	91	4.16	1,170	53.42	2,190	100	Guatemala
1	0.03	2,595	85.96	-	-	43	1.42	380	12.59	3,019	100	Jamaica
3,809	6.17	34,667	56.16	12,618	20.44	5,142	8.33	5,498	8.91	61,734	100	Mexico
120	1.15	5,760	55.42	1,044	10.05	1,753	16.87	1,716	16.51	10,393	100	Peru
215	0.91	9,962	41.94	9,845	41.45	2,966	12.49	764	3.22	23,752	100	Venezuela
12,784	4.53	150,110	52.82	34,899	12.28	44,182	15.55	42,226	14.86	284,201	100	Total

Source: CEPAL, on the basis of official figures. In the case of vegetable fuels, figures were estimated by CEPAL. Data on coal and commercial energy for Cuba and Jamaica were taken from United Nations, World Energy Supplies, 1950 - 1974.

(a) This energy was expressed in calorie units considering the consumption of Kilocalories that, in the average, were used by power plants to produce 1 KWH (Kcal / KWH).

structural connection between lifestyle and development patterns in Latin America.

The emerging, dynamic, "modern," "Western," or what I have elsewhere called "transnational" segment of the economy and society because of its worldwide diffusion, is highly capital- and import-intensive. The stagnating or shrinking segment that is being displaced is highly labor-intensive and is based on local natural resources. It follows that—under certain conditions—the latter will probably fail to absorb the growth of the labor force and may even release labor, while the former, although growing very fast, will require only a small amount of additional labor. Job creation in the new segment will not compensate for job destruction or stagnation in the existing segment, giving rise to growing structural unemployment and underemployment. Labor will be released and pushed out of the activities that are being displaced and disrupted or are stagnating, and the skills of these workers will become obsolete, while the new activities will constitute areas of attraction for labor with new skills, even if they fail to absorb it in sufficient amounts.

Furthermore, the expanding dynamic segment of the industrial structure will place a heavy burden on the balance of payments, due to its massive reliance on imported material, technological, and financial inputs, while the demand for local natural resources will tend to be relatively stagnant.

As required by the economics of scale of a highly capital-, energy-, and import-intensive technology and by other factors, most of the new activities—industries, trade, finance, public works, new government departments, housing schemes, health and educational services—tend to be sited in the larger towns, and particularly in the capital city, while those activities that are being displaced and disrupted or are stagnating, were at least partly located in rural areas, declining regions, and smaller cities. In particular, the "modernization" of agriculture, in which the largest proportion of the population is engaged, releases large amounts of labor, which may accumulate in poor rural sectors, colonize frontier regions, or leave the rural areas altogether.[14] All these push and pull factors have led to a massive emigration of population from rural areas and declining regions and towns to the main cities, and especially to the capitals, resulting in a large-scale and very rapid urbanization process.[15]

A number of factors—given the limited resources available for the expansion of public consumption and the urban infrastructure of basic services (partly due to the use of imported standards, designs, and technologies), the process of urban land speculation, and the low and often unstable incomes of a large share of the urban population—have produced heterogeneous structures in cities. Urban areas are characterized by a mixture of expanding high-rise government and business downtown areas, suburban residential sectors in the transnational style, decaying older middle class and workers' quarters around the urban center and in the industrial areas, all surrounded and infiltrated by a swelling sea of slums. These have come to be called the "marginal" areas and their inhabitants, the marginal urban population of Latin America.[16] But as they grow and proliferate one wonders who is really becoming marginal—the poor slum dwellers or the affluent transnationals.[17]

The Transnational Development Style and the Environment

The foregoing analysis sets the stage for the examination of the nexus between the new lifestyle and development pattern and the environment.[18]

The development policies of the last decades have generated considerable overall economic growth and technological innovation and a significant shift in the composition of consumption and production, both within and among economic sectors. This has been accompanied by very important changes in the distribution of economic activity between regions and between rural and urban areas. Population has also increased very fast and large migratory flows have substantially changed its distribution.[19] Since production and income have grown even faster than population, per capita income levels and living standards have also increased significantly. This is shown by the improvements in life expectancy, general and infant mortality, and literacy, among other indicators. Nevertheless, these average figures hide the very unequal distribution of the fruits of progress, since most of the increase in income has accrued to the upper- and middle-income groups, who receive a large share of total income, while about 40 percent of the population are considered to be below the poverty line and 20 percent below the extreme poverty line. But even though inequality is great and may even have increased, the absolute standard of living of the poor has also been raised somewhat.

All these very important transformations have had a considerable impact on the environment: a great intensification and large shifts in the exploitation of natural resources, both renewable and nonrenewable, as well as intensive technological change; a considerable spatial redistribution of human activities and in particular massive urbanization and industrial concentration; and a new, vastly expanded, and highly concentrated process of generation of industrial, agricultural, and urban wastes, pollution, and contamination.[20]

Industry has grown nearly 7 percent per annum and has reached 25 percent of GNP for Latin America as a whole, with much higher figures for Brazil, Mexico, Venezuela, and some others. The structure of industrial output has changed in many ways. With respect to its composition, as already mentioned, the production of automobiles, petrochemicals, iron and steel, consumer durables, and electric and electronic goods has increased very fast, while the traditional branches, such as textiles, footwear, food processing, and others, have stagnated. With respect to market structure, large-scale enterprises, frequently branches of transnational corporations, using modern imported technology, have grown rapidly, displacing some middle- and small-sized local manufacturers and establishing in many cases monopoly or oligopoly positions. This concentration of ownership has also implied geographical concentration, as most of the new large-scale firms, particularly the producers of consumer durables, have established themselves near the main urban markets.[21]

This new industrial structure represents the local installation of the productive structure that underpins the new lifestyle. It depends heavily on imported capital goods, raw materials, energy (oil),[22] semifinished products, technology, know-how, designs, trademarks, and marketing skills. There is therefore a shift away from reliance on local natural and human resources, with the consequent burden on the balance of payments, which, in turn, must be financed by increased exports of primary products based on exploitation of natural resources. This may be justified by comparative advantage, but there are also serious drawbacks, as we shall see later on. The noticeable increase in energy consumption has brought along an increase in the international trade of oil. At the same time, this has translated into a series of problems derived from the transportation of the hydrocarbon.[23]

Fast growth, the level of development already achieved, the increasing similarity of industrial technology and production structure in Latin America to those of the industrial countries, accompanied by a degree of geographical concentration that is even more pronounced, and an almost total lack of concern until recently with the problems of industrial wastes have resulted in serious pollution and contamination in all of the main industrial areas of Latin America. Since these mostly coincide with the main cities of the region, the quality of life of the urban population has been gravely affected.

Agricultural mechanization, the building of large dams and irrigation schemes, and the "green revolution" package have also had very serious social and ecological consequences.[24] One of the main effects has been increased individual productivity in the modernized farms and the consequent displacement of rural labor. Many of these displaced workers have emigrated to the cities, as already mentioned. But others have stayed in the rural sector and either remained in areas of minifundia and marginal soils or migrated into new frontier lands.[25] These changes in agriculture are shown in tables 5.2–5.5.

Table 5.2

Structure of Land Use, 1950 - 1975
(Thousands of Hectares)

	1950/1955	1970/1974
Cultivated Area	52,938	87,857
Pastures and Prairies	344,818	520,002
Forests and Mountains	979,000	1,035,708

Source: CEPAL, CEPAL/FAO Joint Agricultural Division, **25 Años en la Agricultura de América Latina.**

Table 5.3

Indicators of Growth of the Agricultural Sector

	1950	1974
Irrigated Area (hectares)	7,300,000	11,550,000
Number of Bovines	159,115,000	259,201,000
Cultivated Area (hectares)	52,000,000	84,500,000

Source: CEPAL, CEPAL/FAO Joint Agricultural Division, **25 Años en la Agricultura de América Latina.**

Table 5.4

Evolution of Cultivated Area
(Millions of hectares)

	1950	1974
Cereals	29.0	49.6
Roots and Tubers	2.8	4.4
Oil producing	3.1	9.2
Sugar producing	3.2	5.5
Fruits	1.8	2.5

Source: CEPAL, CEPAL/FAO Joint Agricultural Division, **25 Años en la Agricultura de América Latina.**

Table 5.5

Growth of the Supply of Tractors

	1948 - 52	1961 - 65	1971	1974
Units	146,498	438,762	669,356	746,873
Index (1948 - 1952 = 100)	100	300	457	510
Cultivated hectares per tractor	361	-	-	122

Source: CEPAL, CEPAL/FAO Joint Agricultural Division, **25 Años en la Agricultura de América Latina; Cuadernos de la CEPAL, 1978.**

Since most of the best agricultural lands of Latin America had already been cultivated by the 1950s, the opening up of new lands has taken place mainly in tropical and semitropical areas. This process started more or less spontaneously as a consequence of rural modernization and the increased pressure of population on the land, but it was stimulated by a number of large road-building projects aimed at the penetration of the interior. The result has been massive deforestation of tropical and semitropical forests. Given the fragile soils and heavy rainfalls of these regions, this has led to the rapid degradation of the ecosystems, particularly the soil, of the cleared lands, forcing the colonizers to move ahead and clear new areas, with similar consequences: a vicious cumulative dynamic with devastating ecological results.[26] According to Food and Agriculture Organization (FAO) calculations, the annual rate of deforestation in Latin America is around six million hectares, which is equivalent to five times the annual wood production figure for the region. The annual losses of some countries and subregions can be seen in Table 5.6.

In the area of minifundia and marginal lands, population pressure is increasing, leading inevitably to overutilization of soils and thus to erosion (Table 5.7). As these lands are usually on the hillsides of fertile

Table 5.6

Estimates of Losses of Forests between 1958 and 1973
(in thousands of hectares)

Country or Region	Total	Annual Average Decrease
Mexico	43,664	3,115
Central America	813	58
CARICOM	585	42
Other Caribbean	214	15
Andean Pact	21,315	1,523
Brazil	21,350	1,525
South America (South East)	3,650	260
TOTAL	91,571	6,540

Source: FAO, Evaluación de los Recursos Forestales de la Región Latinoamericana.

Table 5.7

Percentage of Eroded Soil in Three Countries

Country	Percentage Eroded	Type of Erosion
Colombia	30	Grave
Chile	62	Moderate to very grave
Mexico	72	Moderate to very grave

Source: CEPAL, El Medio Ambiente en América Latina.

valleys that are frequently provided with dams and irrigation schemes, erosion contributes to the silting of the reservoirs.[27]

Modernization itself has well-known ecological consequences. Irrigation schemes produce salinization in many cases and contaminated river waters poison foodstuffs. The massive use of pesticides contributes to the development of resistant varieties of insects, altering natural ecological balances and facilitating the revival of pests and diseases, like malaria, that had apparently been brought under control. These problems are illustrated in Tables 5.8 and 5.9.

Furthermore, the heavy use — frequently the overuse — of chemical inputs has reached the point of decreasing returns in many cases, which means that increasingly large doses may be required simply to maintain production. The consumption of fertilizers grew at the astonishing annual rate of 13.9 percent between 1951 and 1972, as shown in Table 5.10. Another very serious problem in the semiarid zones of Latin America is desertification, which has advanced dramatically in the past few years.

As mentioned before, one of the most important recent changes has been urbanization.[28] The population of Latin America is now more urban than rural, with a heavy concentration in only one or two very large cities in each country. Mexico City, Buenos Aires, Rio de Janeiro, and São Paulo are now among the largest cities in the world, and a number of other capitals have more than three or four million inhabitants. They con-

Table 5.8

Consumption of Pesticides in Cotton Fields

Country	Year	In Cotton (100 Kg)	Per Capita (kg/person)	Per Km^2 Kg/Km^2	Per Cultivated Area (Kg/person)
El Salvador	1973	10,892	3.06	512.02	109.55
Guatemala	1974	9,235	1.77	84.80	89.09
Honduras	1974	196	0.07	1.75	23.39
Nicaragua	1973	7,809	4.12	66.10	43.02

Source: Project PNUMA/ICAITI, Estudio de las Consecuencias Ambientales y Económicas del Uso de Plaguicidas en la Producción de Algodón en Centro América, Guatemala, September 1975.

Table 5.9

Population with Malaria Problems
(El Salvador, Guatemala, Honduras and Nicaragua)

Number of Inhabitants	2,765,789
Affected Area	46,945 km^2
Causes of the Problem	Resistance of the sector to insecticides

Source: Sylvio Palacios, "Situación Actual y Estrategia de los Programas de Malaria en las Américas", PNUMA/OMS, Reunión sobre Control Bio - Ambiental de la Malaria, Lima, Peru, December 1975.

tinue to grow at rates as high as 5 percent per annum (Table 5.11).

This process has many consequences for the environment. The great demand for urban land, which is usually concentrated in very few hands, causes intense real estate speculation, steeply rising prices, and a consequent redistribution of income from the many buyers to the few sellers.[29] It also means that in urban development schemes a large proportion of public resources is spent on very expensive land. Furthermore, given the very unequal distribution of income, a large majority of the urban population cannot afford to buy land and must pay high rents to landlords. One effect is the geographical extension of cities, as rural areas or small adjacent towns provide cheaper housing. But this often leads to the destruction of highly fertile agricultural soil, since cities were originally sited in the best agricultural valleys. Table 5.12 provides some data on the geographical growth of some Latin American cities.

This "suburbanization" has been facilitated by the great expansion in the use of private automobiles and public buses. But as this process has

Table 5.10

Growth of the Consumption of Fertilizers

	1949 - 1953	1961 - 1963	1971 - 1973
Consumption (thousands of tons) (a)	294.4	1073.2	3481.2
Annual rate of growth	15.5	12.5	13.9
Consumption per cultivated hectare (Kg / ha)	5.5	15.5	42.3

Source: CEPAL, CEPAL/FAO Joint Agricultural Division, 25 Años en la Agricultura de América Latina: Cuadernos de la CEPAL, 1978.
(a) Thousands of tons of nutrients NPK (N, P_2O, K O)

Table 5.11

Size and Growth of Some Latin American Cities

	1970 (millions)	Annual rate of Growth	Period
Buenos Aires	6.7 (a)	2.7	1947 - 1960
Bogota	2.5	7.4	1957 - 1964
Caracas	1.3	6.6	1950 - 1961
Lima	2.7	5.0	1940 - 1961
Mexico D. F.	8.6	5.5	1960 - 1970
Rio de Janeiro	6.9	4.1	1950 - 1970
Santiago	2.8	4.1	1960 - 1970
São Paulo	7.9	5.7	1960 - 1970

Source: L. Herrera and W. Pecht, Crecimiento Urbano de América Latina, BID-CELADE, Santiago, 1976.
(a) 1960.

Table 5.12

Geographical Growth of Some Latin American Metropoles
(Square Kilometers)

	1940	1950	1960	1970
Bogota	-	42.1	73.6	136.1
Cali	6.6	11.7	35.6	47.2
Lima	-	108.7	145.1	254.8
Mexico D. F.	99.4	175.7	411.7	742.2
Monterrey	58.6	77.1	102.5	155.3
Santiago	113.3	155.7	228.8	294.8

Source: L. Herrera and W. Pecht, **Crecimiento Urbano de América Latina**, BID - CELADE, Santiago, 1976.

continued, urban transportation congestion has become a real night-mare. Heavy investments in the large freeways and related paraphernalia of modern urban transport networks have only increased congestion and chaos: The average speed of cars in cities like Mexico, Caracas, and Rio de Janeiro is now hardly more than twice the speed of walking.[30] The increase in the number of motor vehicles in various countries is shown in Tables 5.13 and 5.14. The duration of the round trip between home and work has also increased; it is estimated at four hours a day for an industrial worker in São Paulo. Air pollution is far above reasonable standards in many Latin American capitals (Table 5.15), and road accidents have become one of the most important causes of death. Income levels are generally rising, but the quality of urban life is deteriorating.

The most dramatic urban problems in Latin America are undoubtedly massive poverty, unemployment, underemployment, and the precarious housing conditions that characterize a large, and in many cases growing, proportion of the urban population. The so-called marginal populations have very limited access to urban land and public services. They settle down along river banks and canals, industrial quarters, railroad stations and tracks, steep hillsides and ravines, and other areas that are not otherwise used and valued because of their perilousness, unpleasantness, the health risks that they entail, difficulty of access, etc. They lack the most elementary public services, such as paved streets, running water, sewage and waste disposal, electricity, public transportation, and police. Their dwellings are makeshift constructions, constructed of all kinds of discarded materials.[31]

These are heavily overcrowded urban areas, where people subsist under the worst possible environmental conditions. The polluted air, the contaminated water and soils, the domestic animals amongst which people live all breed large populations of rats, insects, and other carriers of

Table 5.13

Estimates of the Number of Automobiles and Commercial Vehicles in
Selected Countries of Latin America in 1950, 1962 and 1974
(in thousands)

Country	Cars 1950	Others a/ 1950	Cars 1962	Others a/ 1962	Cars 1974	Others a/ 1974
Argentina	318.1	234.0	624.3	483.3	2027.5	879.8
Bolivia	1.7	9.0	7.6	4.7	22.0	16.4
Brazil	257.0	198.0	819.2	771.0	3795.0	1001.9
Colombia	37.0	27.0	132.8	93.0	328.8	110.0
Chile	39.9	31.9	72.6	95.4	235.3	165.3
Guatemala	7.7	5.9	31.5	12.1	70.8	39.1
Mexico	173.0	129.7	512.5	349.3	2053.2	728.9
Peru	31.1	27.4	100.0	79.0	264.0	139.9
Dominican Rep.	4.3	3.4	15.5	7.4	64.8	32.2
Venezuela	69.6	61.3	279.9	113.3	957.9	200.0

Sources: Various issues of the United Nations **Statistical Yearbook**; International Road Transport Union,
World Transport Data, 1976. These figures do not always coincide with published statistics. It
was necessary to reinterpret the numbers so as to make them consistent. The growth rates for
commercial vehicles are sometimes unreliable because the figures used are inconsistent.

a / Commercial vehicles (trucks and buses)

Table 5.14

Annual Growth Rates in Stock of Automobiles and Commercial Vehicles in
Selected Countries of Latin America, between 1950 - 1962 and 1962 - 1974
(Percentages)

Country	Cars 1950 - 1962	Others 1950 - 1962	Cars 1962 - 1974	Others 1962 - 1974
Argentina	5.78	6.23	10.31	5.12
Bolivia	13.29	- 5.27	9.26	10.98
Brazil	10.14	12.00	13.63	2.21
Colombia	11.24	10.86	7.85	1.41
Chile	5.11	9.56	10.30	4.69
Guatemala	9.48	6.17	6.98	10.27
Mexico	9.47	8.61	12.26	6.32
Peru	10.22	9.23	8.43	4.88
Dominican Republic	11.28	6.70	12.66	13.04
Venezuela	12.30	5.25	10.80	4.85

Note: Statistics for commercial vehicles were not corrected and, therefore, those growth
rates may be inaccurate.

Sources: Various issues of the United Nations **Statistical Yerabook**; International Road
Transport Union, **World Transport Data**, 1976.

Table 5.15

Air Pollution in Selected Latin American Cities

City	Dust (mg/cm^2)	Carbon Monoxide p.p.m.	Ton/day	Sulphur Dioxide (microg./m^3)
São Paulo	169.0	-	-	70.0
Buenos Aires	167.4	-	-	70.0
Mexico	145.3	-	-	146.6
Caracas	-	-	1350	135.6
Santiago	-	-	-	81.0
Lima	-	40	830	-
Tolerable Limits	100.0	-	-	70.0

Source: CEPAL, El Medio Ambiente en América Latina, Document 76 - 3 - 422 - 70, March 1976.

all kinds of diseases. It is not surprising that under these conditions many plagues and pests that had been eliminated or brought more or less under control are reviving in many cities and that indicators such as infant mortality are increasing in some cases after decades of decline.[32] Large and expensive public health campaigns have therefore become necessary to avoid the spread of disease and to improve hygienic conditions in marginal communities.

The environmental situation, combined with precarious employment and income characteristics, has obvious effects upon the social conditions of the marginal population: high delinquency rates, particularly among juveniles, prostitution, vagrancy, alcoholism, etc. But the great majority of this population is determined to survive and to overcome these terrible conditions. This can be seen in the gradual process of improvement that takes place in many slum areas and in most individual dwellings, in the organization of the squatters in order to obtain some basic services from the authorities, and in various other kinds of collective effort to improve the environment and create some minimal social organization.[33]

Suitability of the Transnational Development Style to Latin America

After reviewing some of the main interrelations between lifestyles, development patterns, and the environment in the last decades, one is bound to ask whether the emerging transnational development style in Latin America is sustainable over the long run and whether it can substantially improve the standard of living of the majority of the population. As has been shown, the emerging style is largely of imported origin, and its expansion feeds cumulatively on continuing imported technological innovation.[34] The substantial economic and social structure that has been built in this way in the region over the last decades, mainly an urban structure, is in the last resort sustained by the exploitation of its natural resources and the exportation of the primary products derived from them. One may well ask if it is not too risky and dangerous to finance a lifestyle and a development pattern that cannot sustain themselves by exporting more or less limited and replaceable natural resources, which are also subject to the instability of international markets.

The following questions must be clarified: Can this development pattern eventually generate a more diversified export potential, including manufacturing, sufficiently large and dynamic to finance most of its own import requirements? Is this possible without a substantial change in the international economic order?[35] What are the extent and quality of the reserves of natural renewable and nonrenewable resources? Are these resources being managed rationally with a view to maintaining an adequate resource base for future generations? Are the financial resources being generated by the exploitation of natural resources being used wisely, i.e., in order to maintain and enhance the resource-capital of society in the long run? Is the technological capability required for all these tasks being developed?

These questions become even more pressing when the problem of satisfying the basic needs of the majority of the population is brought into the picture. There is no doubt that the present development strategy has failed to achieve that objective, in spite of fast economic growth, and that there is extreme inequality between the affluent and the poor. Thus, policies aimed at satisfying the basic needs of the poor will have to be implemented. In other words, the production of basic foods, clothing, and footwear and the provision of basic services such as social security, shelter, education, and health will have to be expanded. Is this compatible with the continuation of the present development pattern in terms of financial resources as well as real material renewable resources? Is it possible with the massive underutilization of human resources that the present development strategy implies? Is it compatible with the existing trends towards administrative centralization, economic concentration, massive urban concentration, and heavy reliance on capital-, energy-, and import-intensive technology?

Furthermore, the level achieved by the problem of wastes, pollution, and contamination, at least in some of the more advanced countries of Latin America, can no longer be ignored. It is already having deleterious effects on the health of the population, particularly the poor, and on the quality of urban life generally, and large and growing expenditures — both public and private — are needed to repair and prevent its effects. Economic growth and urban concentration, under the present style of development, are beginning to become self-defeating: The benefits of higher incomes and consumption levels are being increasingly undermined by the deterioration of the quality of life and the higher expenditures needed to compensate for it.[36]

The *problematique* enunciated in the last few paragraphs has not been thoroughly examined and clarified in Latin America.[37] It is particularly important that the capability of the environment to sustain the present style of development in the long run be studied, because to pursue the present path without regard to its environmental requirements and effects (quite apart from its other problems of inequality, dependence, and underemployment) could ultimately have catastrophic consequences.[38]

An Alternative Development Style

This does not imply the need for a moratorium on economic growth. The development of the productive forces of society is a necessary prerequisite for the improvement of the quality of life of the population. But as I have attempted to show in this chapter, different development styles have different consequences in terms of the utilization of resources, the degree of geographical concentration, and the incidence of wastes, pollution, and contamination. Growth has to continue in Latin America in order to generate the means required for the satisfaction of the basic needs of the population, but it will have to be part of an alternative style of development.

One can only suggest some of the basic characteristics of an alternative style that would be compatible with the satisfaction of the basic needs of the majority and with the preservation and enhancement of the resource base and the environment. It will have to gradually reduce dependence on fossil sources of energy (particularly oil) and utilize more renewable and less polluting sources of energy, to develop more labor-intensive and resource-appropriate technologies,[39] to be based much more on recycling wastes, and to manage natural resources on ecologically-based knowledge and technologies. It will also require much more administrative and political decentralization and local self-reliance and management, and it must contain overconcentration in gigantic cities and consumerism.[40]

These changes may sound hopelessly utopian. But this may not be quite the case. They do, of course, all go against the grain of the present development style, but this style is generating some major crises, which in turn are dialectically generating some interesting responses. The oil crisis is the best known of them, and it has been having some major consequences.[41] To mention only one, it is inducing large efforts to develop alternative sources of energy. This is not a minor effect. The present development style is very largely based on the massive utilization of cheap oil—in oil-generated electricity, petrochemical products, automobiles, aviation, consumer durables, rural mechanization, maritime transportation, fertilizers, detergents, plastics, artificial fibers—by very large, highly concentrated firms. The dramatic change in the oil price and the supply situation may have quite substantial economic, social, and political consequences.[42]

The urban crisis is also producing major changes: Circulation of vehicles is being restricted and rationalized; local organization and decentralization are being stimulated and communities are organizing themselves to deal with their main problems; efforts at industrial and geographical decentralization are being made. The crisis in the health services is reducing reliance on large, highly centralized, and sophisticated institutions in favor of small-scale, decentralized, participatory services and is even vindicating the pragmatic knowledge assembled by healers and other practitioners without formal training. A revolution is looming in architecture as the transnational style is collapsing due to its heavy reliance on energy-intensive and imported or highly import-intensive materials. The use of traditional local materials and designs, appropriate to and making use of climatic and other local characteristics, and of the traditional construction skills of the population, are reversing the earlier trend towards transnational homogenization. The younger generation everywhere is adopting lifestyles quite different from the consumerist passion of the past generations.[43]

Does all this add up to the emergence of an alternative lifestyle and development pattern? It is hard to know, for we know so little of what is really going on and how important and extended the changes are. But there is no doubt that something is going on, and that it is the result of the very serious problems inherent in the present development style, in both industrial and underdeveloped societies. To transform these multiple and widespread reactions to the present crisis, together with our knowledge of the limitations and drawbacks of the prevailing development style, into a viable program for an alternative development pattern, one that would satisfy the fundamental needs of the majority of the population on a sustainable basis while maintaining an ecologically sound management of the environment, is surely one of the main tasks that now confronts us.[44]

Acknowledgments

The author wishes to thank Nicolo Gligo for his assistance in preparing this chapter.

Notes

The footnotes refer to papers that were prepared for the CEPAL/UNEP Regional Seminar on Development Styles and Environment, Santiago, 19-23 November 1979. These documents are synthesized in the global report presented to the Seminar under the title "Estilos de desarrollo y medio ambiente en América Latina" (Borrador de Informe Global, E/CEPAL/Proy. 2/R50).

1. The mutual historical conditioning between environment and development is analyzed in Nicolo Gligo and Jorge Morello, "Notas sobre la historia ecológica de América Latina," document E/CEPAL/Proy. 2/R34.

2. The changes in industrial development are examined in Hernán Durán, "Estilos de desarrollo de la industria manufacturera y medio ambiente en América Latina," document E/CEPAL/Proy. 2/R43.

3. Various approaches and schools of thought have attempted to define the human environment, many of them considering the aspect "quality of life." On this point see Gilberto Gallopin, "El medio ambiente humano," document E/CEPAL/Proy. 2/R32.

4. The basic concepts that define the styles of development can be found in José J. Villamil, "Conceptos de estilos de desarrollo: Una aproximación," document E/CEPAL/Proy. 2/R49. Regarding ecological questions see Jaime Hurtubia, "La evolución del pensamiento ecológico," document E/CEPAL/Proy.2/-R45.

5. The environmental dimension of the transformations of the international relations of underdeveloped nations are explored in Osvaldo Sunkel and Luciano Tomassini, "La dimensión ambiental y el cambio de las relaciones internacionales de los países en desarrollo," document E/CEPAL/Proy. 2/R44.

6. See Durán, "Estilos de Desarrollo."

7. These changes are studied in Ian Thomson, "An Analysis of some of the Social Consequences of the Automobile in Latin America," document E/CEPAL/Proy. 2/R9.

8. The implications of the process of agricultural modernization and its features are described in Nicolo Gligo, "Estilos de desarrollo, modernización y medio ambiente en la agricultura latinoamericana," document E/CEPAL/Proy. 2/R11.

9. See Constantino Tapias, "El medio oceánico y la actividad pesquera," document E/CEPAL/Proy. 2/R16.

10. The situation of forest resources is assessed in Sergio Salcedo and José Leyton, "El sector forestal latinoamericano y sus interrelaciones con el medio ambiente," document E/CEPAL/Proy. 2/R10.

11. This aspect is covered in Giorgio Solimano, "The Impact of Socioeconomic Development and Ecological Change on Health and Nutrition in Latin America," document E/CEPAL/Proy. 2/R18.

12. The great expansion in the consumption of oil as the principal energy source is examined in Jorge Trénova, "Perspectivas de la energía solar como substituto del petróleo en América Latina hasta el año 2000," document E/CEPAL/Proy. 2/R15.

13. This phenomenon can be readily perceived in processes like the expansion of tourism, a subject examined by José J. Villamil in "Impacto del turismo: La experiencia del Caribe," document E/CEPAL/Proy. 2/R23.

14. Some of these questions are addressed by Emiliano Ortega in "Interrogantes en torno a la agricultura campesina y el deterioro del medio ambiente," document E/CEPAL/Proy. 2/R47.

15. This theme is treated comprehensively by Armando di Filippo in "Distribución espacial de la actividad económica, migraciones y concentración poblacional en América Latina," document E/CEPAL/Proy. 2/R25.

16. See Centre International pour le Développement, "Medio ambiente marginal y estilos de desarrollo en América Latina," document E/CEPAL/Proy. 2/R40.

17. The dramatic situation of marginal sectors is studied in Lucio Kowarik, "El precio del progreso: Crecimiento económico, expoliación y la cuestión del medio ambiente," document E/CEPAL/Proy. 2/R8.

18. I have attempted to introduce the principal lines of thought regarding this relationship. Sergio Melnick has reviewed them in his study "Desarrollo y medio ambiente: Principales escuelas, tendencias y corrientes de pensamiento," document E/CEPAL/Proy. 2/R21.

19. See Alejandro Rofman, "La 'interiorización' espacial del estilo de desarrollo prevaleciente en América Latina," document E/CEPAL/Proy. 2/R21.

20. A useful conceptual work on the subject is Jorge Morello, "Ecología y atributos del ecosistema," document E/CEPAL/Proy. 2/R33. Another related work is Juan Gastó, "Ecosistema: Componentes y atributos relativos al desarrollo y medio ambiente," document E/CEPAL/Proy. 2/R27.

21. The consequences of industrial location are analyzed in Alberto Uribe and Francisco Szekeley, "Localización y tecnología industrial en América Latina," E/CEPAL/Proy. 2/R42.

22. The growing use of energy in industry is discussed in Alcibíades Azolas and Hernán Durán, "Consumo energético en la industria manufacturera: El caso de Brasil," document E/CEPAL/Proy. 2/R46.

23. The massive use of oil has been the major cause of ocean pollution. See Ignacio Vergara, "Transporte marítimo y contaminación en América Latina," document E/CEPAL/Proy. 2/R37.

24. Reference has already been made to this theme in note 8. The ecological viewpoint is presented in Juan Gastó, "Bases ecológicas de la modernización agrícola," document E/CEPAL/Proy. 2/R28.

25. See Nicolo Gligo, "Estilos de desarrollo."

26. Three regional case studies are excellent illustrations of this problem: Carlos Barrera et al., "Economía y ambiente: Análisis del subsistema regional chaqueño," document E/CEPAL/Proy. 2/R3; Charles Mueller, "Expansión de la frontera agrícola y medio ambiente en el Brasil," document E/CEPAL/Proy. 2/R4; and Jorge Adamoli and Patricio Fernández, "Expansión de la frontera agropecuaria en la cuenca del Plata," document E/CEPAL/Proy. 2/R48.

27. An interesting alternative technological form of land use by peasant sectors is examined in Lowell Jarvis and Emilio Klein, "Generación de empleo y la con-

servación de los recursos naturales; un programa para El Salvador," document E/CEPAL/Proy. 2/R30.

28. Shifts in economic location have generated a process of expansion of small urban centers. The subject is examined in Juan Antún, "Centros de crecimiento explosivo en América Latina," document E/CEPAL/Proy. 2/R7.

29. See Guillermo Geisse, "Renta de la tierra, heterogeneidad urbana y medio ambiente," document E/CEPAL/Proy. 2/R12.

30. Additional information on these questions can be found in Ian Thomson, "Social Consequences of the Automobile."

31. See Lucio Kowarik, "El precio del progreso."

32. See Giorgio Solimano, "Impact of Socioeconomic Development."

33. Two works that throw light on strategies for survival and marginal organization are Carlos Borsotti, "Estilos de desarrollo, medio ambiente y estrategias familiares," document E/CEPAL/Proy. 2/R5; and Larissa Lomnitz, "Organización social y estrategias de sobrevivencia en los estratos urbanos de América Latina," document E/CEPAL/Proy. 2/R24.

34. For more details see Warren Crowther, "Technological Development, Development Styles and Environmental Problems," document E/CEPAL/Proy. 2/R35.

35. These questions are addressed by Raúl Prebisch in "Biósfera y desarrollo," document E/CEPAL/Proy. 2/R22.

36. The experience and possibilities of alternative strategies are explored by Jorge Wilheim in "Metropolización y medio ambiente," document E/CEPAL/Proy. 2/R17.

37. Marshall Wolfe has analyzed the principal political problems that arise when considering the environmental issue in "Perspectivas: El medio ambiente en la palestra política," document E/CEPAL/Proy. 2/R6.

38. Several efforts have been made to incorporate the environmental variable into development planning. See Alvaro García and Eduardo García, "Las variables medioambientales en la planificación del desarrollo," document E/CEPAL/Proy. 2/R39; and Rubén Utria, "La incorporación de la dimensión ambiental en la planificación del desarrollo: Una alternativa de guía metodológica," document E/CEPAL/Proy. 2/R20.

39. In this regard see Amilcar Herrera, "Desarrollo, medio ambiente y generación de tecnologías apropiadas," document E/CEPAL/Proy. 2/R1.

40. See José J. Villamil, "Conceptos de estilos de desarrollo."

41. On this point see Alfredo del Valle, "Los nuevos problemas de la planificación energética en América Latina," document E/CEPAL/Proy. 2/R31.

42. For an analysis of the Brazilian situation see Fernando H. Cardoso, "Perspectivas del desarrollo y medio ambiente: El caso de Brasil," document E/CEPAL/Proy. 2/R38.

43. Evidently, any substantial change in lifestyles and values will require an environmental education policy. See Vicente Sánchez, "Papel de la educación en la interacción entre estilos de desarrollo y medio ambiente," document E/CEPAL/Proy. 2/R29.

44. The incorporation of the environmental dimension in national develop-

ment plans and programs is a constant concern in Latin America. Important contributions on this question include Santiago Torres, "La incorporación de la dimensión medioambiental en la planificación regionál: Aspectos operacionales," document E/CEPAL/Proy. 2/R14; Warren Crowther, "Information, Development Styles and Environmental Problems in Latin America," document E/CEPAL/Proy. 2/R26; Lety Gaete, "Información medioambiental para la planificación," document E/CEPAL/Proy. 2/R13; and Guillermo Alonso, "Antecedentes jurídicos del medio ambiente en América Latina," document E/CEPAL/Proy. 2/R41.

Part Three
Overcoming Dependency:
Selected Strategies

6
Negotiating a New Bargain with the Rich Countries

Mahbub ul Haq

If history is to be our guide, the world may well be on the threshold of a historical turning point. On the national level, such a turning point was reached in the United States in the 1930s, when the New Deal elevated the working classes to partners in development and accepted them as an essential part of the consuming society. At the international level, we still have not arrived at that philosophic breakthrough when the development of the poor nations is considered an essential element in the sustained development of the rich nations and when the interests of both rich and poor nations are regarded as complementary and compatible rather than conflicting and irreconcilable. And yet we may be nearing that philosophic bridge.

However, if we are to cross this bridge, the rich nations must place the current demands of the Third World in their proper historical perspective, agree on a strategy of serious negotiations, help crystallize certain negotiating areas and principles, and determine the negotiating forums where mutually beneficial agreements can be thrashed out. It is in this spirit that the following few concrete suggestions are offered.

This chapter is reprinted with permission from Guy F. Erb and Valeriana Kallab, eds., *Beyond Dependency: The Developing World Speaks Out* (Washington, D.C.: Overseas Development Council, 1975), pp. 157–162. It is based on remarks made by the author at a Conference on New Structures for Economic Interdependence (cosponsored by the Institute on Man and Science and the Aspen Institute for Humanistic Studies, the Overseas Development Council, and the Charles F. Kettering Foundation) held at the United Nations and at the Institute for Man and Science, Rensselaerville, New York, May 15–18, 1975. For the report of that Conference, see *New Structures for Economic Interdependence* (Rensselaerville, New York: Institute on Man and Science, August 1975).

Perspective

It is important that the current demands of the developing countries for a New International Economic Order be perceived in correct perspective.

First, the basic objective of the emerging trade union of the poor nations is to negotiate a new deal with the rich nations through the instrument of collective bargaining. The essence of this new deal lies in the objective of the developing countries to obtain greater equality of opportunity and to secure the right to sit as equals around the bargaining tables of the world. No massive redistribution of past income and wealth is being demanded: in fact, even if all the demands are added up, they do not exceed about one percent of the GNP of the rich nations. What is really required, however, is a redistribution of future growth opportunities.

Second, the demand for a New International Economic Order should be regarded as a movement—as part of a historical process to be achieved over time rather than in any single negotiation. Like the political liberation movement of the 1940s and the 1950s, the movement for a new economic deal is likely to dominate the next few decades and cannot be dismissed casually by the rich nations.

Third, whatever deals are eventually negotiated must balance the interests of both the rich and the poor nations. The rich nations have to carefully weigh the costs of disruption against the costs of accommodation and to consider the fact that any conceivable cost of a new deal would amount to a very small proportion of their future growth in an orderly, cooperative framework. The poor nations have to recognize that, in an interdependent world, they cannot hurt the growth prospects of the rich nations without hurting their own chances of negotiating a better deal.

Strategy

The international community must also move quickly to develop a negotiating strategy with a view to:

(a) Reaching agreement that serious negotiations are acceptable on all elements of a New International Economic Order. The rich nations should declare their willingness to enter into such negotiations within the UN framework, and the poor nations should accept the fact, in turn, that the meetings of 1975 have merely begun the process of negotiation;
(b) Narrowing down the areas of negotiation to manageable proportions in the first instance and selecting the priorities fairly carefully so that the dialogue can move from the least divisive issues to the more difficult ones

in a step-by-step approach. Conferences can seldom produce decisions unless agreement has been reached quietly in advance. At present, such quiet efforts are needed to reach preliminary understandings and a political consensus on the nature and form of the negotiations between the rich and the poor nations;

(c) Developing and agreeing on certain negotiating principles as an umbrella for future discussions. While detailed negotiations may have to proceed on a case-by-case basis, negotiation of an overall umbrella is absolutely essential in the first instance if the advantage of collective bargaining is to be retained;

(d) Formulating specific proposals for implementation. These proposals should bring out various alternatives and their implications for each side; and

(e) Determining the negotiating forums through which agreements can be reached on these proposals in a specified period of time.

Negotiating Principles

It may be useful to focus on a few critical areas to illustrate how the international community can move toward the formulation of certain negotiating principles.

International Trade

What is really wrong with the present economic order from the point of view of the poor nations? First, the exports of about twelve major primary commodities (excluding oil) account for about 80 percent of the total export earnings of the developing countries. The final consumers pay over $200 billion for these commodities and their products while the primary producers obtain only about $30 billion—with the middlemen enjoying most of the difference. Second, the export earnings from these commodities fluctuate violently at times. Third, the purchasing power of these primary exports keeps declining in terms of manufactured imports. Fourth, the manufactured exports of the developing countries often face tariffs and quotas in the industrialized countries and constitute only about 7 percent of world manufactured exports.

In order to improve this situation, at least certain negotiating principles can be articulated in the first instance:

(a) Producing countries must get a higher proportion of the final consumer price for their primary commodities. The present marketing and price structure should be examined to determine whether a better return to producers can be ensured by further processing of primary commodities, reduction of present imperfections in the commodity markets, squeezing of middlemen's profits, and organization by the producing countries of their own credit and distribution services;

(b) A better deal on primary commodities must be obtained *before* efforts are made at price stabilization or indexing—as in the case of oil—since stabilization of present low earnings will not achieve much. Possibilities of establishing an international commodity bank should be considered, both to improve present earnings and then to stabilize them;

(c) The consuming countries must be given long-term assurances of the security of supplies, without any deliberate interruptions or embargoes;

(d) Producers' associations in primary commodities should be accepted as legitimate instruments of collective bargaining to offset the present considerable concentration of economic power at the buying end; and,

(e) Present restrictions in the industrialized countries against the manufactured exports of the developing countries should be relaxed, and intra-developing-country trade in these manufactures expanded with a view to increasing the present share of the developing countries in world manufactured exports.

International Monetary System

Let us survey the situation in yet another key area—the present monetary system—from the point of view of the developing countries.

As Professor Triffin has convincingly argued, international liquidity is largely created by the national decisions of the richest industrialized nations as their national reserve currencies (e.g., dollars, sterling) are in international circulation.[1] During 1970–1974, international decisions on special drawing rights (SDRs) acounted for only 9 percent of the total international reserve creation; even these decisions are primarily dictated by the needs of the rich nations. Not surprisingly, the developing countries obtained very little benefit from the creation of international liquidity: out of $102 billion of international reserves created during 1970–1974, the developing countries received $3.7 billion, or less than 4 percent. As in any banking system, the poor get little credit.

As such, negotiating principles in this area will have to include the following:

(a) national reserve currencies should be gradually phased out and replaced by the creation of a truly international currency—like the SDRs—through the deliberate decisions of the International Monetary Fund (IMF);

(b) the volume of this international liquidity should be regulated by the IMF in line with the growth requirements in world trade and production, particularly to facilitate such growth in the developing countries;

(c) the distribution of this international liquidity should be adjusted so as to benefit the poorest countries, especially by establishing a link between the

creation of international liquidity (SDRs) and long-term assistance; and
(d) in order to carry out these reforms, the present voting strength in the
IMF should be changed to establish a near parity between the developing
and the developed countries.

International Resource Transfers

Another area of constant controversy between the rich and the poor
nations—the present "aid order"—can serve as a final example. What is
really wrong with it from the point of view of the developing countries?
First, the present resource transfers from the rich to the poor nations are
totally voluntary, dependent only on the fluctuating political will of the
rich nations. Second, although a kind of international "deal" was made
by the rich nations in accepting a target of 1 percent of GNP, with 0.7
percent in Official Development Assistance (ODA) to be transferred annually to the poor countries, in actual practice ODA has declined in
1975 to 0.3 percent for all member countries of the OECD's Development Assistance Committee (DAC) and to 0.2 percent in the case of the
United States. Third, not enough attention has been paid to the terms of
international resource transfers, so that the developing countries have accumulated over $120 billion in financial debt whose servicing takes away
about one half of new assistance every year.

If a negotiated framework for international resource tranfers is to
emerge, a fresh start needs to be made on a number of fronts:

(a) An element of automaticity must gradually be built into the international resource transfer system—e.g., through an SDR link with aid, certain sources of international financing such as royalties from seabed mining, and a tax on nonrenewable resources—so that these transfers become
less than voluntary over time;
(b) The focus of international concessional assistance must shift to the
poorest countries, and, within them, to the poorest segments of the population. As such, this assistance should be mainly in the form of grants,
without creating a reverse obligation of mounting debt liability at a low
level of poverty;
(c) International assistance should be linked in some measure to national
programs aimed at satisfying minimum human needs. Such a target for the
removal of poverty can be easily understood in the rich nations; it can be
the basis of a shared effort between the national governments and the international community; it provides an allocative formula for concessional
assistance; and it establishes a specific time period over which the task
should be accomplished;
(d) One possible formula for international burden sharing could be to combine an expanding volume of financial funds at commercial rates from the

liquidity-surplus members of the Organization of Petroleum Exporting Countries (OPEC) with subsidy funds made available by the industrialized countries and the richest OPEC countries. Such a formula is likely to provide resources on intermediate terms, with a grant element of about 50 to 60 percent;

(e) Multilateral channels should be used for directing this assistance in preference to bilateral channels, since this will be consistent with greater automaticity of transfers, allocations based on poverty and need rather than on special relationships, and a more orderly system of burden sharing; and

(f) Arrangements must be made to provide a negotiating forum for an orderly settlement of past debts, possibly by convening a conference of principal creditors and debtors.

Conclusion

It is not the intention of this paper to attempt to prepare a concrete blueprint of a new "planetary bargain" that the poor nations seem to be seeking at present—a task that in any case would be impossible in the time available—but rather merely to illustrate a more positive approach toward reaching such a bargain. The report of the Group of Experts on the Structure of the United Nations System is aimed at providing sensible negotiating forums within the UN framework for an orderly dialogue on the elements of a New International Economic Order.[2] Technocratic proposals are easy to formulate. But what is really required for the success of the deliberations between rich and poor nations is political vision of an unprecedented nature that is inspired by the promise of the future, not clouded by the controversies of the past nor mired in the short-run problems of the present.

Notes

1. See Robert Triffin, "The International Monetary System," in *New Structures for Economic Interdependence* (Rensselaerville, New York: The Institute on Man and Science, August 1975). Proceedings of a conference co-sponsored by the Institute on Man and Science and The Aspen Institute for Humanistic Studies, the Overseas Development Council, and the Charles F. Kettering Foundation.

2. Report of the Group of Experts on the Structure of the United Nations System, *A New United Nations Structure for Global Economic Cooperation,* U.N. Doc. No. E/AC.62/9 (New York: United Nations, 1975).

7
The Revolution of Being:
A Preferred World Model

Gustavo Lagos

This article is part of the transnational research endeavour known as the World Order Models Project (WOMP). The WOMP was created in the early 1960s by a few United States citizens who wanted to address the theme of war prevention within formal academic environments. Nevertheless, it became apparent that the question of war prevention could not be studied in isolation from four other problems that humankind faces and which transcend the nation-state system: poverty, social injustice, environmental decay and alienation. The concrete task then was to develop an analytic framework that would provide intellectual tools for coping with these five problems. This conclusion was reached by a group of social scientists from different parts of the world, including Africa, Asia, Europe, Latin America and North America, that gathered under the auspices of the Institute for World Order to study these issues from a regional perspective in order to enrich the global approach.

This body of social scientists criticized the prejudice still prevailing in some social science circles against all research founded on preferences and values. But, WOMP is not a "utopian" undertaking in the conventional way. The objective is to formulate *relevant utopias*, that is, world order systems that clarify alternative worlds and the necessary transition steps to these worlds. In fact, each participant was asked to attempt a *diagnosis* of the prevailing world order, make prognostic statements based on that evaluation, state his *preferred future* world order, and advance coherent and viable *strategies of transition* that could materialize that future. A stringent time-frame, the 1990s, served to discipline and focus thought and proposals.

This chapter presents a Latin American view of a preferred world.

The Roots of the Revolution of Being:
The Failure of the Revolution of Having

A stratified international system has always existed, but it revealed itself in full force only after the Second World War. The emergence of the Soviet Union and the United States as superpowers — far ahead of the rest of the world in economic, scientific, and technological capacity, in military strength and prestige — has generated an international process of dependence and inferiority and resulted in a deterioration of the real status of the other nations, termed *atimia*.[1] Atimia, when it affects such world powers as Britain, France and Germany, is partial; when it affects other nations, especially the countries still termed underdeveloped or developing, it is generalized or complete.

An analysis that portrays the system of international relations as being stratified need not be derived only from the construction of abstract indicators to measure the real status of a country in terms of economic, scientific, and technological power and military strength, with their repercussions on national prestige. My first real appreciation of the stratified international system grew out of personal encounters as a Latin American and a Chilean participating in international meetings and negotiations. These personal experiences, which became the psychological basis of my theory of atimia, had shown me that by the mere fact of my belonging to an underdeveloped country and region of the world, the characteristics of the real status of that country and that region — dependence, a sense of inferiority, generalized atimia — were somehow, consciously or subconsciously, transmitted and ascribed to me. In other words, through an indefinable process, involving a sort of irrational fatalism, the characteristics of the national-regional group to which I had belonged from birth became my own. Nor am I alone in this; in one way or another, the same thing has been felt and experienced by all Latin Americans who move or have moved in international life, whether in financial, business, or academic circles, or in any of its other manifold spheres of action.

This same feeling of atimia, which I and many other Latin Americans have experienced in the real-life encounters of the international stratified system, exists for many more human beings within their own countries. Latin American *national* elites become second-class citizens in the *international* area. But these national elites are surrounded within their own states by masses of second-class and third-class citizens, human beings who do not have the economic power to travel outside their country, much less the political power to represent their country internationally.

At the beginning of the second half of the twentieth century, within the framework of the United Nations, the concepts of development and underdevelopment made their appearance as a theoretical attempt to account in scientific terms for an appalling situation that is still smiting the conscience of the world. At last our region was discovering a "rational" explanation for poverty, dependence, privation — death in life.

At that time Latin America believed that by conquering underdevelopment it would attain the promised land. Development came to constitute a value in itself. Thanks to the demonstration effect, Latin America aspired to become a developed continent, in the likeness of the developed models already existing: Western Europe, the United States, Japan, and the socialist countries. To this end it needed technical, financial, and educational assistance from "the models."

The international economic structure, however, continued to maintain the pattern of exploiting centre and exploited periphery, thus widening the gap between rich and poor countries.

The figures are not exactly encouraging for our continent. A population of 270 million human beings, which is increasing at the whirlwind annual rate of 2.9 percent, has an annual gross national product that in 1969 averaged $450 per capita for the region as a whole. For comparative purposes, it should be noted that GNP per capita in 1969 was $4,200 in the U.S., $2,460 in France, and $1,200 in the Soviet Union.[2]

The Latin American's expectation of life is 55 years, against 70 years for an inhabitant of the U.S., Europe, or the Soviet Union.

Similarly, illiteracy figures in our countries average nearly 32 percent, against a percentage very little above zero in the industrialized countries.

With regard to the quality of diet, suffice it to say that the intake of a Latin American averages 2,500 calories a day, whereas the corresponding average in the industrialized world is approximately 3,500 calories.

These figures, so disheartening for our region, cannot be analysed without brief reference to the influence exerted on the foregoing process by the U.S., which is at present Latin America's principal hegemonic center. This influence must be viewed in a historical perspective, as the region's contemporary problems have their roots in its past history.

Latin America was drawn into international relations as a result of the incorporation of its peoples in the colonial systems set up by Spain, Portugal, and other powers in the region. This colonialization was the starting-point for a situation of absolute dependence for Latin America that took the form of economic, political, and cultural domination.

This absolute colonial relationship was abruptly metamorphosed when our nations won their political independence. Spanish restrictions on trade between the colonies and the countries of Europe and the rest of America, already weakened by contraband, were abolished altogether and replaced by free trade. Thus Latin America opened its gates to the industrial progress of Europe and the U.S.

At that time Britain was witnessing the apogee of the Industrial Revolution, which convulsed the entire structure of commerce and production. This industrial phenomenon demanded new markets for British products, and it was in newly independent Latin America that a good many such markets were found.

By the time the Industrial Revolution had been consolidated in Britain in the mid-nineteenth century, British commercial, financial, and industrial capitalism had already penetrated Latin America. During the second half of the century its influence increased: British vessels carried a major share of cargo to and from Latin American ports; British capital was invested in railways, public utilities, and government securities; British banks issued credit at half the rate of interest charged by their competitors. London was the financial clearinghouse for international payments to exporters in the European countries and the U.S. against sales to Latin America.

While the Industrial Revolution was being consolidated in Britain, on the other side of the Atlantic development processes were brewing which were to convert the U.S. into a new centre of industrial and financial capitalism that would supersede Britain, its former metropolis. Once this objective had been attained, the U.S. made its presence inexorably felt in Latin America.

The new hegemonic center constituted by the U.S. grew into an exporter of capital. The policy of trade expansion in world markets had emerged as the accepted doctrine for contending with the frequent depressions experienced in the U.S. economy. This notion had a profound and calamitous effect on U.S. foreign policy, helped to lay stress on the ideology of "Manifest Destiny," and led to an aggressive search for new markets and new investment opportunities in Latin America. This was the origin of the "Big Stick" policy, which implied the unbridled use of force for imperialistic purposes, as was demonstrated by the process that culminated in building the Panama Canal. This expansionist policy too was the origin of dollar diplomacy, which meant that U.S. bankers were made the instruments of ousting European interests in Latin America, not excepting the use of force whenever it seemed necessary or expedient.

In the course of time, the violence-oriented policies pursued by Latin America's new hegemonic centre underwent a gradual change of tone, thanks to the action of certain progressive statesmen in the U.S., and also in some measure to a belated stirring of consciousness on Latin America's part.

The Latin American countries began to demand, separately rather than collectively, a change in their relations with the U.S., and this objective was apparently attained with the establishment of successive inter-American policies. But all these endeavours ended in crashing failure, an outstanding case in point being that of the defunct Alliance for Progress, the most recent of the U.S. attempts to rectify its policy on Latin America.

A few statistics may help to give a clearer idea of the magnitude of Latin America's situation of dependence, in which the U.S. plays a primary role. These data, in Tables 7.1, 7.2, and 7.3, are so telling that no explanation is needed.

These were the reasons that the Chilean Minister of Foreign Affairs, Gabriel Valdés, together with the Latin American ambassadors to the U.S., personally delivered to President Nixon on June 11, 1969, the Consenso de Viña del Mar, which had been adopted by the Comisión Especial de Coordinación Latinoamericana (CECLA) the preceding May. In his introductory speech at the delivery ceremony, Mr. Valdés made this comment: "It is a generalized belief that our continent is receiving real aid in the financial field. Figures demonstrate just the contrary. We can really say that Latin America is contributing to financing the development of the United States and other industrialized nations."

The figures given likewise shed light on the role played by transnational corporations in the region. In Latin America there are more than 2,000 subsidiaries of some 200 U.S. companies. From 1954 to 1967, direct exports of U.S. private capital to our region amounted to $3,361 million, the total profit earned was $12,403 million, and the amount repatriated was $10,839 million. It may also be added that 17 percent of the financing came from the U.S.

But the harmful effects of the transnational corporations are not only economic and social. What the figures do not make clear is that these gigantic entities constitute a threat to the sovereignty of the countries in which they are installed. The danger becomes even more acute in view of the inordinate degree of protection some governments—notably that of the U.S.—accord these private enterprises, which is reflected in all sorts of international pressures exerted by the mother country on any nation that dares to defy the private interests in question. In this connection, Cuba, Peru, and Chile have faced or are facing obstructive action on the part of the U.S. Nevertheless, it would be a mistake to impute the generalized crisis Latin America is currently experiencing simply and

Table 7.1

Movements of and Returns on Foreign Capital in Latin America, 1950 - 1967

	Inflows	(Millions of dollars) Outflows	Balance
Movements of foreign capital:			
- Direct investment	9,601.2	947.2	8,654.0
- Medium - term and long - term loans	20,360.4	13,102.2	7,258.2
- Compensatory loans	11,418.7	8,753.0	2,665.7
- Net movement of foreign capital			18,577.9
Returns on foreign capital:			
- Profits and dividends		18,430.6	
- Interests on loans		5,751.3	
- Total income		24,181.9	- 24,181.9
- Balance of movement of foreign capital and income			- 5,606.2

Source: Data from the Economic Commission for Latin America (CEPAL) and the International Monetary Fund (IMF), tabulated by researchers working on the subject of dependence in the Center for Socio - Economic Studies (Centro de Estudios Socio - Económicos - CESO) of the Universidad de Chile.

Table 7.2

Sources and Uses of Direct Private U. S. Investment in Latin America
1960 - 1964

	(Millions of dollars)
Sources:	
Profits	4,782
Depreciation and depletion	2,899
Funds obtained in Latin America	1,361
Funds from the U. S.	404
Total	9,446
Uses:	
Plant and equipment	3,567
Inventories	562
Receivables	993
Other assets	601
Distributed Profits	3,723
Total	9,446

Source: U. S. Department of Commerce, **Survey of Current Business**, November 1965.

Table 7.3

Latin America: Exports, Imports, and Trade Balances, by Principal Regions
and Countries, 1958 - 1968

	Exports (f. o. b.)		Imports (c. i. f.)		Balance	
(Millions of dollars)						
	1958	1968	1958	1968	1958	1968
United States	3,831	4,186	4,312	4,770	- 481	- 584
European Economic Community (founder members)	1,297	2,277	1,518	2,229	- 221	+ 48
European Free Trade Association	926	1,094	833	1,157	+ 93	- 63
Western Europe	161	729	105	1,072	+ 56	- 343
Japan	169	617	138	515	+ 31	+ 102
Latin America	762	1,368	898	1,535	- 136	- 167
Total	8,396	11,799	8,589	12,405	- 193	- 606

Source: ECLA, on the basis of official statistics.

solely to unfair and arbitrary international structures.

According to some partial data, in several of the less developed Asian countries the existing inequalities are not as great as in Latin America.

These inequalities in our region have been summed up as follows by UN experts. In terms of income strata the distinctive features of distribution in Latin America are the following: The highest income group has a much larger share of total income than in the industrialized countries; a correspondingly smaller proportion falls to the bulk of the population in the wide middle ranks of income distribution. The poorest groups and those immediately below the highest group receive proportions similar to those of the same groups in the industrialized countries.

The reader may perhaps be surprised to learn that the poorest groups in Latin America and in the industrialized countries are in much the same position in this respect. But the apparent contradiction vanishes when the study goes on to point out that the poorest groups differ greatly from one type of country to the other. In Latin America they are made up of active members of the labour force, whose place in the lowest income strata is permanent; in the industrial countries, on the other hand, a very low income is not for the most part a permanent state, and most of the groups concerned consist of "special cases," many of whom are not active members of the labour force.[3] Nevertheless there is always a lower income group frozen proportionately. The ratios of rich to poor in the U.S. have hardly changed, at least in this century. The U.S. has always had a powerful class structure and is a stratified system, but there is mobility of individuals within the system, which itself remains almost completely unaltered with respect to wealth.

Table 7.4 shows the respective shares of the various income groups in Latin America and the U.S.[4]

If we now take into account the fact that the GNP of the U.S. is $861,623 million, with a population of 203 million inhabitants, and the GNP of Latin America is $119,842 million, with a population of 266 million,[5] the conclusion to be drawn is abysmally depressing. The 5 percent group in the highest income bracket in the U.S. receives more in monetary terms than all the groups in Latin America put together; in other words, 10 million privileged inhabitants of the U.S. receive more than the entire Latin American population. Consequently, those who live in the industrialized world must realize that the inequality of income distribution is not merely an internal problem deriving from the exploitation and domination existing within national societies, but also, and primarily, a problem deriving from the unfair, arbitrary, and abusive structures of international relations in the political and economic spheres, which have opened this gulf between income levels in the industrial countries and in countries of the Third World. This at least is the opinion of many prominent Latin American political leaders and social scientists.

In view of these tragic disparities, economic development has taken on the status of a value in itself. Our societies, as we have already said, have aspired to become developed countries. Only now are some Latin American intellectuals and leaders beginning to grasp the fact that development in the countries ranking highest in the stratified international system does not necessarily imply true wellbeing. Latin America must never fail to bear in mind the need to forestall the emergence of development models calculated to turn its countries into sheer copies of the more developed countries, capitalist or socialist, as such modelling signifies the creation of veritable culture media to breed the same problems the advanced

Table 7.4

Percentage of National Wealth Belonging to Each Income Class
in the United States and in Latin America

Income group	Latin America		United States
Lowest 20 percent	3.1		4.6
30 percent below the median	10.3	80 % of the population have 37.5 % of the wealth	18.8
30 percent above the median	24.1		31.1
15 percent below the top 5 percent	29.2	20 % of the population have 62.6 % of the wealth	25.5
Top 5 percent	33.4		20.0

countries are facing at present. Our nations must learn from the developed countries to avoid stumbling into the same pitfalls as they. It is absolutely essential that our creative endeavour should be directed towards the formulation of genuinely Latin American solutions. Hence there is no point in persisting in a race for development that takes no account of the values inherent in developed society.

The convergence of socialism and capitalism in the late twentieth century makes these pitfalls increasingly easy to identify: both go in for capital-intensive strategies of economic growth; for heavy industry using complex machinery; for massive and complex machine-driven economies of scale that threaten the world environment and local diversity. They do so in large part of course because of the dynamics of their chauvinist great-power rivalries. Capitalism as a global economic order has increased poverty gaps. Socialism has remained nationalistic and relatively indifferent to the plight of the developing countries. China and the Chinese economy so far constitute partial exceptions to these remarks, which are directed mainly at the other large industrialized countries.

The developing countries therefore need a profound new development strategy. It must be made quite clear that this is no new proposal. On the contrary, since the last century there has been a far-reaching movement on the part of authentically Latin American thinkers to lay systematic stress on the necessity of applying solutions of our own to problems of our own. A case in point is afforded by a great Uruguayan philosopher, José Enrique Rodó. Imbued with a profound romanticism, Rodó says in his *Ariel* (1900) that

> one imitates somebody in whose superiority or prestige one believes. Thus it is that the vision of an America delatinized of its own free will, without the coercion of conquest, and then regenerated in the image and likeness of the northern archetype, now hovers over the dreams of many who are concerned for our future, inspires the satisfaction with which at every step they draw the most suggestive parallels and finds expression in constant proposals for innovation and reform.

Lighting upon a response to the drama of Latin America far ahead of his time, Rodó wrote in *El Mirador de Próspero* (1913):

> The Hispano-American peoples are beginning to acquire a clear and steadfast consciousness of the unity of their destinies; of the indestructible solidarity which has its roots in the very essence of their past and stretches out into the infinity of their future. Auguste Comte expressed his profound faith in the future consciousness of human solidarity, when he said that humanity, as a collective being, does not yet exist, but that it will exist some

day. Let us say that our America, the America of our race, is beginning to "be" as a collective person, conscious of its identity.

Rodó's prophetic vision extended to the U.S., and in *Ariel* he voiced what must have been one of the earliest criticisms of the consumer society:

> The life of the United States does in fact describe the vicious circle indicated by Pascal in the eager pursuit of material welfare, when this is made the be-all and the end-all in itself. Its prosperity is as great as its inability to satisfy even the most moderate conception of man's destiny. A titanic achievement, by virtue of the enormous willpower it represents and of its unprecedented triumphs in every sphere of material aggrandizement, that civilization unquestionably produces a singular impression of inadequacy and emptiness. And the reason is that if we exercise a right conferred by the history of thirty centuries of evolution over which the dignity of the classical spirit and the dignity of the Christian spirit have presided, and venture to ask what is the guiding principle involved, what the motive underlying the immediate concern with those positive interests which set that formidable mass vibrating, all that will be found as the formula for the ultimate ideal is that same concern with material success.

The time has come when the visionary summons of Rodó can no longer be disregarded. It is incumbent upon us therefore to work out an original solution for our weighty problems. And it is precisely in this context that we formulate the proposition of the revolution of being, which we consider applicable to all countries alike, industrial or underdeveloped, affluent or poor, socialist or capitalist. But we would stipulate that the revolution of being must take into account the situation of each region, respecting the idiosyncrasies, the customs, and the propensities of every people and of every nation.

The Nature of the Revolution of Being

What then are the values that ought to orientate and guide what we call "the revolution of being" that would lead to the integral development of man? Of course, if we are not to lapse into an idealistic position, these values must be embodied in socioeconomic and political structures to make them operative. It would be illusory and hypocritical to talk of the integral development of man, to issue declarations in favour of democracy and human rights, unless at the same time socioeconomic and political structures are changed in such a way as to permit the implementation of the values in question.

Marxist thought has dismissed as unscientific the exaltation of values as the driving forces behind the historical process, formulating its famous thesis of the predominance of the economic base or infrastructure over the superstructure, which includes the juridico-political structure corresponding to the state and the law as well as ideologies. In this scheme of things the world of values would pertain to the superstructure, which would ultimately be determined by the economic base.

If we consider contemporary sociological thought, especially Anglo-Saxon thinking, and within that the ideas current in the U.S., we are frequently assured by these sociologists that a process of interaction does take place between the economic base and the juridico-political structure, which correspond to the state and the law, and the ideological structure. This idea of interaction between the two components seems to approximate very closely Engels' assertion that the infrastructure is related to the superstructure in a dialectical process of cause and effect, in an interplay of actions and reactions.[6] Thus "bourgeois" sociology would appear to coincide with this fundamental Marxist conception and in doing so to demonstrate that Marxism lacks a scientific basis, as it is impossible to prove that *ultimately*—which may mean in the course of ten, twenty, fifty, or a hundred years—either the infrastructure or the superstructure will be predominant. All that can be scientifically affirmed is that there does exist a process of interaction between the two, to which the Marxists apply the term *dialectic* and bourgeois sociology simply calls *interaction*.

Given these premises, let us see by what values the revolution of being should be guided. Its values would be those of peace, economic welfare, social justice, participation, harmony between man and nature, liberty, all of which in combination and embodied in socioeconomic and political structures should lead to the integral development of man, that is, to the revolution of being.

The antivalues are the values of the powerful capitalist and the socialist societies. The values of the revolution of being are those by which a humanistic society is guided in the pursuit of man's liberation, of his complete self-fulfillment as a human being.

These are the characteristics that give expression to the values that inform the essential dimensions of the revolution of being:

1. Multidimensional man (versus the unidimensional man of capitalist and socialist societies, the former being alienated mainly from the base, the latter mainly from the superstructure).

2. Community spirit guided by an ethic of solidarity (versus the rampant individualism of capitalist societies and the grim collectivism of socialist societies).

3. Work for the benefit of man (versus work for the benefit of the corporation or the state).

4. Tendency towards rationality in consumption oriented to being more rather than to having more (versus the tendencies towards unlimited production of goods in socialist societies and towards unlimited consumption in capitalist societies).

5. Liberating pedagogy oriented to the construction of the world: teaching-learning society (versus pedagogy oriented to the installation of the socialist system and pedagogy designed to preserve the status quo or establishment of capitalist societies).

6. Dialogic society: dialogue between generations, social groups, ideologies, civilizations (versus the nondialogic societies of the socialist countries and the limited dialogue of capitalist societies).

7. Tendencies towards equalitarian income distribution (versus tendencies towards equal distribution limited by the emergence of a new class in socialist societies and wide disparities in income distribution in capitalist societies).

8. Participation of all sectors of society (versus marginality of sectors not belonging to the new class in socialist societies and existence of numerous marginal sectors in capitalist societies).

9. Rationality oriented towards the integral development of man, and subordination of economic growth to this goal (versus rationality oriented towards the attainment of economic growth that dominates both capitalist and socialist societies).

10. Rationality oriented towards integration with other national societies with a view to maximizing peace, economic welfare, and social justice at the world level (versus rationality enclosed within the framework of the national society in the capitalist countries and rationality oriented towards the ideological, political and economic conquest of other national societies in socialist countries).

11. Limitation of sovereignty by practical implementation of cooperation and solidarity at the world level (versus unlimited conception of sovereignty, except for satellite countries, prevailing in both capitalist and socialist societies).

The historical implementation of the values of the revolution of being entails the suppression of all kinds of violence, direct or structural. Direct violence in the international field may be perpetrated through war, preparation for war, trade in armaments, military alliances, and so on. By direct violence at the internal level, within a given nation, is meant all acts of direct repression deriving from the socioeconomic structure, from the juridico-political pattern followed by the organization of the state or from the prevailing ideologies or ideology: for example, action taken by the police or the army to repress street demonstrations of protest against the government in the exercise of a legitimate right to freedom of assembly and speech.

Structural violence, the kind of violence that is not direct, is exerted through innumerable channels not so immediately visible to all observers as for instance war is. These in contrast are disguised, more or less dissimulated forms of violence, occurring either at the external level, that is, within the international system, or at the internal level, within national societies. At the external level this structural violence comprises the domination-dependence systems in force between the industrialized world and the so-called developing countries. It may take such forms as colonialism or neocolonialism and all the manifestations of imperialism in its various cultural, economic, political, scientific, technological, and other aspects. Internal or intranational structural violence consists of all those systems conducive to the economic exploitation of man by man; all systems that, operating at the social, economic, political and cultural levels in relation to the structure of production, produce alienation (estrangement from society or estrangement from self through society); and, lastly, all those structures of society whereby the individual human being may be prevented from participating in the various processes of social life that are the necessary and inevitable channels for his integral development.

Within this context peace is a synthesis value. Why is this so? Because, in a society pursuing the full liberation of man through the revolution of being, peace entails the implementation of a number of integrant values: it demands a measure of economic welfare, it requires social justice, it calls for participation, it necessitates the creation of a harmonious relationship between man and nature; in short, it involves all the values just pointed out as essential to the revolution of being.

Peace presupposes the suppression of both direct and structural violence at the internal level: within national societies it presupposes the maximization of the integrant values through the execution of the project of the revolution of being. At the external level, that is, in the international system, peace likewise presupposes the abolition of direct and structural violence as well as the maximization of the aforesaid values. The revolution of being implies a new conception of modernity, inspired neither in capitalism nor in socialism, both of which have meant in historical terms the revolution of having, the expression of the acquisitive spirit, the predominance of money, of trade, of business, that is, of economic motivation as the driving force of human activity, incarnated in the religion of GNP.

Being modern, in our view, is not living to have but living to be. This is the conception implicitly and explicitly embodied in the revolution of being.

The revolution of being implies the establishment of a biological and an educational structure for being. It implies what was said long ago by St. Thomas Aquinas, a modern man of the thirteenth century: a minimum of material welfare is necessary for the practice of virtue. That is, man must have at his disposal a minimum amount of material goods and services if he is to be able to develop as a human being. Hence our assertion that the revolution of being must be based on a biological and an educational structure for being. What is meant by a biological structure for being is a minimum of material welfare for each and all which will guarantee everyone human standards of diet, health, and housing, in other words an economic base of goods and services that will enable every man to enjoy the sound body the Greeks extolled as the prerequisite for the development of a sound mind. The biological structure for being accordingly implies a society in which the economic base and the juridico-political structure, that is, the state and the law, are organized to provide each and every man with this minimum of material welfare that will ensure integral development from the biological standpoint.

A structure for being further presupposes that the cultural system and the educational system of society are oriented to education for being, to training man for being more rather than for having more, because in such a society the economic base and the structure of the state and law will suffice in themselves to safeguard the biological structure. The biological structure for being, which permits the development of a healthy body, must be the precondition of education for being.

Education for being in its turn entails the establishment of a *teaching-learning* society. A teaching-learning society is one in which the classic educational systems are superseded, the systems under which it was assumed that an educated man was one who had passed through the primary, secondary, and university levels of education. In the teaching-learning society, the assumption is that education for being lasts throughout a man's life, and that within society all men learn and teach at the same time through a continuing process of dialogue. This dialogue stems from the common search for truth, which does not mean that everybody's truth is the same. On the contrary, it means that through dialogue the members of the teaching-learning society starting from different ideologies and cultural orientations, pursue the truth and educate themselves and others. Society is organized as a great laboratory in which all men teach and learn concurrently through social communication. This basic concept of the teaching-learning society implies a revolution in the classic systems of education.

If we had to sum up the essential characteristics of such a society, we might say that over and above the aforesaid teleological element, it is a society that allows continuing self-criticism of its own defects and those imputable to the human being within it. It does not imply that truth is possessed by any one social group or man or class but by the concurrence of all its members in a joint quest for truth. Self-criticism is therefore one of its cornerstones. Self-criticism implies the capacity not only to criticize oneself but to go on from there to criticize society and other people, not in defense of the possession of truth—for truth is beyond posses-sion—but in pursuit of man's eternal search for truth, through words, which are his means of communication, and not through violence, the symbol of noncommunication. Accordingly the teaching-learning society is anti-Manichean. In it men are not divided into the possessors of good or the possessors of evil. Its basic premise is that society is made up of real human beings with defects and virtues, aiming at self-development through dialogue with their fellows. Dialogue implies that those taking part in it find themselves in the presence of a truth that transcends them. None of them possesses truth, but through dialogue each tries to discover it.

This quest for truth has been pursued by all religions, and different ideologies have claimed to have discovered the right path to it. All of them have failed. Mankind needs cultural revolutions, taking place in different national societies and international systems or subsystems (regions), to make the teaching-learning model of human communica-tion and understanding operational on a world scale.

The teaching-learning society is only one aspect of a self-managed society in which a maximum of government is combined with a minimum of state. A self-managed society is one whose members participate in all the socioeconomic and political structures, both in the economic base and at the level of the juridico-political structure of the state and the for-mulation of law. It stems from the grass-roots of the people themselves, of man himself, rising to its peak authorities by way of intermediate steps in the scale of government. It might be described as a community made up of other groups whose members participate in all the social structures with the conscious aim of enabling society to govern itself. This is why we said that in a self-managed society there must be a maximum of government through this range of communities, which extends from those of the lowest rank, with less decision-making power as units, by way of those at the intermediate levels up to the great national commu-nity.

Nor will there be any concentration of power at the national level.

Here too it begins at the bottom and is represented by a state apparatus that incorporates a system of checks and balances, thereby making it impossible for power to concentrate in a single pair of hands or a single branch or a single structure. On the contrary, it is self-regulated by virtue of a new system, a reformulation of the theory of the balance of power that Montesquieu propounded long ago in his *De l'Esprit des Lois* and Hamilton, Madison, and Jay examined in their classic defense of the U.S. Constitution, the series of papers entitled *The Federalist*.

But a self-managed society presupposes a self-managed economy, given the constant interaction between the juridico-political structure of the state, the law, and the forms of social consciousness, or ideologies, on the one hand and the economic base on the other. The essence of the self-managed economy is that it must guarantee the biological structure and the educational structure for being we have described as the basis for the integral development of the human being in body and mind.

The economy of the new society must be based on a genuine and effective balance between man and nature. This new balance must be the product of a national decision that fully respects the relevant international agreements, to obviate the possibility that some countries will adopt measures for the conservation of the environment that might be prejudicial to the other members of the international community. It must end the irresponsible and indiscriminate abuse of natural resources and must make for a true return to nature: for example, a compulsory minimum should be fixed for the amount of green space per inhabitant in the great cities, which have nowadays become dreary concrete jungles; steps should be taken to prevent soil erosion, destruction of landscape, pollution of the air and of lakes, rivers, and oceans, and so forth.

Economic planning will have to determine the national economy's priorities and must faithfully reflect the decisions of the grassroots organizations of society. This implies decentralized planning, which obviously cannot be absolute, as it will have to be smoothly and efficiently fitted into an over-all plan agreed upon by the national community.

Resources for financing the development of national societies will have to be drawn from domestic savings and from foreign exchange earnings from exports, external financing being acceptable for specific projects and purchases of technology indispensable to the plan. Such external financing should be channelled through international agencies whose membership provides for effective representation of the recipient countries, to forestall the exertion of inadmissible pressure by the countries or institutions granting capital.

There can be no doubt that multinational integration is a genuinely positive solution for countries whose individual markets are too small to permit the installation of enterprises large enough to reap the benefits of economies of scale.

With regard to the ownership of the means of production, basic sources of wealth should be nationalized in the self-managed economy in accordance with the right every community can exercise under the principles recognized by the UN.

The general principle in respect of ownership in the new society must be that of workers' enterprises in which industrial employees and manual workers will take over the management of an industry and share in its profits within the framework established by law. Thus labour will replace capital in the management of enterprises. The ownership of capital will not be necessarily in the hands of the workers, although of course this possibility will not be excluded; in any case, capitals will receive only a dividend fixed by law, with a ceiling. The state will however have to keep the ownership and management of monopolistic and strategic enterprises in its own hands, although still with the participation of the workers, as this is a human and economic *sine qua non* of the new society. In the case of small-scale industries or small farms or businesses that depend essentially on the personal work and capabilities of the entrepreneur, cooperatives afford an appropriate framework for their development.

An indispensable feature of the national community's over-all plan is the formulation of tax and social-security policies and of other similar measures conducive to effective income redistribution at the level both of individuals and of enterprises in order to prevent the accumulation of profits, which in practice leads to the emergence of privileged groups or classes. To that end, income distribution must guarantee every human being a minimum livelihood, while in addition a ceiling must be set above which the income of no member of the community must be allowed to rise. Work will be the main source of income for everyone of working age: it will not be permissible for dividends or rents from accumulated and inherited savings or goods plus income from labour to surpass the ceiling.

Thus in a self-managed economy work becomes a right and a duty for everyone, and policies of full employment and education for being, both based on true equality of opportunities, will ensure the effective exercise of that right and the effective performance of that duty.

A self-managed society, based on a self-managed economy and a teaching-learning society that guarantees the proper biological structure and appropriate cultural and educational structures for the revolution of being, culminates in a self-managed political system. Under such a system the political constitution gives expression to the idea of the self-managed society as the global concept by which all social institutions and processes are inspired. It reflects the power structure required to permit the operation of the teaching-learning society, the self-managed economy, and the self-managed political system itself.

We do not intend to make the mistake of over-precisely describing the pertinent institutions, as every self-managed society must grow out of the sociopolitical, economic, and cultural context of each individual country. It would therefore run diametrically counter to the very idea of the self-managed society to try to present a general model supposed to be valid for such societies of all types. Each national society must find its own way to the new world of self-management, the new world of participation, the new world in which all human beings play a part in order to achieve their integral development through interaction with others. The self-managed society is that of the socialization and the personalization of man.

The balance-of-power system is essential to the creation of a system of checks and balances, both within the central organs of the state, the juridico-political organization, and the law and within society itself, with the object of preventing the concentration of power in the hands of specific groups or parties.

In a self-managed society, alongside the three classic powers of the state—the executive, the legislative, and the judicial—there should in our view be other additional powers; but as we are not proposing a universally valid model, for the reasons given, these ideas are put forward as suggestions that should be studied in relation to the characteristics of each national society. These new powers we have in mind—purely, we repeat, as approximations or suggestions—would be:

1. An independent controlling power established in the political constitution to supervise the legal validity of the acts of the executive, as already current under the legal systems of certain countries.

2. A power responsible for the official defence of human rights. Here the idea would be to install, likewise under the terms of the constitution, an attorney-general of human rights, permanent in tenure, the system of appointment being designed to facilitate the choice of a person with the qualifications and the integrity needed for the discharge of his office. His function would essentially be to arraign before the court of justice any individual (even the head of state), any group, any institution that violated human rights in the self-managed society. His would be a monitorial power to see that human rights were not violated by any of the other powers existing in the self-managed society, the juridico-political apparatus, and the legal machinery of the state.

3. A constitutional tribunal to settle disputes between the executive and the legislature. The structure and membership of such a tribunal and

the system of appointing its members would be of vital importance for its satisfactory operation. Just and upright men would have to be chosen to form it.

4. The people and the teaching-learning society as the ultimate source of control over possible deviations on the part of the powers established in the organs of the state or the powers established in the society through its various integrant communities and their expression and reflection in the state machinery. Our view in this connection is that the plebiscite or the referendum, as a properly regulated institution, might afford the people an opportunity of making pronouncements on certain issues of fundamental importance for the life of the self-managed society. It could be convened by any of the state powers (executive, legislative, or judicial) or by the attorney general of human rights, and also in certain cases by the constitutional tribunal, so that the people themselves might adopt decisions on basic problems or questions arising in the self-managed society in the event of differences of opinion between the institutions pertaining to the juridico-political machinery of the society and of the state.

To carry the idea of plebiscite somewhat further, a specific percentage of the electorate, or of youth or the female population, might also conceivably act as a controlling power if, in the circumstances indicated, they were given faculties to convene a plebiscite or referendum. To go farther still, it might be thought feasible for other social groups too — intellectuals, for example, or a given percentage of workers — to have recourse to a plebiscite. It is worth repeating that at bottom this would mean creating a system of checks and balances between the various powers, so that the people could adopt decisions as the ultimate controlling power if at any given moment the state institutions fail to meet the requirements of the process of change.

But a country cannot always resort to a plebiscite, and limits must therefore be set to the availability of this recourse lest it become an organ that paralyses state or societal action and government policy. In the future the progress of electronics might make it possible for the population to be periodically consulted on specific problems that might or might not be matters for a plebiscite. Such direct consultation of the people by the use of electronic techniques would be a way of achieving what in the Athenian democracy was done through the people's assembly, the number of whose members according to Plato's rule for his utopian republic should not exceed 5,000. In self-managed societies this number might range from several millions to several tens of millions of persons. The refinements of modern electronics would be placed at the service of the self-managed society to obtain the direct opinion of the people, of the members of society as a whole, as often as possible on specific questions or on the actual running of the society.

Let us now analyse the international dimensions of the revolution of being. The following characteristics give expression to the values and antivalues that inform the essential dimensions of the revolution in the international arena:

1. Ecumenical and solidaristic conception of the international system, which consists of the interaction of national interests seeking their maximization through integration and participation in regional communities and in the world community (versus the nationalist conception of the system in the present-day world, which consists of the interaction of national interests seeking their own maximization in an antagonistic context).

2. Conception of sovereignty shared at the regional and world levels: the nation-states delegate part of their sovereign powers to supranational integration agencies in which they are represented. Thus sovereignty is shared by the state members of the system (versus the unlimited conception of national sovereignty existing at present).

3. Existence of an international society by virtue of values shared at the world and regional levels (in the present-day world no international society exists, for want of values shared at the world level).

4. Peace in the sense of a synthesis-value that implies the suppression of direct and structural violence at the level of the system and of its component units and the promotion of humanist values and therefore the overthrow of antivalues (whereas warfare, preparation for war, trade in armaments and military alliances form an essential part of the international system in the present-day world).

5. National autonomy and regional autonomy in the framework of world solidarity: these concepts relate to the sovereign decision-making capacity of the nation-states and of the economic and/or political communities.

Thus nations must pursue full participation in the structures, institutions, and processes of the regional communities and of the world community. This participation implies that the nation-states take an active part in the decision-making process of the communities in question (versus the existence of areas of influence and the domination-dependence systems at the economic, scientific-technological, cultural and military levels, existing in the present-day international system).

6. Dialogue between teaching-learning societies and civilizations: cultural pluralism. This concept implies that nations develop their own cultures, not in isolation but through dialogue with other cultures and civilizations (versus the cultural domination by hegemonic nations existing in the present-day world).

7. International division of labour based on the harmonious and balanced development of the national economies (versus the international division of labour deriving from domination-dependence systems).

8. Fair distribution of the benefits resulting from the interaction and integration of the regional economies and of the world economy (versus the widening economic and technological gap deriving from the unfair structures of international trade and the other forms of interaction existing in the world economy).

9. International ownership of scientific and technological inventions, of the world system of satellite communications, of the moon and other celestial bodies, and of the resources of the seabed (versus the present-day system of private and national ownership of scientific and technological know-how and of communications systems).

10. A world and regional levy for the purposes of solidaristic development (versus the present-day voluntary and insignificant contributions to the development of other nations).

11. A new type of international stratification in which the national and regional communities that have succeeded in affording their inhabitants a high quality of life will be those enjoying the greatest international prestige and constituting poles of humanist development to influence other systems as models of the new society (versus the existing international stratification based on military and economic power and on prestige deriving basically from these variables).

The international structures and processes of the revolution of being should emerge as the product of two types of interaction, interaction between societies that have adopted or are in the process of adopting the model of the self-managed society and others that have not yet done so, and the interaction between the said societies and the power structure represented by the system of international stratification.

The idea underlying the revolution of being at the international level is that the nation-state is a feudal state, of which the most perfect example is to be found in the Marxist-Leninist socialist states that have nationalized the land and the means of production. The feudal state is nothing more nor less than the concentration of property and sovereignty in the hands of a single power. The Marxist socialist state is the owner of the land and all the means of production, besides possessing political sovereignty over its territory. Consequently, by a dramatic paradox, in a world on the brink of nuclear catastrophe, ecological disaster, and world revolution, the Marxist-Leninist state has reverted to feudalism holding both property and sovereignty in its hands.

The basic orientation of the revolution of being at the international level is towards the elimination of the feudal state created by socialism as well as the feudal patterns of capitalism, which through other media (military-industrial complexes, security agencies, transnational enterprises) has also set up a feudal state within a pseudodemocracy.

The only way to abolish the feudal state in both its socialist and its capitalist forms is to move towards socialization of the means of production, of the mass communication media, and of other areas of international activity through institutions forming part of or dependent on the UN. This entails establishing within the UN or its agencies a balance-of-power system similar to that described in connection with the self-managed society; but in this instance, the checks-and-balances system would have to operate at the world level, and its object would be to forestall the concentration of power in a technocracy that might set up a world dictatorship. Should that happen, there would not even be a loophole for any citizen of any country to escape from the world power structure, precisely because of its global scope. But as the revolution of being will be brought about through a lengthy historical process, in the course of which societies of the new type will display varying degrees of development, steps must be taken to ensure that the mobility of persons from one country to another is guaranteed by the attorneys-general of human rights referred to in the context of the revolution of being at the national level. A further possibility worth studying would be to appoint as part of a restructuring of the UN regional and world attorneys-general of human rights who would exercise functions similar to those of their counterparts in national societies, but at a multinational level.

The socialized areas of the world economy would be:

1. World agency for the seabed: The main objectives of this institution would be to exploit those seabed resources outside the limits of the jurisdiction of states and regional economic communities and to establish a system of research, investment and exploitation which would permit rapid development of the physical, chemical, geological and biological resources of the seabed.

2. World agency for science and technology: Its objective would be to administer the rights to the use of all scientific discoveries and/or technological innovations, taking special care to promote the development of the relatively less-developed regional economic communities and nation-states. The agency would in due course acquire ownership of the rights to the peaceful use of scientific discoveries and technological innovations.

3. World agency for global mass-communications media: This strategic and outstandingly important agency would acquire ownership of the world system of mass communications and administer it in such a way as to guarantee the regional economic communities and states

members access to the use of the system, to provide constant and factual information on world events, and to ensure real pluralism so that the agency's programmes would represent the various ideologies and political and cultural currents of the world's peoples.

4. World agency for outer space: This agency would establish norms for the exploration and utilization of outer space and the celestial bodies for the benefit of all countries and regions, whatever their degree of economic and scientific development. All areas of the celestial bodies would be freely accessible, and freedom of scientific research on them would be guaranteed under the principles of the UN.

5. World agency for ecological balance: This new world institution would seek an increasingly satisfactory balance between the lifesustaining systems of the earth and the demands — industrial, agricultural and technological — its inhabitants make upon them.[7] It would organize, share, and deploy knowledge and expertise, identify priority problems and coordinate national measures within an effective global framework. The agency would be empowered to establish standard and compulsory world norms for the conservation of the environment and would be endowed with the appropriate means to police and enforce its decisions.

6. World agency for development planning and financing: This agency would establish an indicative plan for world development in close collaboration with the agencies for ecological balance, the seabed, science and technology, outer space, and global mass communications media. The plan would contemplate an equitable international division of labour to secure the harmonious and balanced development of the national and regional economies and of the world economy and an equitable distribution of the benefits resulting from the integration of rational economies and the world economy.

This agency would also pursue the aim of establishing a monetary system to afford sufficient liquidity for international payments. Special drawing rights would be allowed mainly to economically less-developed regions and countries.

The new institution would have to be empowered to provide long-term credits at low rates of interest to finance specific projects or development programs; grants for the purposes specified; technical assistance of every kind (in close collaboration with the agency for science and technology).

7. World agency for the control of transnational corporations: It would lay down a code of good conduct for the operation of transnational corporations, backed by the appropriate means of policing and enforcing its decisions.

The creation of these world agencies would entail a drastic revision of the UN Charter. This organization would be replaced by a new one, the world community of peoples, whose members would be regional communities and nation-states.

The term regional community is used here in a broad sense. It may signify either a country, such as the U.S., Japan, or the Soviet Union, or a group of countries organized as an economic community, for example, the European Economic Community, or the future economic community that may emerge from Latin American integration.

The general assembly of this new organization would be formed by representatives of each regional community elected in proportion to the size of its population. For example, each region would have the right to two votes and to one or two additional votes for every hundred million inhabitants. Each state would have the right to one vote. All representatives from each regional community and from each member-state would be elected by popular vote. The assembly would elect the directors of the agencies by a majority of two thirds of its members, with no possibility of a veto for any region or state.

The secretary-general of the world community of peoples, together with the directors of the world agencies, would submit the programmes of the respective agencies to the general assembly, which would be required to pronounce on them within a given period after hearing the reports of the specialized commissions it would itself appoint. The plan would be implemented by each world agency in its sphere of competence. The agencies existing at present, such as UNESCO, ILO, FAO, WHO, and UNCTAD, would be sweepingly reformed, and their work would be carried out in co-ordination with the new agencies to obviate duplication of effort.

What must be stressed as of unquestionably paramount importance is that the decisions of these agencies would be binding on all the regions and countries of the world. For example, if certain norms were adopted for world trade, IMF, UNCTAD, and other related agencies would be obliged to apply them. If certain programmes were formulated, in education, science, and culture, UNESCO would have to play a salient part in structuring the teaching-learning society at the world level by promoting a dialogue between civilizations through projects similar to the East-West intercourse currently in progress, reformulating it in a world dimension, allocating it resources appropriate to that scope, and gearing it to the basic ideas of the teaching-learning society just analysed.

ILO, for its part, would have to direct its whole effort towards the study, analysis, and implementation of workers' enterprises (self-management) on the basis of technical assistance.

FAO in turn would have to draw up a radically reformulated world food program designed to ensure the necessary biological basis for the revolution of being in the field of nutrition. A similar course of action would be incumbent upon WHO in respect of health.

Thus UNESCO, FAO, and WHO would have an important role to play in seeing that the biological and educational bases for the revolution of being were established; but in fact all the mechanisms and agencies of the world community of peoples would be oriented towards attaining, within their specific fields of competence, the objectives of that world metamorphosis that constitutes the revolution of being.

To give a final example, the world agency for the control of transnational corporations would not only formulate a code of good conduct laying down precise regulations covering the activities of these important enterprises (in respect of profits, salaries and wages, discrimination by nationalities, tax declarations) but also directly supervise the implementation of the code through the appointment of specialized official inspectors to audit the accounts and review the legality of the acts of such corporations. By this means the enterprises in question would be prevented from proceeding with impunity in some of the less-developed countries whose administrative and legal structures are not efficient enough to counteract the tremendous power of these transnational bodies.

The Transition to the Revolution of Being

We will now endeavor to identify some of the basic features of the historical process whereby the transition might be made from the world of today — particularly Latin America — to the world of the revolution of being.

The first point to be stressed is that the period of transition is *permanent*. This is apparently a paradox, for the existence of a transition towards something implies that a stage will be reached at which the process of transition ends. But as the French philosopher Renan put it, contradiction may sometimes be a sign of truth. What is maintained here is that the transitional period is permanent, that there are transitions within the transition, and that the goal is never reached. Why not? Because arrival at the goal would signify the final triumph of the revolution of being, the entry into the promised land. It would signify the integral development of the human being in a stateless and classless society such as Marx dreamed of, a society in which man would be perfect, in which he would be freed from every form of alienation, in which he would achieve full and limitless self-expression. If the period of transition were *temporary*, the goal would one day be attained. But that uttermost human perfection will never be reached. The revolution of being will never be fully consummated, for that would mean the ultimate triumph of the new man, the ultimate triumph of the liberation of man, a human paradise on earth.

The period of transition is permanent, and in this contradiction in terms lurks the profound truth that man cannot change his nature. But it is not a pessimistic assertion, for although it is true that human nature cannot change it is equally true that man is infinitely more than man, as Pascal maintained. In other words, man can strive for self-perfection, can discover within his own being unsuspected potentialities that enable him to rise above himself. History is full of amazing cases in which man's capacity to surpass himself is revealed.

There is no society in the world, whatever its degree of development and whatever the yardsticks by which that development is measured — the religion of the gross national product or the quality of human life — which has at its disposal all the means and instruments wherewith to attain the targets implicit in the revolution of being. The new man of whom St. Paul spoke, as did Marxism-Leninism somewhat later in the day, cannot grow spontaneously out of the old Adam. In fact, the old Adam is continually laying ambushes for the new man, to confound him through selfishness and turn him back into what he was, or into something even more primitive. The transitional period will therefore advance under the banner of conflict — conflict between the new man and the old Adam, conflict between those who want man's liberation and those who want to perpetuate the exploitation of man by man. This has been the eternal conflict throughout the course of history, the conflict that has engendered all social contradictions from time immemorial.

In a recent work entitled *Masse et Classe*, François Perroux goes deeply into the evidence that the Marxist theory of the conflict between labour and capital is no longer valid in the world of today. The struggle between two organized classes, he says, is not the only, nor can it be the chief, factor accounting for conflictive situations, whether in a developed country, in an underdeveloped country, or on a world scale. The coordinates of this struggle are to be found in conflicts of politically mobilized masses under the direction of power groups, which modify and expand the content and scope of the original Marxist conception. In the twentieth century the dependent wage-earner class no longer has a monopoly on the fighting spirit, suffering, and work.[8]

The object of Perroux's analysis is to establish a central fact through which he shows that the Marxist analysis is not inapplicable, at least to a large extent, to the realities of the twentieth century. His central contention is that the contradiction between capitalists — owners of private capital — and wage-earners is only a species of the genus. What does he mean by this? He means that beyond the contradiction diagnosed by

Marx is the contradiction between the masters of the machines and the servants of the machines. The masters of the machines are those who hold the power within the socioeconomic, juridico-political and legal structure, and the servants of the machines are those who do not. Apart from this basic contradiction, which holds good whatever the existing system of ownership and social pattern and was quite unforeseen by Marx, there are yet others: the contradictions between the political state and the public administration, between innovation and routine, between creative types and cyclical types, between cultural poverty and genetic poverty, between elemental imperialism and the peoples' sense of solidarity.

Perroux ends his analysis with the observation that the simple opposition of two adversaries, sharply defined by their economic roles and doomed to destroy each other or to exchange their respective roles, turns into a singularly complicated matter in the multiple conflict of masses organized by political élites.

Consequently the content of exploitation and domination in conflictive situations today has a meaning quite different from the original interpretations Marx put forward.

Owing to the diversity of these twentieth-century contradictions the historical process of transition to the revolution of being becomes not only a process of permanent transition but also one in which conflicts of all kinds are waged on a variety of strategic and tactical fronts in the society of masses, classes, and nations.

Accordingly our next step will be to identify those groups that might be able to do away with some of the highly complex contradictions described by the French economist. The question is, which human groups can put the revolution of being into effect? Which groups will be the bringers of the future, whose aim is the true liberation of man through the resolution of these conflicts? We shall call these groups *prospective actors*, with reference to the revolution of being at the world level.

Our hypothesis consists in the assertion that the worldwide crisis brought about by such conflicts generates the emergence of the prospective actors — that is, the agents of change — by its own dynamics, through three processes: (a) the marginalization and progressive alienation of social groups; (b) rebellion on the part of significant segments of these groups against the social structures and cultural objectives of society; (c) politicization of this rebellion through the quest, formulation and adoption of a new model of society to supersede the old. The dialectic of the contradictions in question does in fact place huge social groups — even entire nations — in a marginal position. When the marginalization process is intensified and the groups affected become *marginality-conscious*, the result is alienation from the existing order of things; and the marginal groups deny the objectives and the institutionalized media of a given national or international system.

We define the alienated marginal groups therefore as those that have not been socialized within the existing system and repudiate its objectives and institutional media, which they regard as arbitrary and illegitimate. The alienated marginal persons concerned are not necessarily members of the proletariat, although these may be in the majority: they may belong to the middle strata of the population, and even to the upper middle class. Their sole common feature is their denial and repudiation of the existing social order. Consequently it is precisely to such alienated marginal persons, who rebel against society as it stands and postulate a new society, that we give the name of prospective actors.

In Latin America a historical bloc of prospective actors formed by quite heterogeneous groups can be identified:

1. The various political parties whose prospective action will take the precise form of the conquest of power. These parties are legion in Latin America, and it is impossible to discern a unitary political structure throughout the whole region, as every country's political parties are completely different from those of its neighbour. Nevertheless, no one can doubt the fundamental importance of the role these parties are called upon to play in the attainment of the objectives of the revolution of being.

2. The political, trade-union and social grassroots movements. This group of prospective actors includes the powerful federations of industrial workers' trade unions, the federations of agricultural workers, and the millions of shanty-town dwellers who form veritable hunger belts around the larger Latin America cities. The future role of these groups depends upon the degree of freedom of association that the Latin American governments are prepared to allow. All too often the governments of the region have been implacable in their persecution of the industrial trade unions and have sought — successfully, alas — to prevent the emergence of agricultural trade unions that could make a stand against the interests of the powerful owners of latifundia in many Latin American countries.

3. Youth and university movements. In speaking of the prospective actors it is indispensable to stress the essential part that youth must play. We are living in an age when the youth sectors are steadily gaining importance because they have not yet been absorbed into the traditional establishment groups. Moreover, in the specific case of Latin America the preponderance of these sectors is absolute: 43 percent of the popula-

tion of the region is under 15 years of age against 25 percent in Europe, 30 percent in the U.S. and 32 percent in the Soviet Union. Consequently, no serious attempt at change can hope to prosper and become irreversible without the sponsorship, enthusiastic support, and mass collaboration of youth groups. These groups have a better right than any other to participate in the construction of their own future.

4. The progressive intellectuals. This group of prospective actors comprises intellectuals, social scientists, social philosophers, and scientists in general who are disposed to level sweeping and well-grounded criticisms at the development model in force and to seek and formulate appropriate ways and means of attaining the new societies' objectives. In this process of discovery and formulation, pluralistic dialogue between the various ideological schools of thought must be an essential part of the work.

5. The radicalized church. In speaking of the bringers of the revolution of being in Latin America an institution of paramount significance for the region cannot be overlooked. The Catholic church has played an immensely important role in the historical development of Latin America. During the nineteenth century and a considerable part of the twentieth it was a mainstay of the ruling sectors, because it effectively supported the established order.

Today the Catholic church in Latin America is coming out more and more strongly in favour of change, and even in those countries where the conservative sector of the clergy is still predominant the church seems to be abandoning its former commitment to the ruling classes and seeking new paths and new attitudes.

A good example of this progressive trend on the part of the Catholic church is afforded by the open letter addressed by Cardinal Raúl Silva Henríquez to the Christians of the Netherlands in February 1972.[9] The Chilean cardinal quoted a passage from the prophet Isaiah: "To loose the bands of wickedness, to undo the heavy burdens, and to let the oppressed go free, to break every yoke, to deal thy bread to the hungry, is not this the fast that I have chosen, saith the Lord." The cardinal also spoke of the people who cannot fast of their own free will during Lent because they have fasted perforce throughout the whole year. The progressive, and in many cases revolutionary, tendencies of the church will become more marked as time goes by, and it will thus become a true protector of the oppressed classes and a factor of change in the region.

6. Another sector of transcendent importance for the region, both in the past and in the present, is the armed forces. In Latin America these forces had their origin in the national armies that fought against Spanish rule and won political independence for our countries, often using the tactics of guerilla warfare.

Once the independence movement was over the role of the armed forces necessarily underwent modification. Moreover, the Latin American armies began to absorb powerful influences, first from Europe and later from the U.S., completely forgetting how to make use of guerilla tactics, as has been pointed out in a brilliant article by a former president of Colombia, Alberto Lleras Camargo. In many countries the armies became veritable pretorian guards of the existing régimes, justifying by the use and abuse of force what could have been justified in no other way. Elsewhere, they filled the power vacuum created by anarchy and political *caudillismo*. In short, they played all sorts of roles.

At the present the armed forces are passing through a third phase, of which the training of the troops, warrant officers, and officers constitutes a salient feature. In various war academies interesting training programmes are being implemented through which members of the forces are attaining high standards of specialization in the most widely varying fields, including social science subjects such as sociology and economics.

Consequently, in many countries the armed forces are becoming an active and dynamic factor of social change. Happenings in Peru are a highly significant case in point.

Politically speaking, this trend is represented by the formation of joint civil and military governments within political systems, and an impressive degree of topical interest is beginning to attach to such coalitions in the region. These new patterns of government may be the result of freely concerted agreements between civil and military sectors or may simply be imposed by the armed forces.

7. We cannot conclude this enumeration of prospective actors without referring to a development which has characterized the social structure of certain Latin American countries, for example Argentina. In some countries the middle class already represents a substantial proportion of the total population. In all probability this development will spread through the other countries of the region, and sizeable intermediate strata will be formed in the national societies concerned, consisting of professionals, employees, government officials, small and medium entrepreneurs, shopkeepers, and skilled workers.

Members of these intermediate strata have frequently become the most dynamic factors in Latin American societies. But it would be a mistake to suppose that the middle class *en bloc* exhibits a uniform ideology or political role, for which reason this socioeconomic phenomenon may have widely different projections in the future. We cannot, therefore, include the middle strata as such among the prospective actors, but only some segments and members of them.

The time has now come to indicate some of the arduous tasks that will have to be initiated or continued by this comprehensive and heterogeneous group of prospective actors in Latin America. Fortunately many of these tasks can be identified with tendencies which are already discernible in our region. A word of warning: we make no claim to deal definitively and exhaustively with the subject. On the contrary, all we shall attempt is to establish a few salient landmarks that give some idea of the road on which our region is, and ought to be, setting out. For the purposes of this analysis we are not going to turn to the past, nor will we lapse into the unhealthy fatalism of some intellectuals who believe that our future is completely predetermined by our colonial inheritance or by existing circumstances.

The Grand Strategy of the Revolution of Being and Its Specific Strategies

The main distinction between grand and specific strategies needs to be made here: The implementation of the revolution of being is the grand strategy of prospective actors in Latin America as elsewhere in the world; specific strategies are only part of this grand strategy.

Among specific strategies we shall indicate those of the greatest importance:

1. *The elimination of economic underdevelopment and external dependence.* The new Latin American economy will necessarily imply an economic restructuring designed to satisfy the basic needs of the population and involving therefore the programming of economic activity at the national, subregional, and regional levels. One indispensable measure will be the application of drastic controls to limit all those forms of nonessential consumption now transmitted to the Latin American economy through the propaganda and sales systems of the great transnational corporations and through mass-communication media.

The introduction of radical changes also necessitates the regulation of foreign investment and technology. Clearly defined policies—such as those designed by the Andean group, the emergent subregional market—must be adopted with respect to the huge transnational corporations that are becoming the chief instrument of the region's economic domination by foreign interests.

Actually the nationalization of basic sources of wealth and means of production in the hands of foreign capital is unquestionably the Latin American trend that has had the greatest impact on powerful and influential groupings of industrial countries, in particular the U.S. Argentina, Bolivia, Chile, Cuba, Mexico, Peru, and other countries have at some time in their history carried out nationalization. Although this process has taken radically different forms, it has invariably been vigorously resisted by the countries affected.

Because this trend towards nationalization will intensify as time goes by, there will certainly be a tightening of the tension between our countries and the U.S., whose government so far seems always to have made common cause with the great transnational corporations. The only way of relieving these possible tensions is for the U.S. and other governments concerned to adopt a new criterion that recognizes the distinction between the public interests of a nation and the private interests that control large enterprises and have been affected by nationalization.

It is not superfluous to recall that in resolutions of the UN General Assembly express and solemn recognition has been accorded to the permanent sovereignty of states over their sources of wealth and natural resources and to their faculty to nationalize these in accordance with their own norms.[10]

Another reaffirmation of the new independent trend of our countries is represented by the strenuous campaign to secure recognition of the Latin American stand on the 200-mile limit for patrimonial waters.

We should make it clear that this struggle against the dependence by which we have so long been oppressed does not seek to convert the region into an isolated unit, cut off from economic intercourse at the world level. Our sole aim is to reach a stage at which we can speak of an interdependent region that plays its part with perfect freedom in trade with all the world, unhindered by blackmail by the powers that have dominated us hitherto. Unfortunately there are countries that fail to understand the challenge this implies and believe that the best way to escape the shameful dependence into which they were plunged by one power is to fall directly into the sphere of economic dependence dominated by the rival hegemonic power, as has been the case with Cuba.

2. *The reaffirmation of regional and national autonomy.* Since the end of the 1950s there has been a noticeable trend towards depolarization of the international system, which from the Second World War up to that period had approximated a bipolar structure. Several indicators make this apparent: (a) the revolts in Cuba, Yugoslavia, Albania, and, up to a point, Romania, which have broken the monolithic character of the areas of influence of the two superpowers; (b) the reconstruction of Europe, its economic recovery and its high level of development, which in conjunction with the formation and strengthening of the European Common Market have set Western Europe on the road to becoming a new economic power on a world scale—a tendency strengthened by the accession of Britain, Ireland, and Denmark; (c) the emergence of China

with the status of a nuclear power, its dramatic rupture with the Soviet Union, and its recent opening to the western world through trade with the U.S.; (d) the Anglo-Saxon loss of monopoly of the manufacture and supply of arms to countries of the Third World; (e) Japan's access to the status of a world economic power: and (f) the successive crises that have undermined the dollar as a leading international currency.

It would be incumbent on the prospective actors to strengthen such trends in Latin America, because in the first place they imply a decentralization of the international system and second, they help create multinational regions that are viable from the standpoint of modern economic development. The decentralization of the international system would pave the way for an international system with a polycentric structure, in which our region should find its appropriate niche. Latin America should stress the obsolescence of the old system of military alliances that the cold war zones of influence organized in defensive and offensive blocks.

The Latin American countries are giving proof of a clear-cut and indisputable tendency towards autonomy. The time has gone when some of our governments seemed to follow the dictates of the U.S. State Department to avoid offending their powerful neighbour to the north.

Particularly since the end of the Second World War our countries have become conscious of their former submissiveness within a stratified international system and have started international action to improve their real status in the system. Some international economic organizations have helped on occasion to clarify our countries' situation in this respect and have been instrumental in the region's efforts to raise its status. Further, in some instances the creation of such organizations has constituted a political act whereby the Latin American countries have asserted their will to change the distribution of power within the international system with the object of making it more democratic.[11]

This determination was evidenced when the Latin American countries — acting on Chile's proposal — insisted that the Economic Commission for Latin America (ECLA) be established despite opposition from the industrial countries. Creation of the Inter-American Development Bank (IADB) at the regional level was likewise the product of lengthy negotiations between the Latin American countries and the U.S.

Our countries have also demonstrated their increasing autonomy at the various sessions of UNCTAD, where they have directly confronted the industrialized countries with demands for the adoption of specific measures to reduce the gap between rich and poor countries. A Latin American, Raúl Prebisch, strove with inexhaustible energy for the creation and effective operation of this conference.

Another manifestation of our countries' new struggle for independence is to be found in the establishment of the Special Committee on Latin American Coordination (CECLA), the aim of which is to unify criteria in respect of relations with the U.S., Europe, and the rest of the world. In this perspective CECLA appears as the first valid attempt to set up a Latin American subsystem of nations to enable the region to formulate policies of its own with due regard to the interests of all the countries in it.

3. *The integration of Latin America.* This process, closely related to the preceding point, is one of the region's most noteworthy tasks and has incalculable implications for the future.

New models for the integration of national economies in the world economy should be designed to further the rapid progress of regional integrational movements and new economic policies at the national level closely linked to the integration process. It is therefore indispensable that the Latin American integration movements should be based on the programming of development and not exclusively on schemes for the liberalization of trade. The objective of the new policies should be the production of industrial goods at levels of efficiency comparable with international standards to enable Latin America's products to compete in world markets and augment intraregional flows of manufactured goods.

In this context, it must be acknowledged that the line followed by the Latin American Free Trade Association (LAFTA) does not exactly coincide with these propositions. Many problems and contradictions have turned this important agency into a mere forum for negotiating the liberalization of trade in specific products, and even here major difficulties have arisen.

By way of reaction to this stagnation of the regional integration process a new integrationist trend has come into being, and is reflected in agreements at the subregional level. A case in point is the Andean pact, which represents one of the most ambitious subregional integration projects in the whole world.

The signatories to the pact (Bolivia, Chile, Colombia, Ecuador, Peru, and recently Venezuela) have adopted common measures with respect to foreign investment and transfers of technology, a question on which no integration project had dared touch before. Another salient feature is the adoption of a major sectoral development project for the metal-transforming industry covering the entire subregion.

Subregional integration will therefore presumably start booming in the next few years, provided a solution is found for various political and economic rivalries and problems that presently cast a shadow on integration processes.

4. *The democratization and stabilization of political régimes that guarantee full popular participation.* When we speak of democratization we are not referring to the abolition of repressive dictatorships and their replacement by democratic régimes in the style of the republican-liberal system prevailing in western countries. On the contrary, the appalling conditions of exploitation and poverty existing in so many Latin American countries will not end with the establishment and observance of a few formal liberties deriving their inspiration from liberal thought in the eighteenth and nineteenth centuries. It is useless to proclaim equality in the sight of the law when the great majority of people lives out of reach of the administration of justice and to introduce universal suffrage when there are vast areas where powerful political *caudillos* impose their own opinion on the masses, who have nothing to do with major political decisions affecting them. What is the good of freedom of speech when a few enterprises, nine times out of ten under foreign influence or management, play false with the people's right to be told the truth? What is the good of freedom of association when the oligarchies and their hangers-on refuse to countenance the formation of agricultural trade unions and workers' federations? These values, worthy in themselves of all respect, become truly meaningful only when accompanied by real and effective popular participation at all levels of society. Accordingly, everything that we have said of participation in the revolution of being is fully applicable to Latin America.

Another point to be clarified is the concept of stability. Many sectors in the international hegemonic centers have displayed great concern over Latin America's chronic political instability. What they are anxious about however is the uncertainty of the future outlook for foreign investment in the region. We, on the other hand, interpret stability as the only alternative that will allow a social process to mature and strike permanent root in a given nation. Otherwise changes would never be irreversible, and processes could never be consolidated.

In the context of democratization and increased popular participation, a pause to dwell on national integration is worthwhile. National integration is a task of vital importance for Latin America because there are millions of human beings in the region who are completely cut off from their national communities by an inextricably tangled thicket of geographical, political, cultural, and socioeconomic factors.

We therefore believe that measures should be taken to ensure that these huge marginal sectors formed by indigenous population groups, illiterates, shanty town dwellers and the like are integrated in their respective national societies. Only through radical structural changes in the political, social, educational, and economic spheres, to secure effective participation, will it be possible for this objective to be attained.

National integration also implies the adoption of formulas for participation through communitarian grassroots organizations at the level of neighbourhoods, trade unions, youth groups, women's institutes, sports clubs, and so on. In this connection some of the measures carried out in Chile by the Christian-Democrat Government (1964–1970) may constitute an interesting precedent. More recently Peru too has been conducting noteworthy experiments in economic self-management and popular participation through the creation of agricultural and industrial communities in which rural and urban workers play an essential role. This trend is in striking contrast to the ideas of traditional Marxism-Leninism, which aims at replacing the old employers by highly centralized bureaucratic bodies under which the workers are just as far removed from the decision-making process as they were under the capitalist and neocapitalist systems.

5. *Land reform.* Outstanding among the structural changes in progress and in need of acceleration is land reform. Various countries have embarked with greater or lesser degrees of success upon the difficult and controversial task of changing obsolete agrarian structures. It could hardly be otherwise, as the structure of agriculture in Latin America is in many cases a mere prolongation — sometimes lightly modified or "modernized" — of the old structures of colonial times. In many countries the scourges of the *latifundia* system, ignorance and poverty, still keep the broad rural masses under the yoke of an up-to-date version of slavery.

For some time now Chile, Cuba, and Peru have been putting interesting and much-debated land reform programmes into effect. Other countries such as Mexico and Bolivia have made experiments of this kind in the past.

The great majority of the countries of the region are conscious that agrarian reform is an inevitable phase in the battle for national welfare, and this consciousness will no doubt be reflected in political and social movements to introduce structural changes. Obviously such processes will not follow the same lines everywhere. Some countries may adopt the classic Marxist-Leninist model in the Cuban fashion, which will finally culminate in absolute socialization, with the state becoming the owner/manager of the land. Others will perhaps choose the path of communitarian socialism, leading to self-management at the agricultural level; yet others will perhaps prefer to carry out a reform that will turn the agricultural workers into owners of individual farms in the framework of a neo-capitalist society; again, various combinations of these formulas may possibly be devised. In short all that is clearly foreseeable is that radical changes — widely differing and even opposite in their content—will be brought about in agrarian structures. As the agrarian problem has very different nuances in each country, it is impossible to make recommendations of generalized feasibility to bring about rapid and effective land reform in Latin America.

6. *Educational reforms.* Sooner or later our countries will find themselves compelled to change and intensify the aims of education at the primary, secondary, university, technical and other levels. These changes and aims will constitute important components of the process of creating teaching-learning societies in Latin America. Reforms seem likely that will take into account the necessity of formulating educational policies consistent with the realities in which they are applied and repudiating programmes imported from regions whose special characteristics have nothing to do with those of the recipient peoples. Thus the deep-rooted European and American influences in our education should begin to give way before educational systems created by Latin Americans and inspired by our own national values.

One important branch of activity will consist of intensive campaigns, aimed at wiping out the illiteracy that blights the lives of millions of Latin Americans.

To sum up: The different aspects of the Latin American reality just analysed show the unity and multiplicity, the variety and uniformity of this immense human and geographical world that is Latin America.

This reality, in which heterogeneity and homogeneity are mingled within and among the nations of the region, is full of contradictions that embrace socioeconomic, cultural, and political systems in the society of masses, classes, and nations.

Different groups, social and political movements, are emerging from the very heart of these contradictions, antagonisms, conflicts, and oppositions. Some of them are carriers of the future; they are the prospective actors mentioned at the beginning of this section.

If they can really interpret the deep aspirations all Latin Americans cherish in this continent—the continent where, if direct violence in the form of warfare does not exist, structural violence does, partly created from within but mainly fostered from outside—these prospective actors may come to be the builders of the revolution of being.

Notes

1. See Gustavo Lagos, *International Stratification and Underdeveloped Countries* (Chapel Hill: University of North Carolina Press, 1963), especially pp. 24–30.

2. These figures are taken from International Bank for Reconstruction and Development (IBRD), *World Bank Atlas* (population, per capita product, and growth rates), 1971. The estimate of GNP has a wide margin of error, mainly because of the problems involved in deriving it at factor cost from net material product and in converting the estimate into U.S. dollars.

3. We have based our analysis on the ECLA study *Income Distribution in Latin America* (UN publications, Sales No.: E.71.II.G.6).

4. Ibid., p. 33.

5. Data taken from the IBRD, *World Bank Atlas.*

6. Letter from Engels to Franz Mehring, quoted by Marta Harnecker in *Los conceptos elementales del materialismo histórico* (Santiago, Chile: Siglo Veintiuno Editores S.A., May 1972).

7. The ideas about the functions of this agency have been taken from the speech delivered by UN Secretary-General U Thant at the University of Texas (Austin), on May 14, 1970, under the title "Human Environment and World Order."

8. François Perroux, *Masse et Classe* (Paris: Casterman, 1972), p. 44.

9. Published in the periodical *Mensaje,* Santiago, Chile, March-April 1972.

10. Resolutions of the UN General Assembly, N. 1303 (XVII), December 14, 1962, and N. 2158 (XXI), November 25, 1966.

11. Gustavo Lagos, "The Political Role of Regional Economic Organizations in Latin America," in *International Organisation: World Politics*, edited by Robert W. Cox (London: Macmillan and Co., Ltd., 1969), p. 43.

8

The Need for an Ambitious
Innovation of the World Order

Jan Tinbergen

What Makes the Need for a More
Organized World Order So Urgent?

There is a wide discrepancy between the intensity with which evil forces shaping our common future — or no-future — are operating and the intensity of the forces needed instead. Designers, producers, and dealers of armaments are more active than ever; Western politicians involved in the preparation of new forms of international cooperation lack the willingness to give up old structures. These politicians, as well as their voters and commentators, are skeptical about any innovation; they lack imagination and instead concentrate on the defence of established structures, especially the nation-state and non-competitive industries. Destructive forces, including the senseless overkill capacity of weaponries, physical and psychological pollution, an increasing adherence to doctrinaire instead of innovating thought, an appalling neglect of the interests of young children by the too easy attitudes of parents with so-called modern ideas, are spreading, often without any other base than some sort of vogue.

Preponderant among the evil forces is the pursuit of *polarization* by the ideologically formulated *geopolitical desires* of a few actual or prospective superpowers. Such polarization, combined with the present "state of the art" in matters of armament, can only be propagated by stupid or by criminal ideologists. Preponderant among the skeptical and unimaginative politicians are those sticking to national autonomy which is supposed to maintain independence — a non-existing "ideal" in a world of rapidly growing interdependence from which nobody can escape. This rush towards disaster can only be stopped if the constructive pro-

This essay originally appeared in the *Journal of International Affairs,* vol. 31, no. 2, 1977, pp. 305–314. It is published here with the personal authorization of Professor Tinbergen.

grammes available are carried out with the energy shown by today's "evil forces." Among other things the situation requires that nobody considers himself an onlooker to the world's drama, but, on the contrary, that everybody feels involved, as in fact we are, and acts accordingly.

The World Looked at from a Management Scientific Point of View

Since business has been much more successful in overcoming narrow national points of view than have governments, most politicians and the general public, it may be useful to look at the world from a *management scientific* viewpoint. This implies that we try to answer the question, how the activities necessary to provide mankind with the goods and services needed for maximum welfare have to be organized without the *precondition* of the existence of nation-states. In the answer we will find of course that nation-states nevertheless are among the institutions needed, but with *a few tasks less* than they have claimed on accidental historical grounds, tasks which are now threatening human values of a higher order than *nationalist* values (in contra-distinction to *national* values).

As a matter of fact the organization of transnational enterprises (TNEs) has been remarkably successful in avoiding the sort of silly frictions between persons of different nationality, which have almost completely paralyzed an efficient solution of an increasing number of major international problems. If transnational enterprises are able to avoid these frictions in order to solve production and trade problems, governments, whose tasks are often felt to be of a "higher order," should certainly make a considerable effort not only to look critically at, but also to learn from, transnational enterprises. The general intellectual framework needed for efficient performance of large numbers of people is exactly the concern of management science. The overwhelming part of the applications of management science does deal, of course, with business problems, but the approach is equally applicable to more general problems. Put in some more detail, the main problems to be dealt with are what *activities,* to be carried out by what *institutions* with what competences, so as to maximize *world welfare*, that is the balance of positive satisfaction from needs fulfilled and of dissatisfaction connected with the efforts needed for that fulfillment. In the further elaboration an important distinction can be made, namely, the one between qualitative and quantitative aspects of the social order defined by the institutions required and their tasks.

The central question arising in the *qualitative* part of the analysis may be called the question of the *optimal level of decision making* needed for the attainment of optimum welfare. This question may be restated as one of needed *hierarchy trees,* complete with horizontal *cross-connections* between vertical and hierarchical lines. The complex organizational structure just described is sometimes called a *matrix organizational structure,* which essentially means a two-dimensional organizational structure. We must keep open the possibility that more than two-dimensional structures are needed which we may call *tensor* structures. The concrete elaboration depends, first of all, on the concrete nature of human welfare, as expressed in what socio-economists call a *welfare function.* It specifies the needs of the people as well as the positive or negative value attached to the efforts that have to be made in the processes of production and distribution. Next, the concrete elaboration of the optimum order depends on the nature of these *processes of production* and *distribution,* described by socio-economists with the aid of what they call production functions.

Thus, if among the human preferences the *need for participation* in decisions plays a signficiant role, this need will require that many decisions are taken at low hierarchical levels — such as the levels of the person, the family, the shop floor, the enterprise, the municipality and so on. In short, the need for participation will require a good deal of *decentralized decision making,* characterized by small units of production, small geographical political units and so on. We come back to this qualitative aspect in the next section.

The quantitative aspect of the optimum social order deals with such questions as the volumes of production and consumption of goods and services relevant for the satisfaction of the world's population, their *rates of growth* over time, and the distribution of the efforts of production and the welfare derived from consumption over the world's population. In the socio-economist's language, the *macro-aspects* of these concepts are often referred to as the level and rates of growth of income, total and per capita, and the distribution over geographical areas and social groups. These quantitative aspects will be discussed in more detail in the last three sections.

Limits to Decentralization;
Where Centralization is Crucial

We mentioned the importance of decentralization in decision making for human beings who desire participation in the decisions which affect their present and future welfare. Generally such a desire is one of the basic human features and shows up in the preference for autonomy in many areas of life. This desire also grows with a rising *level of education* and is stronger in advanced than in "backward" cultures. On the other hand it is less easy to be satisfied in "modern" cultures since these have developed very complicated processes of production and distribution, characterized by technologies not easily understood even by relatively educated individuals. There are *technological* and *natural forces* at work in today's world which set limits to the social effectiveness of decentralized activities. Examples are not only to be found in some of the most recent phenomena which mankind has to face, such as *pollution, over-fishing* or *nuclear energy*. There are also a number of long-standing, natural and technical phenomena which impose limits to human autonomy, such as erosion and *desertification* and the development of *manufacturing industry*. The common element in all these phenomena is that decisions made by person A, municipality B, or the nation C do not only affect the welfare of A, B or C, but also that of outsiders D. If A's decision creates pollution which also reaches D's environment, something tends to go wrong. Similarly, if person A works on the shop floor of a factory and produces parts which D must compose into a more complicated tool, if municipality B cuts a forest and causes erosion to the detriment of D's welfare, or if nation C prevents D's products from entering C's market, outsider D is affected by A's, B's or C's decisions and yet cannot raise his voice: participation is refused to D if we preserve A's, B's or C's autonomy. Already *in the name of democracy,* we must organize processes of decision making in which D participates: that is, decisions made at a higher, more centralized level. On top of that, this centralization may be needed to insure optimum welfare. So the rule of maximum decentralization *does not apply here.* Centralization even *beyond the national level* may be necessary and the optimal social order may require centralization at the *world level.* The criterion which determines when centralization is part of our optimum decision process is whether lower level decisions have significant effects on outsiders, or, again in the socio-economist's language, whether there are *external effects.*

Thus, the management scientific approach to our present world problems teaches us that, dependent on the *objective nature of the problems* we have to solve in order to attain maximum human welfare, decisions can be made at low levels if external effects are virtually absent, but have to be taken sometimes at very high — supranational — levels if important external effects exist.

The crucial question then is to identify the problem groups whose nature is such that decisions at the world level — or as close to the world level as attainable — are part of the optimal social order. In the RIO report (Tinbergen et al., 1976) ten such problem groups are identified.

Space does not permit us to detail why these groups have external effects; they will only be briefly listed here, together with some international institutions which deal with them at present, although not necessarily to a sufficient degree of efficiency, and often to a low degree:

(i) monetary problems: International Monetary Fund;
(ii) financing of investment and income redistribution; World Bank Group, Organisation of Economic Co-operation and Development, Council for Mutual Economic Assistance;
(iii) food production and distribution: Food and Agriculture Organisation, Organisation of Economic Co-operation and Development, Council for Mutual Economic Assistance;
(iv) industrialization, international trade: United Nations Industrial Development Organization, General Agreement on Tariffs and Trade, United Nations Conference on Trade and Development;
(v) energy, ores: International Atomic Energy Agency;
(vi) transfer of technology; various United Nations agencies;
(vii) transnational enterprises: a centre of information at United Nations headquarters;
(viii) environmental problems: United Nations Environmental Programme, Organisation of Economic Co-operation and Development, Council for Mutual Economic Assistance;
(ix) ocean management problems: United Nations Conference on the law of the seas;
(x) problems of armaments reduction: United Nations disarmament conference.

The necessity of an order in which a number of important problems have to be dealt with in a centralized way excludes, as a viable order, one where the only power is exerted by some 150 autonomous nation-states and a considerable number of TNEs. No efficient management is possible with such an organizational structure. Some *political superstructure* is needed for the handling of problems with external effects. Within this superstructure a *rule of thumb* for proper management must be applied, namely that an efficient council has a number of members of the order of ten rather than of a hundred. In other words, a council of some ten to fifteen members should be the top executive for world management in each of the fields mentioned, but also in a *coordinating body of the necessary matrix or tensor structure,* that is, with the necessary cross-connections. The ten to fifteen council members should represent an equal number of regions, such as Latin America, the Arabic region, China or Western Europe. The same degree of urgency we see for the solution of the world's most pressing problems (cf. the first section) applies to the question of integrating Western Europe, not only for the sake of its external problems but even more for the contribution to the solution of today's world problems.

If the communist-ruled regions, such as Eastern Europe (including the Soviet Union) or China, are not willing to join in such a world super-structure, we must do it without them. It would be far more attractive, of course, if they were to join.

The coordinating body referred to should simultaneously contain experts in each of the ten *subject* areas and this, then, reflects the *matrix structure* previously mentioned. If, on top of that, still other aspects of world society need to be reflected, a tensor structure is called for, as mentioned above.

What Geographical Differences in Welfare Will Be Acceptable Around the Decade of 2010–2020?

Let us now turn to some of the most important *quantitative* aspects of the optimal world order some forty years from now. These have been dealt with in a few reports or books; among them the Leontief et al. study for the United Nations (1977), the Doubling the World Population study by Linnemann et al. (1976), the RIO report (Tinbergen et al., 1976) and the Bariloche Foundation (Herrera et al.) report to the Club of Rome. This list is not complete. Perhaps the RIO report has based its views in the clearest way on some explicit attempts to answer this vital question. This does not necessarily imply that these attempts are the most realistic ones for the forty year period. These attempts started from the conviction, expressed in the first section, that around 2010 to 2020 the world must be a *well-organized community* in order to survive various threats (wars, famines, pollution, shortages of energy and some vital non-renewable resources). Next the RIO report attempted to view the density or intensity of *information* and *communication* ties between the world's peoples in comparison to what they were around 1970. The impression that led the authors of the RIO report is that by the years 2010–2020 the inhabitants of the world will know as much of each other as might the inhabitants of a large country know about their own citizens in 1970. Travel, television and migrant workers are the carriers of this information. Travel by rich tourists demonstrates a high level of living to the poor of Asia and Africa, television acts like movies, although the peoples shown are real, not theatre actors. Migrant workers observe in the most penetrating way the gap between incomes in their home countries and the "host" countries, where the dirtiest, the hardest and the most uncomfortable jobs are left to them. Fascinating examples of these reductions in distance are given by McHale (1969).

This being so, we may conclude tentatively that the *geographical differences in well-being* between the various regions of the world in 2010–2020 are comparable with the differences tolerated within well organized countries around 1970. We happen to have some figures about such regional differences for a number of industrialized countries around 1970, and for two of them—the United States and France—a century ago. By geographical income differences we mean income differences for people of comparable status in different geographical areas, not income differences between people in the same town with different occupations. The latter are far larger than the former and their reduction may be of greater importance for people's welfare. We will come back to that question in the last section.

The ideal method to measure geographical differences is to collect figures about income for identical occupations in different regions. These are hardly available for the past century; but we have average incomes for the states of the United States and for the "départements" in France. The measure chosen to express the degree of geographical income inequality is called *decile ratio*. It is the ratio of the average income of the upper decile to that of the lowest. Each decile contains ten per cent of the country's population; the upper decile starting with the geographical unit (state or département) showing the highest income, followed by the one with the next highest income, until ten per cent of the country's population is included. A similar procedure for the lowest geographical decile starts with the unit showing the lowest average income, and so on. The assumption implied in taking this measure is that the economic structure of the units does not differ too much. The measure is misleading if, for example, the lowest average income units are entirely rural and the highest urban; unfortunately this tendency will exist.

The results obtained have been given elsewhere (Tinbergen, 1978); they can be summarized by the statement that the *geographical decile ratio is well below three* for the USA, German Federal Republic and France around 1970, in contradistinction to (i) the USA and France around 1870 and (ii) the European Community of the Six around 1970, where it was also around three.

Consequently, the RIO report considers a desirable goal for the decade 2010–2020 to be a *geographical decile ratio for the world at large* of 3; for 1970 it is estimated to be 13, after two corrections in the official income figures given by the *World Bank Atlas* (Washington D.C., 1973), described in Tinbergen (1976).

To reduce the *geographical decile ratio from 13 to 3 in forty years is a very ambitious goal.* Recognizing this, the RIO report also shows projections in which a reduction from 13 to 6 is taken as the target. Leontief's

Scenario X attains a comparable figure of 7 in the year 2000. This scenario also appears to be ambitious in that it implies that developing countries as a group have to invest some 30 to 40 percent of their income (both taken gross).

One conclusion imposes itself: the quantitative aspect of the world's "problématique" is frightening; and the strength of the "forces needed" in international politics (as indicated in the first sentence of this essay) is completely out of line with this statement. Whatever the latter's value or credibility, it is at least provocative! If better figures can be derived in a different way, let these be formulated.

The Feasibility of a Five Percent Annual Growth in Per Capita Income as an Average over Countries over the Forty-Year Period

Development of the developing countries over a forty-year period is not only determined by the target discussed in the previous section, namely the reduction of the geographic decile ratio from 13 to 3 or 6. More important determinants will be discussed in the final section. Within rather wide limits, the RIO report comes to the conclusion, however, that the average rate of growth of *per capita* income of all developing countries over the whole forty-year period must be about five per cent per annum. This is just another way of saying that an ambitious target has to be fulfilled. How ambitious? That we are now going to discuss.

Our argument is that the figure is less ambitious than it seems to be, although it is a high figure in comparison to what has been reached so far. Some of the exceptions to the low figure may help to find the ways and means to attain the five percent. First, there is the category of the *oil countries*, before as well as after the oil price increase of 1973. Before 1973 some of them, for instance Libya, already showed a very high rate of growth. The price rise of 1973 made all oil exporting countries exceptions. They would seem to illustrate that the discovery of some *new resource* or the increased *scarcity* of others—natural as well as organized scarcity—are among the factors which make for a better performance. An appropriate *population policy*, if adopted within the next decade, may create a relative scarcity of manpower, which would be a step in the right direction. Mrs. Gandhi's somewhat abrupt action in this field presents an example of what is possible.

Another set of exceptions to the rule of slow growth are the well-known examples of South Korea, Singapore, Taiwan and Brazil. In an earlier half century Japan was an example, with which the Korean and the Taiwanese examples have some relationship. It must be admitted that Taiwan is a special case since its population contains a disproportional number of enterprising refugees from the mainland. Korea and Taiwan were an exception in that they received *financial assistance* of some seven percent of their national income *over a prolonged period.* Although dependent on a better financial assistance policy of the developed countries, this exception may be made a rule. The Brazilian case constitutes an example of forceful, capitalist policy. For Asian agriculture, Myrdal (1968) makes just that recommendation.

That brings us to a third example of quick growth, namely *communist* rule, especially in Eastern Europe. This is an alternative to Brazil, and one that may develop with some automatism *if the policies of the middle-of-the-road are kept so unambitious* — both in the developing and in the developed countries, the latter as their real "partners" in the sense of the Pearson report (Pearson et al., 1969).

In fact this is a crucial question to the more tolerant countries: do we have to admit that tolerance and high performance are incompatible, or, in other words, that the Western type of society cannot mobilize the forces needed to survive? Is this *testimonium paupertatis* — a test of lack of imagination — the end of our type of society, the American "liberal" or the European democratic socialist type? I refuse to believe that, but their performance in international co-operation and integration is clearly much below what is needed. Among our blunders are our lack of co-operation with the Indian Congress before it turned authoritarian, the lack of co-operation with Arab socialism of various types or with Latin American democrats in the fifties and the early sixties — we were too inward looking.

My conclusion tends to be that a "great coalition" — notwithstanding the negative connotations the word has for many of us — of all tolerant progressive forces from North American liberals (and radicals, maybe — cf. Bowles and Gintis, 1976), via Western European socialists (and perhaps "Eurocommunists") with Latin American democrats, Arab socialists and the innovated Indian Congress — if that can be innovated — is the "movement" that can make the world a better place to live, with the five per cent as its goal.

The Need for Slower Material Growth in the Rich Countries

There are some *limits* to the world's *material growth.* They are related to the Meadow's "limits," although we may escape some of these limitations. For the time being, the *food* limit, as shown by the Linnemann report, is the most visible and urgent one. The nature of the food limit is socio-political, however, rather than physical or biological; at least so it seems to us today. It is also *psychological* in the sense that the rich countries have become *too materialist*. The better distribution of welfare still needed in the rich countries does require some further growth; and so do the *partnership obligations* the rich countries have to fulfill vis-à-vis the developing world. Slower material growth of the developed nations as a whole implies a reduction in real income of the highest-income groups, especially the intellectual and managerial *elites* (cf. Tinbergen, 1977). This reduction can be attained with the aid of market forces: a relative increase in the supply of intellectuals and managers in comparison to the demand of them is likely to continue.

Slower growth in material welfare will have to be compensated for, at least partly, by increased non-material welfare, for instance more satisfaction from work and education and improved quality of products.

The distribution of growth in the next forty years over *time* and over *developed* and *developing* countries should be co-ordinated. In the early part of the period, the rate of growth of developed countries should be raised as a means to further the growth of developing countries. Step by step, however, the dependence of the developing economies upon developed nations should be loosened. One way of attaining this lower degree of dependence is the expansion of the production of *capital goods* in countries such as India, Brazil, Venezuela and others. This will enable developing countries to buy these goods without having to earn the amounts needed from exports to developed countries. At the same time raw material producing countries will *process a larger part of their raw materials* to earn more from exports to developed countries, even if the latter reduce their growth. In the latter phases of the forty-year period, the rates of growth in the developed countries should be falling and those of the developing countries rising. The figure of five percent growth per annum by the latter is conceived as an average over the forty-year period, as set out in the previous section.

Many economists believe that *slow growth* is an *impossible requirement*. They fear that some of the essential prime movers of an economy will tend to be weakened if a low rate of growth is adopted as a political goal. I do not share this vision. Theoretical arguments to the contrary are that, whatever an economy's rate of growth, it remains a community of *continually changing generations*. Older people are retiring and younger generations have to take their places. This implies the maintenance of *incentives* for the younger. Slow material growth does not prevent competition between *qualities* of various products, both between and within product groups.

An *empirical test* of these theoretical arguments seems to support the latter. Such a test is also given in Tinbergen (1978), where an attempt is made to estimate the impact of the rate of growth of per capita income on the level of efficiency of developed countries, including as other independent variables physical capital per capita and the level of education. While the latter two independent variables show highly significant regression coefficients, the regression coefficient of the rate of growth is not significantly different from zero. The measure of efficiency (the dependent variable) chosen is income per capita.

We did agree (cf. the fourth section) also in favour of a reduction of income inequality *within* countries, in the sense of smaller differences in incomes between people with different occupations. These differences are too large to be satisfactory to a clear majority in most, if not all, countries. The subject is not included in this essay, since it constitutes a problem outside the range of subjects listed in the third section. It might have been included, however, since countries with a more equal distribution of personal income do experience some external effects from countries with a more unequal personal income distribution: high-income people may try to emigrate from the former to the latter, sometimes to avoid taxes, sometimes to profit from a labor market situation more favourable to them.

Let us finish this essay by a brief *summary*.

We see an urgent need for innovation in the international socio-economic order. We base this view on the technical and natural forces which have made the world much more interdependent. This is not only true for some novel phenomena such as environmental pollution and the levels of production of all sorts of goods needed for a growing population or required by the relatively well-to-do who produce with the aid of technologies not known before. The increased interdependence is also due to phenomena with which we have long been familiar, but whose expansion has created increased interdependence, such as the demand for food, energy and raw materials in short supply. This increased interdependence requires a management scientific approach. This approach has qualitative and quantitative aspects. Among the qualitative aspects, the questions of optimal decision levels and the size and structure of executive boards are pertinent. Decision levels must be as low as possible, but high enough to avoid external effects which are undemocratic. Boards must be of a manageable size and co-ordinating cross-connections require a matrix or even a tensor structure (more than two-dimensional cross-connections). Quantitative aspects require a distribution of growth over the various parts of the world such that political stability can be attained. It is possible that forty years from now information and communication will have spread to such a degree that only drastic reductions in geographical income differences can "keep the world together." Some very tentative estimates have been made of the required growth rates; constructive criticism is invited.

References

Bowles, S., and H. Gintis, *Schooling in Capitalist America*, New York, 1976.

Herrera, A. O., et al., Fundación Bariloche, *Report to the Club of Rome,* Ottawa, International Development Research Center, 1976.

Leontief, W., et al, *The Future of the World Economy (A United Nations Study)*, New York, 1977.

Linnemann, H., J. de Hoogh, M. A. Keyzer, and H.D.J. van Heemst, *Food for a Growing World Population*, Econ. and Social Inst., Free University, Amsterdam, 1976.

McHale, J., *The Future of the Future,* New York, 1969 (and later publications).

Myrdal, G., *Asian Drama,* New York, 1968.

Pearson, Lester B., et al., *Partners in Development: Report of the Commission on International Development,* New York, Praeger, 1969.

Tinbergen, J., co-ordinator, *Reshaping the International Order*, New York, 1976.

_____ . "How to Reduce the Incomes of the Two Labour Elites?", mimeo.

_____ . "Some Remarks on Slow Growth," in C. H. Hanumantha Rao and P. C. Joshi (eds.) *Reflections on Economic Development and Social Change*, Bombay, Allied Publishers, 1979.

9

The Politics of Self-Reliance

Johan Galtung

It should be emphasized from the very beginning that to talk about the politics of self-reliance is to talk not about a strategy of transition to something utopian, but about a process that is very much alive, that takes place for everybody to watch, talk about, and participate in — or fight against, as many do and more will do as the process gains momentum. It already involves roughly one billion human beings — a quarter of humankind is in the active, forerunner phase, with the remaining three-quarters on the sidelines being apathetic or talking about developmental processes of yesteryear. Of this one billion human beings the majority are Chinese.[1] The group also includes many of the peoples of former French Indochina and many in India and Sri Lanka still touched by Gandhi's *sarvodaya* theory and practice. Efforts to implement the process elsewhere include the *juche* of the People's Republic of Korea (although more at the national than the local levels);[2] *ujama'a* in Tanzania; similar attempts in Ethiopia; the important developments in Albania; the beginning of a program in Madagascar; efforts at increased local self-reliance in many places in Western Europe, particularly in the Nordic countries;[3] and others scattered all over the world, unknown to us because nobody has yet been trained to count this way. Hence, the politics of self-reliance is an important part of contemporary history — an effort to undo five centuries of dependency on the West, to turn the tide started when Columbus traveled west and Vasco da Gama east (both of them too far), and to work for a world where "each part is a center."[4]

Self-Reliance Ideology

An Image of a World of Self-Reliance

If self-reliance is the antithesis of dependence, then understanding can be gained by using the English language as a guide. For "dependence" has two negations in English, both of them implicit in the idea of self-reliance: *in*dependence and *inter*dependence. Independence is autonomy, that invaluable combination of self-confidence, a high level of self-sufficiency, and the fearlessness out of which invulnerability is forged. Interdependence is equity, which means a style of cooperation that does not engender new patterns of dependence. Very often this can best be done by cooperating with ones' geographical neighbor, but there may also be more relevant social neighbors further away. Thus one might envisage a future pattern whereby some people in what today is called a "developing" *country* would cooperate directly with "developing" *districts* in rich countries, the benefits being shared equally as is the case in any equitable relations. The truly autonomous will never fear to cooperate with others, knowing there is something to fall back upon in case the ties should turn out to become so vertical that a *de*coupling has to take place again before *re*coupling can be put on the political agenda (when there has been sufficient change in the system). This is in no sense unproblematic: The world has much experience with independence and with dependence, but very little with truly equitable interdependence. The world went very quickly from autonomy to dependence on the self-appointed Western center and is only now trying to evolve patterns of autonomy in the context of a highly interconnected world. We all have to learn through practice how to combine independence with interdependence, autonomy with equity.[5] It is this combination that is called self-reliance.

Imagine now that the wave of self-reliance continues, not unabated, as nothing ever does in human affairs, but at an even quicker pace than during the last twenty-five years and at all levels: local, national, regional. What kind of world would we get? It would be a world with very many centers, not in the Western sense of a center controlling a periphery dependent on it, but rather in the Chinese sense of a center of concern. Each would be largely self-sufficient in food, assuming a world population distribution consonant with this. (After fundamental restructuring of patterns of ownership in the "countryside" has taken place, this would, above all, be a problem for the metropolitan areas, some of which would have to "de-develop.") Each would be self-reliant in the satisfaction of other basic material needs: clothes, shelter, and educational and medical services. Each would have an energy system compatible with production for these needs on a nonluxury basis. Beyond this, there would be patterns of exchange, centered not only on goods, but also on experience, on a reciprocal basis. There would be several levels of self-reliance, starting with individuals and small groups like families (magnitude 10^{0-2}), going on to the local (magnitude 10^{2-4})[6] and the national levels (magnitude 10^{5-7})[7] and to the regional level (magnitude 10^{8-10}).[8] At the top there is the globe itself, which still has no choice but to be self-reliant.

This would be a world almost the opposite of the one we have today, with chains of dependency radiating from the metropoles in the capitalist (and to some extent the socialist) West through a system of internesting regions, nations, and districts down to the most remote rural village, typically ending with an old, underfed, underclad, unsheltered, illiterate, perennially diseased woman, who is exploited by everybody. Just as the basic key to the politics of dependency is to tap the resources of the periphery through the mechanisms of capital drain, resource drain, body drain, and brain drain, the key to the politics of self-reliance is to regain control over resources — over capital, raw materials, labor, and the most precious of them all — human creativity. The whole theory of self-reliance hinges on one fundamental hypothesis: that together these resources constitute a reservoir, now partly drained away, partly misdirected, and largely underutilized, that is sufficient for the satisfaction of basic human material needs all over the world within a short time span of, say, five to twenty-five years. The necessary conditions for self-reliance are local power control and mass participation. These conditions constitute at the same time one of the keys to the satisfaction of basic nonmaterial needs: being the subject of one's own need-satisfaction rather than an object, a client at the end of a new dependency chain topped by managers of various kinds. In short, a self-reliant world would be as different from the world of today as the latter is from the world before Columbus and da Gama.

The Struggle for Self-Reliance

Self-reliance means struggle. This statement has one implication that is both trivial and terrifyingly important: The politics of self-reliance has been and will continue to be resisted both from within and from without. It will be a politics of struggle because of the vested interest in the present world order for those at the top. This should be interpreted not only materially, in terms of the way the periphery is treated as a vast reservoir whose resources are siphoned off in the direction of the minor and major centers, but also nonmaterially, in terms of power as a *bene per se*. If the resources of the peripheries were really controlled by them and released for their own purposes, a major restructuring of the world would take place.[9]

Nowhere is this seen so clearly as in the case of China: In 1948–1949 it was a part of the global slum generated mainly by the Western onslaught; twenty-five years later it is a center in its own right, a place no leader from the center can afford to ignore, not only as a market but as a place to learn why and how a non-Western center could become a reality. No wonder there is such agreement in the West that the only factors that can explain the Chinese achievement are "Chinese culture" and "five thousand years of history" or "more than two thousand years as a unified state," with little or no attention given to the generalizable elements in the struggle for local, national, and regional self-reliance.[10] The prospect of Latin American, African, Arab, South Asian, or Southeast Asian centers, in addition to China, must be less than heartwarming for people used to thinking of Washington, London, Paris, Bonn, Moscow, and Tokyo (with their subcenters), singly or combined, as the centers of it all almost by the laws of nature. No wonder the Western countries are making such energetic efforts to incorporate China into their system.

Thus it is to be expected that the struggle for self-reliance, initiated with the decolonization struggles and processes after the Second World War, will continue to be a bitter one. This does not mean that all phases will be violent. But it is as important to have an idea of the likely counterstrategies of the enemies of self-reliance, so as to be better prepared to meet them, as to have some notion of the strategies of self-reliance themselves. The following is written with this double purpose in mind, with a particular view to elucidating the dialectic of strategy and counterstrategy as the struggle gains momentum—a dialectic that we shall assume will have its ups and downs. We are not heading for a nice linear, or even exponential, growth in the phenomenon of self-reliance around the world; the resistance will also gain increasing momentum.

Self-Reliance as a Multilevel Ideology

In the following I shall assume that politics is a phenomenon with phases, not necessarily temporal, that can be described in terms of five components: consciousness-formation, mobilization, confrontation, struggle proper, and transcendence.[11] Many political offensives get stuck after the first, second, third, or fourth and never come to the crowning achievement. I shall, further, make use of the distinction between individual and collective (local, national, regional) levels of self-reliance, keeping in mind that nonterritorial units (such as associations or organizations) may also act more or less self-reliantly. The first problem to be dealt with is consciousness-formation: How does the *prise de conscience,* the inner awakening, take place?

I can give my own formula of how I see my ideology, one among many, of self-reliance. I see it as a combination of a vision of human beings; of local organization, particularly in its relation to the state; of the structure of social interaction in general and economic production and consumption in particular; and of international relations. The ideology of my vision encompasses some insights about inner man found in Buddhist thinking in the East and existentialist thinking in the West; anarchist thinking on the significance of local autonomy; liberal thinking on freedom and outer man in general, i.e., man in society; Marxist thinking on social structure; and antiimperialist theory and practice from recent years. All of this is tied together in ways that draw upon modern versions of federalism, with a strong emphasis on decision making at the lowest possible level, and tempered with ecological considerations of respect for the environment, in solidarity with present and future generations. Thus, it goes beyond the ideas contained in the United Nations Environmental Programme, of satisfying the inner limits of man (basic needs) without transgressing the outer limits set by our finite earth.[12] Any ideology of self-reliance would also have to fill in the details on what to produce and how, how to distribute it, and the kind of structure most likely to yield these results.

Thus, my ideology is a multilevel ideology. I think it has to be, for reasons to be spelled out below. It is inspired by, but also richer than, any kind of neo-Marxism with which it may be confused. At the global level self-reliance ideology has much in common with the stance taken by the Third World in favor of restructuring international relations, and not only the economic relations. At the domestic level there is much similarity with standard socialist thinking: nationalization of some of the key components of economic life in order to ensure that the first priority in production and in the utilization of surplus is given to the satisfaction of basic material needs for those most in need. At the local level there is much similarity with anarchist thinking, but also with liberal and even with some capitalist practice. Thus, it is basic to the whole idea of self-reliance that the local community is in command of its own resources; that creativity and initiative — one might even say entrepreneurship — are encouraged. This can happen only in an atmosphere of freedom, particularly freedom of expression,[13] so that people may bring ideas and insights together and convert them through discussion into something that can be used locally, in a unit that might be a federation of villages, a city ward, or anything with some promise of viability and providing a setting for participation and identification. Self-reliance ideology might be similar to capitalism in its emphasis on creativity and initiative, but highly dissimilar in its emphasis on mass participation (thus, the entrepreneur would not be a private individual or the top management in a private or state corporation, but the participants in the community) and an equitable relation with other units. In order to produce one would not start by creating a periphery from which capital, resources, and human labor, skilled and unskilled, could be drawn (either by moving production factors to the center or by letting standardized forms of production take place in the periphery); one would start with what is available locally and what is needed locally and build from there in circles of equitable exchange.

To many, an ideological stance of this type looks like eclecticism which implies that there is a certain newness to the combination. Used pejoratively, "eclectic" implies some sort of unintegrated combination of ideological elements with no real-world viability or feasibility. In view of the Chinese experience, it would be hard to level such accusations at self-reliance ideologies. They may be confusing combinations for minds trained in considerably narrower bands in the ideological spectrum. This has something to do with a certain habit in Western thought: the tendency to single out for attention a very limited range of variables and build an ideology around them, to the exclusion of all others, assuming that changes in these variables will have large-scale repercussions throughout the system. In this sense, Marxist ideology and liberal ideology are very similar. Marxist thinking has been as mesmerized by the idea of collective ownership of the means of production as liberal thinking has been by the opposite — private, competitive ownership — and neither can see how both the systems they have promulgated have been put at the service of the state system that matured after the "peace" of Westphalia in 1648. Both have assumed that the local and international levels will somehow take care of themselves once the national levels are set right. Thus both are essentially single-level ideologies.

In the present version of self-reliance thinking there is no such assumption. Rather, one may be impressed by the extent to which the local, national, and international levels of action can work at cross-purposes with each other if the development of human beings is the yardstick and not, for instance, national aggrandizement. Self-reliance theory and practice should never be referred to as such if it degenerates into single-level self-reliance only.

Higher-Level Self-Reliance Not Sufficient for Lower-Level Self-Reliance. Imagine that regional self-reliance has been implemented at the level of the Third World as a whole, at some continental level, or at subregional levels. In practice this would mean full control over Third World factors of production and production for and by Third World groups. But which groups? Given the present world structure, the center-periphery gradients are all there to be used by the strongest among today's poorer countries. Thus, regional self-reliance might protect the Third World against dependence on the First and Second Worlds (and for that reason be strongly resented by them), but would not offer any protection against penetration of the poorer countries by the Brazils, the Irans, and the Indias, and later by the Nigerias. The subimperial connections of today may become the raw material for forging the imperial connections of tomorrow; the logic would be the same, as would the basic mechanisms, which might even include visions of a *mission civilisatrice*, possibly based on myths or realities about empires of the past (as in the Iranian case under the shah).

Likewise, national self-reliance would not meet the bill either. In fact, this is what many nationalist regimes have practiced, e.g., on the basis of the theoretical rationale of the physiocrats, which today takes the form of "economic nationalism." The result is often the same whether the regimes are to the right or the left: increased centralization. The argument in the preceding paragraph may be repeated one level lower: national self-reliance may serve as a protective shield against penetration by other countries, but at the same time it leaves the domestic scene at least as open to exploitation of the masses by the national elites as before. The elites may simply use the dependency chains forged in the past colonial and the present neocolonial eras as raw material out of which solid exploitative structures may be built for the future. *National* self-reliance is compatible with exchange with others "at the same level of technical development" (whatever that may mean in precise terms), but it is also compatible with production for export rather than for the needs-satisfaction of the population. It is easier for the elites to control economic surplus in the form of money and other financial instruments that pass through the national banks than in the form of goods produced locally, and the surplus is more easily spent in ways decided by the national elites.

The difference between rightist and leftist regimes in this connection is mainly theoretical and is measurable in the frequency of statements that this is all in the true interests of the masses. It is usually the rural population that will suffer most because they are least able to fight back. They are less organized due to their settlement pattern and their ties to some minimum production of their own food— one reason why it is in the interest of the national elites to keep this residual production. In addition, the elites may hope to save the cities through imported foodstuffs, thereby protecting themselves against delivery strikes on the part of the rural population.

It is also generally a mistake to believe that it is easier to fight one's own elite than foreign-based imperialism, for in the latter case the national bourgeoisie may side with the masses in a war of national liberation. The same applies to local self-reliance: We know too much about villages and groups of villages to assume, gullibly, that the village left to itself will automatically satisfy human needs. Local self-reliance may protect the village from the parasitic elements in the nation. (Today perhaps these are, above all, national planning elites, who plan "for the country as a whole" and "not for parochial interests," shifting surplus towards the urban, industrialized, commercialized, and bureaucratized center.[14]) But this would leave the village open for local exploitation of the weak by the strong. The strong are those who control two basic production factors: capital (goods) and land. (In the age of slavery they controlled even human labor, but discovered that there are advantages in relaxing control a little, just as they later discovered that they could also give up control over land and still keep control of the means of production.) Hence we are thrown back to the lowest level: mass participation and individual self-reliance, and the obvious (socialist) conclusion that there has to be local control of all local factors of production.[15]

No doubt the politics of mass participation ultimately means that the masses take power, including the means of production, into their own hands and start producing for their own needs. This may not require a revolution *strictu sensu*; often some form of cooperative movement might be both necessary and sufficient to gain control. But it would imply a provision for local decision making on the basis of direct democracy. The unit to which this decision making would apply must be one with a sufficient amount of economic potential to offer a guaranteed minimum material basis to fulfill basic material needs. This is where local self-reliance differs so fundamentally from *self-management* (*autogestion*).[16] The latter implies general participation and direct democracy in decision making in a *unit* of production (a farm, a factory, a firm); self-reliance implies control, including decision making, over the entire economic *cycle*. On that basis — and here we recognize the Marxist concern for an adequate material basis — a whole edifice of activities and institutions in other social fields can be constructed, e.g., culture and what today is called "leisure," but more profoundly integrated with work rather than kept in separate compartments, as in our sectorally organized, segmented societies.

Lower-Level Self-Reliance Not Sufficient for Higher-Level Self-Reliance. The argument against single-level self-reliance works equally well in the opposite direction. Thus, local self-reliance is not enough. Even if each community had the idyllic character attributed to it in utopian literature in general, and anarchist literature in particular (integrating farm and factory, for instance),[17] at least two problems would remain. In a future world consisting of 150,000 such communities of roughly equal power, rather than 150 states as at present, a system based only on local self-reliance might be viable. But that is not our world. In the world of today the local community can be kept going on such a basis as long as there is sufficient normative fervor and normative production locally, in addition to inspiration from the outside. But it may crumble due to outside influence as soon as the production of ideology is reduced to a trickle and routine sets in, as was seen clearly in the hippie communities of the 1960s. (This is less true of many European communes of the 1970s; perhaps they do not have the same pretensions of being all-embracing.) In the world of today the transnationals and other forces will move into an unprotected local community with their demonstration effects on both the production and the consumption sides, and stronger communities might also very easily prevail over weaker ones. This may also be true in any future world; anarchist thought has always been weak on the problem of how all these communities are to be integrated into a reasonably peaceful whole, just as little thought has been devoted to the relation between local and national planning in a self-reliant society.

The Role of the State

Hence, local self-reliance can succeed only if it involves the great majority of the population in a setting of national self-reliance. Concretely this means not only the negative task — very important and difficult though this is — of not standing in the way when local communities try to develop a self-reliant basis; there are also a number of positive functions that can best be performed at the national level. There will always be some economic cycles that transcend the local level. The production of fertilizer, for example, need not only be by local biogas formulas; there will also be some scope for large chemical plants. But such cycles should be under collective control by people accountable to the masses affected by their decisions. In other words, there should be direct control of the managers of such nationalized plants, not only indirectly by controlling (through elections on an institutionalized basis) the politicians who presumably control the managers. The system known in Yugoslavia as "self-management" (*samo upravljenje*) is insufficient for this purpose for the simple reason that managers and workers in such plants may have a joint interest in sharing the spoils that accrue to them from exploiting other parts of the economic cycle.[18] Neither parliamentary elections nor workers' control has proven sufficient. The Chinese pattern, or nonpattern, of cultural revolution is probably better, but it is difficult to institutionalize; the moment that happens, it is lost. Needless to say, the pattern would not fit in with Western paradigms for nation-building based on elite-controlled and predictable institutions with little scope for spontaneity.

Obviously, the national center must also provide a good infrastructure for cooperation between the local units. The transportation and communication networks of a dependent country are not centralized. One of the first tasks of a self-reliant national government would be to use the economic surplus to build roads between outlying villages, i.e., connecting the periphery with the periphery so as to permit interdependence on the basis of concentric solidarity and to give second priority to the roads and telecommunications connecting the capital with the district capitals and the district capitals with "reliable" centers in the villages. Thus, it is naive to believe that a dedication to self-reliance does not have profound effects at the national level as well: The state cannot simply retire in favor of a laissez-faire "villageism" based on the bicycle and an improved wheelbarrow (with rubber wheels of the same type as the bicycle and a handle that is compatible with erect walking). In some cases this will have to be subsidized by the state, especially in the mountains where road-building may be absolutely essential yet far beyond local means, as in the Sierra Maestra in Cuba.

But the state has another very important function, a much more problematic one. Although the relations between the local units may be equitable, they may not be equal. No unit exploits the others, but they may differ in their "factor-endowments," some having more and some less of potential and actual nonhuman and human resources. For example, one unit may be much more able to inspire and be inspired by the masses so as to release creativity beyond the critical threshold, beyond which it becomes self-generating. The units may all practice "serving the people," but not all practice "trusting the people"—those that do may discover that they are amply rewarded. Hence, there is scope for the state to intervene at some point to prevent the most successful from converting their surplus into tools of inequity. A state based on a very low level of local self-reliance may have the centralized bureaucracy and the power apparatus needed to take from the rich and give to the poor through taxation and welfare state practices; a self-reliant country may not have this power to intervene. What needs to be put on a more equal footing is no longer individuals but local units. To tax the units collectively and transfer resources to the less fortunate may impair the self-reliance of rich and poor units alike; not to do so may lead to destructive imbalances. A Chinese answer would be to have the richer communes transfer the surplus into the industrial sector, which is more centrally controlled (apart from the countless very small "factories"), and to use the control over the industrial sector to level off inequalities. In a country where 80 percent work primarily in agriculture this may be an answer, at least for a time; it would not be in a country where less than 20 percent work in agriculture. Hence, there is not only scope, but a burning need, for social creativity.

Thus, self-reliance at the national level consists of more than assuring the conditions for autonomy of the units at the local level and an equitable pattern for exchange and cooperation among them of *their* choice. The state will also have to supplement and complement local production patterns, at least to the extent that the "economies of scale" doctrine has some validity and is not merely an ideology to protect expansionism and centralization. The production of labor-saving devices to avoid unnecessarily hard and degrading work is particularly important here. The state may also have to provide a protective shield against outside penetration, partly by producing its own ideology. Some of this shield will initially have to come from the national centers, since the masses have been deprived of self-confidence and have been tapped for resources for too long. Production for satisfaction of material needs may have to take place on a national scale till local units are in a position to do so themselves (which will take time given the strength of the center-periphery gradients inside the country). In addition, the state must provide national defense against interventionism of various kinds that will try to destroy the emerging patterns of self-reliance. The defense may be nonmilitary or military, national (conventional "modern" army) or local (guerrilla); preferably all four possibilities would be combined in a web of determination and will to survive that in and by itself *is* self-reliance.

To reiterate: National self-reliance, particularly in the Third World, is not enough. Most of the national units are too small and weak alone, measured against the giants in the Western center and Japan. Like local units, they can too easily be conquered from the center when they are alone, fragmented, and marginalized, without any self-confidence, dependent (or so they believe) on the center for material and nonmaterial goods and services, and paralyzed by fear (which is not strange, given the interventionism to which the Third World — including the small countries in Eastern Europe — has been exposed in the years since the Second World War). No doubt the solution here is solidarity: the regional self-reliance of the Third World and subgroups within it, working for more equitable patterns of exchange, and for a higher level of autonomy. In the economic field this has so far taken the form of action for better terms of trade and increased processing in the Third World. It is unnecessary to repeat that the actions of OPEC could not have been pulled off by one oil-producing country alone; yet this example also clearly shows that regional self-reliance is not enough to satisfy *human* needs — *vide* Iran. That brings me back to the first chain of reasoning against single-level self-reliance, from the higher toward the lower levels.

Self-Reliance as a Three-Pronged Dynamic Approach

Evidently, then, the answer—and this *is* the doctrine of self-reliance if there is one at all—is to combine all three levels—regional, national, and local—in a three-pronged approach, with the development of human beings everywhere as the goals. But this is a general strategic consideration; how is it to be converted into political tactics? More precisely, if it is impossible to work on all three levels at the same time, which level should be given the priority? Does one start with the individual *prise de conscience*, or with mobilization, confrontation, fighting at the local, or the national, or the regional level?

Answers to these questions cannot come out of general theoretical speculations. Everything depends on the "political situation." But that, in turn, is not only a question of objective circumstances; it also depends on subjective goal-setting, on consciousness-formation, and on the level of mobilization. The political situation offers an opportunity for confrontation only when there is a minimum of consciousness and readiness to act. Thus, the October 1973 war was an objective situation that helped increase the level of Arab solidarity. Many of the Arab states into which the Arab nation is divided are oil-producing countries, but this would have meant nothing if they had not had—for some time at least—a vision, a goal of substantially improved terms of trade. They used the mobilization brought about by the confrontation over another issue to inject the goals of their consciousness into the struggle—no doubt leading to some kind of partial transcendence of the world order. In other cases both consciousness and mobilization may be there waiting for an opportunity to launch a confrontation (e.g., when some old man, a symbol of an *ancien regime* dies socially or biologically). All other combinations may also be meaningful except two: consciousness without any action (the other four), or action without any consciousness. But these are not given, static entities; they develop as the process unfolds itself, dialectically, not linearly.

The conclusion from all this would be to seize opportunities when they arise, that is, when the forces favoring dependency are weak, whether at the local, national, or international levels. Recently international action has perhaps been most consistently dynamic, or at least this is the image given by the press, which always caters to the elite levels. Third World elites have exhibited remarkable solidarity and through their actions and organizations (Group of 77, the nonaligned) have succeeded in changing the thinking about and to some extent the practices in the world economic order. But this solidarity extends to the level of regional self-reliance only. The moment there is any talk of national self-reliance the countries whose elites prefer to stay in the capitalist system (but on better conditions) differ sharply from those with a more socialist orientation. Among the latter there is a similar distinction between those who consider national self-reliance on their political agenda. Whereas many Third World countries today are moving towards some pattern of national self-reliance in the sense of nationalizing some key industries (usually to put them under the control of the military rulers of the country), only a few can be said to steer the surplus systematically in the direction of those most in need, and among these only a handful may be said to go in for local self-reliance. Together, however, as was pointed out in the introduction, the population in this "handful" of countries, together with others at the local levels in other countries, may comprise as much as a quarter of humanity.

Should one then argue against the New International Economic Order (NIEO), which represents self-reliance at the regional level only, with some excursions into the national level but with no mention of either the local level or individual human beings with their needs and goals? No. It should be seen as one among many necessary, but not sufficient, steps, adding up to a *process* of fighting against dependency. It arose because the international level provided better opportunities for confrontation than the other two levels, since the less developed countries were more conscious and better mobilized than ever before while the other side was delegitimized and lacked new ideas. The Vietnam wars served to reveal the true nature of the Western world, which was divided into those who did the killing, those who supported them, and those who failed to protest until it was clear that the Vietnamese were "defeating" the "most formidable power the world has ever seen." Of course, there have also been openings at the national and local levels, but with the exception of China and the countries of former French Indochina these have been less spectacular in recent years. Substantial progress has been made at the national levels, though, in such countries as the People's Republic of Korea and Cuba. The three examples of China, Korea, and Vietnam together seem to indicate that it may be advantageous for a country to have a philosopher as leader, rather than one who feels called upon to give "on the spot guidance" on anything from chicken breeding to factory layouts. What is left for the local population but "to do and die," if not in a military battle at least in the battle of production, when the leadership is in the hand of a (self-appointed) universal genius?

Having a positive attitude to NIEO as a part of a much more comprehensive process, however, does not, or should not, blind us to its weaknesses.[19] For instance, the First and Second Worlds may soon discover that Third World solidarity is to their advantage, for it means that the majority, which rejects both national and local self-reliance, will dominate the socialist minority among Third World countries, which includes both the more classical (Soviet) style and the more recent (Chinese-style) varieties. One obvious result will be that the focus will be on the Third World as a whole, not on restructuring or creating new structures within and among Third World countries. This, in turn, gives the capitalist West a chance to appear in a new guise, using their subsidiaries in the Third World—now "nationalized" companies—or joint ventures for the transfer of technology, etc.[20] The patterns of dependency can be recreated in these ways, and the waste of resources in the production of nonbasic material goods in a way that also works against the satisfaction of basic nonmaterial needs can continue more or less unabated. After all, this is essentially what happened in Eastern Europe and the Soviet Union, and because these countries will have to turn their failure to develop more genuine patterns of socialism into a virtue, they will probably support such practices and continue to argue in favor of increased trade, even when it can be shown to be antithetical to development as defined here: satisfaction of human needs for those most in need.

Clearly, the Western countries prefer such countries to those that go in for genuine national self-reliance, not to mention those that add to this a pattern of local self-reliance—although the pre-UNCTAD pattern was even better in Western eyes. As a consequence it may be predicted that Third World solidarity will break up, for beyond a certain point—which may already have been reached—it becomes regressive rather than progressive. Then solidarity among Third World countries that practice national self-reliance and those that also practice local self-reliance may see the light of day and become an important factor even when they are not geographical neighbors. Such solidarity may also serve to highlight the problems of national and local self-reliance rather than the perennial theme of "terms of trade" (a very limiting approach) and to push more countries into more advanced development patterns. If this happens the continued need for Third World solidarity in another field will become evident: Solidarity in case of outside intervention in Third World countries will have to proceed from the verbal stage and UN votes to concrete action. "Intervention, if one of us expands the pattern of self-reliance, is an attack on us all" will have to be a political formula leading to collective defense.

Thus, in the years to come, Third World solidarity will probably strengthen and weaken at the same time, but in different fields. It takes little imagination today to envisage a Third World secretariat, for instance, having the Third World Forum[21] as one of its sources of inspiration. But a secretariat of that kind, doing for the Third World what OECD and the EEC Commission (backed by such organizations as the Trilateral Commission) do for the capitalist world would also quickly reveal cracks in solidarity, particularly if (or when) the Brazils, Irans, and Indias start behaving as the big powers have done in the UN since its inception. There is also the problem of imbalances in the production of development intellectuals, which is high in Latin America and South Asia and low elsewhere. But these are problems that will have to be faced. The contradictions will have to come to the surface and be handled by the Third World itself.

It is assumed that as the regional level of self-reliance matures and gains momentum, the other levels will also come into motion throughout the developing world. One reason this is so is negative: It will very soon become evident that the level of living of the masses will not necessarily improve with such measures as nationalization of key industries, because the basic distribution structure remains the same. Another reason is positive: The achievements of self-reliant regimes will continue to gain recognition, as has by and large been the case with China so far, and it will be more difficult for other regimes not to make at least some steps in the same direction.

For some time to come, however, the movement will tend to get stuck at the level of national self-reliance, if for no other reason than that the social group most capable of overthrowing a capitalist regime in favor of national self-reliance is likely to be the armed forces, who are also the most capable of resisting attempts towards autonomy at the local levels, especially if there is an ethnic component in these attempts. In many countries, consequently, the politics of self-reliance will for some time be reduced to the politics of the armed forces, the struggle between those recruited from the national periphery (often the army) and those who are drawn from the center and who have a more professional, less populist vision of development (usually overrepresented in the navy and the air force). So far the world has no experience with a popular uprising against a national or even a socialist government with impeccable antiimperialist credentials—except, perhaps, in Eastern Europe. That experience will soon be part of contemporary history. In all probability the experience will show what was hinted at above: that it is more, not less, difficult to fight a well-entrenched, self-righteous "progressive" national elite than it was to fight the old imperialist configurations—among other reasons, because so many of the national elites were on the progressive side in that struggle.

The Reaction of the Capitalist World

What will be the reaction to all this in the Capitalist West? In the beginning—that is, now—the West will watch from the sidelines, calling self-reliance a "fad" and trying to debunk it with frequent references to a return to the Stone Age or the Middle Ages.[22] The basic message — "we are going to set our own goals and choose our own means" — will not be lost, but will be received with a mixture of disbelief and anger. The rapid gains in the living standard of the poorest in the poor countries[23] will be measured not against the misery they are escaping from, but against the living levels attained by the richest in the rich countries of the world on the basis of centuries of exploitation. Like Marxism in an earlier day, self-reliance will be debunked as an ideology of leftist intellectuals in Western Europe, the sons and daughters of directors and professors, sometimes joined by their parents, something one can afford when one is rich, not when one is poor.[24] They will enthusiastically ally with those in the Third World who feel that self-reliance is something second-class. All the evidence to the contrary, especially that based on comparison of pairs of similar countries, will be discounted as based on special circumstances; all failures and negative experiences will be seen as typical. As Western elites have done this continuously since 1917 there is considerable expertise available in writing commentary of this kind.[25] It will be put to work in the mass media factories of human unconcern. For self-reliant countries elsewhere in the world this no longer matters; they are not taking their leads from status quo–oriented Western ideology.

What should the role of the West be? Just as the minimum task of the state is not to impede moves toward local self-reliance (as long as such moves are compatible with the self-reliance of other units), the minimum task of the Western center is not to stand in the way. This will be hard on all the "development agencies," which make up a booming industry in the West, providing jobs for bureaucrats and professionals, new outlets for excess capital, food surpluses, etc. — even under governmental guarantee — and a smooth continuation of Western colonial practices by extending the life expectancy of the roles of missionary, benefactor, administrator of other peoples, and large-scale manipulator.

Under self-reliance there is still some scope for Western "development assistance," but this will have to be of entirely different kinds, such as:

- efforts to restructure their own productive machinery so as to make it less dependent on factors from, and markets in, Third World countries;
- joint exploration by developed and developing countries of the technologies of local self-reliance, particularly making experiences in communities in rich and poor countries visible to each other;
- financial assistance, particularly in the form of untied grants, for some of the programs under national self-reliance; and
- some functions in connection with regional self-reliance (e.g., in

connection with integrated commodity programs) and possibly in connection with the redirection of trade.

One desirable assistance pattern in the Western world is the competition among development agencies, with the Dutch, Swedish, and Canadian agencies leading the field in understanding self-reliance and rejecting some of the development assistance practices of the 1950s. However, the West does not like to be rejected, particularly in what it perceives as selflessness.[26] The result may easily be the interventionist aggressiveness so well known from the post–Second World War era.

However, as dangerous as the conventional form of development assistance (a clear antithesis to self-reliance because it leads not only to dependence on more aid but to a habit-forming pattern of international begging, which China was first to reject) is the possibility that the capitalist countries may "invest in self-reliance." The slogan is a good one: It has appeal and is semantically close to the capitalist idea of "self-help." The stupid capitalist fights this and stimulates Western countries to engage in military, political, economic, and cultural interventionist practices; the clever capitalist spies on progressive groups to get ideas and starts marketing equipment "for your self-reliance" and "to help overcome the first hurdles." Much of this could be compatible with new orientations in the field of technical assistance, adding up to a rich package of "if you can't lick 'em, join 'em" elements that may constitute the most dangerous form of attack on self-reliance.

A more subtle form of attack, but one with some of the same consequences, might come from the political left in the center countries through offers to serve as catalysts in the processes needed to undertake structural change. Unless there is a clear program for phased withdrawal, or a genuine pattern of joining the local communities, such practices amount only to a continuation of the dependency structure. The obvious alternative would be for such groups to promote self-reliant structures in their own territorial or nonterritorial environment, thereby weakening the power of those very same center countries to intervene in weaker countries that are moving towards self-reliance. This is important because one of the most obvious implications of a program favoring local and national self-reliance would be the rejection of techniques that presuppose that other local, national, or regional units should fulfill the role of delivering the raw materials or labor. But such policies tend to be resisted!

Self-Reliance in Capitalist Countries

At this point, however, another factor enters the global politics of self-reliance: efforts in the same direction in the First and Second Worlds. In materially overdeveloped countries the euphoria of rediscovering the local community, agricultural work, and forms of togetherness that are productive and not merely consumptive—in short, self-reliance in its various manifestations—is now quite well known to many. What is not so well known is that there *may* soon be similar movements under way in the Second (the conventional socialist) World. Generously interpreted, the call at the Twenty-fifth Congress of the Communist Party of the Soviet Union for more emphasis on nonmaterial aspects of life may be considered to offer some openings in this direction. Given the general propensity of these countries to imitate the West, it is likely that inspiration may come from leftist theory and practice in capitalist Western Europe rather than from another member of the socialist community—China. For the socialist countries have great difficulties in learning from China. The Second World is blinded by fear and by general Western superiority complexes[27] that seem to take on the special Marxist form of accusing the Chinese leaders of catering to petit-bourgeois elements and inclinations in the Chinese peasantry.

Thus, in the richer parts of the world the motivation pattern for self-reliance will be different. What in the Third World is a necessity, a matter of survival, because other forms of development have been proven inadequate, or even catastrophic, is to many in the First World a way of escaping material overdevelopment as well as nonmaterial underdevelopment. It is partly stimulated by the increasingly well-known negative aspects of modern industrial societies, partly by visions of something better, of a higher quality of life achieved *because* the material standard of living is somewhat reduced. At the same time it also offers a solution to the obvious problem of double-edged dependence. It is not only Third World countries that are dependent on imports and exports; First World countries depend equally on exports and imports, and the solution is self-reliance.

As the Third World becomes decreasingly available for the old exploitative trade patterns, the volume of production in the First World becomes increasingly disproportionate to the demand. The old methods of enlarging geographical markets through more or less imperialistic practices and increasing demand through fads and planned obsolescence have served the system well, but the second method will be decreasingly available as Western consumers mature and become less manipulable—in other words, more self-reliant. Excess production leads to well-known problems, one of them being structural unemployment. But there are solutions to the problem of excess production that are compatible with more self-reliant patterns of life in the overdeveloped countries. Present levels of productivity could be maintained while reducing the working hours so as to introduce opportunities for richer life-styles; or productivity could be reduced, not only by making work more labor-intensive, but by making it more creative, which would mean trading off some of the standardized mass production of today's industrial society for a more artisanal type of production. Of course, these two methods are not mutually exclusive but are both very sensible reactions to the changing structure of world economic relations, as well as solutions to problems of material overdevelopment and nonmaterial underdevelopment. Or do these countries need wars to make them discover self-reliance?

Self-Reliance in Socialist Countries

In the Second World the problems will be put differently. There is much less dependence on the Third World for trade, and one cannot as yet speak of material overdevelopment, except in some elite segments of Second World societies. On the contrary, there are patterns of material underdevelopment, not in the fields of schooling, medical treatment, and clothing, but definitely in the fields of shelter and food.[28] (The contrast between Chinese and Soviet achievements in food production points to the significance of local self-reliance.) This might one day constitute a very powerful source of motivation for peasant revolts against primitive accumulation (of which Eastern Europe has a long history). But there is also considerable motivation to be found in the nonmaterial underdevelopment of the socialist countries in Eastern Europe—both in the fields of alienation (which they would share with the capitalist countries in Western Europe) and in the field of repression. There is more scope for local initiative, for designing and practicing one's life according to one's own inclinations, without wanting to return to capitalism. It may well be that this kind of motivation would be most strongly felt among intellectuals, which brings us back to the formula of an alliance between the intelligentsia, the peasants, and some of the "minorities" as one possible formula for the mobilization for self-reliance in these countries. In due time the yearning for more freedom may lead to new forms of self-reliance in China, too.[29]

Conclusion

Let me now try to summarize. I have been working analytically with

- *three levels of self-reliance*: local, national, and regional, with the individual level underlying it all;
- *five stages in the political process*: consciousness, mobilization,

confrontation, struggle, and transcendence;
- *two fields of motivation*: material and nonmaterial; and
- *three worlds*: the Third, the Second, and the First (and a fourth — China — in the background).

What I have tried to do is to indicate how all these can be seen as elements in a historical process that has been going on for some time, that is unveiling itself before our eyes, and that in all probability will gain more momentum in the future. The basic point of the present analysis is not that it contains new elements or ideas about what self-reliance could be, but that an effort has been made to establish some kind of relatively credible scenario for how it may proceed to more levels, involve more phases in the political process, and spread geographically to new areas, always liberating more people more effectively in more fields. This can be accomplished partly by demolishing anti–self-reliant structures and partly by the inspiration of good examples. No doubt this process will get stuck many times on the way: being limited to one level (e.g., the regional or the national); to one phase (e.g., the talking/writing phase, or consciousness-formation only); to one field (only the material needs of humankind); or to one part of the world (the Third World). In saying this, however, I am already referring to the past: we are far beyond this combination. But we are also very far from overturning dependency patterns, creating a world of self-reliance at all levels, in all fields, and in all parts of the world.

Nevertheless it is reasonable to predict that this movement will continue, not only because self-reliance seems to speak so much better to the human condition in all parts of the world than any other short formula in today's arsenal, or supermarket, of political slogans. It is because self-reliance as a method is entirely compatible with self-reliance as a goal. It is so different from competitive, social-Darwinist capitalism and totalitarian, repressive socialism with all their talk of liberating human creativity and bringing about the brotherhood/sisterhood of all, while in reality forging new chains of enslavement. It is so different that I would like to conclude by paraphrasing the greatest thinker and practitioner in the field next to Mao Tse-tung (and one who was much less different from him than people tend to think), M. K. Gandhi, stressing the unity of goals and means: There is no road to self-reliance — self-reliance is the road.[30]

Notes

1. For one inspiring article about Chinese self-reliance see Tony Durham,

"Think Big, Think Little," in Peter Harper et al., *Radical Technology* (London: Braziller, 1976). The Chinese have for a long time made the distinction between *yang fa* ("foreign ways"), *t'ufa* ("earth methods"), and *hsin fa* ("entirely new methods") and the idea of combining them, walking on not only two, but many legs. After Mao there has no doubt been a trend towards *yang fa*, but over time the Chinese strategy is self-reliant (not self-sufficient).

2. John Gittings, in his article "Keeping the Country on Its Toes," *Guardian*, 20 May 1976, writes: "The Fatherly Leader, Kim Il Sung, has in the past thirty years visited 2,896 places in Korea to give On the Spot Guidance. Some places he has visited more than once, making a grand total of 9,030 times." Unfortunately there is usually some relationship between this incredibly high level of mobilization of a no doubt very dedicated leader and some kind of demobilization of the people. Gittings also argues against the idea that *juche* means self-reliance; but it does mean that "people rather than things are regarded as the essence or mainstay of development."

3. In these countries it is known under such names as "the green wave," "green socialism," or "populism," and the political momentum is often carried by the youth movements, peasants' parties, or parties that are particularly strong in the countryside and are now looking for a new, more comprehensive political basis. Characteristic of them, as one of the more important authors in the field, the Norwegian professor of sociology and politician Ottar Brox, has pointed out, is the idea of taking the *community* as the basis for political theory and practice, not the *sectors,* as liberals/capitalists do, or the *classes,* as marxists/socialists do. A society can be analyzed in terms of sectors and classes, but political practice along such lines will tend to be abstract, above the level of the community with which people can identify. To focus only on the community, however, leaves out the national sector and class contexts. It should also be pointed out that Brox himself is a leading member of the Norwegian Socialist Party.

4. The Cocoyoc declaration, (Declaration by UNCTAD/UNEP Expert Seminar, Cocoyoc, Mexico, UN General Assembly, 1974). The precise wording in the part of the Cocoyoc declaration spelling out self-reliance is: "The ideal we need is a harmonized, cooperative world in which each part is a center, living at the expense of nobody else, in partnership with nature and in solidarity with future generations."

5. The alternative would be a less interconnected world, which would be difficult, perhaps even impossible, given the high population density relative to the pre-1500 world. Hence, the argument in this paper is not against interconnection, but against the present structures: they have to be redirected and become more equitable. Isolationism is not identical with self-reliance.

6. As pointed out, the Chinese commune seems to be of the magnitude 10^2 (team), 10^3 (brigade), and 10^4 (the commune itself). As to *ujama'a* (meaning "familyhood" in Swahili): "The size of an *ujama'a* village depends on the land available, and the number of people in each village ranges from 50 to 4,000, although 500 to 2,500 is normally viewed as the desirable village size" (J.H.J. Maeda and Ibrahim M. Kaduna, "Self-Reliance and *Ujama'a*: Tanzania's Development Strategy," in *What Now?*, 1975 Dag Hammarskjold Report on Development and International Cooperation, [Uppsala: Dag Hammarskjold

Foundation, 1975], pp. 54–59). See also Jimoh Omo-Fadaka, "Tanzanian Way to Self-reliance," *Ecologist*, Vol. 2, no. 1, February 1972. Other sources indicate that out of 7,000 villages, 700 are *ujama'a* villages.

7. There are some countries today with a population in the order of magnitude of 10^8 (above 100 million). They should be regarded as regions—some of them more successfully integrated than others—rather than as countries, particularly since, with the partial exception of China, they are all highly multinational.

8. The inclusion of the magnitude 10^{10} (ten billion and above) implies that this is regarded as an acceptable population figure for the world—but not 10^{11}.

9. To take but two examples: oil and sunshine as sources of energy. The less developed countries are by and large also the countries with most sunshine, which may indicate that the energy balance of the world would turn in their favor if societies became more sun-based than they are. On the other hand, this also applies to oil, which gives a clue to the obvious strategy of the rich countries in order to preserve the present "order": to monopolize the converters, assuming they cannot buy the sunshine the same way they bought the oil. (They may send the clouds in that direction, though.)

10. In the book *Learning from the Chinese People* (Johan Galtung and Fumiko Nishimura, [Oslo: Gyldendal, 1975], also available in Danish, Swedish, and German editions) the position is that Chinese culture and history were necessary conditions for the Chinese patterns of self-reliance—certainly not for self-reliance as such.

11. This is elaborated in Johan Galtung, *The True Worlds: A Transnational Perspective* (New York: Free Press/Macmillan, 1979), chapter 4.3.

12. See the Cocoyoc declaration for formulations.

13. In the case of China, as pointed out by Sartaj Aziz (in a communication to the Fifth World Future Studies Conference, Dubrovnik, 28 March–2 April 1976), there is a trade-off between equality and the freedom to choose occupation and probably also the place to work and live. On the other hand, there is considerable freedom of expression and impression. Whether other countries will make similar or different trade-offs on the way to self-reliance remains to be seen. Something probably has to be sacrificed before a society with reasonable security, economic well-being, freedom, and identity for all is achieved.

14. The author has some experience with the former Indo-Norwegian fisheries project in Kerala, India (see CERES, no. 41, 1974). During a short follow-up study in January 1976 it became clear that the proletarianization of the local fisherman population had gone even further, making it likely that in some years they may no longer be able to engage in regular fishing, but will be entirely dependent on the export market. Shrimps, prawns, and lobster—in short, luxury seafood—have the same relation to household fish as luxury cash crops have to staple food products.

15. This does not exclude individual self-reliance in the sense that individuals or very small groups (families and what in the West are called "communes") also can be owners of means of production, land, and their own labor as long as they produce for their own consumption and do not exploit others. There is no objection in self-reliance ideology to the family farm—but the feudal landowner is ruled out. Nor is there any objection to small-scale capitalism, if it remains small scale.

16. This is why the Yugoslav experiment to some appears as micro-socialism combined with macro-capitalism: a high level of sharing in decision making inside the factory, e.g., about how the factory shall participate in what may one day become indistinguishable from a capitalist market.

17. The classic here is the work of Kropotkin, which contains visions very similar to present practice in Chinese people's communes. Will the picture of Stalin on the walls in Chinese communes one day disappear in favor of that great Russian, or will, in the spirit of self-reliance, all the foreigners in the usual Marx-Engels-Lenin-Stalin-Mao Tse-tung (Hua Kuo-feng) quintet gradually disappear?

18. Take the example of a tourist agency. The Yugoslav model would provide for an open discussion between guides, secretaries, drivers, clerks, and managers—but there is nothing in the model that would guarantee the inclusion of a rather important group, the tourists themselves. A self-reliance model focusing on the total cycle would build their participation into any model of decision making in order to hear their views and to protect them against coordinated exploitation.

19. See "Self-Reliance and Global Interdependence: Some Reflections on the New International Economic Order," *Papers*, Chair in Conflict and Peace Research, University of Oslo, 1976.

20. For an exploration of this, see Johan Galtung, "East-West Security and Cooperation: A Skeptical Contribution," *Journal of Peace Research*, Vol. 12, no. 3, 1975, pp. 165–178.

21. This important group of Third World intellectuals is an excellent example of a new actor created as the dynamics of Third World self-reliance gets under way. Its weakness is that, true to the tradition of intellectuals, it is much stronger on regional and national self-reliance than on local self-reliance and is probably also weak on the theory of intellectuals and their efforts to constitute a new class. The rise of intellectuals as a class is closely linked to the rise of the nation-state and centralized capitalism; small communities are less dependent on intellectual analysts to the point that their presence might even look ridiculous.

22. No doubt there is much to learn from these periods, especially as to satisfaction of basic material needs and needs for identity. But the issue is not well put: the issue is whether one can have some of the positive sides of those periods in human history without also having to accept the negative aspects. Thus, ill health is hardly a desirable concomitant.

23. The experiences of the four best known Third World countries that are socialist (Cuba, China, North Vietnam and North Korea) seem to indicate that periods from five to twenty-five years are sufficient to bring the masses in countries at the bottom of the world capitalist system above an acceptable floor where basic necessities are concerned.

24. All parts of a sentence like that are wrong: self-reliance is *reflected* in some leftist and even some conservative intellectuals in the West, but as *practice* it is very much the product of the East and of the intellectuals and nonintellectuals alike. The record of self-reliant versus dependent countries serves to indicate that the masses in the latter cannot afford to stay dependent, that a change towards self-reliance is a necessity.

25. For an example, see C. F. Kindleberger, "World Populism," *Atlantic*

Economic Journal, Vol. 3, no. 2, 1975, pp. 1–7. (A very minor point: the present author is referred to as a "Marxist sociologist by the name of Johann [sic] Galtung." I am neither a Marxist nor a sociologist. One can be inspired by Marxism and yet feel that much more is needed as a guide to practice in our complex world; sociology is certainly too limited—hence approaches like peace research and development studies.)

26. A typical example is catastrophe aid and the aggressiveness with which China's lack of interest in receiving such aid after the earthquake that shattered Tangshan on 29 July 1976 was received. So many of China's policies are designed precisely to meet such calamities on a self-reliant basis, knowing that catastrophe aid is *one* of the instruments used by rich countries to forge dependence (although at the same time it is no doubt also inspired by selfless considerations). Perhaps most important, underlining that self-reliance is a psycho-political rather than merely an economic category, the attitude with which the Chinese people seem to be able to face such situations is practical and nonpanicky—in other words, self-reliant.

27. It is interesting to note that the two big Western powers, the United States and the Soviet Union, both seem to assume that China is not on her own social dialectic but will have to go through the same stages that they think they have been through. The American assumption is typically that the Chinese system of self-reliance will yield when GNP per capita rises; the Soviet assumption is that it will disappear when China comes out of her present "stalinist" phase and enters the more technocratic phases that succeeded it in the Soviet Union.

28. Jomoh Omo-Fadaka, ("Escape Route for the Poor," in Harper et al., *Radical Technology,* pp. 249–253) cites the examples of China, Tanzania, Albania, North Korea, Vietnam, Burma, and Cambodia as examples of self-governing, self-regulating, and self-supporting economic structures. He also argues against the Soviet model, claiming that it is authoritarian; that the pace of growth for agriculture is very low—"yields . . . still compare unfavorably with those of 1913"; and that the system has led to increasing preoccupation with material possessions and the emergence of new and privileged classes.

29. One is thinking particularly of forms that would permit more freedom of choice of occupation, place, and work and perhaps in general more individual creativity in creating one's own lifestyle, in full solidarity with others.

30. The original reads: "There is no road to peace, peace is the road."

10
Collective Self-Reliance: The Case of the Caribbean Community (CARICOM)

Kenneth Hall
Byron Blake

Collective self-reliance has recently become widely accepted as the most appropriate strategy for overcoming the constraints on development experienced by the Third World, both at the national and international levels. At the same time, however, the existing arrangements for regional economic integration among Third World countries are experiencing considerable difficulties that raise doubt as to whether conditions permit the implementation of collective self-reliance as a viable practical strategy in the proximate and medium-term future. Collective self-reliance appears contradictory, particularly at the international level, where it is being enunciated simultaneously with the declaration to establish a New International Economic Order. The issues raised by the record of regional economic integration and the simultaneous attempt to pursue policies of collective self-reliance and the creation of a New International Economic Order suggest the need to reexamine the premises on which existing regional arrangements have been made, their achievements, and the nature of their current problems and to propose new measures to achieve the goals and realize the aspirations so frequently enunciated in international and regional fora. The experience of the Caribbean Community (CARICOM) will be used as a basis for this examination.

CARICOM

CARICOM comprises the Commonwealth countries of the Caribbean: Barbados, Guyana, Jamaica, Trinidad and Tobago, Antigua, Belize, Dominica, Grenada, Montserrat, St. Kitts-Nevis-Anguila, St. Lucia, and

St. Vincent. The Bahamas maintains informal links with CARICOM, while other Caribbean countries participate in some of its activities. It is the most recent stage in a long history of efforts to achieve political unity, economic integration, and general cooperation among those countries. Its most immediate predecessors were the West Indies Federation, which lasted from 1958 to 1962, and the Caribbean Free Trade Association (CARIFTA), which was established in 1968 and ultimately gave way to the present arrangements.

CARICOM pursues activities in three areas: economic integration through the common market arrangements; functional cooperation and the operation of common services such as education, health, transportation, communications, culture, and sports; and coordination of foreign policy. Major CARICOM institutions are the Heads of Government Conference, the Common Market Council of Ministers and several other ministerial institutions, and the CARICOM Secretariat, the principal administrative organ. Integration and cooperation are also pursued through independent institutions, called associate institutions, such as the Caribbean Development Bank, the University of the West Indies, the West Indies Shipping Corporation, the Caribbean Investment Corporation, and the Caribbean Food Corporation. Conceptually and organizationally CARICOM is intended to achieve the fullest cooperation in a wide variety of issue areas to achieve the objectives of regional development. Specifically, it is intended to achieve the strengthening, coordination, and regulation of economic relations among its member states in order to promote their accelerated harmonious and balanced development, the sustained expansion and integration of economic activities, the equitable sharing of benefits derived from those activities, and a greater measure of economic independence and effectiveness in dealing with other states and international organizations. It also aims at promoting the efficient operation of certain common services and activities for the benefit of the population, the promotion of greater understanding among the Caribbean people, and their social, cultural, and technological development.

Collective Self-Reliance and CARICOM

At its most general conceptual level collective self-reliance denotes the desire of countries to rely collectively on their own resources in the attainment of their development objectives. At the policy level it implies not autarkic development but rather a dynamic interrelationship between one group of countries and the rest of the international community in the areas of trade and the transfer of technology. The critical criteria for collective self-reliance are that the policies pursued in international economic relations should be determined by specific deficiencies of the participating nations and that they should be intended to strengthen and/or complement deficiencies in resources and indigenous scientific and technological capability and to achieve genuine reciprocity among countries sharing similar aspirations. At the internal level collective self-reliance implies structural transformation designed to promote social justice and effective utilization of local resources, to satisfy the basic needs of the population and to engender public participation and democratization in the development process.

It has generally been conceded, however, that few if any Third World countries or groups of countries are now pursuing these policies. Collective self-reliance has therefore assumed an operational definition that is significantly different from its theoretical and conceptual formulations. At the operational level it calls primarily for two sets of policies. First, Third World countries should combine their bargaining strengths so that they can better exploit their bargaining positions and negotiate a more advantageous arrangement with the industrialized countries. Secondly, economic transactions and social and cultural links among Third World countries should be expanded so that a greater utilization of their material, spiritual and cultural resources can be achieved.

CARICOM is more consistent with the objectives of the operational definition of collective self-reliance than the theoretical and conceptual requirements suggested by the more comprehensive definition. In this context CARICOM is perceived not merely as a desirable but as an essential strategy in overcoming the development problems in the region. For some of its members CARICOM represents the only feasible strategy if they are to maintain their economic, financial, and political viability as independent countries. Like other Third World island nations, CARICOM countries are small, have limited resource bases, and experience problems resulting from a legacy of political and economic fragmentation and a high level of economic dependence and geographical and physical fragmentation. These problems provide a very strong case for collective self-reliance among the countries.

Policies of Collective Self-Reliance:
Achievements and Problems

The Treaty of Chaguaramas, which established CARICOM, is substantially in keeping with the measures for economic cooperation among Third World countries agreed upon at the Conference on Economic Cooperation among Developing Countries held in Mexico City,

September 13–27, 1976. At the operational level, decisions have been taken and activities have been pursued in trade and related areas, production, infrastructure and services, monetary and financial measures, technical cooperation, external economic relations, health, education and culture, industrial relations, communications, insurance, tourism and intraregional travel, meteorology, and harmonization of laws. Furthermore, the institutional arrangements provide adequately for the participation not only of heads of governments but are decentralized to include all the portfolios at the national level through regular ministerial and official meetings.

There is some controversy over the significance of the achievements of CARICOM to date. One school of thought views the whole process as one of gradual implementation through a series of stages. Others have placed more emphasis on the slow pace of implementation, on the current difficulties, and the lack of activity in certain key areas; they are therefore less impressed with the range of activities that have been undertaken.

There is no doubt that, since its conception, achievements have been registered in the three broad categories of policy options, namely, strengthening the bargaining position, mutual assistance, and increase in the economic transactions among members and cooperation in a wide range of other areas. Thus the volume of intraregional trade expanded by more than sixfold between 1967 and 1975, the percentage increasing from 8 percent of total trade in 1967 to 11 percent in 1973. A common external tariff has now been agreed upon, together with a scheme for the harmonization of fiscal incentives for regional production. The establishment of an interim balance-of-payments facility and an expansion of the intraregional clearing scheme have facilitated expansion in trade and further eased the restrictions due to monetary problems. Trinidad and Tobago has also provided substantial grants and loans to most members of the community to assist in meeting their financial and balance-of-payments difficulties, particularly those arising from increases in the price of oil. In the area of sectoral integration, the Caribbean Food Corporation has been established as the first step in the implementation of a regional food plan, and the Corn/Soya Company in Guyana has begun operations. There has also been some industrial programming, with priority being given to pulp and paper and sea island cotton.

In the field of external economic relations, CARICOM successfully worked as a single unit in negotiating the Lomé Convention and was instrumental in the establishment of the African, Caribbean, and Pacific (ACP) group of countries. A new economic and technical cooperation agreement was concluded with Canada in 1979; a similar agreement was earlier concluded with Mexico. The establishment of a new West Indian Shipping Corporation, the Caribbean News Agency, the Caribbean Examinations Council, and the Caribbean Broadcasting Union gives some indication of steady and increasing activity across a wide range of fields.

Whether these achievements justify the optimism sometimes expressed about CARICOM as a viable instrument of collective self-reliance is questionable. The experience of the organization since 1976 casts serious doubt on the capability of the existing arrangements to operate effectively and to achieve its declared objectives within a reasonable time. These doubts derive from several trends observable within CARICOM. There has been a reduction in economic transactions between the member countries; the volume of regional trade as a percentage of total trade has dropped significantly from 11 percent in 1973 to 6 percent in 1976. More important, there has been a tendency for member governments to adopt unilateral action in pursuit of national or ideological interests. The dissatisfaction of several members of the community with the distribution of benefits further suggests that one of the prerequisites of successful collective self-reliance, namely the capacity for trade-offs, has not yet been fully developed.

These developments have led to predictions that CARICOM will either collapse or stagnate. It has been suggested, for example, that in the near future there will be a halt in activities in new issue areas, that there will be no further developments in certain critical areas such as foreign investment and exchange rates, that the proposals for joint ventures will not be implemented, and that there will be a reversal of the progress that has been achieved in the free trade regime and in the operation of arrangements for the intraregional trade in commodities.

These difficulties raise the futher question of whether the preconditions exist for the successful operation of CARICOM as an instrument of collective self-reliance. Some contend, for instance, that there are not enough resources to permit substantial compensation for those who are presently nongainers until such time as the potential of the activities being undertaken are fully realized. Furthermore, national alternatives have increasingly been adopted in a context where CARICOM is no longer perceived as consistent with the priorities of some of its members and offers a less attractive alternative in the pursuit of national goals. The current difficulties are also assumed to be fundamental in nature rather than temporary and amenable to compromise. Finally, it is suggested that the community at present lacks internal dynamic and that there is little prospect of acquiring new sources. This view is, however, not universally shared, especially by those who regard the institutional framework as basically sound and the current difficulties as the result of temporary problems traceable directly to the international economic recession in the mid-1970s.

Some Problems and Proposed Solutions

It is generally agreed that the present arrangements have not worked as effectively as was anticipated and that new instruments and renewed effort will be needed to regain lost momentum if CARICOM is to continue as an attractive alternative to national options and not to become an increasingly irrelevant vestige of Caribbean economic, political, and social development. In this connection, proposals have been submitted that suggest the need for a reexamination of the basic assumptions underlying CARICOM, its objectives, and its operations. These proposals have derived from an identification of certain key issues.

At the institutional and decision-making level a major problem is the implementation of decisions. Estimates vary with regard to the number of decisions that have been implemented but it is known that the proportion within the time frame specified is rather low, particularly in areas requiring domestic legislation in member countries or in sensitive areas of national concern. Some governments have complained about the inconvenience, and in some cases the negative impact, created by nonimplementation of decisions by other states. This is particularly significant, as the CARICOM Treaty contains a significant proportion of declaratory goals that leave the specific mechanisms, timing, and method of implementation to the ministerial bodies and member governments. Questions have also been raised with regard to the decision-making process itself, which requires the consensus of all member states, each member having a veto. This has resulted in a time-consuming process characterized by compromises that limit the effectiveness of the measures agreed upon. Equally important, many governments lack the capability to implement decisions even when they are willing to do so.

These problems suggest the need for measures to strengthen and speed up the collective decision-making and implementation processes. Proposals have been made to improve the process by the establishment of a commissioner system, reorganization of the secretariat to give it greater emphasis on implementation, and decentralization of its activities on the basis of functional areas so that units could be nearer the points of implementation and more readily accessible, especially to those governments that require assistance. At the national level, it has been suggested that there should be institutional organization to permit more effective national coordination with regard to regional issues. Proposals have also been made for the creation of joint administrative departments to permit a greater degree of effectiveness, especially among the smaller members of the community. Implementation of these proposals would remove some of the bottlenecks that currently impede the achievement of the objectives of CARICOM.

A much more important issue, however, is the divergence of policies being pursued at the national and at the regional levels. The adoption of collective self-reliance at the regional level presupposes complementary policies of self-reliant development at the national level and a willingness on the part of national governments to coordinate their planning to achieve appropriate complementarity in policy and production. Recent experience suggests, however, that some governments have attempted to formulate and implement policies of self-reliant development consistent with domestic priorities while others have not pursued similar policies. This has resulted in operational and policy differences between member states and has prevented either the adoption or the implementation of decisions in major areas covered by the treaty. In some cases it has even led to the restriction of trade in items that are considered nonessential by some countries but that are significant in the export component of others. Thus, the whole common market arrangement experienced serious difficulties when Guyana and Jamaica imposed import restrictions on "inessential" products, partly because of their very serious balance-of-payments problems and partly because of the adoption of basic needs strategies at the national level. The adoption and implementation of the recommendations submitted to the Common Market Council by a group of Caribbean experts with regard to licensing and quantitative restrictions, regional import programming, trade in agricultural products, state trading and public-sector procurement, and financing intraregional trade would go a long way toward meeting some of those difficulties. Urgent measures are also needed to implement projects in the industrial and agricultural sectors that give priority to the use of regional resources.

Perhaps one of the most controversial issues that has arisen recently deals with the question of the distribution of benefits, specifically the dissatisfaction expressed by the Leeward and Windward Island member states, which are the less developed countries in CARICOM, that they have received few benefits, particularly in relation to their inputs. This implies that mechanisms such as the special regimes for the less developed CARICOM countries have not operated effectively to prevent polarization of economic activities and disparity in the distribution and allocation of benefits and resources. It also implies that the member states are not yet ready for the "trade-off" strategy of development, which requires the willingness and capability to offset certain types of costs against other types of gains at different times. In part this situation is the result of the impact of the world economic crisis of the mid-1970s on the economies of most member countries. More importantly, it is directly related to the inability of all member states, except Trinidad and Tobago, to absorb additional costs and postpone anticipated benefits for an indefinite period. This was in direct conflict with the assumptions on which CARICOM was based. In 1973 it was optimistically expected that Barbados, Guyana, Jamaica, and Trinidad and Tobago would be able to carry the main burden of implementing policies of collective self-reliance, but in 1976, instead of being able to contribute substantially to the costs of collective self-reliance, the first three of those countries were experiencing serious economic problems of their own and had to be assisted by Trinidad and Tobago or by other sources. To the extent that the problem is temporary, there is some hope that solutions can be found in the near future, but if, as seems likely, these are fundamental structural problems, then the existing disequilibrium is likely to continue and could conceivably be solved only by the expeditious adoption and implementation of more concrete and far-reaching measures of collective self-reliance.

CARICOM also appears to lack the support of the population, which could bring to bear the requisite influence on decision makers at the national level that would force them to pursue national policies consistent with the objectives of collective self-reliance at the regional level. This is the result of the institutional structure, whereby CARICOM is essentially an arrangement between governments and more specifically between national bureaucrats. Unless structural and institutional reorganization is undertaken at the national level to permit public participation in the development process, CARICOM is likely to remain divorced from the popular will. Efforts will then be needed to democratize and decentralize economic and political decision making at the local level, so that regional policies will become an integral part of national planning and decision making. Proposals for worker participation at the national and regional levels are consistent with these ideas and should be encouraged. This would also provide new resources from which a new dynamism could develop.

Another area to which some of the current difficulties are related is the question of the capability of CARICOM as a whole to pursue meaningful policies of collective self-reliance at both regional and international levels. It is being increasingly suggested that CARICOM will become viable only if it is linked with a larger area or combines its own negotiating strength with those of other developing countries, which would enable it to enter into arrangements that are complementary to the pursuit of collective self-reliance. The experience with the Lomé Convention, the formation of the ACP, and other efforts at the international level lend support to that view. The tendency of some member countries to look outside the region for solutions to their national problems also suggests that some countries, at least, have doubts about the viability of CARICOM as an instrument of collective self-reliance. In this connection urgent steps should be taken to implement the proposals and decisions to strengthen the machinery for the coordination of external economic relations and to participate in the wider international efforts at Third World collective self-reliance.

Conclusion

CARICOM's experience of collective self-reliance suggests the necessity for the adoption of policies of collective self-reliance if the region as a whole is to overcome the constraints of development. It also implies, however, that the consistent pursuit and attainment of those policies are plagued with difficulties, even in a situation where the countries involved have a common heritage, are located in the same region, have a history of close working relationships, have common problems, and are at more or less the same stage of development. CARICOM has also demonstrated the wide gap between the declaration of goals of self-reliance and their transformation into concrete and successful policies. In addition, the CARICOM experience has pointed out some of the constraints imposed on collective self-reliance by the situation of small Third World island countries and suggests that the achievement of collective self-reliance will depend, at least for those countries, as much on their own efforts as on the wider collective self-reliance of all Third World countries. CARICOM cannot be regarded as a failure, however, since it continues to implement many of the treaty measures, operating programs of cooperation in a wider group of areas than any other regional movement among Third World countries. Its achievements in some of these areas have been significant. Furthermore, while there are undoubtedly some serious problems, many people in the region are of the view that those problems can be solved and that the experiment will continue to be significant in any assessment of collective self-reliance as a viable, feasible, and successful strategy for Third World countries.

References

Brewster, H. and C. Thomas, *The Dynamics of West Indian Economic Integration* (Mona, Jamaica: ISER, 1967).
Brewster, H., "Self-Reliance and Economic Co-operation Among Developing

Countries," *African International Perspective* (1976:3), pp. 20–22.

_____. "The Theory of Integration and the Caribbean Community Process: Ten Years On," paper presented at the Conference on Contemporary Trends and Issues in Caribbean International Affairs (Port of Spain, Trinidad: May 1977).

Caribbean Community Secretariat, *The Caribbean Community, A Guide* (Georgetown, Guyana: 1973).

Demas, W. G., *Essays on Caribbean Integration and Development* (Mona, Jamaica: ISER, 1976).

_____. *West Indian Nationhood and Caribbean Integration* (Barbados: CCC Publishing, 1974).

_____. "The Caribbean and the 'New International Economic Order'," *Journal of Interamerican Studies and World Affairs* (1978:3), pp. 229–263.

Hall, K. O., and B. Blake, "The Caribbean Community: Administrative and Institutional Aspects," *Journal of Common Market Studies* (1978:3), pp. 211–228.

_____. "Major Developments in CARICOM: 1975," in Leslie Manigat (ed.), *The Caribbean Yearbook of International Relations* (Leyden: A. W. Sijthoff, 1977) pp. 387–399.

Lewis, V., *The Caribbean Community: A Political Analysis* (Barbados: Barbados Advocate News, 1973).

_____. "Problems and Possibilities of Caribbean Community," *Social Studies Education* (1976:7), pp. 26–33.

Lewis, V. (ed.). *Size, Self-determination and International Relations: The Caribbean* (Mona, Jamaica: ISER, 1976).

McIntyre, A., "Decolonization and Trade Policy in the West Indies," In F. M. Andic and T. G. Mathews (eds.), *The Caribbean in Transition* (Rio Piedras, Puerto Rico: Institute of Caribbean Studies, 1965), pp. 182–212.

_____. *"Evolution of the Process of Integration in the Caribbean and the Current Situation and Perspectives of CARICOM"* (Georgetown, Guyana: Caribbean Community Secretariat, 1976).

Ramphal, S. S., *Dialogue of Unity: A Search for West Indian Identity* (Georgetown, Guyana: Caribbean Community Secretariat, 1975).

_____. *To Care for CARICOM* (Georgetown, Guyana: Caribbean Community Secretariat, 1975).

Ramsaran, R., "CARICOM: The Integration Process in Crisis," *Journal of World Trade Law* (1978:3), pp. 208–217.

11

The Future of Latin America: Between Underdevelopment and Revolution

Rodolfo Stavenhagen

Three Ways of Looking at the Future

There are three ways of facing future social and economic problems. The first is a normative or voluntaristic approach which envisions the realization of an ideal model which may or may not be utopian. A second approach, which is essentially fatalistic or passive, deterministically denies man the capacity to forge his own destiny. A third way of facing the future is based on an analysis of current tendencies and trends as they can be inferred from historical processes, thus tracing alternatives available to mankind. The relative viability of each alternative depends not only on the validity of the analysis which precedes it, but also, and I would say above all, on the conscious action of men dedicated to transforming the conditions of their existence. Within this perspective the future appears to take the evocative title of one of Borges' stories, "The Garden of the Forking Paths."

Of course this approach neither denies previous theoretical positions nor the value systems of those who employ them. However, instead of ignoring them with a false claim of "scientific impartiality" or converting them into dogmatism (as would be the case with the two previously mentioned approaches) we feel that a theory of society which neither falls into dogmatism nor claims impartiality is a basic prerequisite for forming a valid strategy for the future.

It is within this latter context that we propose to discuss some of the problems of underdevelopment and development in Latin America.

This is a condensed and revised version of an article that originally appeared in *Latin American Perspectives*, vol. 1, no. 1, Spring 1974, pp. 124–128. It is published here with the permission of Professor Stavenhagen and the editors.

Before beginning one must recognize that when speaking of an area which has more than twenty countries and almost 300 million people, our generalizations will necessarily encompass great internal differences and many specific phenomena. Thus the problems posed must be discussed at a level of generality which will not do justice to either the diversity or complexity of the social and political structures.

Underdevelopment in Latin America

We will begin with the obvious by stating that underdevelopment in Latin America is not simply a question of being "behind" the industrialized nations in a manner which can be measured by comparing the gross national product, per capita product or other such indices; but rather underdevelopment is the product of a specific historical process. Underdevelopment is the state of being of Latin American countries in modern times, just as "colonial society" was its state of being during three centuries of Iberian domination. Furthermore the two phenomena are closely related, since underdevelopment is the historical continuation of colonization.

Given this understanding of the problem, one finds that the great task of social and economic development in Latin America is not just "technocratic" manipulation of the rates of investment and savings, modernization of business firms, or more intensive use of natural or human resources. Instead, nothing less than a profound transforming of all social and economic relations within the nations of Latin America will be necessary, as well as a qualitative change in Latin America's external relations with industrial countries, that is, with the world market in which Latin America finds itself.

It is only in recent years that the problem has come to be formulated in these terms, since for many years technicians and statesmen considered that economic development had nothing to do with social structures and political systems. In fact, from the end of the Second World War until the middle fifties there was general optimism concerning the future of Latin American economies. International prices of exportable raw materials stayed high; some of the countries had accumulated considerable foreign exchange reserves; in some nations the industrialization process had made undeniable progress; and the superficial signs of a certain degree of prosperity spread through the middle classes of the growing urban centers. But this image was a mirage, made all the more dangerous since high rates of economic growth and favorable trade balances blinded the eyes of many not only to the serious problems which were still unresolved, but especially to the inherent contradictions in the development process itself. In recent years early optimism has given way to more realistic appreciations and to the recognition that building the future cannot be done without eliminating the causes of past failures. At this historic turning point, Latin America needs to identify and confront the tasks which face it in the last third of the twentieth century and choose the route which will permit their completion. With some simple statistical projections we can see the scope of these tasks for the next few years.

Tasks for the Future: Some Projections

It is well-known that Latin America has one of the highest rates of population growth in the world. If the population continues to increase at the same rate it has (and there is no reason to think otherwise), in the year 2000 (in less than 30 years) our population will have increased 125 percent over the 1970 level, that is, there will be 355 million new mouths to feed. At the same time the population will continue to be concentrated in urban centers, and 235 million new residents will live in our cities. It is easy to imagine the problems which these urban concentrations will pose in terms of housing, public services, education, urbanization, and employment. In fact it has been calculated that 85 million new workers will need jobs. More than six million new housing units will have to be built each year until the end of the century in order to house the growing population, without considering the necessity of improving existing housing, whose average quality leaves much to be desired. More than a hundred million new students will need schools and teachers. We could continue to enumerate other such needs, but these data are enough to indicate the magnitude of the problems.

Given these problems, what are the real possibilities for Latin American economies? The response to this question can only be found in an analysis of recent trends in Latin American development and their implication for the coming decades. Available data, which generally come from official United Nations statistics, show us that the recent evolution of Latin American economies cannot in any way be considered satisfactory.

The Need for Structural Reforms

Internal colonialism is one of the structures of Latin American underdevelopment which must be broken in order to get out of the vicious cycle of poverty, backwardness, external dependence and internal domination. The great problem posed by Latin America today is how to break this vicious cycle. The various social forces involved in this problem promote different alternative models for social change.

The present dynamic of economic growth requires increasingly high rates of increase in production, for which statesmen and technicians demand higher investment coefficients and increases in work productivity. A decade ago the ill-fated Alliance for Progress had already proclaimed unattainable goals for Latin American development (Levinson and de Onis, 1970). Now annual growth rates of 7 and 8 percent are suggested as minimum goals for the next decade, but the means proposed are the same ones which have proved to be ineffective in the past (see Prebisch, 1970). In order to maintain and increase the rate of economic growth and give the appearance of development as measured by statistical averages, it is probable that Latin American leaders will continue favoring and devoting special attention to the modern sector of the economy. Of course this policy is important from many points of view, but as we have noted previously, it increases the characteristic structural disequilibria of underdevelopment.

On the other hand, these same disequilibria have produced increasingly strong social and political pressures from the masses which demand greater benefits from economic growth, a better income distribution, new sources of employment, as well as increasing participation in the political processes. The forms which these pressures assume are diverse (and we will return to some of them later on), but all of them lead to the proposal of major structural reforms which the dominant classes in Latin America have been more or less successful in opposing. Within the limits of existing laissez-faire economics it is impossible for these structural reforms to take place. Such reforms would affect the positions of privilege and domination of the ruling oligarchy and bourgeoisie as well as the domestic and foreign beneficiaries of internal colonialism and foreign dependence.

State Capitalism and the Double Standard of Development Policy

In order to meet these social and political pressures and channel them, in so far as it is possible, without modifying the existing power structure, the State has emerged as a public entrepreneur and as a fundamental element in directing the development process. In this way, what might be called a double development policy has been created. On the one hand, it reinforces as much as possible (through foreign financing, subsidies to private foreign investment, state participation in certain types of enterprises, tariff protection, manipulation of exchange rates, regional economic integration, etc.) the dynamic modern sector (rapid-growth industries, export agriculture) and on the other hand distributes token benefits to the marginal masses.

These token benefits range from "social" investments (public housing, basic urban services) to minifundia agrarian reforms. However, the growing unemployment problem and structural marginality make the formation of policies to provide employment and income for the marginal masses unavoidable. It is quite probable that in the coming years steps will be taken and minimal investments will be made to create employment at low productivity levels for the increasing work force. In this way perhaps the socio-political pressures of the masses will be lessened for some time, but in any case they will be kept within a closed circle of "underdeveloped development." By accelerating the growth of the modern sector without basic modifications in the structures responsible for underdevelopment, labor and production in the marginal sector will be tied to a low consumption market which is increasingly distant from the high consumption market tied to the modern sector. As a consequence, such double standard development policies, instead of contributing to the integration of one national market, create two markets with few ties between them, and thereby reinforce internal colonialism in Latin America. If these are indeed the present tendencies, it is doubtful whether the double standard of such development policies will manage to contain the increasingly severe tensions and conflicts inherent in the system.

The Failure of Liberal Democracy and Populism

One of the clearest manifestations of these contradictions has been the failure of liberal democracy as a viable political structure in Latin America. Traditionally (until the end of the last century or the beginning of the present one in some countries, until the depression of the thirties in others and until more recent times in the rest), the power structure has been based in the rural and urban oligarchies which were tied to the external sector of the economy. The great majority of the population were excluded from institutional participation in the political process. Progressively the urban middle class and the industrial working class demanded and obtained political representation to a greater or lesser degree (and with very important variations from country to country). Thus arose the so-called middle class political parties and the industrial labor unions. While keeping in mind the shortcomings of any broad generalities, it can be stated that the incorporation into the political system (which one writer has called "broadened participation") (Germani, 1962) of the urban middle class, and later, of the organized proletariat, coincides with urban growth, the first attempts at industrialization, and the formation of an internal market.[1] In certain countries this evolution has led to regimes and movements called "populist," of which the best known (for filling an entire epoch of the history of their countries) are Peronism in Argentina and Getulism in Brazil, although there cannot be an exact definition of populism in Latin America.[2] The principal characteristic of such regimes seems to be the mobilization and manipulation of the "available" working masses in order to build a broader base and provide more maneuvering room for unstable coalitions between certain competing factions of the ruling classes. The figure of the charismatic leader using demagogic language is a secondary characteristic of these movements.

Populism certainly played a political role for the bourgeoisie during the period of "inward oriented growth"[3] of Latin American economies, and at the same time it was a relatively primitive expression of the urban masses' intent to participate in the political system. But this sytem ceases to be functional when those who ran it try to incorporate the marginalized masses so as to broaden their political base. Given that there is no room for marginal groups in the context of dependent development, their appearance on the political scene as participants in populist movements constitutes a danger for the stability of the system, and ultimately for the hegemony of the ruling classs. As a consequence, when these ruling classes feel themselves overwhelmed by such movements they try other solutions.

Military Regimes

In order to fill the political vacuum, military regimes have been coming to power with increasing frequency. In the last four decades there have been almost a hundred successful military coups in Latin America. In the last ten years alone more than twenty have taken place in eleven countries, without mentioning the unsuccessful ones. These new regimes no longer have anything to do with the arrogant military caudillos of an autocratic and personalistic nature who were characteristic of earlier times. Today the take-overs are institutionalized with power being seized by a well-organized, highly professional technico-bureaucratic military apparatus aspiring to modernity. Sometimes the military justify their interventions in order to "put the house in order" before giving power back to the civilians. More recently they have stated that they want to stay in power to carry out development policies which they feel civilian regimes are incapable of. The new military take-overs are not the product of a military caste with aristocratic pretensions tied inseparably to the interests of the traditional oligarchy. Rather they are linked to the rise of the urban middle classes in what has been called the "crisis of hegemony" of the traditional ruling groups (Nun, 1969). In other words in certain Latin American countries, given the inability of liberal democracy to function and given the inherent instability of populist regimes, military regimes are the only ones capable of keeping the process of dependent development functioning by institutionalizing what one author has called the "norm of illegitimacy" (Horowitz, 1969).

The new military regimes not only seize power; they also try to control the state administrative apparatus, strengthening its entrepreneurial tendencies and its growing intervention in the economy. Frequently they are closely linked to multinational corporations in their countries, due in part to their professional role as "organization men," and in part to the fact that the military apparatuses are themselves consumers of great quantities of modern, expensive technology.

Some of the recent military regimes have based their political action on the ideology of "defending Western civilization" within the global context of the Cold War, which they have tried to wage within their own boundaries, in what is now becoming an almost classical neo-fascist strategy (with political executions, torture of prisoners, etc.). In this manner they play the role the Pentagon has assigned them in its scheme of "hemispheric solidarity" and at the same time carry out, at least in the southern part of the continent, what one author has called a "subimperialistic strategy" (Marini, 1969).

Nevertheless the military's hegemonic calling does not prevent the development, on occasion, of a certain amount of nationalist ideology. In addition to grandiose "national projects" of geopolitical inspiration, some military men also adopt the traditional demands of the left for the nationalization of the basic natural resources of the country. Since the investments in these sectors are no longer the principal interests of foreign capital in Latin America, the nationalization of these resources enables the military to improve their image in areas of great political sensitivity, without affecting the fundamental interests of foreign capital nor the basic characteristics of external dependence (ECLA, 1970: part 4, chapter I, tables 2 and 3).

It is evident that the military regimes, by their very nature, represent a bureaucratic, elitist, technocratic intervention in the national political process. Military intervention excludes by definition the political interplay of parties and movements of different social classes, although on occasion it may attempt to simulate a democracy with political parties. In contrast it does not exclude the very active, but restricted, interplay of certain economic and political pressure groups which takes place below the apparent institutional calm. In any case, the military apparatuses in power are not linked to the political currents of the great majority of the population. They cannot, without danger of losing control, play the part they have assigned themselves—or which has been assigned them—without systematic political repression and on occasion extremely violent suppression of any opposition movement which attempts to gain political power. Military repression is not only directed against opposition political parties, but against labor unions, peasant movements, students, and other groups which only claim the limited rights which the law grants them. Thus one of the principal characteristics of Latin American military regimes has been the reduction of salaries and living standards of workers and peasants, which is no more than one of the expressions of polarized, dependent development to which we have referred.

Popular Movements

The power structure controlled by the traditional oligarchies, the consular bourgeoisie or the military regimes, have been increasingly challenged by the demands and the political movements of the popular masses. These movements have taken different forms based on national and historical circumstances, but for simplicity's sake we can classify them into two main types: those which want greater participation within the existing system (which can be called reformist) and those which demand fundamental change in the economic and social system (which can be called revolutionary). We must note that this distinction refers to the content and range of goals and not to the form of struggle or the tactics for taking power. Thus some reformist movements can take power in a revolutionary manner, while other movements which put forth revolutionary objectives may do so within the electoral system. The distinction between what is revolutionary and what is reformist in specific historical contexts is not always clear, and certainly some popular movements oscillate between the two extremes for tactical or strategic reasons.

As examples of reformist movements we can cite the "national-popular" parties which are based on wide sectors of the urban middle class, working class and peasants. Some examples of political movements of this type are the Mexican Revolution during its first stage (until 1940), the Movimiento Nacionalista Revolucionario (MNR) of Bolivia, the Alianza Popular Revolucionaria Americana (APRA) in Peru, the Brazilian *trabalhismo* before the 1964 military coup, the Acción Democrática party in Venezuela, etc. Given the increasing contradictions in the model of dependent development mentioned above, it is hardly likely that this type of political movement has much of a future in Latin America. If these movements attain power they tend to become bureaucratic corporate states (as has been the case in Mexico); if they do not attain power, or lose it, they tend to dilute and are then overtaken by the left or absorbed by the right.

A question which has been widely discussed in Latin America is whether industrial labor movements (which in some countries have significant political and numerical strength) are "revolutionary" or not. In these discussions political ideology based on other socio-political contexts has been more important than Latin American realities. The organized working class, even when it is numerically small, has been incorporated into a system of privileges and benefits (protective legislation, minimum wages, collective bargaining rights, social security, etc.) which generally were not the result of generations of long, hard struggle, as in Europe, but rather the product of protective, paternalistic governmental policies. In exchange for certain concessions, many organized labor movements have become closely associated with government structures or certain parties in power. In addition, given their relative position of privilege compared to the peasants and marginal masses (that is, as beneficiaries of internal colonialism), the organized working class tends to be more demanding on economic issues than revolutionary in political matters.

This is not to underestimate a real tradition of revolutionary struggle in many of the Latin American labor movements, which in some countries began in the late nineteenth century. But the largest part of the industrial working class emerged, and became organized, during the period of import-substituting industrialization (i.e., after the Great Depression). It is a young working class, not only in age, but in historical tradition. It is composed, in large measure, of rural emigrants, who during the post-war period found avenues of upward social mobility in urban-industrial employment. In most countries, this industrial proletariat is tightly controlled by a self-perpetuating (and often corrupt) elite of union bureaucrats who are closely linked to reformist political parties (APRA in Peru, Acción Democrática in Venezuela, *trabalhismo* in Brazil, Partido Revolucionario Institucional [PRI] in Mexico, Peronism in Argentina).

At the various periods in recent history, some of the labor organizations have radicalized their demands, and they have either directly contributed to creating revolutionary situations, or they have become involved in them in other ways. The Cuban revolution and the short-lived socialist government in Chile are cases in point. In some other countries, where military regimes have systematically repressed workers' organizations, it is possible to detect an increase in workers' radicalization at the grass-roots level. Examples of this are to be found in wild-cat strikes in

Brazil, among the Bolivian tin miners who reject military rule, among numerous sectors of the Argentinian working class (particularly in the Córdoba area in 1969-1971), Uruguay, and even, at the present time, in Peru (whose military government has consistently adopted a nationalist and populist stance, but which has tightly controlled organized labor). It is an open question what line the Chilean labor movement (much of whose leadership has up to now survived repression) will now take against the fascist dictatorship.

In contrast to labor organizations, peasant movements have traditionally been of a more radical nature, with some exceptions, due principally to the rigid, repressive social and political structure in rural areas which makes any peasant demand, however modest it may be, a frontal attack on the power of the landed oligarchy. More than any other social groups, peasants in Latin America have suffered the most violent, systematic repression. Thus some peasant movements have become, especially in relation to agrarian reform, important revolutionary forces. It is very probable that in the next few years the incidence and intensity of peasant movements will increase in countries which are not carrying out rapid intensive land redistribution. Also it is likely that these movements will be repressed with increasing efficiency by governments fearing that ties between peasant movements and other revolutionary groups could lead to far-reaching social revolution.

Revolutionary Struggle

The sixties which, as we have seen, were a period of increasing foreign dependence and increasing domestic polarization in Latin America, were also a decade of revolutionary guerrilla struggle in several countries of the continent. The success of the Cuban revolution, as well as the institutional and military obstacles to any significant political change in the majority of Latin American countries, has inspired young Latin Americans (especially students) to take part in guerrilla struggles. In no fewer than fourteen Latin American countries there were guerrilla organizations at some time in the past decade, and in seven of them revolutionary combat has, or had at one time, considerable political significance.

The objects, strategy, and tactics of these movements have varied and the Latin American left has had major internal splits over questions concerning these matters. The pros and cons of rural guerrilla warfare tied to peasant movements or urban guerrilla struggle linked to marginal groups and other sectors and the relative merits of a guerrilla "foco" and a "mass revolutionary party" have been widely debated and will continue to be so in coming years. The purely military successes of these movements have been few, due in no small part to the considerable advances in counter-insurgency warfare by Latin American armies trained by the United States. Despite the assassination of Ché Guevara in Bolivia in 1967, which signaled the end of an era of guerrilla struggle in Latin America, it is likely that guerrilla warfare will continue to be used sporadically as an instrument of political struggle as it has been for many centuries. But it is hardly likely that any of these movements will obtain a total victory in the forseeable future, unless a particularly favorable situation occurs.

In contrast to their military achievements, the political repercussions of guerrilla movements have been considerable, and their impact in various countries still cannot be objectively evaluated.[4] In some countries there has been an escalation of repression and violence which has resulted in increased isolation (but not necessarily a weakening in the short run) of the military regimes in power. In others they have contributed to exposing the structural crisis and the governments' inability to resolve it. Finally in still other countries the dramatic guerrilla experience served as a catharsis to raise the consciousness of other sectors of the population (including the military), thus permitting a political opening in the system toward certain revolutionary reforms (massive land reform, nationalizations) whose final direction still cannot be determined with clarity.

Nevertheless, the lack of rapid and significant success (the victory of the Sandinista Movement in Nicaragua is a recent exception) and the growing difficulties for guerrilla movements on the continent during the last decade have not led to the abandonment of the revolutionary model for social change. In any case the result has been the search for other strategies and the recognition by revolutionary groups themselves that social realities and the political dialectic in Latin America were more complicated than they had imagined initially. Of course the future of revolutionary movements (guerrilla or not) depends not only on the relations between domestic forces in each Latin American country, but also on the international situation.

Whatever the final evaluation of Allende's policies will turn out to be (and that will depend, of course, on who does the evaluating), voices on the left are already heard to say that the Chilean experience demonstrates the uselessness of electoral politics in the revolutionary struggle. This would be, in the authors' opinion, a premature judgement, just as the repeated failure of guerrilla activity does not preclude the possibility of its eventual success in some Latin American country, given the right historical circumstances.

Revolutionary activity, as the history of revolution shows, has many facets, and it is indeed true that the world has seen more revolutions that have failed than those that have succeeded. The lessons of the Chilean experiment will take some time to appear clearly. To the outside observer, however, there are already some elements that appear important: a) The explosion of the myth of the "apolitical" professionalized armed forces; b) the stubborness of right wing ideology among the officer corps; c) the economic interests of the urban middle sectors and the extent to which these groups will be able to organize themselves politically to defend their privileges; d) the dangers inherent in the initial redistribution of income and consumer spending when the socialist State is not yet in a position to combat effectively the systematic sabotage of the country's productive capabilities by its internal and external enemies; e) the lack of solidarity among different factions of the organized working class, and the key role played by a corrupt "labor aristocracy," placed in strategic sectors, in blocking certain governmental measures; f) the demonstration, once again, that the "democratic" parties of the bourgeoisie (in this case the Christian Democrats) would rather have fascism than even the slightest hue of socialism.

Certainly the role of the United States was also crucial in the Chilean tragedy. The "invisible boycott" that Allende denounced several times, and through which Chile was denied international credits (which have since been heaped upon his fascist successors), was engineered by the U.S. government. The machinations of a number of multinational corporations closely tied to the Nixon administration; direct intervention by the Central Intelligence Agency (CIA) and the Pentagon (as reported from many sources, including United States senators and congressmen) in support of the groups that were preparing the coup; all of this has been crucial in the (now) "Chilean road to fascism." Allende was overthrown not because his experiment was a failure, but because it was too much of a success. It remains to be seen what the strategy of the democratic forces will be in Chile in the future, in their struggle to regain their liberty.

Future Alternatives

Rarely in history has there existed over an entire continent, as there currently is in Latin America, such a generalized awareness among the most diverse social groups as to the necessity of carrying out major modifications of the political and social structure. Perhaps the closest approximation of this widespread consciousness was the African anti-colonial movements in the post-war years. Even though everyone is in agreement concerning the existence of a crisis, there is no possible agreement as to solutions, since ideological currents and proposed models for change are a function of the interests of social classes and of the conflicts between opposing social forces.

There is nothing in the present Latin American situation which would indicate the possibility of one single pattern of development which could be followed by all countries. Nor is there anything which would permit one to suppose that the current situation of underdevelopment, internal polarization and external dependence can be maintained indefinitely. But it is also clear that any model for change which can be adopted will not be implemented without encountering obstacles, contradictions, tensions and conflicts. Based on the analysis made thus far we can indicate three major alternative models for the future of Latin America.[5]

1. *The continuation of dependent development.* Current tendencies may continue in some countries for some time, passing from crisis to crisis, each time sinking deeper into what has been called the "development of underdevelopment" (Frank, 1970). Although apparently this process contains the "seeds of its own destruction," there is no doubt that the forces that maintain it have sufficient capacity and flexibility to impede the germination of these seeds, at least until powerful counterforces arise which manage to displace the forces of the status quo. If this process continues for some years the subordination and integration of Latin America into what one author has called "the New Roman Empire" will doubtless be complete, and Latin American countries will pass from being satellite dependencies to being provincial dependencies (Jaguaribe, 1969). This "puertoricanization" of Latin America, toward which present economic tendencies lead, will without doubt have unforeseeable political repercussions.

Among the forces which support the present model of dependent development (or growth without development, or polarized expansion, as it can be called interchangeably), are of course the multinational corporations whose activities, if they were given free reign, could in a short time considerably limit the freedom of action of various national governments (the economic power of some of these conglomerates, measured by their sales, is larger than that of many small countries measured in terms of GNP). And behind these economic interests one must mention the political and military strategy which the United States has manifested through various direct and indirect interventions into the internal affairs of Latin American countries during the last few decades.

To this combination of extra–Latin American forces which support the continuation of dependent development, one must add the interests of the Latin American consular bourgeoisie and the neo-fascist, "subimperialist" ideology of certain military regimes notably those of Brazil and Chile. So long as there are no changes in the interests of each of these protagonists, or conflicts between them, the only forces which oppose this constellation of powers will be the nationalist and anti-imperialist ideological currents of certain sectors (including elements of the bourgeoisie and middle strata, as well as the armed forces and the church) and popular revolutionary movements (which may or may not opt for armed struggle, according to their circumstances).

2. *Autonomous capitalist development,* based on a broad alliance of social classes and a developmental, nationalistic ideology. This model has been tried at certain times in certain countries, and its failure until now does not mean that it will not be attempted again and again in the future. This could happen if the political and social costs of the previous model become too high for the dominant national and foreign classes. This would imply the necessity of reversing some of the present tendencies of dependent development, which could only take place in the context of State capitalism and Latin American economic integration, with powerful public enterprises and state planning organizations carrying out the tasks which Latin American bourgeoisies are incapable of completing themselves.

The viability of this alternative results from the possibility which certain active elites (multiclass political parties, military groups, technocrats and government planners) have of converting external dependence into interdependency, and polarized development into integrated development, without destroying the present class structure: In order for this to happen they would have to know how to obtain widespread mass support, active or passive, which would permit them to limit the power of the dominant classes and negotiate with foreign interests from a position of relative force. At the same time they would have to know how to manipulate and incorporate into the system these same popular forces to prevent being overwhelmed by the left. Thus while the previous model signifies governing *against* the people, this model would have to govern *without* the people.

The possibilities for this model depend on a strategy which is both political and economic and which until now has not been successfully implemented in Latin America. Those that have controlled economic strategy generally have been incapable of controlling the political process, and those who have held political power have generally lacked a viable economic strategy for this model. As a consequence it is likely that attempts at this model for development will again be transformed into the previous model of dependent underdevelopment or will be carried by their own momentum into the socialist revolutionary model, which is the third alternative we will consider.

3. *Revolutionary socialism.* Since the victory of the Cuban revolution,

and especially since the socialist government took power in Chile in 1970, the alternative of revolutionary socialist development has been objectively proposed as a possible model for development in Latin America. If "socialism" in this context refers to a certain kind of political ideology and social and economic organization, the adjective "revolutionary" does not refer so much to the manner of taking power as to social changes in the modes of production and class relations. For reasons expressed previously it is hardly likely that guerrilla movements will be successful in the near future. The road of electoral politics for revolutionary parties does remain open in some countries, but as the Chilean experience showed, even before the fascist coup, revolutionary measures can be blocked by a well-organized parliamentary opposition. In Latin America in the seventies it is not realistic to believe in the sudden, revolutionary overthrow of the capitalist system, either through guerrilla struggle or by electoral means, in any country. Rather, it will be necessary to envisage a "period of transition" between current dependent underdevelopment and the possible socialist development of the future. This transition would require particular political and economic strategies.

In the political area, it will require the mass mobilization of peasants and workers and large sectors of the middle classes. Under pressure of guerrilla movements and revolutionary parties (which, except in Chile, do not have mass followings), this might lead to a realignment of some traditional political forces, including sectors of the army, the "national populist" parties and the Church. Again, there is as yet no successful attempt of such a political realignment, which might serve as a model. In Chile it failed; in Peru, after a weak-kneed beginning, the military backed away from this course and turned sharply to the right; some hoped that the return of Perón would herald such a course in Argentina, but his death, followed eventually by another military coup, removed that possibility.

In the economic sphere, the transition to socialism will require the most difficult step of all: breaking external dependency, i.e., breaking the stranglehold of the multinational corporations and of financial and technological dependence. If this can be achieved (Cuba did it, Chile tried it, and Mexico speaks of it), then many other measures of economic policy will come naturally: redistribution of income, elimination of structural marginality and internal colonialism, increase in standards of living of the population, popular participation in decision making, etc.

Just as there is no recipe for socialism, there is no recipe for a strategy of transition. The contradictions and the internal and external conflicts which any socialist strategy (no matter how mild) will encounter appear formidable indeed. But one of the weaknesses of those who create the future is precisely their strength: an incurable optimism and an unbreakable faith in the potential capabilities of humanity. The revolutionary alternative in Latin America cannot take place, as Ché Guevara had already foreseen, without a new morality and a new kind of human being. But this new human being can only arise in the crucible of revolutionary struggle.

Notes

1. The best analysis of this process is in Cardoso and Faletto (1969).
2. Literature on this subject is abundant. We will simply cite some of the important works: Di Tella (1964 and 1965); Graciarena (1967); Ianni (1968); and Weffort (1965).
3. "Inward oriented growth" refers to the stage of Latin American development in which demand produced by the internal market began to have an important role in the dynamic of economic growth. See CEPAL (1969).
4. There have been few objective analyses of recent guerrilla experiences of Latin America, and socio-political studies of the subject have yet to be done. One of the few attempts is that of Gott (1970).
5. The practice of political futurology has attracted a number of specialists from the social sciences in Latin America. The most stimulating essays are dos Santos (1970); Jaguaribe (1969); Pinto (1968); and Sunkel (1967).

References

Cardoso, F. H. and E. Faletto (1969). *Dependencia y desarrollo en América Latina,* Mexico City: Siglo XXI.
CEPAL (Comisión Económica para América Latina) (1969). *El pensamiento de la CEPAL,* Santiago, Editorial Universitaria.
Di Tella, Torcuato (1964). *El sistema político Argentino y la clase obrera*, Buenos Aires: Eudeba.
_____ (1965). "Populism and Reform in Latin America," in *Obstacles to Change in Latin America*, edited by Claudio Véliz, London: Oxford University Press.
dos Santos, Theotonio (1970). "Dependencia y cambio social," *Cuadernos de Estudio Socio Económicos,* 2.
Economic Commission for Latin America. *Economic Survey of Latin America,* New York: United Nations, 1967, 1968, 1969, 1970, 1971, 1972.
Frank, André Gunder (1970). *Latin America: Underdevelopment or Revolution*, New York: Monthly Review Press.
Germani, Gino (1962). *Política y sociedad en una época de transición*, Buenos Aires: Paidos.
Gott, Richard (1970). *Guerrilla Movements in Latin America*, London: Nelson.

Graciarena, J. (1967). *Poder y clases sociales en el desarrollo de América Latina,* Buenos Aires: Paidos.

Horowitz, Irving Louis (1969). "The Norm of Illegitimacy," in *Latin American Radicalism,* edited by Irving Louis Horowitz, Josué de Castro, and John Gerassi, New York: Vantage Books.

Ianni, Octavio (1968). *O colapso de populismo no Brazil,* Rio de Janeiro: Civilizao Brasileira.

Jaguaribe, Helio (1969). "Dependencia y autonomía en América Latina," in *La Dependencia Político-Económica de América Latina,* edited by Aldo Ferrer, Mexico City: Siglo XXI.

Levinson, J. and J. de Onís (1970). *The Alliance that Lost its Way,* Chicago: Quadrangle Books.

Marini, Rui Mauro (1969). *Subdesarrollo y revolución,* Mexico City: Siglo XXI.

Nun, José (1969). *Latin America: The Hegemonic Crisis and the Military Coup,* Berkeley: Institute of International Studies.

Pinto, Aníbal (1968). *Política y desarrollo,* Santiago: Editorial Universitaria.

Prebisch, Raúl (1970). *Change and Development: Latin America's Great Task,* Washington: Inter-American Development Bank.

Sunkel, Osvaldo (1967). "Política nacional de desarrollo y dependencia externa," *Estudios Internacionales,* 1.

Weffort, Francisco (1965). "Estado y masas en el Brasil," *Revista Latinoamericana de Sociología,* 65(1).

12
The Evolution of Cuban Development Strategy, 1959–1980

Joel C. Edelstein

The revolutionary government in Cuba has evolved a succession of approaches to the task of fostering independent national development with remarkable speed. In 1959 the anti-Batista movement came to power under the leadership of Fidel Castro and with a reformist program. Castro's 26th of July Movement (M26J) dominated a broad coalition of forces. Since its emergence in the unsuccessful attack on the Moncada military barracks in 1953, M26J had been distinguished from other political forces solely by its call for unity among opposition forces and its insistence that armed struggle rather than negotiation was the only effective means of achieving change, i.e., was the only road to reform.

Once Castro was in power and the promised reforms had been introduced, internal polarization and an escalating pattern of foreign threats and attacks resulted. The government responded by taking over the holdings of its opponents, both foreign and domestic. The biggest wave of nationalizations occurred in the summer of 1960. Thus in order to secure the reformist regime, the revolution became socialist. In the midst of the April 1961 invasion at Playa Giron, Castro used the term *socialist* openly for the first time, calling upon Cubans to defend their socialist revolution. Seven and one-half months later, he declared himself a Marxist-Leninist. Despite this rapid ideological transformation, the central goals of the revolution had not changed. The petit-bourgeois humanism of M26J had become Marxist humanism. The earlier demands for national sovereignty through economic diversification were transformed into a policy of expanding sugar exports to reduce a growing foreign debt. By 1966, the resultant need for a massive increase in agricultural labor propelled the government to adopt labor mobilization policies based on collective "moral" incentives. For the next four years, Cuba attempted to rely upon the communist spirit among the people to develop an independent socialism while simultaneously constructing communism.

The period of communist construction culminated in the 1970 sugar harvest. Eight and one-half million tons of sugar were produced at the cost of the disorganization of the rest of the economy. The Cuban leadership came to recognize that planning and management systems could not operate the economy efficiently with the high degree of centralization utilized in the period of communist construction nor could the Cuban people work at a constantly high level without individual material incentives. The views of the leadership concerning both domestic economic organization and foreign policy came to coincide more closely with those of Cuba's major trading partner and source of both economic and military support, the Soviet Union. Since 1970, the Cuban leadership has accepted the hard reality that the period required to achieve socialist transformation, economic development, and independence must be measured not in years, but in decades if not generations. Soviet advice and assistance have been sought and accepted, while in every forum open to Cuba, this help has been gratefully acknowledged. Although efforts to achieve economic diversification and the multilateralization of external relationships continue, the Cuban leadership has implicitly accepted a period of dependency as necessary on Cuba's path to independent socialist development.

Discussion of the Cuban revolution by foreigners has generally been characterized by heated polemic, incorporating naive and sometimes intentional distortion. Many myths and misunderstandings have been put forth: that the acceptance of Marxism marked a rejection of the goals elaborated in the 1950s; that the use of moral incentives reflected a romantic escape from concern with economic development; that Cuba has merely exchanged dependency on the United States for dependency on the Soviet Union. This chapter sets out to provide a context in which to better understand why policy choices have been made, the significance of the outcomes of these choices, and the conditions limiting alternatives realistically available to the Cuban leadership.

The Cuban Development Strategy: Historical Stages

The Background

During the first half of the twentieth century the course of Cuban development was determined largely by external forces. The upper class, always dependent upon Spanish support during the colonial period, was constricted by a large U.S. economic presence following the demise of Spanish rule. In return for removing U.S. forces from the island, the

United States extracted Cuban agreement to a U.S. military base as well as the right of military intervention. The United States sent troops to Cuba three times in the first quarter of this century, partly at the invitation of the Cuban upper class. Cuba's monocultural economy was dependent on world economic conditions. Sugar prices dropped precipitously in the Great Depression, and the militant labor and student movements that had developed in the 1920s were able to overthrow the dictator Machado, who had been installed following the U.S. occupation of 1917–1923. The revolution of 1933 resulted in a struggle for power among the forces that had participated in bringing down the Machado regime. Again the U.S. intervened. In this instance a warship appeared off the coast while Special Ambassador Sumner Welles worked to secure a regime compatible with U.S. interests. The outcome was the first regime of Fulgencio Batista, who ruled from behind the scenes until 1940 and then as president for an additional four years.

In a very real sense, power did not reside in Cuba at all. Not only was Cuba generally vulnerable to fluctuations in the price of sugar, but much of the Cuban economy was directly controlled by U.S. investors. Moreover, the possibility of U.S. military intervention was always present. The importance of the U.S. market for Cuban sugar and tobacco subjected the Cuban economy to highly technical aspects of legislation passed by the U.S. Congress concerning postal regulations and the shipment of tobacco products (Smith, 1960). Thus, politics was not a struggle over the determination of policies that would determine the future of the country, but a fight for jobs and bureaucratic careers among those with education and little opportunity outside the government sector. A logical consequence was massive corruption within both the elected governments of the 1940s and Batista's second regime, which came to power in a coup in 1952.

Cuba in the 1950s was marked not only by political corruption but also by the still broader perversion of social life and institutions caused by tourism, much of it under U.S. Mafia control, combined with lack of employment. The economy was blocked. Sugar production, which accounted for about 80 percent of total exports, was effectively limited by a quota allotment set in the United States. A reciprocal tariff agreement also fixed the proportion of sugar exports to the United States that could be in a refined state to 22 percent. Since the agreement also provided that tariffs on U.S. products be fixed at low levels, economic expansion outside of the sugar sector was precluded by foreign competition. Opportunities for Cuban industry were also limited by the small national market. Rural poverty and unemployment were widespread (Zeitlin and Scheer, 1963:15–19). Approximately 400,000 cane cutters were employed only for the four-month sugar harvest each year. The large sugar plantations did not cultivate large portions of their land, but held the land nonetheless in order to deny the *macheteros* an alternative to seasonal labor. Those wishing to escape conditions in the countryside migrated to the cities, where they contributed to a surplus of labor and consequent low wages.

The government, particularly during Batista's second regime in the 1950s, was involved in distributing benefits among organized interests, from the allocation of sugar production quotas to intervention in wage settlements. The result was stagnation. Producers had neither the incentive to invest in modernization to increase productivity in the sugar sector nor the ability to compete with foreign imports for the limited domestic market. At the time of the revolution, annual per capita income was $200, as it had been at the beginning of the century (Bray and Harding, 1974:602).

Revolution for Reform (1953–1959)

In the course of the struggle against Batista, M26J, usually through its leader, Fidel Castro, issued a number of declarations and pamphlets. Despite some inconsistencies, these statements put forth a coherent set of objectives, an analysis of Cuba's problems, and a program for Cuban development.

At the most general level M26J sought dignity for all Cubans as individuals and for the nation. In the face of the existing corruption, M26J called for honesty. It promised fundamental economic security for all citizens through full employment and social welfare for those who could not work. Thus, Cubans would be able to reject such indignities as prostitution and military service in the army of a dictator. In contrast to the prevailing opportunism, the statements proposed that caring for the poor and forgotten, *los humildes* (the humble), would create a compassionate and just society made strong by its social solidarity. Together with a program of economic diversification through industrialization, the resultant unity would provide a basis for Cuba to regain independence.

Employment for those who could work and social welfare for those who could not were to be achieved through state guidance and assistance of an economy based on private enterprise. The key to the program was land reform, which would reduce rural unemployment and raise rural incomes. Better conditions in the countryside would keep the rural population from migrating to the cities, thus reducing the size of the urban work force and causing urban wages to rise. With protection for Cuban entrepreneurs and state help in mobilizing private capital for investment, manufacturing for an enlarged domestic market could flourish. State enterprise was explicitly rejected for all but utilities, which had discredited themselves through a history of low levels of investment, poor service and high rates. Even funds originally gained through corruption, when recovered, were to be used for social welfare rather than state investment. Foreign private investment was not precluded.

The program reflected the thinking then current among nationalists of the United Nations Economic Commission for Latin America, who argued that the long-term decline in prices of agricultural commodities and minerals relative to those of manufactured goods prevented development in monocultural export-oriented economies. They argued for domestically oriented economic diversification to reduce dependency on foreign imports, thus reducing the need to export primary products to earn foreign exchange for the purchase of imports. Onto this strain of progressive bourgeois Latin American thought was grafted the North American conventional wisdom of development — that import-substitution industrialization would create an enlightened and democratic middle class that would bring forth a reign of stability and progress.

Politically, the reformist program called for a multi-class coalition on behalf of *los humildes* for the benefit of all. In Castro's defense speech at the trial following the failure of the Moncada attack, he held out something for nearly everyone — education for all, land for the landless, full employment, better wages, lower rents and utility costs for workers, career opportunities for the middle sector, and business opportunities for the industrialists. He even called upon the soldiers and officers of Batista's military to recover their honor by joining with the revolution. The few large landowners who would be negatively affected were to be compensated for their losses. As for political organization, the program called for the reinstitution of electoral democracy. Unlike the sham of the 1940–1952 period, the government would be authentically democratic because the honesty and patriotism of its new leaders would call for active citizen participation from all sectors, thus insuring the continued democratic responsiveness of the government.

Despite the limited, reformist character of the M26J program, the movement insisted that its objective was radical social transformation. In a statement to a group of supporters at the Palm Garden in New York in November 1955 (which Castro apparently felt was sufficiently important to repeat in an article in *Bohemia* the following month) Castro stated:

> Look, the Cuban people want something more than a simple change of command. Cuba longs for a radical change in every aspect of its political and social life. The people must be given something more than liberty and democracy in abstract: decent living must be given to every Cuban. The

state cannot ignore the fate of any of its citizens who were born and grew up in this country. There is no greater tragedy than that of the man capable of and willing to work who suffers hunger with his family because he lacks a job. The state is unavoidably obliged to provide him with a job or to support him until he finds a job. (Bonachea and Valdes, 1972:283)

Rarely has such a limited economic program been expected to bring about so much social and political change. At the same time, ending corruption and providing the conditions for individual and national dignity would, in humanistic terms, have constituted a true revolution. As the revolutionary movement came to power at the beginning of 1959, it remained to be seen whether the economic reforms could provide private employment and public funds to accomplish the social goals. Moreover, the viability of a multi-class commitment to a program on behalf of the humble remained in question. If the program of economic reform proved to be insufficient to achieve social goals, which of the two would be discarded? And if some social classes opposed the new government, creating serious instability, would the leadership forsake its program in favor of the electoral mechanisms that permitted unity to be threatened?

Transition to Marxism-Leninism (1959–1961)

Upon coming to power, the new government enacted the urban reforms, including reduction of rents and utility charges that it had promised. The Rebel Armed Forces stepped up the combination of seizing and distributing land and securing military control that had begun in the later stages of the armed struggle. The first agrarian reform law was promulgated in May of 1959 and the previously rather hasty activities gradually became more orderly.

Almost from the first, the two premises upon which the reformist program was based proved to be invalid. After only a month in power, Castro decried the government's inability to deal with unemployment: "Here everybody speaks of unemployment. Here we must take measures to put an end to unemployment, but no one says how. Here everybody says that we must develop industry, that we must industrialize the country, but no one says how. With public works? With public works, can we give a job to a million unemployed? And where are we going to find the money for so many undertakings which will give jobs to the unemployed?" (1959:181) The government lacked the resources to generate employment. (As will be explained shortly, this is not to say that the reforms got a full chance to work.) Secondly, support for the regime among the upper classes quickly waned as the seriousness of its reformism became apparent. Despite symbolic gestures by a few entrepreneurs, such as the donation of tractors to support agrarian reform, a process of polarization soon began and grew rapidly. Moreover, the U.S. presence in the Cuban economy was so great that virtually any measure to reorient the economy would immediately affect U.S. interests. The United States quickly moved into opposition.

The preeminence that Castro had achieved during the armed stuggle was consolidated in the new government after some jockeying with the first president and his cabinet, who were generally moderate representatives of the middle sectors. Castro became the principal focus of government actions. As Edward Boorstein, a foreign economist working for the government, later reported, Castro oversaw and coordinated the growing struggle with the government's enemies and its efforts to mobilize supporters; political survival dominated the revolution. No other individual or agency could give comparable coordination to the organization of the economy (Boorstein, 1968). Although actions that fundamentally altered the character of the economy were taken, their impulse was initially political. As some entrepreneurs ceased production in order to reduce employment in an effort to bring down the government and others left the island, expecting to return in the wake of a U.S. invasionary force, the government intervened or nationalized their enterprises to maintain operations and employment. Nationalization of domestic enterprises was undertaken to strike against domestic opponents and against foreign holdings to retaliate for hostile actions by the United States. In June 1960, a commission was established to draft a new law governing the operation of foreign private corporations. Four months later there were no such corporations. The outcome of political conflict was the takeover of most of the private sector by the state, seemingly without coherent plan or intent.

The transition to Marxism-Leninism was characterized by a central continuity in the goal of a society characterized by justice and compassion in which Cubans individually and as a nation could maintain their dignity. Social solidarity as well as economic diversification, including import-substitution industrialization, were still seen as essential for national sovereignty. Ideological changes came about as adaptations to rapidly changing circumstances. Most important was the shift in the political base of the revolution. As the reality of social polarization undermined the concept of a multi-class coalition on behalf of the humble, the latter was replaced by a simplified Marxian class analysis that more accurately accounted for political developments. The basis of national unity was no longer to be a compassion shared among all classes, but solidarity of the working class in coalition with the peasantry. While all Cubans were invited to be part of the new society, the revolution was to be carried out by those classes who were to directly benefit from it and who formed, in fact, its strongest and most reliable support. As the political struggle led to nationalization of foreign holdings, these actions were supported by the concept that the economy must be in Cuban hands. And with the nation defined as a society of workers and peasants, only enterprises owned collectively could be considered to be under the control of the nation. Thus was the nationalization of domestically owned private firms explained.

With a class perspective came other elements of Marxism. The concept of exploitation had been completely absent from the statements of M26J. Concern had been expressed for the humble and the forgotten, and poverty and its attendant human degradation had been the focus, with little discussion of inequality per se. In all of his speeches and writings during the struggle against Batista, Castro had used the term *exploitation* only once. Even then, it referred not to a Marxian understanding of labor as the only creator of value and of wage labor as the appropriation of surplus value from the worker; rather, it was used only as a polemical expression to describe an instance in which bus drivers had been forced to accept a reduction in their wages. With the acceptance of a class perspective the labor theory of value followed naturally—that workers (and their peasant allies), who were the basis of the revolution and the future society, were the sole producers of value by their labor.

Adoption of the labor theory of value was also promoted by the need of the leadership to call upon the people to work and to accept pay in accordance with productivity. Economism in the labor movement had created a widespread impression that with socialism would automatically come wealth comparable to that formerly enjoyed by the bourgeoisie. In the early 1960s, the government emphasized the fact that government policies could aid only in the distribution of what wealth society had—that to the extent that justice consisted in providing adequate consumption levels for all, it would have to be achieved through development of the economy to a level that could provide the goods to satisfy these needs. The Marxian understanding of alienation followed naturally from class analysis and the labor theory of value as an extension of the petit-bourgeois radical humanism that had been expressed throughout M26J statements.

Somewhat later, the Leninist concept of political direction by a vanguard party was integrated into the perspective of the revolutionary government. The first cabinet of moderates had put off elections until the new government had become more secure. Subsequently, Castro attacked as hopelessly abstract the idea that institutional mechanisms can guarantee democratic government, pointing to the failure of bourgeois democratic regimes to act on behalf of the majority of their citizens. He related democracy solely to the output of government—who benefits—rather than how policy is made or decision makers selected. He proclaimed that, since the Cuban government manifestly acted on behalf of Cuban workers and peasants, the Cuban political system was far more democratic than those of nations with electoral systems. Elections were also deemed inappropriate at that point, since they encouraged division at a time when maximum unity in the face of foreign hostility was required. The question of future political arrangements was left open. For the time being, Cuba was a society in transition to be directed by its leaders, who obviously had the enthusiastic support of most workers and peasants and who engaged in and responded to a constant dialogue with the people. Because the goal was the transformation of society, it was necessary that a vanguard party be built, incorporating those who were at once the hardest workers and most morally upright, who also had the clearest vision of the socialist future.

Independent Socialist Development (1962–1965)

During the first three years of the revolution political survival was the near-exclusive preoccupation of the government as it implemented the initial reforms, engaged both foreign and domestic enemies, and organized and mobilized its supporters. Mobilization was both political and military, and included the antiilliteracy campaign of 1961. Other steps were taken to meet commitments to the peasants, such as construction of rural housing and provision of new health, educational, and cultural services to the countryside. While nationalizations had changed the role of the state in the economy, development planning was still focused on diversification of the economy and import-substitution industrialization. Sugar was a hated symbol of colonial oppression, and in 1960 and 1961 up to 20 percent of it was plowed under to plant crops that had formerly been imported.

Because the revolution had succeeded in large measure due to previous economic stagnation, it was not surprising that the first year or so of the new government saw a satisfying prosperity. Redistribution programs provided a market that stimulated the economy. Underutilized land and capital came into production. Moreover, stores and warehouses held sizable quantities of goods for which demand had been absent. The boom brought a wave of optimism to Cuban economists, who projected an incredible growth rate of approximately 15 percent per annum. Foreign visitors were only slightly less bullish. It appeared that the Cuban economy could simultaneously provide expanded incomes and services, invest for accelerated growth, and cope with the costs of diversification.

Concerned with avoiding debt that would threaten the country's newly-won independence, the government was conservative in its use of foreign exchange, at least to the extent permitted by its disorganization and weak controls. Only when the threat of economic blockade appeared were enterprises encouraged to go on a buying spree for imports regardless of cost.

In late 1961 and 1962 economic difficulties began to emerge. Shortages appeared and rationing was adopted to assure that commodities in short supply would be shared equally. An apparent preoccupation with quantity to the detriment of quality in production led to a major economic conference in August 1962. Economic planning, organization, and administration became priority issues. Moreover, it became clear that import-substitution industrialization would initially be import intensive. The purchase of capital plant for new industries required a huge amount of foreign exchange, and Cuba was going into debt at a rapid rate. In May of 1963 Castro announced that increasing debt could not be tolerated and that Cuba would expand sugar production to pay for its industrialization.

The significance of the reemphasis on sugar and even the origin of the decision to expand its production are not clear. In part it reflected knowledge gained in the first three years: that the upswing of the first year could not be projected into the future because it was based on the existence of unutilized capacity and an abundance of goods; that importation of capital plant was then beyond Cuba's means; that the infrastructure required by industrialization was lacking (e.g., the change of the primary trading partners from the United States to one six thousand miles away required the development of warehouses to hold imports for distribution, since in the past goods had been ordered in the quantities needed and had been available on short notice due to the proximity of ports in Florida and the U.S. Gulf Coast); that the flight of most of those who had experience in management had left the nation without a pool of personnel with the requisite skills to operate an industrial economy; and that replacement of sugar by other crops had resulted in a net loss of foreign exchange, because savings on foreign exchange earnings gained through reduction of agricultural imports had been less than the losses in sugar export earnings.

The expansion of sugar production made sense as what has been called a turnpike strategy (Barkin: 1973). Diversification and industrialization remained the goals, but it would be necessary to travel to this desired destination via the mechanization of agriculture and the expansion of sugar production — a longer route, but a faster and safer one. Sugar exports could pay for imports and avoid or reduce the growth of foreign debt. The emphasis would include not only sugar, but the modernization of all agriculture as part of a rural development project. Thus, diversification would be achieved in the entire agricultural sector, reducing the need for importation of food products (e.g., before the revolution, Cuba had consumed most of the lard output of Chicago's stockyards) while ensuring that the people would not lack food. Rural development would minimize if not eliminate the alienation of the rural population that was so dominant a part of the history of the Soviet emphasis on industrialization. Moreover, the concentration of national resources in the cities while the countryside was impoverished had been identified as a distorted pattern of development created by neocolonialism. The mechanization of agriculture would develop the industrial techniques and the management skills needed for the expansion of manufacturing in Cuba. Thus, the turnpike strategy appeared to be a way to guard Cuban economic independence while establishing the human and the financial bases for industrialization.

A question arises as to the origin of the reemphasis on sugar: Castro had made the commitment to an eight-million-ton harvest (raised to ten million tons a few months later) at the end of the decade upon his return from a two-month visit to the Soviet Union. The Cuban leadership was concerned at the rapid growth of debt, but Cuba's creditor was no doubt displeased with the situation as well. As in other instances in which Cuban and Soviet views coincided after a period of divergence, it is not certain whether the Cuban leadership had come to agree with the Soviet position or had been forced to concede to Soviet pressure. Cuba was experiencing economic difficulties and was dependent on Soviet sugar purchases because of the U.S. blockade. The threat of another military attack from the United States was quite real. Under these circumstances the Soviet Union could well have dictated a change in Cuban economic policy. The Soviet motive could have been a straightforward desire to receive payment for Soviet economic support, thus reducing the cost to the Soviet Union of its assistance to Cuba. Conceivably, the Soviet leadership may have wished to lock Cuba into a sugar monoculture, creating a permanent economic dependency. On the other hand, the Cuban leadership had all of the reasons just described to favor a turnpike strategy as a path to eventual economic independence. Additional support for viewing the decision as one initiated by or at least accepted willingly by the Cuban leadership lies in the proximity of the decision to the October missile crisis. Cuba had just been humiliated by the Soviet Union, which negotiated with the United States on matters vital to Cuban sovereignty and did not even have the courtesy to consult with the Cuban leadership. It had been made clear that the fruits of dependence on the USSR could be no less bitter than those of the earlier neocolonial relationship with the United States.

By the end of 1962, the disparate elements of the anti-Batista movement had been integrated into the United Party of the Socialist Revolution (PURS) under Castro's leadership, together with former members of M26J and of other elements of the coalition who had accepted the direction that the revolution had taken. The organizational strength of the Popular Socialist Party (PSP), the prerevolutionary, Moscow-oriented communist party, had been used to consolidate the revolution in the face of anticommunist opposition. In 1962, elements within the PSP that sought to challenge the predominance of the leadership focused around Castro were disciplined. Those who had opposed the radicalization of the first three years had either left the island or been subordinated. The U.S. campaign to overthrow the revolutionary government had been defeated in each of its escalating steps, from diplomatic pressure to economic sabotage and blockade to armed invasion. The balance of the 1960s would bring a secret war of sabotage and terror carried out by 600 to 700 U.S. operatives and over 1,400 Cuban counterrevolutionaries based in Florida, all working for the Central Intelligence Agency. In 1963, these agents would receive some support from farmers in the Escambry Mountains of south central Cuba; this led to a military response from the Cuban government, together with increased rural development efforts and a second agrarian reform law. Nonetheless, by 1962 the focus of the revolution had shifted from political survival to the organization of Cuban socialism.

Between 1962 and 1965, a debate took place over what kind of socialism Cuba would attempt to develop (see Silverman, 1971). The more conservative position advocated *auto-financiamiento* (self-finance), a more decentralized form of administration that permitted each state enterprise to finance its own investment plans through retention of earnings. This position argued that the greater autonomy of the firm that self-finance implied was a more efficient way of organizing production. Managers would be in direct control and would be able to deal more effectively with day-to-day operating problems. Moreover, prices would be established in relation to the cost of production and managerial behavior with respect to cost and quality control would be under the discipline of the market. Self-finance was also associated with the use of wage differentials, relating wages to actual contributions to production in order to motivate workers and maintain work discipline. It was argued that greater centralization was beyond Cuba's present capacity to plan and administer the economy, while reliance on the consciousness of managers and workers to stimulate optimal work performance was a voluntaristic hope beyond the level of development of the forces of production.

The opposing point of view, led by Ché Guevara, advocated *el sistema presupuestario de financiamiento* (central budgeting). Central budgeting was considered superior because it gave planners the capacity to mobilize resources for the transformation of the economy and the achievement of social justice. Self-finance, in this view, would allocate investment to the enterprises and sectors that were already strong, thus perpetuating the economic structure and the production mix established in the neocolonial period. Maintaining a close relation between prices and production costs would make production unresponsive to the needs of those with low incomes. Central budgeting advocated pricing based on social values rather than on costs. While recognizing serious problems that had already arisen in planning and administration, this position held that the difficulties were flaws in the new system that could be ironed out with experience and with efforts at raising the levels of consciousness of those in responsible positions. It was further argued that consciousness was not tied to the level of development of any single nation, but was a worldwide phenomenon, and that an advanced level of consciousness, in Cuba as in the rest of the world, had arisen in reaction to an advanced level of U.S. imperialism on a world scale. The feasibility of introducing collective incentives, basing wages not on individual contributions to production but relying on consciousness to stimulate work behavior, was said to have been demonstrated during the October crisis. In that instance production had risen despite the withdrawal from the work force of thousands of workers who had taken up positions to defend the nation. Moreover, use of market mechanisms and individual material work incentives were held to be destructive of the further development of socialist consciousness and progress toward communism.

As Bertram Silverman (1971) has pointed out, the components of each position – degree of centralization of investment planning, pricing policies, and work incentives – did not necessarily have to be put together as they were. For example, it is possible to set pricing policies to conform or depart from costs in either system of finance. Moreover, the Cuban version of *auto-financiamiento* was itself rather centralized. However, while the debate was ostensibly about economic organization, in reality it concerned distinct visions of the transition to socialism, one emphasizing efficiency and growth, the other popular mobilization and radical egalitarianism.

Fidel Castro expressed no opinion about the debate until 1966, although he advocated a fiscal conservatism that coincided more closely with self-finance. During this period, both systems were used in various sectors of the economy. At the end of 1965, the debate ended and the journals in which it had been aired were closed. Cuba embarked on communist construction.

Communist Construction (1966–1970)

In the 1962–1965 period, advanced socialism or communism was seen in rather conventional terms as a distant goal. First, it would be necessary to pass through a lengthy stage of socialist development in which both the level of the forces of production and socialist consciousness would be advanced. In 1966, however, communism became an immediate consideration in day-to-day decision making.

Communism was defined nationally as an economy operating without exchange relationships. "From each according to his ability" meant that people would work as a social duty; "to each according to need" meant that goods and services would be distributed without charge. A great mobilization campaign was undertaken in which people participated in agricultural work on a voluntary basis. Thousands went to farms near their homes after completing full workdays on their regular jobs and on weekends. They also worked on farms for periods of a month or more, particularly during the *zafra* (sugar harvest), while their coworkers who remained behind put in "guerrilla workdays" of up to fourteen hours to make up for the absence of the volunteers.

The volunteers did not receive extra pay for their extra work. However, workplaces that by their performance in both normal production and voluntary work contributions had earned the designation of advanced workplaces paid a full wage for sick pay and pensions and absenteeism was not disciplined by a reduction in pay. Instead, it was hoped that the example of the volunteers' enthusiasm would affect the slackers' consciousness.

An effort was also made to expand the free goods sector. No fees were charged for education, health services, some utilities, sports events, and local bus rides and telephone calls. Rents were set at a certain portion of income, with a 10 percent maximum. Rent was no longer collected on some housing units and it was proposed that in 1970 all rents would be eliminated. Volunteer work camps on the Isla de Juventud (Isle of Youth, formerly the Isle of Pines off the south coast) functioned essentially without money.

Work without monetary remuneration and the distribution of goods without charge were considered "islands of communist practice" — communist areas within socialist society. The path to communism would be through quantitative growth of these islands until they became dominant, representing a qualitative transformation of society. Thus, communism was not a completely separate stage of development following a lengthy period of socialist development. While Cuba was not yet a communist society, communism existed within socialism. Development meant the simultaneous construction of communism and socialism with the goal of ultimate qualitative change. Indications of progress were to be found in further cutting the tie between individual contributions to production and individual consumption: more voluntary work and expansion of the free goods sector with the ultimate aim of the extinction of exchange relationships and the significance of money.

In fact, money did lose much of its power to influence behavior. During this period, the rate of investment rose to over 30 percent of GNP. Only essential commodities were available, and virtually all of them were distributed through a rationing system at low prices. Consumption was allocated and limited by rationing as it had been previously by money (though, of course, with greater equality). The only items in the state sector for which money served as an allocative mechanism were meals in restaurants. Most people who did not trade on the black or gray (legal, but discouraged) markets could not spend their incomes. A sizable portion of the population had dresser drawers full of excess cash.

When asked about their future career plans, militant young Cubans enthusiastically responded that they would go wherever the revolution sent them to do whatever Cuba needed to be done. As Robert Bernardo (1971) has pointed out, the allocation of labor was no longer performed by the market. Moreover, the entire economic structure was centralized along the lines of the central budgeting position that Ché Guevara had advocated in the earlier debate. Administrative allocation of resources became still more dominant when in 1968 bars and other small private businesses, said to be undermining egalitarian distribution in the state sector through black market activities, were nationalized.

The use of moral incentives to construct socialism and communism simultaneously was explained as the use of consciousness to create wealth. Throughout the history of the Soviet Union, emphasis has been placed on development of the forces of production to a level at which more advanced relations of production would be possible. The Cuban leadership proclaimed its rejection of this strategy of creating wealth to build consciousness. Hardly disguising its references to the USSR, the Cuban leadership insisted that the use of individual material incentives as the basic stimulus in the economic development effort resulted in "selfishness amidst abundance." Instead, it was proposed that appeals to a consciousness of social duty would bring about the effort needed to raise the level of productive forces. The fruits of this labor would make it possible to expand the free goods sector and provide for greater social welfare for those unable to work. Experiencing the benefits of the collective effort would reinforce and advance consciousness still further. In this fashion socialism would be developed, while communist practice would expand until the realm of exchange relations was limited to a number of shrinking islands in the midst of a communist society.

While romantics and those familiar only with Marx's early work were exhilarated at Cuba's daring experiment, most foreign economists, Marxist and bourgeois alike, shook their heads. Reliance on collective incentives contradicted equally the concept of economic man on which bourgeois economics has been based and the Marxian understanding that the social relations of production cannot transcend the level of development of the forces of production. The Cuban leadership had a history of overoptimism, setting unrealistic goals, and wasting resources in the effort to fulfill them.

Given the risks involved in such a heretical violation of accepted economic truths, it seems unlikely that the moral incentives strategy was chosen exclusively because it appeared to avoid the possibility of achieving economic development while failing to develop socialist consciousness. An alternative explanation, proposed in part by Bertram Silverman (1973), focuses on the need to expand the agricultural workforce. Sugar cane is a perennial grass, yielding cane for several harvests. Weeding the cane fields had previously required large amounts of labor, but the use of herbicides applied by aerial crop-dusters had drastically reduced the size of the workforce needed for this phase of cane culture. Thus, the harvesting of cane, traditionally done throughout the Caribbean by the arduous and monotonous wielding of the machete, presented the greatest problem in expanding sugar production. As noted earlier, the goal of a ten-million-ton harvest in 1970, more than twice Cuba's average annual output, was announced by Castro upon returning from a visit to the Soviet Union. During that visit, the Soviet Union made a commitment to provide Cuba with cane-cutting machines. Early on, it was made clear that the mechanization of the harvest was regarded as essential. The problem of labor for the *zafra* was due not only to the size of the harvest; there was a shortage of *macheteros* because many had taken advantage of new opportunities to enter more desirable kinds of work. In 1965, Castro remarked that it would continue to be difficult to obtain labor for the harvest, though the situation was expected to improve with the arrival of cane-cutting machines by 1967. At this time Castro still endorsed a conservative fiscal policy, suggesting that he was not about to advocate full acceptance of central budgeting and moral incentives.

A few months later the moral incentives strategy—constructing communism and socialism at the same time—was implemented. It may be that the deciding factor was information that the mechanical harvesters would not be forthcoming. Just why the Soviet Union failed to deliver is not certain. Design of a machine was not easy. A harvester must cut the cane very close to the ground so that the cane will grow properly the following year; it must cut the tops and strip leaves that grow on the stalks; often it must perform these tasks while moving across hilly ground; and it must deal with a plant that does not grow in neat rows and that often lies at an angle rather than perpendicular. Machines were developed that could perform some of these functions, but it was clear that the expansion of sugar production would require a massive increase in the agricultural workforce, since most of the crop would nonetheless be harvested by hand.

Raising the needed workforce might have been accomplished through individual material incentives. However, given the physical hardship that cane cutting entails, substantial wage incentives would have been required to induce workers to leave offices or even factory jobs for the cane fields. Such incentives would have increased costs considerably, and the productivity of cane cutting is relatively low. The cost would have greatly reduced the net earnings derived from the industry. As it was the late 1960s was a period of severe austerity for the entire Cuban population. The use of material incentives would have meant concentrating the austerity among those not participating in the workforce. In concrete terms, it would have meant starvation for the old and ignoring the needs of children and those too ill to work. This would have violated a long-standing central value of the revolution. Moreover, strong material incentives to attract labor to the harvest would have rewarded unskilled labor at a higher rate than some other activities requiring greater skill or education. This would have undermined major efforts being made to prepare the workforce to develop the capacity to handle industrial operations, which remained an essential goal of Cuban development.

Aside from the moral incentives strategy with the unknowns it contained and the use of material incentives, two other options were available to the Cuban leadership to bring about the needed increase in agricultural labor. One was forced labor. This could have been accomplished by levying an extra work requirement upon all able-bodied citizens, to be enforced by severe punitive sanctions for those who did not comply. Or, a portion of the population could have been isolated from the rest, based on some real or invested characteristic, and that group interned in labor camps. During the moral incentives period, hierarchy in the workplace was increased, including the use of a military style of organization of the harvest. However, there is no evidence that the use of forced labor was even considered.

Finally, there were the options of giving up the economic goals of the revolution or accepting a very slow rate of growth. There is no indication that either of these options was considered. On the contrary, the moral incentive period was imbued with an attitude of aggressive optimism that identified the stage as one of austerity and sacrifice but expected extraordinarily rapid gains. The leadership appeared to believe that a few years of effort would bring a permanent solution to Cuba's problems. Developing the sugar industry would provide export earnings sufficient to finance industrialization without increasing indebtedness, and the program was to include much more than sugar. Throughout the period, Castro insisted that the effort in sugar was not intended to draw resources away from other sectors. Agricultural diversification and modernization were to continue and accelerate as well. In crops from garlic to rice and in dairy animals the plan was to hold down consumption in order to use most of the present yield for reproduction until the expanded production fulfilled domestic needs and even provided a surplus for export. There was a feeling that the need to import agricultural products as well as the problem of export earnings insufficient to finance industrial development could be brought to an end "once and for all." Cuba would emerge from the years of sacrifice with an economic base that could provide for independence and industrial development. Moreover, successful economic growth would enable the free goods sector to expand, reinforcing a growing communist consciousness and expanding the sector of communist practice.

On July 26, 1970, before more than a million people gathered in the Plaza of the Revolution, Castro offered his resignation. He blamed the leadership, including himself, for failing to effectively manage the industrial side of sugar production. Although production had exceeded the previous record harvest (of 1952) by about 20 percent, it was one and a half million tons below the goal of ten million tons, and the cost inflicted on the rest of the economy had been severe. In many areas of production output was only half what it had been. Castro praised the Cuban people, who had harvested enough sugar cane to exceed the goal by 10 to 20 percent, if the ratio of raw cane to processed sugar had been maintained at normal levels. Instead, the schedule for the modernization and expansion of grinding capacities in the mills had lagged. In some cases the work had not been completed until the big harvest was well underway. Breakdowns occurred due to problems in the newly installed capacity, which should have been solved before the cutting began, and because of inadequate maintenance of many of the old *centrales* (sugar mills). The cut cane lost much of its sugar content when breakdowns resulted in delays in milling.

A massive operation had been required to transport cut cane to operating *centrales* at greater-than-normal distances from the fields because closer ones had failed. This sometimes desperate effort had left much of the economy without transportation. Although production of steel rods to reinforce concrete had continued, the finished rods lay in the yards because they couldn't be moved to the cement plants. Breweries capable of their normal output lacked trucks to transport the finished product. Part of the problem was attributed to a failure to maintain the quality of the industrial workforce and its management and maintenance capabilities. Castro also blamed the economic organization, which had been centralized to a level that planning and management systems could not efficiently operate. He criticized technical and administrative personnel in the sugar sector for taking advantage of the priority that sugar had been given, drawing from other sectors resources that were not needed for sugar and that, in some instances, had not even been used.

In the period that followed the 1970 harvest, a critique of the moral incentives strategy was developed, beginning with the failure of consciousness alone to motivate the workforce or to guide managers toward efficient utilization of labor and material resources. By the November 1973 Congress of the Cuban Workers Federation (Confederación de Trabajadores Cubanos — CTC), this critique had been broadened and consolidated into a complete rejection of the theory of simultaneous construction of socialism and communism.

Dependent Socialist Development (1970–Present)

Whether the moral incentives strategy was adopted as a new road to communism or as the only acceptable means of increasing the agricultural workforce, it was rejected for its failings. A significant portion of the workforce was not stimulated to work solely by a desire to develop society; workers benefited not in relation to individual contributions, but as members of the collectivity without regard to individual work performance. Absenteeism was high and work productivity was low. Some jobs involving night work or other hardship (e.g., nursing) went unfilled. Some commodities whose consumption was not restricted by price or ration were wasted. For example, no charge was made for water, regardless of usage; as a result, leaks were not fixed. Managerial attention to conservation of resources was no higher than that of the general population. Without the discipline of either the market or effective central cost controls, emphasis was placed on meeting output goals. Workers were hired when they were not needed. Voluntary labor was evaluated by some managers at its cost to the enterprise and was employed in marginal ways as if it had no value.

Centralization caused a number of problems. The consequences of errors in planning and administration became more serious as centralization increased. As administration of many services became more distant from those who were served, a bureaucratic isolation grew. If stores and restaurants were poorly maintained, those who frequented them had no recourse. Conditions of mobilization and austerity led to greater hierarchy in the workplace. Unions declined, and the most able party cadres were drawn away from political tasks into administrative positions. As a result workers were unable to take the initiative when their instructions were inadequate or wrong. When management acted without concern for efficiency in the use of resources or for the welfare of the workforce, the workers could do little to correct the situation.

By 1970 discontent was considerable. Some of the causes were the years of austerity and shortages during 1970 caused by disorganization of production outside the sugar sector. There was frustration on the part of some of those who had contributed extra effort in voluntary work only to find their product consumed by slackers or wasted by inefficiency, as well as with the inability of workers to affect conditions in the workplace and of consumers to affect conditions in stores and restaurants. The leadership responded to the deficiencies of the moral incentives strategy and to the disagreement with a variety of measures intended to improve production, efficiency, and conservation of resources. The means adopted were reestablishment of the links between individual contributions to production and individual consumption, and decentralization and increased popular participation in the operation of economic and political institutions.

The reacceptance of individual material incentives as the principal source of motivation for work involved several measures. Following the socialist dictum, "to each according to his work," wage differentials were broadened, providing higher pay for jobs requiring greater skills, training, effort, or hardship. Higher pay was used to attract workers into less desirable occupations. The establishment of norms of satisfactory work performance was given priority, and overtime work was remunerated. The practice of maintaining historic salaries was stopped. (Previously workers had continued to receive the highest wage or salary they had ever earned, even when they had been transferred to lower-paying positions or when salaries for their positions [e.g., doctors] were reduced below prerevolutionary levels.) These changes were consolidated in a comprehensive salary reform initiated in July 1980. This reform increased salaries for the lowest paid workers and established pay scales within positions, rewarding job experience by setting salaries of workers with many years of satisfactory job performance at twice that of entry level pay. "Profit" sharing in the form of bonuses for workers in enterprises that exceed profitability norms was included, as well as reductions in benefits of workers in enterprises that do not meet expectations. Bonuses were instituted to reward exceptional work by individuals.

In order to make pay differentials effective in influencing work performance and career choices, it was necessary to reduce the quantity of money in circulation. Under previous policies the money supply had ballooned. In contrast to the past attacks on the use of money as means of allocating consumption, money had to "mean something" again. This was accomplished rapidly by reversing the trend toward free rent and expansion of the free goods sector and by making more consumer goods available for purchase. After much discussion throughout the country, a new social security law was promulgated that reduced pensions of workers who had retired from enterprises that had achieved the right to pay 100 percent pensions.

The leadership expressed regret at the necessity of reducing pensions, but affirmed the concept that rights can only be as advanced as the level of development of the forces of production. The effort to use consciousness to create wealth was criticized as an idealistic error. It was accepted that Cuba's level of development could not support reliance on consciousness as the principal stimulus for work or conservation of resources, for the expansion of the free goods sector, or for a high level of centralization in the organization of the economy. The new strategy adopted in the 1970s accepted inequality in consumption levels as necessary in the transition to socialism. Another aspect of the strategy moved toward a kind of equality that is more important in terms of assuring long-term development toward communism—mass participation in decision making.

In the second half of 1970 and the beginning of 1971, nearly all of those holding responsible positions were publicly criticized by Castro (who included himself among those deserving of criticism). Specific failures in performance were brought up as well as a general accusation that the leadership, which had been charged with the task of raising the consciousness of the masses, instead had much to learn from the workers. Hierarchy as well as overcentralization were criticized. The message was that the masses were at least as concerned as managers that production and other tasks be carried out efficiently and that they should have more power to solve problems in the workplace and elsewhere. Moreover, the leadership had learned much through very costly mistakes. If the masses committed errors, they too would learn from the process.

Decentralization and participation were introduced in several ways. In the workplace the unions, which had all but vanished in the late 1960s (Perez-Stable, 1975), were revitalized. They were rebuilt on a basis more democratic than any Cuba had previously known. The open elections and single slates that had characterized the unions for several decades were replaced in the 1970s by competitive elections for local leaders by means of secret ballot. While ultimate responsibility for each enterprise remained with management, roles were established for the union (to protect the interests of the workers in the enterprise), and for a local party representative (to reflect the general interests of society). Monthly assemblies were initiated in which individual workers could express complaints and grievances, which the management was required to investigate and to report on at the following assembly. Involvement of the workers in the formulation of the economic plan for the enterprise and in the establishment of work norms was also begun.

The workplace also became a site for worker participation in decisions related to distribution. While a portion of the expanded production of consumer goods is sold with no restrictions on the open market, workers' assemblies are also authorized to assign the right to purchase goods on credit at reduced prices. Their decisions are based on merit as evaluated by the workers, emphasizing work performance but including as well social contributions in activities such as voluntary work, participation in community projects, making blood donations, and serving as aides in schools. New housing built by workers in the enterprise is also distributed in this fashion.

In the 1970s voluntary work was refocused toward construction of housing and community facilities that are more directly and tangibly related to the benefit of those who volunteer. Although workers do not necessarily live in the apartments they have built, participation in voluntary work has been a component of merit that is considered in the allocation of housing. The program for the construction of housing and community social facilities, known as "plus work," also contains a new element of decentralization and self-reliance. Communities are encouraged to make proposals for projects to meet community needs. Resources are allocated by local, provincial, and central governments and the communities supply the labor. In this way, local initiative is developed. Also, in cases such as operation of a vehicle to provide emergency transportation for isolated towns, tasks such as maintenance become the responsibility of the community rather than of a centralized agency. At the beginning of the 1980s, the use of volunteers for housing construction was deemphasized, although other volunteer programs continue.

One of the most significant efforts to increase popular participation has been the creation of the Organs of Popular Power (Organos de Poder Popular – OPP). These institutions, begun on an experimental basis in a single province in 1974, oversee the operation of all local-level social services, schools, and economic enterprises within their jurisdiction. (Large enterprises of regional or national significance are administered by their respective national ministries.) Part-time representatives, who maintain their normal employment, are elected in jurisdictions of approximately eight hundred to twenty-five hundred citizens. The representatives meet together in municipal councils and attempt to resolve community problems and handle individual complaints and difficulties. Each representative must hold an assembly four times a year to hear complaints and suggestions and to report on past problems and what has been done about them. They are subject to recall, and several have been recalled since the program was begun. The municipal representatives elect provincial delegates, who deal with problems at that level and also elect delegates to the national level. The OPP has a limited role in policymaking, which is otherwise the responsibility of the Communist Party. It has reduced the distance between the citizen and local institutions, providing a level of power for local communities and performing an ombudsman function.

By 1970 most of the nation's human and material resources had been mobilized. In three areas, efforts have since been made to complete the process of incorporating the able-bodied population into the workforce. First, a portion of the plus work program contributes to more effective use of the workforce. Since many enterprises have been overstaffed, some workers were assigned to construction rather than to enterprises where they were not needed. At the beginning of the 1980s, management was given greater autonomy, but under the discipline of shadow profit calculations.[1] This change motivated managers to dismiss unneeded workers. Some of those dismissed (who receive government support while out of work) find employment in the Ministry of Construction, which is carrying out the projects formerly done by workers on leave from their enterprises. This change also accepts the possibility of some unemployment as a price worth paying to achieve more efficient management. Second, in 1971 a "law against parasitism" was promulgated after discussion in the mass organizations. This law provides that those who have no occupation and workers who consistently fail to report to their jobs may be penalized, including being compelled to do agricultural labor. While penalties have rarely been applied, over 70,000 workers who had not worked regularly during the moral incentives period registered for employment during the course of discussion of the law. Third, a major effort has been made to combat subjective as well as objective obstacles keeping women from entering the workforce.

With the process of mobilization virtually complete, it is not surprising that the major thrust, begun in the 1970s and intensifying as the decade ended, has been on increasing efficiency. Under the new system of management, large enterprises (*combinados*) have been broken up and smaller units with more autonomy created. This change has been made possible by the increasing number of trained personnel created in the past two decades of expanded education. Management now has more flexibility in meeting planned targets, and performance is evaluated in part by the relation of returns to costs. At the end of 1979, many changes were made in top ministerial positions, suggesting a deep concern with carrying out the new policies. Another element of economic change begun in the second half of the 1970s was a reduction in the role of the state in activities such as repair of residential electrical and plumbing systems. Individual plumbers and electricians have been licensed to work privately. Early in 1980, the state opened markets in the cities where small private farmers may sell their surplus at prices regulated by the state.

To promote conservation of resources, the government is evaluating enterprise performance with criteria that place more emphasis on costs (e.g., fuel used per ton of sugar produced by each sugar mill). Conservation has been promoted through a rate structure for utilities providing for very small charges for normally necessary levels of water and power usage, with escalating rates as usage increases. These efforts have been reinforced through major publicity campaigns.

Another area of change in economic policy evident at the beginning of the 1980s has been an effort to improve both the quantity and quality of goods and services. A larger quantity of consumer goods, particularly clothing, was taken off the ration list and made available for purchase despite serious losses in agriculture resulting from three epidemics: a tobacco fungus that destroyed virtually the entire 1979–1980 crop, a disease affecting a portion of the country's sugar cane, and an outbreak of African swine fever in the eastern provinces. Although part of the loss may have been made up by the sharp increase in sugar prices in 1980, the increase in consumer goods may also indicate a shift of some resources from investment to consumption. The change began a few months prior to the emigration of over 115,000 Cubans (slightly more than one percent of the population) to the United States. Although the timing of the changes precludes a link between the economic shifts and the emigration, it is likely that the proximity of the United States, a developed mass consumption society, will provide pressure to maintain increasing levels of popular consumption in Cuba.

With respect to quality, a major campaign was launched to encourage criticism of improper conduct and inefficiency of workers and managers and poor quality of goods and services. Efforts are being made to educate service workers to achieve a higher level of service to the public. The criticism campaign includes the creation of letters-from-readers columns in newspapers and a requirement that agencies and enterprises must respond to critical letters. Telephone numbers of agencies empowered to investigate complaints have been publicized on radio and television and in newspapers. The top leadership has also demanded that journalists stop using stock phrases and engage in more profound critical analysis of problems. Thus, the new economic direction combines individual material incentives and the acceptance of inequality based on contributions to production with an effort toward greater popular participation and increased responsiveness of agencies and enterprises.

At the beginning of the 1980s, Cuba is still economically dependent. Although the economy has expanded, sugar still accounts for about the same proportion of foreign exchange earnings as it did before the revolution. Nonetheless, much progress has been made and the economy is now more diversified. A modernized fishing industry provides fish for domestic consumption and export, replacing an "industry" whose technology resembled that in Hemingway's *Old Man and the Sea*. A dairy industry has been created, and agricultural production now includes many crops not previously grown. Infrastructural development in both industry and agriculture has been considerable. (For example, water resources have been harnessed for both flood prevention and irrigation, and electric output has more than tripled.) Industrial production has been diversified to some extent (e.g., production of bus chassis and pharmaceuticals) and expanded. Processes of cane loading and transport have been mechanized. Chemical fertilizers and mechanical cane harvesters are now produced in Cuba. Moreover, one of the most important accomplishments of the last twenty years has been the development of a universally literate labor force, a large and ever-growing proportion of which possesses technical training and skills. Thus, genuine progress has been made toward industrialization. The financing of this process will be enhanced by the development of Cuba's substantial nickel resources, which is currently under way with major loans and assistance from the Soviet Union.

Economic Dependence and Cuban Policy Choices

Since 1970, Cuban concepts of economic organization and Cuban foreign policy have coincided with those of the Soviet Union. Because the USSR is Cuba's major market for sugar as well as a principal source of petroleum and economic and military assistance, it is possible that the USSR is dictating policy to Cuba. This section will briefly examine the context of Cuban policies, which leaves this question in doubt.

Why was the moral incentives strategy rejected in 1970 in favor of one closer to economic concepts used in the Soviet Union? On one hand, disorganization of the economy and significant discontent among the people placed Cuba in a weak position. An ultimatum to conform to Soviet policies or be cast adrift as China had been ten years earlier would have threatened the Cuban leadership. On the other hand, the decision could well have been one of abandoning an approach whose failures had led to this vulnerability. Moreover, by 1970 Cuba no longer had to rely on mobilization. Progress had been made in the mechanization of the sugar harvest, including cutting the cane. (Mechanization increased throughout the 1970s.) Also, in the late 1960s, an institutional net was created that ensures that most Cuban youth will participate in agricultural tasks. Such work is part of the school curriculum, particularly in the schools-in-the-countryside program in which children attended boarding schools where they work for a portion of each day in addition to their studies. The armed forces were given a larger role in the harvest (a tendency that was reversed when Cuba moved toward a military force based on a more sophisticated weaponry). Idle youth who were not attending school, in the armed forces, nor employed elsewhere were conscripted into the Army of Working Youth, which performed agricultural labor. In summary, while Cuba was vulnerable to Soviet pressure, the rejection of the moral incentives strategy could simply have been the outcome of the domestic situation, a reappraisal of the problem of socialist development in light of the experience gained in the second half of the 1960s, and changes that reduced the need to rely on mobilization.

Changes in Cuban foreign policy toward concurrence with Soviet policy present a similar picture. During the period of communist construction (1966–1970), Cuban foreign policy differed from Soviet policy as much as did their concepts of economic organization and incentives. By the start of that period in 1966, the United States had blockaded Cuba and secured Cuba's ouster from the Organization of American States (OAS). In the Western Hemisphere, Cuba had diplomatic relations only with Mexico and Canada. Latin American communist parties allied with the USSR rejected armed struggle and attempted to gain legitimacy and legal recognition in order to participate in electoral politics. The Cuban leadership appeared to believe that Cuba's breaking out of isolation required the establishment of revolutionary socialist regimes in Latin America. Symbolic support as well as training and some financial backing were given to armed struggle. At the meeting of the Organization of Latin American Solidarity in January 1967, literally held under a banner proclaiming that "the duty of every revolutionary is to make revolution," Castro strongly criticized the Moscow-oriented parties. Cuba advocated the *foco* strategy of armed revolution and backed Ché Guevara's ill-fated mission to Bolivia in 1967. The slogan "Two, three, many Vietnams" also suggested that the possibility of a U.S. invasion would be diminished by armed struggle elsewhere in Latin America.

At the beginnning of 1968 Castro responded to a reduction in Soviet oil shipments, stating that "Cuba is alone" (in contrast to his acknowledgement of support in the confrontation with the United States years earlier, when he said, "Cuba is not alone"). Cuba's position with respect to the Soviet invasion of Czechoslovakia eight months later is suggestive of the state of Cuban-Soviet relations. The intervention was condoned as a political necessity, accepting the Soviet explanation that foreign agents and counterrevolutionaries were about to restore capitalism in Czechoslovakia. That concession to the USSR—a fragment of Castro's speech—was preceded by a dismissal of Soviet claims that the intervention was legal because it had been in response to an invitation from the recognized government. The justification for condoning the invasion, political necessity, was a peg on which Castro hung the greatest portion of the statement, a condemnation of the Soviet approach to socialist development, which, after twenty years, led to such popular disaffection that the Red Army was required to prevent a return to capitalism. The speech concluded by noting the dangers to Cuba involved in condoning the invasion of a small country by a large neighbor in violation of international law and suggesting that Soviet troops would not be dispatched to save Cuban socialism if the United States chose to invade. This "support" of the Soviet action was so unpalatable to the USSR that *Pravda* hardly took note of it, in spite of the Soviet desire for evidence of approval in the face of massive international condemnation.

Cuban foreign policy began to move toward concurrence with Soviet policy while Cuba was still pursuing the moral incentives strategy. One of the turning points may have been the progressive military coup in Peru late in 1968. Although it was not a revolution and it soon became clear that the junta was attempting to represent the interests of the weak Peruvian national bourgeoisie rather than the workers and peasants, relations were established between Peru and Cuba. In the next few years, relations were established with Chile, and Cuba and several other Caribbean nations began to participate with other Latin American countries in a variety of multilateral economic associations. The U.S. economic blockade was crippled by the actions of Canada and even Argentina, which forced

U.S. firms operating on their territory to sell their products to Cuba. Contrary to the earlier view, Cuba's reintegration into the hemisphere did not require revolution in Latin America. Meanwhile, the threat of military action against Cuba by the United States had virtually ended with the absorption of U.S. military power in Southeast Asia.[2]

The feasibility of armed revolution in Latin America was also called into question. Ché's death in Bolivia in October of 1967 was painful evidence of deficiencies in the foco theory. The Cubans, in supporting armed struggles in Latin America, had experienced not only failures but cases of fraud, in which material support had been used for other purposes. Cuban foreign policy in the 1970s was characterized by support of nationalist actions of recognized governments in Latin America against U.S. domination. Cuba has taken in and cared for many wounded revolutionaries and the orphans of some who had died in revolutionary struggles (as well as large numbers of Chilean refugees). However, active support for the armed overthrow of existing governments has been limited to the final stages of struggle, when a well-organized movement has developed enough domestic support to succeed. For both positive and negative reasons, it would appear that the shift in Cuban foreign policy was a response to Cuban needs and a reappraisal of conditions, irrespective of Soviet pressure.

Since the mid-1970s the most visible element of Cuban foreign policy has been in Africa. Cuban involvement on the African continent began not long after the revolutionary government came to power. A small number of Cubans in various capacities have developed a first-hand familiarity with the situations of various countries as well as with leaders of many African nations and liberation movements.[3] Cuba's first major armed role in Africa in support of the Popular Movement for the Liberation of Angola (MPLA) government coincided with a Cuban desire to increase its prestige and establish a role as a leader of the Third World. The Cuban leadership has also perceived the involvement in Angola as an opportunity to strengthen the revolutionary consciousness of the Cuban people through this act of international solidarity. Cubans have participated directly in the fighting and have first-hand experience with conditions of poverty and deprivation far more severe than those most Cubans knew even before the revolution. Opinion within Cuba concerning this major involvement is divided. While a consensus exists in support of the ideal of international proletarian solidarity, many Cubans feel that their nation cannot afford the costs of the effort at this time. Although Cuba's interests in Angola are limited to a gain in prestige abroad and a contribution to consciousness at home, the Soviet stake in Angola is also a more general gain in Soviet influence in Africa. Thus, the evidence is not decisive in determining whether the Cuban-Soviet effort in Angola arose out of Cuban or Soviet initiative.

Cuban support for the Mengistu regime in Ethiopia suggests a rather different situation. The Soviet Union has a more direct strategic interest in the Horn of Africa. Some Afro-Cubans trace their origins to the region of contemporary Angola, but no such link exists between Ethiopia and Cuba. Cuba entered the fighting in Angola to combat an intervention in that country's civil war by South African troops. Cubans fought on the side of Ethiopia against Somalia to maintain existing boundaries in the Ogaden region, a position that was endorsed by the Organization of African Unity but that lacked the sort of appeal accorded by the nonaligned movement to the defense of Angola. More recently Cuba has provided logistic support for Ethiopian military campaigns against the Eritrean liberation movement, which Cuba had formerly supported. Although the official Cuban analysis of the Ethiopian regime describes a progressive government based upon enthusiastic popular support (Valdés Vivó, 1977), Cuba has made efforts to provide at least room for maneuver for the left opposition to Mengistu within Ethiopia. It has also attempted unsuccessfully to move the Ethiopian regime to seek a negotiated settlement in Eritrea rather than pursue military victory. Such a settlement would conform more closely to what appears to be the true Cuban perspectives and would provide an opportunity for Cuba to sharply reduce its role in Ethiopia. For all these reasons, the Cuban role appears to be one of attempting to make the best of a bad situation, of attempting to make their involvement more positive from a Cuban point of view since, apparently, it cannot be terminated, possibly because of Soviet pressure for Cuba to remain in Ethiopia.

Military intervention in Ethiopia may be one case in which Cuban economic dependence determined an important foreign policy. Other policies, both domestic and international, would appear to be oriented toward the needs of Cuban socialist development as understood by the Cuban leadership in light of the experience of the revolution and in response to changing conditions. Soviet military and economic assistance were vital to the initial survival of the Cuban revolution. Many Cubans confirm that both the austerity and the militarization of work that occurred in the late 1960s would have been far more severe and of much longer duration without Soviet aid. The end result of aid has been twofold. On one hand, a large debt has been accumulated that ties Cuba to the USSR. On the other, Cuba is developing an economy that will eventually require a lower proportion of trade to national production. The necessity of earning foreign exchange to pay for imports will become a lesser burden in relation to overall economic activity. Moreover, diversification in both the export sector and domestic production will shift exports from excessive reliance on sugar toward a more stable and balanced aggregate, including nickel, citrus fruits, fish, and other products.

Beyond Economic Dependence:
Socialism and Independence

The Cuban revolution cannot be comprehended by those who attempt to understand this complex historical phenomenon as a Soviet plot, whether the Cuban leadership is seen as a naive victim or a sinister coconspirator. Although not every statement of a Cuban leader should be taken at face value, we would assert that the goal of a just, compassionate, and independent society that has been enunciated from the beginning is authentic. In this final section, we will attempt to place the struggle for this goal in historical context. Our objective is to note the significance of some conditions specific to Cuba and others that have confronted all societies to date that have attempted socialist transformation. Our conclusion, in a nutshell, is that Cuba had no choice but to accept economic dependence. The argument is as follows: although the costs, in several respects, of the Ethiopian intervention are indeed significant, the revolution has not been distorted in any fundamental way by economic dependence; economic dependence is not permanent but only a stage during which Cuba is vulnerable; the great danger lies in the possibility that a gap leading to political dependence could open between the leading strata of Cuban society and the masses; and finally, preventing such a gap requires that Cuba successfully deal with the contradictions inherent in breakaway socialism. Before pursuing this point, we must briefly examine some relevant aspects of imperialism and dependent capitalism in order to identify potential similarities in the relations between small breakaway socialist nations and more advanced socialist states and those between imperialist countries and their dependent capitalist clients.

Dependent Capitalism

Imperialism and dependent capitalism form a single phenomenon. Imperialism is the structure of domination emanating from the capitalist system's center. The most obvious mechanisms of control are overt use of military force, manipulation of foreign debt, and control of access to essential commodities. Other manifestations of external control operate within the neocolonial nations, most importantly foreign ownership and control of the domestic economy. The other side of the structure of domination is the establishment within dependent capitalism of comprador classes whose interests are allied with imperialism. *Latifundistas* (owners of large estates) whose land produces crops for export, commercial capitalists who derive their income from import-export trade, nationals employed as local managers of foreign firms, and military commands that rely on foreign sources of sophisticated equipment and training all have a direct stake in maintaining the structure. Other classes that benefit from the status quo are also tied, though less directly, to the extent that the disruption that could be imposed by the center could cause them to be deposed by their own exploited classes. All of these classes function as an internal political constituency in support of imperialism. Cultural penetration reinforces this structure, promoting acceptance of long-term goals (e.g., the consumer society), that are compatible with imperialism.

Internal support of imperialism among the comprador classes maintains the structure, obviating the need for overt actions by the imperialist power in times of normalcy. Within the structure, conflicts exist between the comprador classes and the interests of the center. Efforts by the former to press their interests are constrained to the extent that they rely upon support from the center to maintain their domestic position. They are always somewhat weak because they are in charge of a system of exploitation. Defying imperialism will be costly for any economically dependent nation; comprador classes cannot accept these costs because of their political dependency on the center.

Dependence and Breakaway Socialism

Of course, a state or otherwise collectively owned and planned economy may be subject to economic dependence through reliance on more powerful trading partners and through foreign debt. Foreign control over enterprises is precluded if direct foreign investment is prohibited. State control of the institutions that shape ideology and cultural values permit the state to avoid or limit cultural penetration. While some socialist countries must accept temporary economic dependence, the central problem is preventing the development of political dependence. That is, national solidarity based on an identity of interests between leadership strata and the masses must be maintained. In this way, the danger of developing a comprador party or state apparatus is precluded. On the contrary, solidarity enables the leadership to rely upon the masses to accept great sacrifices, should they become necessary to defy a country that is attempting to use economic dependence to impose policies that fundamentally distort the process of socialist development.

The need to prevent the opening of a gap between leading strata and the masses in the transition to socialism exists in all socialist countries.

However, for those countries able to avoid economic dependence the consequences of such a gap are bureaucratic distortions of the sort present in the Soviet Union. Bureaucratic distortion in economically dependent countries leads to political dependence and client status.

"Breakaway socialism" refers to countries such as Cuba, the USSR, China, the nations of Eastern Europe, and all others that currently describe themselves as pursuing socialist transformation following a Marxian understanding. In all these countries a socialist leadership with state power emerged because of the contradictions of imperialism and imperialist wars, rather than as a result of the contradictions of a fully developed capitalism. These nations have been propelled by a different, though related, set of contradictions to break away from the international capitalist system before the process of integration and closure created the contradictions that can bring about socialist revolution throughout the world capitalist system.

In a variety of critically important ways, socialism is not born directly from the womb of a dependent capitalism that contains strong precapitalist elements. The basic political contradiction for breakaway socialism, which was first confronted by Lenin, is the absence of a numerically dominant, politically conscious, and organizationally adept proletariat. The working class does not rule through the leadership of a vanguard party (Colletti: 1977). Instead, the party leads on behalf of a class still in formation. The basic economic contradiction is a low level of economic development, unsuited to efficient planning, with a level of production too low to support socialist relations of production. When the party uses its power to appropriate the surplus produced by workers and peasants in order to centralize and invest it for capital accumulation, it is performing the task of the bourgeoisie in capitalist development. Within breakaway socialism, there is an ever-present tendency for the party (and the technocrats whose contribution to this process is highly valued) to assume a role comparable to that of a bourgeoisie. The leading strata tend to develop an interest in diverting sociopolitical development from socialism. Instead, it may seek to stall the development of the social relations of production, using power gained in the process of revolution and the struggle for capital accumulation to discipline the workers to press on with economic development, the benefits of which it appropriates.

The Soviet Union has followed a conception of socialist development that envisions a highly segmented, two-stage process. Alteration of the social relations of production in order to eliminate hierarchy in political and economic institutions and, eventually, classes is reserved for the second stage. The first stage, of undetermined length, is preoccupied with raising the level of the forces of production to support the transformation in the second stage as well as to meet the needs of national defense. In this strategy, heavy industry is emphasized as the key in developing the forces of production. Agriculture is placed in a subordinate role; the agrarian sector is to provide a surplus for capital accumulation in industry. Within the industrial sector, light industry is secondary to heavy industry.

The sociopolitical consequences of this conceptualization of socialist development are far-reaching. Capitalist development eliminates the peasant classes, but in breakaway socialism the peasantry is a major, if not the dominant, segment of the population. The policy of placing agriculture at the service of industry dismisses the peasantry as a politically regressive force and accepts its alienation from the project of socialist development. Subordinating light industry to heavy industry, even though the former may be developed more quickly, reduces the capacity to fulfill the immediate needs of the population. The forces of production are conceptualized as the advancement of technology. Specialization, individual material incentives, hierarchy and discipline within the workplace, and the diffusion of mechanization are relied upon to increase productivity and production. Because the understanding of the forces of production emphasizes hardware to the exclusion of developing the working class as part of the forces of production, investment in human resources is secondary to capital accumulation. Ownership of the means of production is seen in juridical terms. In this sense each person, from the factory manager and the state planner down to the sweeper of the factory floor, is both an owner of the means of production and a member of the working class. The possibility of class contradictions in the process of socialist development is denied.

While this strategy of socialist development is in its early stages, it is possible to appeal to the enthusiasm of the worker for voluntary sacrifice. And in times of crisis (such as the defense of the Soviet Union in the Second World War), patriotic nationalism can be a source of identification with the collective welfare. However, the end result is cynicism. The elites[4] are infused with bureaucratic careerism. If conditions permit an increase in levels of consumption, a benign political apathy develops among the masses. If continued hardships are imposed, particularly if the elites appropriate widespread privileges to themselves, the resulting hostile alienation and sporadic resistance among the workers are met by repression. Society seems to stall in the stage of socialist accumulation as management of the masses by the elites becomes a seemingly permanent task, replacing the goal of the transformation of social relations.

Maoism provides the major alternative strategy to that of the Soviet

Union. Shaped by its own experience of struggle with important differences in demographic and historical conditions (for example, see Magdoff, 1975) and with the benefit of the experience of other nations, Maoism gives equal emphasis to the social relations of production and the development of productive forces. A sectoral balance is employed, giving some emphasis to light industry over heavy industry, with industry serving the needs of agriculture. Although taxation of agriculture is used to support industry, it is limited, and agricultural organization is decentralized, with the communes permitted to retain and invest much of the surplus produced. While technological advancement is valued, the policy of "walking on two legs" recognizes the value of traditional, labor-intensive methods as well. Mechanization is employed principally to increase production rather than labor productivity. Regional as well as national self-sufficiency are given priority and efforts are made to diffuse industry throughout the country rather than centralizing investment in areas where some industrial base already exists.

This pattern of investment encourages development of the peasantry as the essential political base for the project of socialist development. The communes are able to benefit from their increases in production, through investment both in agriculture and in light industry. Hierarchy is discouraged in the workplace and in virtually all other institutions. The transformation of social relations, giving participation in decision making to the masses, reduces alienation and strengthens identification with the project of socialist transformation. A mixture of work incentives is used, combining individual material incentives with collective material incentives and the enthusiasm arising from participation in decision making. While participation in decision making involves the masses, the elite strata are required periodically to engage in common tasks, particularly in agriculture, in order to reduce elitist perspectives. Maoism also recognizes that the process of socialist development contains within it a tendency for elite strata to acquire separate interests and a more conservative, technological ideology, in spite of these antielitist, antieconomistic policies. It recognizes an ongoing class struggle within socialist development that is fought continuously on the ideological level.

Emphasis on equality and mass participation, with its attendant constraints on elite strata and the priority given to a general increase in technological advancement among the masses and across regions, reduces the rate of development of advanced technology. As the experience of the Cultural Revolution and its aftermath demonstrated, Maoism carried to extremes results in a literal attack on all specialization and on the development of technical knowledge as well as the disorganization of the economy. Chinese history since 1949 is one of dialectical alternation of periods emphasizing Maoism and those of consolidation, in which major elements of the Soviet strategy have been employed. It is unclear whether or not this dialectical pattern will continue.

Given the dual needs of breakaway socialist countries for development of both the productive forces and the level of social relations of production, a strategy with a single emphasis cannot work. An emphasis exclusively on the forces of production appears to give both power and legitimacy to technocratic strata. These strata tend to develop an ideology and an interest in transforming themselves into a class that appropriates to itself the task of managing a society permanently stalled in the first stage of socialism. On the other hand, overemphasis on the advancement of productive relations appears to create waste and inefficiency to an extent that severely limits economic progress. The masses as well as overburdened managers and technocrats become frustrated, causing a reaction in favor of a radical shift toward emphasis on the productive forces.

This problem is exacerbated for those breakaway socialist states that must accept a period of economic dependence. During this period, any gap between the leadership and the masses can create a dangerous vulnerability to the introduction of political dependence. The gap reduces the capacity of the leadership to call for sacrifices to resist economic sanctions by the power on which the nation is dependent. At worst, a gap so great that mass resistance arises could lead to reliance of the leadership on external support against the masses.

Ironically, policies that stress equality to the detriment of material living conditions tend to increase the gap. Emphasis on economic development and the improvement of material living conditions tends to give rise to elitism within the technocratic strata. By alternating emphases, these tendencies can be controlled by a political leadership that maintains its independence from the technocrats as well as its revolutionary commitment. Historical experience thus far suggests that a balancing political role can be played by a leadership that possesses the vision and the prestige acquired in the initial seizure of state power. The rise of a second generation of leadership brings with it the likelihood of the penetration of the political leadership by technocratic and bureaucratic perspectives.

The Cuban Effort to Achieve Independent Socialism

Bourgeois critics of the Cuban revolution point to Cuba's reliance on the USSR as if economic dependence had been invented by socialism. They ignore Cuba's colonial heritage, the monocultural economy developed under Spanish rule and reinforced rather than ameliorated within the orbit of U.S. imperialism. They also seem to forget that Cuba sought to continue U.S. trade and tourism, while the United States abruptly stopped the purchase of sugar and then established an economic blockade. It was the U.S. effort to bring about the overthrow or the surrender of the revolution that caused Cuba to trade predominantly with the Soviet Union.

Maoist critics seem to imagine Cuba as a miniature China. They fail to recognize that policies of self-reliance were simply inappropriate in Cuba. As a highly underdeveloped country, Cuba's capacity to produce an economic surplus was far more developed than that of China (with a per capita GNP about five times greater). Foreign trade was equal to about 30 percent of GNP, a typical situation with dependent capitalism. Economic activity in sugar, tobacco, and tourism was highly vulnerable to external attack. At the same time, the society was structured to utilize foreign exchange earned in these sectors to import many basic necessities (as well as luxuries). Even if subjective conditions in China and Cuba had been identical, a policy of self-reliance would have had far more severe ramifications for Cuba. For Cuba it would have meant not simply forgoing the more rapid rate of economic growth made possible by foreign technology, but the loss of a capacity to import necessities. And subjective conditions were not the same. Labor unions were more important in Cuba and they were characterized by economism. Cultural penetration and the demonstration effect were far more advanced in Cuba and had oriented the population toward consumer goods and an emphasis on technology as the way to increase production.

The Cuban leadership has consistently demonstrated an awareness of the problems of economic dependence. Given both the objective and subjective conditions, it is not surprising that emphasis has been placed on development of productive forces through acquisition of advanced technology. As noted earlier, the leadership appears to have had an unrealistic optimism concerning what could be accomplished in the initial years of the revolution. In particular, it was thought that import-substitution industrialization, together with agricultural diversification, would ameliorate dependence by reducing the need for foreign exchange earnings to pay for imports. When the effort proved too costly, it was largely deferred to expand export earnings from sugar to finance import substitution without external debt. In the 1970s, the economy recovered from the disorganization produced in preceding years and grew, though as the decade progressed, inflation in the cost of imports from capitalist countries became an increasing burden slowing industrial growth. During this period considerable infrastructure was built and some industrialization occurred. Even though expansion of export earnings was a major element of the strategy, the focus on agriculture also substantially reduced dependence on food imports. Expansion in areas such as cement production and the establishment of domestic production of basic pharmaceuticals has moved Cuba toward economic independence. When nickel development has been completed, Cuba will possess another important source of export earnings. Responding to increasing costs of imports, conservation of resources has been stressed. And the leadership has advocated further diversification of sources of foreign exchange, exporting products initially developed to satisfy domestic needs (Castro: 1978; see also Thomas, 1974, in which small countries are advised to adopt this basic strategy).

Cuba is moving toward economic independence. While the substantial debt to the Soviet Union will be a burden for many years to come, the economy is nationally owned and controlled. Greater internal integration has been achieved, requiring fewer imported intermediate products. A single, very important exception is petroleum, which is needed in growing volume due to increasing mechanization in agriculture as well as industrial development. Since the Soviet Union is expected to curtail its petroleum exports and because Cuba lacks virtually all conventional sources of energy, the Cuban economy will be hard-pressed to finance petroleum purchases and to develop alternative sources such as alcohol from agricultural products, solar energy, and possibly nuclear energy. (Cuba's first nuclear power plant is scheduled to be completed in the mid-1980s.)

Although Cuba has stressed the development of productive forces as a means to independent socialist development, not all elements of the Soviet strategy have been adopted. Most evident is the emphasis on agriculture, which has had a role parallel to that of heavy industry in the USSR. Since much of the peasantry was converted into an agricultural proletariat during the period of capitalist development, the peasantry has been a much smaller segment of the population than in the USSR or China. In contrast to Soviet policy, the private sector in agriculture remaining after the creation of state farms and cooperatives on 70 percent of the land has received favorable treatment. And in part because of the availability of industrial goods from the USSR and Eastern Europe, Cuba has been able to emphasize light rather than heavy industry.

Cuba attempted to use consciousness, presumably a product of an advanced level of social relations of production, to develop the forces of production, but it was not until the 1970s that much was done to transform the social relations of production. Shortly after the revolution came to power Technical Advisory Councils were organized, providing workers with a role in workplace decision making. However, they did not become significant and were phased out. Although investment in human resources has been at a very high level, suggesting an element of Maoist rather than Soviet strategy, change in the social relations of production has been more modest. The use of moral incentives, seen by some as an indication of Maoist practice, was in fact fundamentally different. The period of communist construction in Cuba was accompanied by increased centralization rather than Maoist decentralization. Hierarchy in the workplace was increased and the low level of participation in decision making provided by unions was diminished still further. With respect to transformation of the social relations of production, the period of communist construction was a step backward.

Certainly the moral incentives strategy relied upon the consciousness and enthusiasm of the masses. During the 1962–1965 debate, the argument on behalf of moral incentives contended that an adequate level of consciousness had been developed in reaction to imperialism. During the period of communist construction, material incentives as well as use of the market were criticized as having a negative impact on consciousness because they "put dollar signs in people's heads." The Maoist concept that enthusiasm and reduced alienation flow from participation in decision making was not emphasized until 1970. Despite the efforts at politicization involved in the mobilization of the second half of the 1960s, some of which spilled over into areas such as education, with an emphasis on "red" rather than "expert," policies during that period were closer to mobilization in the USSR during the second war than to the Great Leap Forward or the Cultural Revolution in China.

The policy shift begun in 1970 contains elements that encourage elitism and a growth of a gap between the leadership and the masses as well as others that promote the capacity of the masses to maintain the movement of productive relations toward advanced socialism. Measures undertaken to improve the workings of the economy have a tendency to legitimize inequality and the superior position of managers. Salary differentials and the availability of automobiles and consumer durables create some important differences in living standards. While the crucial areas of access to education, housing, health care, and culture are not affected by salary differences, a portion of the population is acquiring goods that are relative luxuries beyond the income of the majority. These rewards for educational attainment and work performance, together with the threat of unemployment (though the latter is far milder than in capitalist countries), encourage an individualistic, acquisitive mentality inconsistent with advanced socialism. The increased use of economic considerations in management, though vital to improved economic performance, has a similar effect. At the same time, these economic policies are in accord with the nation's level of development. Thus, the gap between the officially sanctioned morality and the morality that can be supported by existing material conditions has been eliminated. This is important because such a gap is a dangerous source of hypocrisy and cynicism.

Measures toward institutionalization have increased popular participation and have legitimized the political role of the masses. Since its beginnings on an experimental basis in 1974, the popularly elected state apparatus (OPP) has continued to expand its role. Strengthening and democratizing the labor unions has given greater legitimacy to the rights of workers, individually and collectively, at the level of the workplace. Decision making by workers' assemblies has had a similar effect. Efforts to increase the participation of women in society—the establishment of more day care centers, strengthening the "Women's Front" caucuses within the unions, the work of the Cuban Women's Federation, promoting the education of women in professional and technical fields, and the legislation of equal rights within the family—have been expanded. This policy contributes to ending the subordination of half the population, preparing women to actively pursue their interests as women and as workers.

Thus far, Cuba's socialist development has been maintained in spite of the unavoidable economic dependence and the contradictions of breakaway socialism. Although the Communist Party makes policy on behalf of the masses, its power has not resulted in privilege or corruption. Recruitment procedures have thus far maintained a high level of prestige of party members among the population. While a minority of the population has disagreed with Cuba's military role in Africa or been impatient with the slow progress in improving material living conditions, no significant gap has emerged between the leadership and the masses on policy questions.[5] Although policies directed toward development of the forces of production sanction inequality, this inequality is related to individual contribution to production rather than bureaucratic privilege. The negative individualistic and potentially elitist attitudes encouraged by these policies are countered by educational efforts such as the inclusion of manual work in the school curriculum and promotion of voluntary work projects of collective benefit.

Cuban independence requires continued economic growth as well as diversification of production for import substitution and diversification of sources of foreign exchange and of trading partners. During the period of economic dependence, popular support must be maintained so that the leadership could rely on mass solidarity (such as that demonstrated in the face of increased U.S. hostility in 1980) should it become necessary to resist Soviet pressure at some time in the future.

Cuban policy choices since 1959 appear to have been formed by immediate situations and problems. From the nationalizations of 1960 in response to domestic and foreign political opposition, to the use of moral incentives to meet the need for increased agricultural labor in the second half of the 1960s, to the changes in economic policy begun in the 1970s to increase efficiency and work discipline, decisions have reflected an effort to meet the requirements of concrete situations while maintaining long-term goals. At present, economic policies have prevented a potential gap between the leadership and the masses by giving more emphasis to improvement of material living conditions. These policies allocate more resources to individual consumption in order to stimulate improved work performance, though no more than appears necessary to accomplish the purpose. Because inequality based on work is perceived as essentially fair, it has not created alienation and therefore does not preclude supplementary collective sources of motivation. The current allocation of resources continues to emphasize collective goods such as education and health care and the satisfaction of popular needs such as housing. Thus, these policies encourage mass support and contribute to economic progress without sacrificing long-term goals.

Progress toward advanced socialism requires that a balance be maintained between an emphasis on productive forces and an emphasis on productive relations. The fruits of economic growth must be allocated to collective forms of consumption to the greatest extent consistent with maintaining motivation to work. Decisions about overall planning, such as the ratio of investment to current consumption or which economic sectors should be emphasized, the management of enterprises, and the degree of hierarchy in workplaces must be made in ways that ensure the maximum levels of worker participation and popular control consistent with efficiency. The role of the masses in governance, including the scope of public dialogue, must also be increased as the capability of the population grows. Historical experience in other societies suggests that the central problem in pursuing these policies will arise from the tendency of second-generation political leadership to use power for bureaucratic privilege and to introduce a technocratic emphasis on production and expanded individual consumption. Although the concept of class struggle within socialism is not part of the Cuban conception of socialist development, institutions for popular participation have provided for a growing body of knowledge and experience among the masses, enhanced by the leadership's encouragement of popular criticism of improper conduct. The future of Cuba's development toward advanced socialism will eventually depend upon the capacity of the masses to resist the tendencies noted above. This, in turn, is dependent in large measure on the performance of the present leadership.

Notes

1. Shadow profit calculations refer to the evaluation of enterprise performance based on the surplus of revenues over costs of production. The "profit" is not realized by enterprise management, although bonuses are often based on shadow profit performance.

2. On a visit to Cuba in 1969 we noted a lack of maintenance of bomb shelters and bunkers, suggesting that concern over an attack had diminished.

3. It is suggestive that some CIA assessments conclude that, at least until the mid-1970s, Cuban knowledge of Africa was superior to that of the USSR and that Cuban-Soviet support of the MPLA in Angola was a Cuban initiative backed by the USSR.

4. The term "elite" is used rather than "class" because the latter term refers to a stratum that passes on its positions and privileges to its children, while the gap with which we are concerned may exist even when individuals from lower strata may have an opportunity to assume elite positions just as children of the elite do.

5. The emigration of slightly more than one percent of the population to the United States in the first half of 1980 has no significance other than a preference by a minority for a society that focuses on consumer goods and has already achieved a high level of mass consumption, combined with the willingness of the leadership of the United States to accept immigrants from an underdeveloped country for propaganda reasons.

References

Barkin, David (1973). "Cuban Agriculture: A Strategy of Economic Development," pp. R261-1–R261-21, in David Barkin and Nita Manitzas (eds.), *Cuba: The Logic of the Revolution* (Andover, Mass.: Warner Modular Publications).

Bernardo, Robert (1971). *The Theory of Moral Incentives in Cuba* (University, Ala.: University of Alabama Press).

Bonachea, Rolando E., and Nelson P. Valdes (eds.) (1972). *Revolutionary Struggle 1947–1958: Volume I of the Selected Works of Fidel Castro* (Cambridge, Mass.: M.I.T. Press).

Bray, Donald, and Timothy F. Harding (1974). "Cuba," in Ronald H. Chilcote and Joel C. Edelstein, *Latin America: The Struggle with Dependency and Beyond* (Cambridge, Mass.: Schenkman Publishing Company).

Castro, Fidel (1959). *Political, Economic, and Social Thought of Fidel Castro* (Havana: Editorial Lex).

———— (1978). *Second Period of Sessions of the National Assembly of People's Power* (Havana: Political Publishers).

Colletti, Lucio (1977). "The Question of Stalin," in Gary L. Olson (ed.), *The Other Europe* (Brunswick, Ohio: King's Court Communications), pp. 226–248.

Magdoff, Harry (1975). "China: Contrasts with the USSR," in *China's Economic Strategy*, special issue of *Monthly Review*, Vol. 27, no. 3, July-August, pp. 12–47.

Perez-Stable, Marifeli (1975). "Whither the Cuban Working Class," in *Cuba: La Revolución en Marcha*, special issue of *Latin American Perspectives*, Issue 7, Vol. 2, no. 4 (Supp.), pp. 60–77.

Silverman, Bertram (1971). *Man and Socialism in Cuba: The Great Debate* (New York: Atheneum Publishers).

_____(1973). "Economic Organization and Social Consciousness: Some Dilemmas of Cuban Socialism," in J. Ann Zammit (ed.), *The Chilean Road to Socialism* (Sussex: Institute of Development Studies).

Smith, Robert Freeman (1960). *The United States and Cuba: Business and Diplomacy* (New York).

Thomas, Clive (1974). *Dependence and Transformation: The Economics of the Transition to Socialism* (New York: Monthly Review Press).

Valdés Vivó, Raul (1977). *Ethiopia: The Unknown Revolution* (Havana: Editorial de Ciencias Sociales).

Zeitlin, Maurice, and Robert Scheer (1963). *Cuba: Tragedy in Our Hemisphere* (New York: Grove Press).

13
Dependence in an Interdependent World: The Limited Possibilities of Transformation Within the Capitalist World Economy

Immanuel Wallerstein

"Dependence" has become the latest euphemism in a long list of such terms.[1] No doubt its original intent was critical. The term itself emerged out of the "structuralist" theories of Latin American scholars and was meant as a rebuttal to "developmentalist" or "modernization" theories and "monetarist" policy views.[2] André Gunder Frank has traced its intellectual origins and its limitations in a combative paper entitled "Dependence is dead; long live dependence and the class struggle."[3]

We live in a capitalist world economy, one that took definitive shape as a European world economy in the sixteenth century (See Wallerstein 1974a) and came to include the whole world geographically in the nineteenth century. Capitalism as a system of production for sale in a market for profit and appropriation of this profit on the basis of individual or collective ownership has only existed in, and can be said to require, a world system in which the political units are not co-extensive with the boundaries of the market economy. This has permitted sellers to profit from strengths in the market whenever they exist but enabled them simultaneously to seek, whenever needed, the intrusion of political entities to distort the market in their favor. Far from being a system of free competition of all sellers, it is a system in which competition becomes relatively free only when the economic advantage of upper strata is so

This article originally appeared in the *African Studies Review,* vol. 18, no. 1, April 1974, pp. 1–26. It is published here with permission of Professor Wallerstein and the African Studies Association.

clear-cut that the unconstrained operation of the market serves effectively to reinforce the existing system of stratification.

This is not to say that there are no changes in position. Quite the contrary. There is constant and patterned movement between groups of economic actors as to who shall occupy various positions in the hierarchy of production, profit, and consumption. And there are secular developments in the structure of the capitalist world system such that we can envisage that its internal contradictions as a system will bring it to an end in the twenty-first or twenty-second century.

The important thing for living men, and for scholars and scientists as their collective intellectual expression, is to situate the options available in the contemporary situation in terms of the patterns we can discern in the historical past. In this task, conceptual clarification is the most constant need, and as life goes on and new experiences occur, we learn, if we are wise, to reject and reformulate the partial truths of our predecessors, and to unmask the ideological obscurantism of the self-interested upholders of encrusted privilege.

The years 1945–1970 were a period of exceptional obscurantism in all fields of study, and African studies has been in this sense typical. Liberal ideology prevailed in the world of social science reflecting the easy and unquestioned economic hegemony of the United States. But liberalism has come onto hard days—not least of all in the anlaysis of "development." If the decline of cold war polarization in the 1960s effectively reduced the political bargaining power of African states, the beginning of a worldwide economic contraction of effective demand of the 1970s is likely to sweep African aspirations aside as those who are on top of the world heap struggle with each other to remain there. In the 1960s, African scholars began to worry about "growth without development." In the 1970s and 80s, there is the clear possibility of neither growth nor development.

To understand the issues, we must successively treat the structure of the world economy, its cyclical patterns including the present conjuncture, and the ways in which the position of particular states may change within this structure. This will, I believe, explain "the limited possibilities of transformation within the capitalist world economy."

The structure of the world economy as a single system has come increasingly in recent years to be analyzed in terms of a core-periphery image, an image which has been linked with the discussion of "dependence." And thus it has been argued, for example, that Third World countries are not "underdeveloped" nations but "peripheral capitalist" nations.[4] This is far clearer terminology, but it leads unfortunately to further confusion if the unicity of the world system is not borne clearly in mind. Ikonicoff argues, for example, that peripheral capitalist economies "operate by economic laws and growth factors [that] are clearly different from those of the economies one might call the model of classic capitalism" (1972, p. 692). This is only so because our model of "classic capitalism" is wrong, since both in the sixteenth century and today the core and the periphery of the world economy were not two separate "economies" with two separate "laws" but one capitalist economic system with different *sectors* performing different functions.

Once one recognizes the unicity of the system, one is led to ask if the conception of a bi-modal system is adequate. Clearly, it leaves much unexplained, and thus we have seen the emergence of such terms as "subimperial" states (see Marini 1969) or "go-between nations" (see Galtung 1972, pp. 128–129). Both of these terms seem to me unwise as they emphasize only one aspect of their role, each an important one, but not in my opinion the key one. I prefer to call them semi-peripheral countries to underline the ways they are at a disadvantage in the existing world system. More important, however, is the need to explicate the *complexity* of the role which semi-peripheral states play within the system as well as the fact that the system could not function without being *tri*-modal.

Before this explication, it is necessary to spell out one more fact. The capitalist system is composed of owners who sell for profit. The fact that an owner is a group of individuals rather than a single person makes no essential difference. This has long been recognized for joint-stock companies. It must now also be recognized for sovereign states. A state which collectively owns all the means of production is merely a collective capitalist firm as long as it remains—as all such states are, in fact, presently compelled to remain—a participant in the market of the capitalist world economy. No doubt such a "firm" *may* have different modalities of internal division of profit, but this does not change its essential economic role *vis-à-vis* others operating in the world market.[5] It, of course, remains to discuss in which sector of the world system the "socialist" states are located.

The capitalist world system needs a semi-peripheral sector for two reasons: one primarily political and one politico-economic. The political reason is very straightforward and rather elementary. A system based on unequal reward must constantly worry about political rebellion of oppressed elements. A polarized system with a small distinct high-status and high-income sector facing a relatively homogeneous low-status and low-income sector including the overwhelming majority of individuals in the system leads quite rapidly to the formation of classes *für sich* and acute, distintegrating struggle. The major political means by which such crises are averted is the creation of "middle" sectors, which tend to think of themselves primarily as better off than the lower sector rather than as worse off than the upper sector. This obvious mechanism, operative in all kinds of social structures, serves the same function in world systems.

But there is another reason that derives from the particular needs of this kind of social structure, a capitalist world system. The multiplicity of states within the single economy has two advantages for sellers seeking profit. First, the absence of a single political authority makes it impossible for anyone to legislate the general will of the world system and hence to curtail the capitalist mode of production. Second, the existence of state machineries makes it possible for the capitalist sellers to organize the frequently necessary artificial restraints on the operation of the market.

But this system has one disadvantage for the sellers. The state machineries can reflect other pressures than of those who sell products on the market, for example, of those who sell labor. What regularly happens in core countries is the operation of a guild principle which, in fact, raises wage levels. It is this to which Arghiri Emmanuel refers when he says: "The value of labor power is, so far as its determination is concerned, a magnitude that is, in the immediate sense, *ethical*: it is *economic* only in an indirect way, through the mediation of its moral and historical element, which is itself determined, in the last analysis, by economic causes" (1972, p. 120).

The rising wages of the workers in the core countries, combined with the increasing *economic* disadvantage of the leading economic producers, given constant technological progress, and heaviest investment in rapidly outdated fixed capital by precisely the leading producers, leads to an inevitable decline in comparative costs of production. For individual capitalists, the ability to shift capital, from a declining leading sector to a rising sector, is the only way to survive the effects of cyclical shifts in the loci of the leading sectors. For this there must be sectors able to profit from the wage-productivity squeeze of the leading sector. Such sectors are what we are calling semi-peripheral countries. If they weren't there, the capitalist system would as rapidly face an *economic* crisis as it would a *political* crisis. (How, incidentally, this shift of capital investment would operate in a world capitalist system composed of only state-owned enterprises is an interesting question, but not one for the moment we are called upon to analyze.)

How then can we tell a semi-peripheral country when we see one? Even if we admit a tri-modal system, it would be an oversimplification not to bear in the front of our mind that each structural sector contains states of varying degrees of political and economic strength. Furthermore, each sector contains some states that are seeking to move (or *not* to move) from one structural position to another (and for whom such a move is plausible) and other states that for the moment are mired in the location where they find themselves.

Nonetheless, it is important to spell out some defining characteristics of a semi-peripheral state, as opposed to a core or a peripheral state. If we think of the exchange between the core and the periphery of a capitalist system being that between high-wage products and low-wage products, there then results an "unequal exchange" in Emmanuel's conception, in which a peripheral worker needs to work many hours, at a given level of productivity, to obtain a product produced by a worker in a core country in one hour. And vice versa. Such a system is *necessary* for the expansion of a world market if the primary consideration is *profit*. Without *unequal* exchange, it would not be *profitable* to expand the size of the division of labor.[6] And without such expansion, it would not be profitable to maintain a capitalist world economy, which would then either disintegrate or revert to the form of a redistributive world empire.[7]

What products are exchanged in this "unequal exchange" are a function of world technology. If in the sixteenth century, peripheral Poland traded its wheat for core Holland's textiles, in the mid-twentieth-century world, peripheral countries are often textile producers whereas core countries export wheat as well as electronic equipment. The point is that we should not identify any particular product with a structural sector of the world economy but rather observe the wage patterns and margins of profit of particular products at particular moments of time to understand who does what in the system.

In a system of unequal exchange, the semi-peripheral country stands in between in terms of the kinds of products it exports and in terms of the wage levels and profit margins it knows. Furthermore, it trades or seeks to trade in both directions, in one mode with the periphery and in the opposite with the core. And herein lies the singularity of the semi-periphery as opposed to both the periphery and the core. Whereas, at any given moment, the more of *balanced* trade a core country or a peripheral country can engage in, the better off it is in absolute terms, it is often in the interest of a semi-peripheral country to *reduce* external trade, even if balanced, since one of the major ways in which the aggregate profit margin can be increased is to capture an increasingly large percentage of its *home* market for its *home* products.

This, then, leads to a second clear and distinctive feature of a semi-peripheral state. The direct and immediate interest of the state as a political machinery in the control of the market (internal and international) is greater than in either the core or the peripheral states, since the semi-peripheral states can *never* depend on the market to maximize, *in the short run*, their profit margins.

The "politicization" of economic decisions can be seen to be most operative for semi-peripheral states at moments of active change of status, which are two: (1) the actual breakthrough from peripheral to semi-peripheral status and (2) strengthening of an already semi-peripheral state to the point that it can lay claim to membership in the core.

The political economies of the various sectors of the world economy show distinct differences in patterns at various moments of the long-run cycles of the world economy. It was rather convincingly established by the price historians who began writing in the late 1920s that for a very long period the European world economy (and, at least since the nineteenth century, the whole world) has gone through a series of systemic expansions and contractions (see a summary and synthesis of this literature in Braudel and Spooner, pp. 378–486). It should be obvious that when the system as a whole is in economic crisis, some part of it may have to pay a price in relative position as a result of the conflict engendered by the enforced redistribution that follows on economic contraction. But what does that mean for the nations of the periphery and the semi-periphery? Is the world economic crisis their bane or their salvation? As one might guess, the answer is not easy.

Clearly, as a general rule, there is more pressure for reallocation of roles and rewards in all systems at moments of contraction than at moments of expansion, since in moments of expansion even groups that are less rewarded may obtain an *absolute* expansion in reward, whereas in moments of contraction even those who are most highly rewarded are threatened with *absolute* decline, in which case one way to maintain an evenness in absolute reward is to seek an increase in *relative* reward. This general proposition applies to world systems as well.

A pressure to reallocate roles and rewards can have two different outlets: one is circulation of the groups who play different roles, and hence what is increase for one is decrease for another. A second is the redistribution of rewards among different roles in a more egalitarian direction. Within the modern world system, much historical change has been justified in the name of the latter objective, but the reality thus far of most such change has been the former. One fundamental explanation is that the framework of the capitalist world system limits critically the possibilities of transformation of the reward system within it, since disparity of reward is the fundamental motivating force of the operation of the system as it is constructed.

To be very concrete, it is not possible theoretically for all states to "develop" simultaneously. The so-called "widening gap" is not an anomaly but a continuing basic mechanism of the operation of the world economy. Of course, *some* countries can "develop." But the some that rise are at the expense of others that decline. Indeed, the rest of this paper will be devoted to indicating some of the mechanisms used by the minority that at given moments rise (or fall) in status within the world economy.

There is an alternative system that can be constructed, that of a socialist world government in which the principles governing the economy would not be the market but rather the optimum utilization and distribution of resources in the light of a collectively-arrived-at notion of substantive rationality. I say this not in order to develop further how such a prospective system would operate, were it in existence, but rather to emphasize that the nationalization or socialization of all productive enterprises within the bounds of a nation-state is not and theoretically cannot be a sufficient defining condition of a socialist system, even if the whole nation thinks of socialism as its objective. As long as these nations remain part of a capitalist world economy, they continue to produce for this world market on the basis of the same principles as any other producer. Even if *every* nation in the world were to permit only state ownership of the means of production, the world system would still be a capitalist system, and although doubtless the political parameters would be very different from what they presently are.

Let me be very clear. I am not suggesting that it does not matter if a country adopts collective ownership as a political requirement of production. The moves in this direction are the result of a series of progressive historical developments of the capitalist world economy and represent themselves a major motive force for further change. Nor am I in any way suggesting the immutability of the capitalist system. I am merely suggesting that ideological intent is not synonymous with structural change, that the only *system* in the modern world that can be said to have a mode of production is the *world* system, and that this system currently (but not eternally) is capitalist in mode.

It is important to cut through the ideological veneer if we are to notice the differences among those countries in the periphery seeking to become semi-peripheral in role, those countries in the semi-periphery seeking to join the core, and those countries in the core fighting against a declining economic position.

The shift to which most attention has been paid in recent years is the shift from being peripheral to being semi-peripheral, although it is usually discussed abstractly as though it were a question of shifting from periphery to core.[8] But this is not the shift that is, in fact, made. Coun-

tries have not moved, nor are any now moving, from being primarily exporters of low-wage products to being substantial exporters of high-wage
products as well as being their own major customer for these high-wage
products. Rather, some move from the former pattern to that of having a
higher-wage sector which produces *part* of what is consumed on the internal market but is still in a dependent relationship for the other part of
national consumption. The essential difference between the semi-
peripheral country that is Brazil or South Africa today and the semi-
peripheral country that is North Korea or Czechoslovakia is probably
less in the economic role each plays in the world economy than in the
political role each plays in conflicts among core countries and the direction of their exported surplus value.

We must start with the clear realization that not all peripheral countries at any given time are in an equal position to lay claim to a shift in
status. As Reginald Green somewhat depressingly puts it: "The attainment of a dynamic toward national control over and development of the
economy must start from the existing structural and institutional position, both territorial and international" (1970, p. 277). We know, by
looking backward in history, that among peripheral countries some have
changed status and others have not. The Santiago meeting of the UN
Conference on Trade and Development (UNCTAD) in 1972 underlined
among other things the differing *interests* of different Third World countries in various proposals. The United Nations has developed a list of
"hard core" poor nations, of which sixteen are in Africa (about half of all
African states), eight in Asia and Oceania, and only one (Haiti) in Latin
America. It is not clear that politico-economic decisions on the reallocation of world resources, such as those that have been favored by the
Group of 77, would in fact do very much to alter the relative status of
these "hard core" countries (see Colson 1972, especially pp. 826–830).

The fact that some make it and some don't is a continuing source of
puzzlement for many writers. For example, Cardoso and Faletto, in their
discussion of populism in Latin American countries as a mode of prof-
iting from world economic crises, note that these movements have been
more successful in some than others. Whereas in some they simply led to
an "intensified oligarchic control of agricultural-exporting groups, usually taking authoritarian-military forms," in others they have led to
"more open polyclass" rule and consequently more industrialization.
They explain differing results as the result of different schemes of
domination that managed to prevail in each country (Cardoso and Faletto 1969, p. 80). This seems less an explanation than a restatement of
the phenomenon.

Similarly, Green notes the limitations of the "staple thesis," suggesting it is unable to account for why the "dynamic external trade sector" with "spill-over demand" worked in Canada and Scandinavia but elsewhere led to "fossilization" (1970, p. 280). He suggests that the key issue is how countries "mobilise and harness the potential resource flows from these enclaves to the creation of national educational, institutional, and productive capacity to create a dynamic for development broader than the original export units" (p. 293). No doubt, but once again this implies some missing element in the equation and assumes all countries can make it.

Is it not rather the case that only a minority of peripheral countries can fit into an expanding world market or conquer part of a contracting one at any given time? And that those who do, of course, manifest their "success" by this missing "extra ingredient." It would seem to be more fruitful to look at the possible alternative strategies in the light of the fact that only a minority can "make it" within the framework of the world system as it is than to search for the universal recipe. We may, of course, be dismayed by the ethics of such a choice — I am myself[9] — but that would only lead us to ask about the possibilities of some more radical systemic transformation, not to look for a reformist panacea.

Basically there are three strategies: the strategy of seizing the chance, the strategy of promotion by invitation, and the strategy of self-reliance. They are different, to be sure, but perhaps (unfortunately) less different than their protagonists proclaim.

By seizing the chance, we mean simply the fact that at moments of world-market contraction, where typically the price level of primary exports from peripheral countries goes down more rapidly than the price level of technologically advanced industrial exports from core countries, the governments of peripheral states are faced with balance-of-payments problems, a rise in unemployment, and a reduction of state income. One solution is "import substitution," which tends to palliate these difficulties. It is a matter of "seizing the chance" because it involves aggressive state action that takes advantage of the weakened political position of core countries and the weakened economic position of domestic opponents of such policies. It is a classic solution and accounts, for example, for the expansion of industrial activity in Russia and Italy in the late nineteenth century (see, for example, Von Laue 1963) or of Brazil and Mexico (see Furtado 1970, especially pp. 85–89) — or South Africa (see Horwitz 1967, Chap. 15) — in the wake of the Great Depression of 1929. A war situation, providing destruction is somewhat limited, and "reconstruction," aggressively pursued, may provide the same "chance." Was this not the case for North Korea in the 1950s (see Kuark 1963)?

In each of these cases, we are dealing with relatively strong peripheral countries, countries that had some small industrial base already and were able to expand this base at a favorable moment. As Theotonio Dos Santos puts it:

> The capacity to react in the face of these [economic] crises depends in large part on the internal composition of the dependent countries. If they possess a very important complementary industrial sector, the latter can profit from the crisis in the following manner: In the course of the crisis, the export sector is weakened, imports diminish and their cost tends to rise because of the financial crisis which devalues national currencies. . . . The consequence is thus an encouragement of national industry which has a relatively important market, a high sales price, and weak international competition; if this sector has some unused capacity, it can utilize it immediately, and with a favorable state policy, it can use the small existing foreign exchange to import cheaply machines, for the surplus production in dominant countries causes their prices to go down relatively. (1971, p. 737)

"Seizing the chance" as a strategy has certain built-in problems for industrial development leads these prospective semi-peripheral countries to import both machines and manufactured primary materials from the core countries, essentially substituting new dependence for the old, from which "no dependent country has yet succeeded in liberating itself" (dos Santos 1971, p. 745). This problem is far more serious today than in the 1930s, and *a fortiori* than in earlier centuries because of the world level of technology. Merhav has argued that what he calls "technological dependence" inevitably

> leads, on the one hand, to the emergence of a monopolistic structure because the scales of output that must be adopted to introduce modern methods are large relative to the extent of the initial market; and on the other hand, these markets will be only practically expanded through income generated by investment, since a large proportion of the capital goods must be imported. In addition, the monopolistic structure itself will restrict the volume of investment. . . . So that the two effects reinforce each other. . . . [10]

Furthermore, such (national) monopolies are created "even in industries which in the advanced countries are more nearly competitive in structure. . ." (Merhav 1969, p. 65). Thus, despite the industrialization, "investment is less than what it could be with the existing resources."[11]

The national political alliance of "development populism" furthermore is subject to internal contradictions in countries based on private enterprise since it involves a temporary coming together of the industrial bourgeoisie and the urban workers to favor certain kinds of state action, but once these actions are engaged in, the two groups have opposite interests in terms of wage scales. Thus, Marini suggests that holding such a "developmentalist alliance" together depends on

> the possibility of maintaining a tariff policy and a monetary policy that allows, at the expense of the agricultural sector and of the traditional sectors, intertwining at one and the same time the rhythm of industrial inversion and, if not a significant rise in real wages, at least an increase in absolute terms of the number of individuals from the popular sectors who are progressively incorporated into the industrial system. (1969, p. 107)

Marini indicates the great political difficulties for Latin America in keeping up such a policy for long periods of time. But hasn't this been equally true for Eastern European countries in the last twenty years, where all enterprises have been state-run? Was not the crisis that brought Gierek to power in Poland the result of the breakdown of the "developmentalist alliance" that Gomulka originally symbolized? Had not Gomulka's backtrackings led to severe worker unrest, as concessions to the agricultural sector were being paid for by urban workers in terms of real wages?

Technological dependence plus internal political pressures from the agricultural sector have a possible solution, as Marini points out. Speaking of the policies of the Brazilian military that came to power after 1964, he says:

> Thus, both by their policies of reinforcing their alliance with the large landowners (*el latifundio*) and by their policy of integration to imperialism, the Brazilian bourgeoisie cannot count on a growth of the internal market sufficient to absorb the growing production that results from technological modernization. There remains no alternative but to try to expand outward, and thus they turn necessarily to obtaining a guaranteed external market for their production. The low cost of production which the present wage policy and industrial modernization tend to create points in the same direction: export of manufactured products. (1969, pp. 85-86)

This same analysis, virtually unchanged, could be used to explain the "outward policy" of the present South African government and their attempts to achieve a common market in southern Africa.[12] At a smaller scale, is this not what has been involved in the abortive attempts of President Mobutu of Zaire to build new structures of economic cooperation in Equatorial Africa?

The image thus far projected is of an attempt by an indigenous "developmentalist" sector in a peripheral country to "seize its chance" and strengthen its "industrial sector," thus becoming a "semi-peripheral" country. Then, we have suggested, over time the combination of internal pressure (the "agricultural sector") and external *force majeure* ("technological dependence") leads to the recuperation of the rebel and the stabilization of the new economic structures such that the development of an "internal market" originally projected is abandoned[13] and an "external market" is substituted, but one in which the semi-peripheral country largely serves as a purveyor of products it is no longer worth the while of the core country to manufacture.

But have we not got beyond the "recuperated rebel" scenario? We may have, as the increasingly sophisticated techniques of the burgeoning multinational corporations seem to enable the world system to arrive at the same result by means of what I am calling "semi-peripheral development by invitation."

The whole system of direct investment across frontiers grew up in part because of the flowering of infant industry protectionism and in part because of some political limitations to growth of enterprises in core countries (such as anti-trust legislation). The multinational corporations quickly realized that operating in collaboration with state bureaucracies posed no real problems. For these national governments are for the most part weak both in terms of what they have to offer and in their ability to affect the overall financial position of the outside investor. As Hymer points out, governments of underdeveloped nations are roughly in the relationship to a multinational corporation that a state or municipal government in the United States stands to a national corporation. While the government of the metropolis can, by taxation, "capture some of the surplus generated by the multinational corporation," the competition among peripheral countries "to attract corporate investment eats up their surplus" (Hymer 1972, p. 128).

Why then do the underdeveloped countries compete for this investment? Because, as the examples of the Ivory Coast and Kenya demonstrate, there are distinct advantages in winning this competition even at the disadvantageous terms such aided development is offered. For example, Samir Amin who has been one of the most vocal critics of the Ivory Coast path of development points out:

> Up to now [1971] every one has gotten something out of the Ivory Coast's prosperity via foreign capitalist enterprise: in the countryside, the traditional chiefs, transformed into planters, have become richer, as have the immigrant workers from [Upper Volta] who come out of a traditional, stagnant, very poor milieu; in the town, unemployment remains limited in comparison with what it is already in the large urban centers of older African countries. (1971b, p. 92)

No doubt, as Amin says, the Ivory Coast has gone from being "the primitive country that it was in 1950" to being a "veritable under developed country, well integrated, as its elder sister, Senegal, into the world capitalist system" (1971b, p. 93). No doubt, too, as Amin suggests, only Nkrumah's pan-African proposals "would have made it possible to begin to resolve the true problem of development" (p. 280). But Nkrumah did not survive, as we know. The effective choice of the Ivory Coast bourgeoisie may not, therefore, have been between the Ivory Coast path and that recommended by Nkrumah and Amin, but between the Ivory Coast path and that of Dahomey. Given such a choice, there seems little need to explain further why they chose as they did (see my discussion in Wallerstein 1971, pp. 19–33).

The path of promotion by invitation seems to have two differences with the path of "seizing the chance." Done in more intimate collaboration (economic and political) with external capitalists, it is more a phenomenon of moments of expansion than of moments of contraction. Indeed, such collaborative "development" is readily sacrificed by core countries when they experience any economic difficulties themselves. Second, it is available to countries with less prior industrial development than the first path but then it peaks at a far lower level of import-substitution light industries rather than the intermediate level of heavier industries known in Brazil or South Africa.

One might make the same analysis for Kenya, except that the neighbor of Kenya is Tanzania, and thus for Tanzania the path of *ujamaa* has survived and is indeed the prime example of the third road of development for a peripheral country, that of "self reliance." Tanzania has been determined *not* to be a "complicit victim," in Sfia's trenchant phrase (see Sfia 1971, p. 580).

A sympathetic analysis of Tanzania's attempts by Green (1970) starts with the assumption that "in Africa the closed-national strategy of structural change for development will be even harder to implement than in Latin America" and that "economic decolonization and development will be agonisingly slow even with efficient policy formulation and execution and the best likely external economic developments" (pp. 284–285). Green terminates with the cautious conclusion that: "The Tanzania experience to date [1969] is that even in the short term a clearly enunciated and carefully pursued strategy of development including economic independence as a goal can be consistent with an accelerating rate of economic as well as social and political development" (p. 324). Let us accept that Tanzania has done modestly well. We may applaud, but may we generalize the advice? One thing to consider is whether Tanzania's path has not been possible for the same reason as Kenya's and the Ivory

Coast's, that it is a path being pursued not by all peripheral countries, but by very few. In this case, both Tanzania's poverty and her rarity among Africa's regimes stand her in good stead of thus far minimizing the external pressure brought to bear against her economic policies. Core capitalist countries calculate risks for Tanzania as well as Kenya. Tanzania's model of self-reliance would seem more convincing if Zambia were successfully to adopt it.

It is from Eastern Europe that we get, interestingly enough, a caution to small countries on the limits of the path of self-reliance. The Hungarian economist, Béla Kádár, sums up his prudence thus:

> The necessity to comply increasingly with world economy as well as the development of international cooperation implies further restrictions in decisions on nationalization. It is an apparent contradiction, and yet in order to ensure national development sacrifices will have to be made by submitting to a greater degree of dependence. This is the price of profits and it is not at all certain that it is bought too costly. Many examples could be quoted showing that excessive striving after autarchy and extreme protectionism lead to increased external economic dependence and to the curtailment of sovereignty. (1972, p. 21)

One of the most pessimistic elements in the analysis of the difficulties of peripheral countries to transform their states is to be found in Quijano's hypothesis of the "marginalization" of the masses. It has become a commonplace of the literature on peripheral countries, that, since the Second World War at least, there has been a steady influx into the towns, in part the result of growing population density in rural areas without corresponding growing need for manpower, in part the secondary effect of the spread of education and facility of movement which makes such moves seem attractive. It is further commonly agreed that this urban influx is too large to be absorbed in the wage employment and is thus "unemployed."

Quijano argues that this process is not reversible within the system because this growing urban manpower,

> with respect to the employment needs of the hegemonic sectors [of the peripheral economic structures] that are monopolistically organized, is *surplus*; and with respect to intermediate sectors organized in a competitive mode and consequently characterized by the permanent instability of these very fragile enterprises with very peripheral occupations, this manpower is *floating*, for it must be intermittently employed, unemployed or underemployed depending on the contingencies that affect the economic sector. (1971, p. 335)

Quijano is pointing essentially to the same phenomenon of which Marx spoke when he referred to "pauperization." Marx was historically wrong about western Europe but that was in large part because he underestimated the politico-economic consequences of the unicity of the world economy.

The point of marginalization as Amin notes is that in peripheral countries wages are not "both cost and revenue that creates demand . . . but on the contrary only cost, demand being found elsewhere: externally or in the revenue of the privileged social sectors" (1972a, p. 711). The conclusion we can draw from such a hypothesis is that at the national peripheral level the problem is relatively insoluble. At best, marginalization can be minimized (as in the Ivory Coast, at the expense of Upper Volta, among others). But it also points to one of the long-run contradictions of the system as it presently exists: for one day, the "demand" of these marginalized workers will in fact be needed to maintain the profit rates. And when that comes, we will be faced, in a way that we are not now, with the question of the transition to socialism.[14]

Let us look, far more briefly, because less relevant to Africa, to the mode by which semi-peripheral countries have historically made it into the core. Which are such countries? England rose from the semi-peripheral status it still had at the beginning of Elizabeth's reign to membership in the core by the time of the seventeenth-century recession. The United States and Germany followed a similar path in the nineteenth century. The USSR is on the same path today. But many other lesser countries have worked their way forward, if to less spectacular heights: Belgium, Sweden, and much more doubtfully in terms of the economic structure, Canada. If I add Canada, it becomes clear that fairly "developed" countries may to some extent still be subordinate to other countries in the hierarchy of the world economy. Still it would be hard to convince anyone in either Canada or, say, Sierra Leone that there were not many significant differences in the way each relates to the world economy, the consequent social and political structure within each country, and the perspectives of the immediate future.

To gauge the degree to which semi-peripheral countries are able today to utilize the classic mechanisms of advancement in the world economy, we should review both how this classic mechanism worked and the role that wage differentials have played in the structuring of the world economy. What in a national society determines the general wage level that so manifestly varies from country to country, and in particular seems always to be relatively high in core countries and relatively low in peripheral countries? Obviously, a given employer wishes to pay the least he can for the services he purchases, given the labor market, and the employee wishes to get as high a wage as he can. From the viewpoint of larger social forces, however, as mediated through the state, wage levels affect both sale of products externally (a motive pressing for lower wages) and sale of products internally (a motive pressing for higher wages). Furthermore, the collective organization of workers leads both to legislation and convention assuring at given times given minima, with the expectations socialized into the psyches of the members of the society. Thus, as Arghiri Emmanuel argues, "Regardless of market conditions, there are wage levels that are impossible, because unthinkable, in a particular country, at a particular period, for a particular racial or ethnic group of wage earners" (1972, p. 119).

Emmanuel argues the case that it is precisely the relative rigidity of national wage levels combined with the tendency to equivalence in international profit margins that accounts for unequal exchange within the world economy. Nonetheless, it is precisely this same rigidity which has made possible historically the shift of semi-peripheral countries, which, in fact, have *medium* wage levels, to the status of core countries.

The problem of breakthrough for a semi-peripheral country is that it must have a market available large enough to justify an advanced technology, for which it must produce at a lower cost than existing producers. Obviously, there are a number of elements involved in this which are interrelated in a complex way.

One way to enlarge a market for national products is to control access of other producers to the one market a given state politically controls, its own: hence, prohibitions, quotas, tariffs. A second is to expand the political boundaries thus affected via unification with neighbors or conquest. Or, conversely, instead of increasing the costs of imported goods, a state seeks to lower the costs of production, thus affecting simultaneously the home market and external markets. Subsidies for production in whatever form are a mode of reallocation of national costs, such that the effective price of other goods is raised relative to the item subsidized. Reducing costs of productions by reducing wage levels is a two-edged sword since it increases external sales at the risk of lowering internal sales, and only makes sense if the balance is positive. A fourth way to increase the market is to increase the internal level of purchasing power which, combined with the natural competitive advantages of low or zero transportation costs, should result in increased internal sales. If this is done by raising wage levels, this is the converse two-edged sword of the previous one, increasing internal sales at the risk of lowering external sales. Finally, the state or other social forces can affect the "tastes," primarily of internal consumers, by ideology or propaganda, and thus expand the market for its products.

Obviously, in addition, it is critical not merely to have optimal cost levels, but to have a certain *absolute* size of the market. Furthermore, the steady advance of technology involving machinery with larger and larger components of fixed capital constantly raises the threshold. Thus, the possibility of a state passing from semi-peripheral to core status has always been a matter of juggling elements that move in varied directions to achieve a nearly perfect mix.

For example, the mix that England achieved in the "long" sixteenth century involved a combination of a *rural* textile industry (thus free from the high guild-protection wage costs of traditional centres of textile production such as Flanders, southern Germany, and northern Italy), with a process of agricultural improvement of arable land in medium-sized units (thus simultaneously providing a yeoman class of purchasers with an evicted class of vagrants and migrants who provide much of the labor for the textile industry), plus a deliberate decision to push for the new market of *low*-cost textiles (the "new draperies") to be sold to the new middle stratum of artisans, less wealthy burghers, and richer peasants who had flourished in the expanding cycle of the European world economy (see Wallerstein 1974a for this argument in detail). Germany, too, in the nineteenth century operated on the advantages of a medium wage level, based on the historic legacy of a declining artisan class to create a sufficiently large internal market, yet with a cost of production sufficient to compete with Britain especially in areas to the east and south where it had transportation advantages. This is not, however, the only mix that can work. There is the "white settler" phenomenon where high wage levels *precede* industrialization and distance from world centres of production (providing the natural protection of high transportation costs for imports). Once again, Emmanuel pushes the point to clarify what is happening. He reminds us that of Britain's five colonies of settlement—the United States, Canada, Australia, New Zealand, and the Cape—the first four have today the highest per capita incomes in the world whereas South Africa is at the level of Greece or Argentina. Yet it had the same colonists, the same links to Britain.

One factor alone was different, namely, what happened to the indigenous population. Whereas in the other four colonies the total extermination of the natives was undertaken, in South Africa the colonists confined themselves to relegating them to the ghettos of apartheid. The result is that in the first four countries wages have reached very high levels, while in South Africa, despite the selective wages enjoyed by the white workers, the average wage level has remained relatively very low, hardly any higher than that in the underdeveloped countries, and below that of the Balkans, Portugal, and Spain. (Emmanuel 1972, p. 125)

The high-wage route (that is, high in relation to the wages in the leading industrial countries of the world) is not likely to be easily repeated. First, it requires special political conditions (a settler population attracted in the first place by the immediately or potentially high standard of living) plus the technological level of a past era, where world distances mattered more and technological dependence (as discussed above) mattered less.

The model of the twentieth century has been the USSR. But what exactly is this model? First of all, let us not forget that the Soviet Union built its structure on a semi-peripheral country to be sure—Russia—but one that was nonetheless the fifth industrial producer in the world (in absolute terms) in 1913. It was not a state in which the process of marginalization had gone very far at all.[15] The state entered into the picture to keep industrial wage levels at a medium level[16] and rural wage levels such that there was an extensive urban labor reserve.[17] Last but not least, the USSR was a very large country, which made possible the relatively long period of autarchy which it practiced. And even then, its long stunting of the internal market because of wage levels has forced it into the Khrushchev-Brezhnev revision of this policy as part of the preparation for future competition in the world market as an exporter of manufactured products. If the USSR with its relatively strong prerevolutionary industrial base, its firm political control over external trade and internal wages, and its enormous size has, nonetheless, if you will, barely made it into the core of the world economy, what hope is there for semi-industrialized countries, true semi-peripheral ones—as the Brazil, the Chile, or the South Africa of today, to take three politically different examples—to expand their market, and primarily their internal market, sufficiently to transform their role in the world economy?[18] All that one has said of the economic processes that are worsening the ability of peripheral countries to maneuver in the world economy points to pessimism here, too, except one consideration which we have not yet discussed: the impact of world contraction on this picture.

If high wages are so advantageous in terms of unequal exchange, why doesn't everyone raise their wage levels, or at least every state? Obviously, because the advantage is a function also of low absolute competition (quite apart from price level). To be sure, capital will always flow to high profit areas, but it "flows." There is always a lag. The way it works, in fact, is that whenever some producer is undercut in the cost of production, there will be a tendency over time to uncover a new specialization requiring a momentarily rare skill, which "in the international division of labor at that moment, is free from competition on the part of the low-wage countries" (Emmanuel 1972, p. 145). And this is possible because we socially legitimate the variety of products which are technologically feasible.

This process, however, can most easily operate in moments of economic expansion, when it is easier to create new markets for new products than to fight over old ones. But in moments of contraction, the calculus changes. As has become clear once again in the late 1970s, core countries are quite willing to expend considerable energy fighting over old ones.[19]

What is the impact of such a fight on the possibilities of semi-peripheral countries moving towards core status and peripheral ones moving towards semi-peripheral status? I believe that the "slippage" of core countries offers, still today, opportunities for the semi-periphery but makes the outlook even more bleak for the periphery.

At moments of world economic downturns, the weakest segment of the world economy in terms of bargaining power tends to be squeezed first. The relative decline in world output reduces the market for the exports of the peripheral countries, and faster than it does the prices of their imports. Peripheral countries may even discover new protectionist barriers against their exports as other countries seek to "take back" areas of production once thought to be of such low profitability as to be worthy only of peripheral countries. To be sure, a few peripheral countries who have the relatively strongest technological base may use the impetus of the crisis to push forward with import substitution. But the bulk of the periphery simply "stagnates."

What happens in the semi-periphery is rather different. In an expanding world economy, semi-peripheral countries are beggars, seeking the "aid" of core countries to obtain a part of the world market against *other semi-peripheral* countries. Thus, becoming the agent of a core country, the subimperial role, is if not a necessary condition of further economic gain at least the facile road to it. It is no accident, thus, that ideologically semi-peripheral countries are often the loudest exponents of particular *weltanschauungen* and the strongest denouncers of evil practices—of other semi-peripheral countries.

As long, therefore, as expansion continues, the mode of economic prosperity for producing groups in semi-peripheral areas is via the reinforcement of dependency patterns *vis-à-vis* core countries. However, when world contraction comes, the squeeze is felt by core countries who proceed to fight each other, each fearing "slippage." Now the semi-peripheral countries may be courted as the outlets for core products become relatively rarer. The bargaining relationship of a core and semi-peripheral country changes in exactly the way the bargaining relationship between seignior and serf changed in moments of economic contraction in the Middle Ages, in favor of the lower stratum, enabling the latter to get some structural and even institutional changes as part of the new exchange.

There is much talk of the new multipolar world of the 1970s. Let us take one such analysis and see its implications for our problem. Anouar Abdel-Malek predicts a period of tripolar peaceful coexistence, in which there will be an attempt to maintain equilibrium between three sectors: Europe, around the USSR; Asia, around China; America, around the USA, the latter spreading out in triangular form to include Oceania and sub-Saharan Africa. Without debating whether this particular geography is accurate, it is difficult to disagree with Abdel-Malek's conclusion:

> The world enters at an accelerated pace into an *era of great mobility* where, paradoxically, the growth of the power potential held by the principal states will permit a dialectic of neutralization-improvement of position (*valorisation*) far more subtle than at present, wherein careful intelligence on the part of national and revolutionary movements in the dependent sector of the world will enable them to take advantage of, in the sense of bringing into being, optimal international alliances, those most likely to bear the enormous autochtonous effort of liberation and of revolution (1971, pp. 63-64)

But will not the economic difficulties lead to increased strife among the core countries? Curiously, as we so clearly see, it does not. It leads them to limit their strife in order to face, each in its turn, the harder bargaining it must do with its dependent semi-peripheral clients. Conversely, we may see new movements towards alliances between semi-peripheral countries, which will take the political form of changes in regimes to place themselves in a position to make such alliances. Can not the former Allende regime in Chile be seen as one such effort? And can not the deteriorating relationship of the USSR with the "revolutionary forces," particularly in semi-peripheral regimes, be seen as the simple consequence of the promotion of the USSR from semi-periphery to core and hence a change in its interests within the framework of a capitalist world economy?

Who in Africa could at the present time take advantage of such a thrust forward by semi-peripheral countries? Not many. South Africa, were the rest of Africa ready to serve as its market. But a segregated South Africa will find political resistance where a Black South Africa would not. And so the African continent may well have to sit this cycle out in terms of the advantages outlined above for semi-peripheral countries.

But if over the next twenty years, a number of semi-peripheral states, using the mechanism of state ownership (wholly or in large part) combined with a transnational, ideologically justified alliance, do in fact manage to make some clear gains, how will that change the world economy? These gains may well be at the expense of some core countries but also at the expense of peripheral ones. Is this more than a circulation of power?

No, if we look at the national and world economics of it. But yes, if we look at its political implications. Establishing a system of state ownership within a capitalist world economy does not mean establishing a socialist economy. It may not mean improving the economic well-being of the majority of the population. It is merely a variant of classic mercantilism. But it does change the world political scene because it clarifies the role of monopolistic limitation via the state in the unequal exchange of world capitalism, and thereby in the long run affects the political mobilization of those forces who are discontented with the "limited possibilities of transformation" within the present system.

If one justifies political changes not because there are clear economic benefits to the world economy as a whole but because they unveil more clearly the contradictions of the present system, the impossibility of maximizing rationally the social good within it, then we must be sure that we do not, by the process of justifying the present changes, in fact create new ideological screens.

But we have been creating these ideological screens for fifty years. By identifying state ownership with socialism, we have contributed to a massive confusion that has had nefarious political consequences. State-ownership countries have, in fact, lower standards of living than those countries that have predominantly private enterprises; and, in addition, social inequality in these so-called socialist countries is still manifestly enormous. This is not because they have state-owned enterprises but because they have been up to now largely semi-peripheral countries in a capitalist world economy.

For twenty-five years liberal reformists have advocated international aid as a major means of overcoming the economic dilemmas of under-developed nations. We have seen how little it has helped. Are we not in danger of falling into the same trap if, using new terms, we create an analogous left-wing myth that self-reliance will overcome, in any immediate sense, the dependence of peripheral countries?

State ownership is not socialism. Self-reliance is not socialism. These policies may represent intelligent political decisions for governments to take. They may be decisions that socialist movements should endorse.

But a socialist government when it comes will not look anything like the USSR, or China, or Tanzania of today. Production for use and not for profit, and rational decision on the cost benefits (in the widest sense of the term) of alternative uses is a different mode of production, one that can only be established within the single division of labor that is the world economy and one that will require a single government.

In the meantime, to return to Africa, what sensible men can do is to use the subtleties of careful intelligence, as Abdel-Malek suggests, to push those changes that are immediately beneficial and to coordinate with others elsewhere the long-run strategies that will permit more fundamental transformation. One step towards more careful intelligence is to call a spade a spade, mercantilism mercantilism, and state-owned capitalist enterprise state-owned capitalist enterprise.

Notes

1. I now believe that the formulations in this chapter are incomplete and can lead to some confusion. In particular I do not clarify the distinctions between semiperipheral states that have socialist governments and those that do not. In a subsequent essay I discuss this question quite specifically: "Semiperipheral Countries and the Contemporary World Crisis," *Theory and Society*, Vol. 3, Winter 1976, pp. 461–483. See also chapter 5 of *The Capitalist World-Economy* (1979).

2. See, as a mere beginning, Bodenheimer (1971), Caputo and Pizarro (1970), Cardoso (1971), Cockcroft et al. (1972), *Bulletin of the Institute of Development Studies* (1971).

3. See Frank (1972a) (French-language version); see also for a similar point of view *Frères du Monde* (1971).

4. See for example, the whole special issue of *Revue Tiers-Monde* (1972), especially the introduction by Ikonicoff.

5. I have argued this at length in my paper, "The Rise and Future Demise of the World Capitalist System: Concepts for Comparative Analysis," *Comparative Studies in Society and History*, vol. 16, no. 4, 1974. Samir Amin makes just about the same point:

> The predominance of the capitalist mode of production expresses itself also on another level, that of the *world system* which constitutes a characteristic of contemporary reality. At this level, the formations (central and peripheral) are organized in a single hierarchical system. The disintegration of this system — with the founding of socialist states, true or self-styled — does not change anything in this hypothesis. . . . Socialism cannot be in fact the juxtaposition of national socialisms, regressive with respect to integrated (but not egalitarian) world character of capitalism. Nor can it

be a *socialist system* separate from the world-system. It is precisely for this reason that there are not two world markets: the capitalist market and the socialist market; but only one — the former — in which eastern Europe participates, albeit marginally. (1972b, p. 13)

6. See Samir Amin: "Central capital is not at all constrained to emigrate because of a lack of possible (investment) outlets in the center; but it will emigrate to the periphery if it can get a higher remuneration there. . . . It is thus here that we insert the *necessary* theory of *unequal exchange*. The products exported by the periphery are interesting to the degree that — other things being equal and here this expression means of *equal productivity* — the remuneration for labor is less than it is in the center. And this is possible to the degree that society is forced by various means — economic and extra-economic — to play this new role: furnish cheap manpower to the export sector" (1972a, pp. 707–708).

7. It would take us far astray to develop this here. What I mean by "redistributive world empire" is defined in the paper cited in footnote 5. It would be interesting to see if it were not such processes as these which account for the stifling of nascent capitalist elements in such ancient systems as the Roman Empire.

8. For example, Samir Amin's discussion (1972a) argues that there are two models of capital accumulation, each a "system," one peripheral and one self-centered (*"autocentré"*). But when he cites a case that uses what he argues is the correct strategy of "self reliance," Vietnam, he talks of Vietnam having reached "an effective first stage of the transition" (p. 717). But what is the structural composition of this "first stage" in terms of the world economy which Amin agrees is single? This is not spelled out. But it is I should think very important to spell it out. Amin is in favor of "self reliance" but not of "autarchy," for example. In practice, Amin distinguishes not only between most peripheral countries and Vietnam, but also between two stages of "peripheral domination," which leads to his calling Brazil a "very advanced underdeveloped nation" (pp. 720–721).

9. R. H. Tawney calls the approach to self-improvement in a capitalist world by individual achievement via the use of talent the Tadpole Philosophy, "since the consolation which it offers for social evils consists in the statement that exceptional individuals can succeed in evading them." And he concludes, "As though the noblest use of exceptional powers were to scramble to shore, undeterred by the thought of drowning companions!" (1952, p. 109). Developmental ideology is merely the global version of this Tadpole Philosophy.

10. Merhav (1969), pp. 59–60. The ways in which technological dependence is both economically irrational and self-perpetuating in the capitalist world economy is explained with great clarity by Urs Müller-Platenburg (1971). However, it is not at all clear from his analysis why the forces he adumbrates (see the summary on p. 77) which force a private entrepreneur in a peripheral country into an irrational technology should not operate equally for a state-run enterprise.

11. Merhav (1969), p. 60. "What it could be" reminds one of Paul Baran's con-

cept of "potential economic surplus" (see Baran [1957], Chap. 2).

12. This has been the clear hope of the South African leadership. See Lombard et al. (1968).

13. See André Gunder Frank: "But this import *substitute* development *did not* create its own market, or at least its own internal market. This development if anything created a post-war internal market for externally-produced and imported producer goods and foreign investment . . . rather than raising internal wages. . . . Instead, to pay for the imports of producer goods required to sustain industrial production, as well as to sustain the latter's profitability, this dependent capitalism again resorted—perforce—to the increasing super-exploitation of labor, both in the export and the domestic sectors, as in Brazil and Mexico (and India?)" (1972b, p. 41).

14. Perhaps to keep his spirits up, Samir Amin seems to suggest in his postface to *L'Accumulation a l'échelle mondiale* (1971a) that we are in the transition now. Yes, to be sure, if we use the word loosely. But no, if it implies in any sense a short run. In any case, he is absolutely right when he says, "For if there is a problem, it is a problem of *transition* and not of perspective" (p. 597). But then he goes on, "The essential point is never to lose from view the necessity of reinforcing the socialist cohesion of the whole of the nation." I fear, as he does at other points, the easy slide of such a concept into ideological justification of a stratum in power. I would say the essential problem is never to lose from view the necessity of reinforcing the cohesion, such as it is, of socialist political forces throughout the world economy.

15. Amin says it was "unknown," but I suspect that this is an exaggeration. See Amin (1972a), p. 714.

16. Emmanuel suggests that this is a distinction between a competitive economy and a planned one, although sixteenth-century England and nineteenth-century Germany belie this explanation. In any case, he is right in his concrete description of what happened in the USSR: "The state being the dictator of specializations of prices, there is no need for high wages to appropriate an increased share in the world economic product. On the contrary, since the share is given by the real potential of production, the state is all the better able to increase accumulation if wages, and consumption generally, are kept down at very low levels" (1972, p. 130).

17. As Amin says, "The *kolkhoz* and administrative oppression fulfilled [the] function [of forcing the masses to be a passive reserve of manpower] that, in the English model, was performed by the enclosure acts and the poor laws" (1972a, p. 715).

18. To "*s'autocentrer,*" to use Amin's awkward-to-translate word. See the discussion in Amin (1971a), pp. 610ff.

19. Actually, the in-fighting began earlier. "When the U.S. balance of payments was strong, its reserves apparently unlimited, and its dollar untouched by any hint of possible devaluation, the government could face the massive outflow of capital by U.S. companies with equanimity. In today's conditions, this is no longer possible. Under President Johnson the government was forced to in-

troduce a number of measures to stem the tide of U.S. investment overseas" (Tugendhat [1971], p. 43).

References

Abdel-Malek, A., ed. (1971). *Sociologie de l'impérialisme.* Paris: Anthropos.

Amin, Samir (1971a), *L'accumulation à l'échelle mondiale.* Paris: Anthropos.

_____ (1971b). *L'Afrique de l'Ouest bloquée.* Paris: de Minuit.

_____ (1972a). "Le modèle théorique d'accumulation et de développement dans le monde contemporain." *Revue Tiers-Monde,* Vol. 13, No. 52 (October-December).

_____ (1972b). "Sullo sviluppo diseguale delle formazioni sociali." *Terzo Mondo,* No. 18 (December).

Baran, Paul (1957). *The Political Economy of Growth.* New York: Monthly Review Press.

Bodenheimer, Suzanne (1971). "Dependency and Imperialism: The Roots of Latin American Underdevelopment." *Politics and Society,* Vol. 1, No. 3 (May), pp. 327-357.

Braudel, F. P., and F. Spooner (1967). "Prices in Europe from 1450 to 1750," in E. E. Rich, ed. *The Economy of Expanding Europe in the Sixteenth and Seventeenth Centuries,* Vol. 4 of *Cambridge Economic History of Europe.* Cambridge: Cambridge University Press.

Bulletin of the Institute of Development Studies (1971), Vol. 3, No. 4 August. Special issue on "Conflict and Dependence."

Caputo, Orlando, and Roberto Pizarro (1970). *Imperialismo, dependencia, y relaciones internacionales.* Santiago: CESO, Universidad de Chile.

Cardoso, Fernando Henrique (1971). *Politique et développement dans les sociétés dépendantes.* Paris: Anthropos.

Cardoso, Fernando Henrique, and Enzo Faletto (1969). *Dependencia y desarrollo en América Latina.* México: Siglo XXI.

Cockcroft, James D. et al., eds. (1972). *Dependence and Underdevelopment: Latin America's Political Economy.* Garden City: Anchor Books.

Colson, Jean-Phillippe (1972). "Le groupe de '77 et le probleme de l'unité des pays du tiers-monde." *Revue Tiers-Monde,* Vol. 13, No. 52 (October-December).

dos Santos, Theotonio (1971). "Théorie de la crise économique dans les pays sous-développés," in A. Abdel-Malek, ed. *Sociologie de l'impérialisme.* Paris: Anthropos.

Emmanuel, Arghiri (1972). *Unequal Exchange.* New York: Monthly Review Press.

Frank, André Gunder (1972a). "La dépendance est morte. Vive la dépendance et la lutte des classes!" *Partisans,* No. 68 (November-December), pp. 52-70.

_____ (1972b). "That the Extent of the Internal Market Is Limited by the International Division of Labor and the Relations of Production." Paper for

IDEP-IDS-CLACSO Conference on Strategies for Economic Development: Africa Compared with Latin America, Dakar, September 4–17. Mimeo.

Fréres du Monde (1971), No. 69 pp. 28–60. "Une lutte historique de classes a l'échelle mondiale."

Furtado, Celso (1970). *Economic Development of Latin America.* New York: Cambridge University Press.

Galtung, Johan (1972). "Structural Theory of Imperialism." *African Review,* Vol. 1, No. 4 (April).

Green, Reginald Herbold (1970). "Political Independence and the National Economy: An Essay on the Political Economy of Decolonization," in Christopher Allen and R. W. Johnson, eds. *African Perspectives.* Cambridge: Cambridge University Press.

Horwitz, Ralph (1967). *The Political Economy of South Africa.* New York: Praeger Publishers.

Hymer, Stephen (1972). "The Multinational Corporation and the Law of Uneven Development," in Jagdish N. Bhagwati, ed. *Economics and World Order.* New York: Macmillan.

Ikonicoff, Moises (1972). "Sous-développement, tiers monde ou capitalisme périphérique." *Revue Tiers-Monde,* Vol. 13, No. 52 (October-December).

Kádár, Béla (1972). "Small Countries in World Economy." Reprint No. 34 of Center for Afro-Asian Research of the Hungarian Academy of Sciences.

Kuark, Yoon T. (1963). "North Korea's Industrial Development During the Post-War Period." *China Quarterly,* 14 (April-June), pp. 51–64.

Lombard, J. A. et al. (1968). *The Concept of Economic Co-operation in Southern Africa.* Pretoria: Bureau for Economic Policy and Analysis, Publication No. 1.

Marini, Ruy Mauro (1969). *Subdesarrollo y revolución.* México: Siglo XXI.

Merhav, Meir (1969). *Technological Dependence, Monopoly and Growth.* Oxford: Pergamon Press.

Müller-Plantenburg, Urs (1971). "Technologie et dépendence." *Critiques de l'Economie Politique,* No. 3 (April-June), pp. 68–82.

Quijano, Aníbal (1971). "Pole marginal de l'économie et main-d'oeuvre marginalisée," in A. Abdel-Malek, ed. *Sociologie de l'impérialisme.* Paris: Anthropos.

Revue Tiers-Monde (1972), Vol. 13, No. 52 (October-December). Special issue on "Le capitalisme périphérique."

Sfia, Mohamed-Salah (1971). "Le système mondial de l'imperialisme: d'une forme de domination à l'autre." In A. Abdel-Malek, ed. *Sociologie de l'imperialisme.* Paris: Anthropos..

Tawney, R. H. (1952). *Equality.* 4th ed., rev. London: Allen and Unwin.

Tugendhat, Christopher (1971). *The Multinationals.* London: Eyre and Spottiswoode.

Von Laue, Theodore H. (1963). *Sergei Witte and the Industrialization of Russia.* New York: Columbia University Press.

Wallerstein, Immanuel. (1971). "The Range of Choice: Constraints on the

Policies of Governments of Contemporary Independent African States," in Michael F. Lofchie, ed. *The State of Nations*. Berkeley: University of California Press, pp. 19–33.

———— (1974a). *The Modern World System: Capitalist Agriculture and the Origins of the European World-Economy in the Sixteenth Century*. New York and London: Academic Press.

———— (1974b). "The Rise and Future Demise of the World Capitalist System: Concepts for Comparative Analysis." *Comparative Studies in Society and History*, Vol. 16, no. 4.

———— (1979). *The Capitalist World Economy*. New York: Cambridge University Press.

14

Towards Another Development

Fernando Henrique Cardoso

The crisis of industrial civilization—as so labelled by some—which gained prominence after the short period of challenge created by the increase in oil prices (already absorbed, according to many specialists) raised a new-old list of lamentations on the present ills and, maybe, the hopes of the future. In this list of key problems—a long one—solutions to which are known though not applied, the following could be pointed out:

- The waste of non-renewable natural resources.
- The use of technologies predatory of nature and, even worse, of labour-saving technologies in societies of high unemployment.
- Increasing environmental pollution.
- Distortions of urbanization, which are related to the more negative forms of association and behaviour prevailing in mass societies (increases in criminality, drug addiction, individual insecurity etc.).

In the countries of the periphery other problems, which in countries of the centre generally affect only the minorities, should be added to these undesired characteristics of industrial civilization:

- The growth in world population (alarming, for the disciples of the Club of Rome).
- The possible food shortage (a painful reality in some areas).
- Inadequate housing, in the same civilization which boasts of steel and glass buildings and pre-stressed concrete bridges.

Reprinted by permission of the Dag Hammarskjöld Foundation from Marc Nerfin (ed.), *Another Development: Approaches and Strategies* (Uppsala: The Dag Hammarskjöld Foundation, 1977), pp. 21–39.

- At times, even the lack of adequate clothing for the majority, contrasting with the refinements of fashion which, through instant communication, offer to the eyes of élites in South-East Asia, Andean America, the heart of Africa and every pocket of misery in the world the fascination of "alternate styles" of fashion, ranging from a "taste for the old" in Balmain, and Cardin's baroque fantasies, to Courrèges' "modernism," or to the false "being-at-ease" of Hechter, in a scandalous waste of imagination and mockery of the world's poverty.[1]
- The sudden jump in infant mortality rates or in the number of "plagues" (e.g., of meningitis or cholera) which, in the mirror image of the narcissist world born proudly after the Industrial Revolution, should have been buried in the darkness of the Middle Ages.
- Statistics on malnutrition and undernourishment that clash with statesmen's high-sounding words saluting the emergence over the last thirty years of countries of "medium development"—which are in fact those on the periphery—capable of embarking on a process of "dependent industrialization."
- Illiteracy, after so many "goodwill" campaigns.

This list would be long if it were to be all-encompassing, as is the list of proposed remedies. Among these, we can mention:

- The rational use of nature, emphasizing the renewable and non-polluting resources (solar energy, or water-power, for example, as opposed to petroleum).
- The combined use of intermediate and advanced technologies, in order to achieve a balance between resources of accumulated capital and available labour.
- Balanced family growth, in favour of the collective welfare (and not "instead of" economic growth), oriented by the criteria of responsible parenthood. This proposal is not as simplistic, needless to say, as zero growth rate, or as the neo-fascist theories of those attracted by the "need" to occupy empty spaces, the crooked geopolitics of those unconcerned with the quality of life in those places.
- The political reorientation of supply, benefiting producers of popular consumer goods (in general, medium and small producers), and of the more than delusive green revolutions or theories of the elastic supply capacity of foodstuffs based on the large capitalistic production unit.

- The acknowledgement that technical-industrial criteria for the definition of what is supposed to be adequate housing are also biased and that, possibly, self-help housing are also biased and that, possibly, self-help housing and direct transfer through expropriation and donation are much more effective than the so-called "self-financed" housing-fund systems, financed by regional or domestic banks.
- The quasi-monastic modesty of non-ostentatious societies, such as the Chinese, avoiding waste and luxury in life style.
- The raising of the living standards of the masses as the only real solution to health and undernourishment problems, especially those of children and mothers, demystifying the clinical, assistance or purely medical approaches, which are elitist and restricted to small segments of the population.

Comparing the world as it exists and the world as some want it to be, the sceptical conclusion may be drawn that there is nothing new in the proposals: utopias, some would say, do not penetrate the "opacity of things." Thus we reach the core of the *problématique* of another development. The "opacity of things," a "situational logic," a "web of vested interests," are roundabout ways of describing without denouncing the problem of exploitation. The problem, to use a phrase that is worn-out but still true, is the exploitation of man by man.

In this sense, even though it is true that much has been said since, say, 1945 about the ills and distortions of industrial civilization, most of it consists of half-truths, starting with the very target of criticism, industrial society, as though it existed as an entity independent of the interests of men, groups, classes, states and nations. As we move from general to more specific problems (hunger in Bangladesh or infant mortality in São Paulo, for example) it becomes apparent that it is not industrial civilization in itself which causes the problems, but rather the (often interrelated) interests of minorities in different countries that offer the ghostly appearance of a civilization of Molochs which devours its own fruits.

Because they fail to recognize this banality—social and economic exploitation, of man by man, of one class by another, of some nations by other nations—so-called "counter-élites" often go round in circles, dreaming of technical solutions. The greatest example of technocratic irrationality endorsed by capitalists and socialists, industrialized and underdeveloped states can be found in the United Nations specialized agencies no less, whose all-capable and all-knowledgeable (in fact) technical programmes are, however, applied through "competent channels," i.e. governments, interest groups, different "situational logics" which, left alone, do nothing but reproduce and replace the conditions that create the problems to be fought against.

This is why sceptics insist that there is nothing new under the sun: maybe deep inside the first dominated man, the first slave, the seed already existed of a rebellious conscience and the impulse of the dialectics which would lead to the destruction of the master. If such processes do not develop it is not because they are not known or not wanted, but because they cannot. Thus, after recognizing that the basic fact that leads to the distortion of industrial societies is the existence of exploitation, and having identified the forms of domination which reflect it, another development should focus, without disguise, on the question of power.

During the nineteenth century, the same theme was already alive. At that time the dispute between "utopian" and "scientific" solutions also created profound divisions among the first universal critics of the industrial revolution, based on the exploitation of man by man. In the redeeming perspective of the greatest critics, the optimistic conviction existed that the progress of civilization and the power of conscience would combine to create the possible conditions for a new, triumphant age characterized by the renewed force of the oppressed.

A century and a half later, the culture crisis erupts in the west. The revolt appears among the children of the rich, the offspring, nauseated by the abundance of an urban-predatory civilization, at play in the universities, which isolate and bribe them with the best and by far the most histrionic means available in the arsenal of technicalities and humanistic resources. Millions of human beings finally discover the contradictions. They find out that man lives on bread and that the majority lack this same bread. They also find out that bread is not enough for those who are already filled. They then go on either to the arrogance of truth discovered ("ah, if you would only do the same as us," French students told workers in May 1968), or to complacency, that of the Berkeley drug-addicts' rebellion, that of the "naturist" communes, that of the horror of civilization, the contemporary form of the Byronic spleen. The generosity and romanticism of a whole generation was spent — almost to its exhaustion — in the counter-techniques, in the building of libertarian ghettos, in the escape through what could be viewed as a type of inverted Jansenism, which sees in the extramundane denial of the world (after becoming disillusioned with the possibility of revolutionizing it), an individual lifebuoy within an unjust social order. Hence the numerous groups of "insurgents," who never really turn into rebels, in order not to be mistaken for revolutionaries. They parade their disgust of the world, under the sign of Aquarius, through the roads of the civilization they detest, in quest of the Nepal of their dreams. The more disciplined exhibit their bald heads harmoniously complemented by white robes and bare feet, in the peripatetic groups of thousands of Zen Buddhists who cross the corner of Fifth Avenue and Central Park, announcing, by their very presence, that they no longer wish to belong to the civilization which began gaining awareness of itself in the Plaza's (ridiculous) architecture and which, all of a sudden, shook off whatever false and fanciful, though charming features it may have had of the euphoric capitalist birthday-cake style of the nineteenth century, in order to reveal, like a blade-thrust among helpless passersby, that sturdy and "logical" building in front—the General Motors building.

But the voices that echoed everywhere in favour of the "wretched of the earth" did not speak out only from the generosity of kind spirits: there were and are voices and actions coming from the ghetto (as in the Marcusian expectation-hope), of black minorities during the hot summers in Trenton, from the Algerian national liberation battlefields, from Viet-Nam, from the remaining colonies in Africa, from Cambodia and even from the spring, which many considered unnecessary and others impossible, in the streets of Prague.

Thus the outcry against the exploitation of man by man, born with industrial civilization itself, led to a beginning in the design of a new utopia—without which no meaningful action is possible—that extended, without suppressing, the vision inherited in the second half of the twentieth century from the past, the vision of the revolutionary classes, the bearers of history. For various reasons, the contemporary ideology of renewal, which may serve as a basis for another development, is more inclusive and less narrowly rationalist than the utopia of the nineteenth century, which, in the order of ideas, precedes it. It does not share so blindly the belief that through the impulse of the very development of productive forces—and thus of technology—the contradiction between private ownership of the means of production and socialization of work will lead to a new order. It adds to this basic platform of rationality an ethical-aesthetic and voluntaristic dimension, embodying the will to revolutionize the cultural matrix of contemporary civilization itself: it attempts to define another style of development.

Its elements—the "new man" of the exemplary revolutionary like Ché Guevara, the cry of Algerians under torture, Giap's people's war, the socialism of Mao's shared hardship—are prolonged contradictorily in other struggles. They are united in an unresolved amalgam—at the level of motivations, in the search for alternatives—with the almost anarchic liberalism of the French May 1968 (*défense d'interdire*), with the anti-racist racism of the "souls on ice" of U.S. blacks proclaimed by Sartre, with the revolted apoliticism of the missionary spirit of U.S. minorities, with feminist movements (how to combine them with socialist Islam?), and even the latent anti-bureaucracy of the Prague spring.

Utopian thought feeds on this confused and contradictory mould (but how can alternative strategies be proposed without utopias?). It arises from a collective will to assert itself which frequently looks like an individual idealistic protest: *"prends mes désirs pour la réalité car je crois en la réalité de mes désirs"* (written on the Sorbonne walls in May 1968).

It is also from this mould—although very indirectly—that the movement for the reconstruction of the international economic order is born. Instead of making a "neutral" analysis of imperialism and its power, and thus of further confirming the impossibility of change, people in the Third World, and some governments, see in the oil crisis and the OPEC union sensitive signs of a will to change which starts with what, in the logic of structures, should be the end: to obtain a fairer order among nations, even before altering the internal order within such nations.

Proposed in such terms the international liberation strategy would seem to be imbued with the same spirit as that of those who believe in the reality of desires more than in the force of reality. Nevertheless, another development does not feed only on the hydromel of utopias. A faithful reading of this will to change could also show that the internal gaps are so many and so deep in the dominating systems—created, it is true, out of the liberation struggles, by minority movements, by urban protest, etc.—that even the highest echelons of the international domination apparatus show cracks in the support structures. Perhaps this is the predominant characteristic of the way in which criticism of oppressing society is currently expressed: in struggle, in pressure from the periphery, in pressure from the societies of the centre, but also in lack of solidarity between the enlightened élites and the dominating classes. This is probably why the fight for the reconstruction of the international order and of the national structures of domination appears as a crisis of values, questioning industrial culture and civilization, as well as the basis on which they are founded. Watergate is as much an episode leading to the new order as are the wrecks that blocked the Suez canal.

If in the nineteenth-century version of utopia it was believed that the overthrow of the dominating classes by the exploited classes would automatically end alienation, inequalities and all forms of exploitation, in the twentieth-century version, the fetishism of *things* seems to be so strong that, symbolically, the utopian turns to machine-breaking, as did the English Luddites in their day. The suspicion is that with advanced technology bureaucratic control necessarily comes about and that with it, even if no private appropriation of the means of production exists, inequality and social plundering will persist which ultimately may maintain exploitation among nations, even in the socialist world.

Thus, confusedly (without necessarily having demonstrated how and why, or more important yet, through whom), the image of a new world arises — idyllic as with all strong values — in which, if nothing is there on the sixth day of creation, the knowledge at least prevails that a value hovers over it all: *equality*, capable of restoring a form of association based on the community, instead of exploiting society. It is at least known, therefore, *for whom* the new order is desired. And this is the keynote of the ideology generated by the disinherited of the affluent civilization which has marginalized the majority. With the impulse of any genuinely negating — and thus dynamic — idea, the new utopia which aims to create another style of development starts with that which the system cannot offer without falling apart. There is no technical reform capable of offering concrete equality (political, economic or social), although there are many technical reforms which may offer better health, more education or more food, conditioned to the maintenance of rigid and convenient differentiations in the appropriation of such goods by some groups. "No longer rich and poor; no longer rich nations and poor nations" is the theme that indicates that the aim is not man in the abstract, but the disinherited of the earth, the poor, the underdog.

But, how?

If the alternative strategies were to deal with final aims, only values and statements of principles would be needed. But, since another development cannot be created without political action, programmes and the reality principle are thus reintroduced; without them values and utopias remain mere hothouse flowers. Nevertheless, it is from them that the strength of the present utopia arises: contemporary industrial civilization created, in fact, the material basis for an equality with decency by increasing the minimum platforms, which are already within man's reach, technically speaking.

It is this contradiction — possibly for the first time in history — between a concrete possibility and a performance so distant from the satisfaction of the needs of all that explains the existence of a malaise even in the industrialized world, which turns every gratification into sin. *Everyone knows that the utopia of our century is materially possible.* It is not rooted only in desires, but exists as a possibility in things; if the "logic" of these does not achieve realization, it is because the desires (and interests) of some minorities do not allow it. This is why the contemporary world suffers as a torment every grain of wheat perishing on the stem. Everyone knows that the interests of some are served to the extent that this wheat is not made into bread. And yet, how the world of instant communications lives each crime committed in Lebanon, each capitulation of national dignity imposed by a banana-growing company when bribing a president, each agreement signed under pressure—be it to depose Dubček in the Kremlin, be it to oblige the confederated countries, through the Ministry of Colonies, as some call the OAS in Washington, to impose embargoes on nations which do not submit. All of this shakes and corrodes the moral fibre and the efficiency of the world order and the strength of the systems of domination. And these, in order to be efficient, cannot rely only on force: obedience requires consent, domination demands hegemony.

Thus, it is not so terrible that the definition of another development not only excites the imagination of the oppressed people, harassed by material wants, but also preoccupies the social and economic thinking of the industrialized nations. In spite of this, the ideology of development concealed until recently another aspect of reality which is now made visible: pockets of misery also exist in the industrialized countries, in which too the most coveted fruit of industrial civilization—success in increasing the gross national product—has created the problems of abundance we have listed: pollution, insecurity, impractical cities, etc. Criticism therefore springs from the situation of the blacks and Puerto Ricans in New York, of Chicanos in San Francisco, of Italians and Spaniards in Switzerland, of Algerians in Paris. And another type of criticism, which generates the urban protest in the popular classes and the fear of the city in the dominating classes, is added: in the suburbs of the rich, the scandalous neighbourhoods of rich Latin Americans, isolated in carefully built ghettos, in the modern fortresses which the luxurious apartment buildings or the large mansions are, are all those who, though theoretically consumers of the abundance civilization, in the end have to live in closed circuits of protection and boredom in order to escape their fear of the cities. Thus, the children of the rich reflect the stigma of being masters of a civilization which denies communality, which creates in fact the situation of the *homo homini lupus* that the thinkers of the eighteenth century tried to avoid through politics.

It is a civilization of poverty for the majority and fear for all.

The alternative to it, beyond the value of equality, lies in its complement, which requires freedom, of the need to *participate*. It lies in democracy, but not a democracy deferred to the quasi-mystical body of a party, or identified with a liberalism relating representativeness to the division of powers and removing all effective political stake to the summit of large state organizations, to parliament, the executive and the judiciary. Participatory democracy, which is an inherent part of another development model, starts by being more demanding and more inclusive.

It turns to the new arenas in which the decisions of contemporary societies are made: the educational system, the world of labour, the organizations which control mass communication.

As the demand for equality is universal, the requisite democratic controls imply denying the authoritarianism of teaching practices which merely reproduce the established order on a larger scale. It must be education not only *for* freedom, but *in* freedom; *a pedagogy of the oppressed* with schools in which the sharing of experiences between generations allows for the emergence of new solutions and not only the codification of what is obvious from the past.

On another plane this approach leads to the search for the means to a cultural revolution. This is taking place not only in China, but also through the actions and intimation of alternatives in the U.S. counterculture, in the mobilization of teaching and work brigades in Botswana,[2] in the generalization of basic education, in never-ending university reforms and student movements. The traditional university, even in orderly societies, is in the process of becoming a museum, surrounded by living experiences of culture re-creation, which penetrate its less conspicuous openings, rejecting an education conceived merely as a conveyor-belt of the dominator's cultural matrix and as a means to impose the culture of the masters upon the dominated classes and peoples.

At the same time, in the absence of a democratic information flow, and in the face of the failure of the large organizations, public and private, to set up forums where the disciplines and the norms of efficiency of the technological civilization can be discussed, understood and agreed to by those who will suffer their effects, the world of the worker will continue to be not only alienating, but also the basis for authoritarianism, in capitalist as well as in socialist societies. This is why another development, which must be based on mass mobilization, will simultaneously be faced with the need to uproot the seeds of totalitarianism through participatory democracy, which such mobilization implies. Participatory democracy means that, before accepting any type of centralization, the what, why and for whom of general decisions will be discussed at the level of the worker, educational and political communities. In a critical review of the values inherited by contemporary societies, the idea of technical progress and rationality is not discarded, but redefined. Instead of the pseudo-rationality of the market—which in fact is the rationality of accumulation and of appropriation by a few of the results of the work of the majority—a social calculation of costs and benefits is now the aim. Instead of an increase in the product, the expansion of collective welfare is the target. This most certainly requires high accumulation and investment levels, but the orientation of investments and the forms of control over the accumulation process thus become the primary focus.

The discussion of this purpose of another development should not be confused with the debate between zero growth and "developmentalism"; with the confrontation between the insane attitude of those who say "blessed be pollution" and the naiveté of those who believe that it is better to stop producing than to contaminate the ecosystem: between those who preach the ruralization of the world and those who proclaim the virtues of urbanization at any price. In such terms, the discussion turns into a dialogue of the deaf.

When the advocates of another development insist that social rationality should prevail over pseudo-technical or instrumental rationality, they are simply reaffirming the fact that the contemporary world can count on richer and more varied alternatives; that if it is true that in order to share it is necessary to grow, it is not true that growth in itself will lead to a fair sharing of the fruits of technical progress among classes and nations.

In an effort of synthesis to express a more egalitarian style of development, requiring more participation and democratic control over decisions by those who suffer their consequences and, at the same time, substantive social rationality in the use of resources, in the use of space, in the choice of technologies and in the responsible consideration of the negative impacts which the process of economic growth may have on the environment, the term *ecodevelopment* was coined.[3] There is no place in ecodevelopment for the cynical position of those in rich countries who propose the non-development and non-pollution (therefore non-industrialization as they themselves conceive it) of the periphery. The supporters of ecodevelopment do not believe in freezing the *status quo* and curtailing the underdeveloped nations' chances of achieving a less needy material civilization, which would be the consequence of zero growth, but advocate instead a differentiated (thus respectful of the cultural, spatial and political characteristics of the Third World) and autonomous growth.

The concept and strategic goal which summarizes this style of development is that of *self-reliance*. This is a political category which rejects the idea that the technological advantage of the great powers is inevitable: self-reliance implies rejection of the monopoly over sophisticated technologies which is the form through which the central economies, and their dynamic sectors — the transnational corporations — seek to guarantee their domination over dependent Third World economies.

Until recently the unquestioned primacy of technology left Third World countries with almost no alternative but to copy the model of the industrial-predatory civilization in order to ensure their national integrity (or to maintain the illusion of it) and in order to carry out a process of industrial growth which would make it possible—maybe, and in the future—to increase the standard of living of their impoverished masses. The military discovery that guerrilla forces can defeat modern armies if and when backed by the people destroyed another technocratic illusion, in the course of a historical experience stretching from the French disaster in Dien Bien Phu to the United States defeat in Viet-Nam (which was considerably aided by the disillusionment of the cultural élites, of minorities and of young people in the United States, with the aims of the war).

Today, not only are there peoples pursuing other alternatives, but in the highly critical conscience of the more advanced techno-scientific spokesmen of the Third World countries, a conviction is being formed that:

- The technological model exhibited by the industrialized countries cannot be applied without provoking deep disturbances, if it is not accompanied by strong redefinitions of political control and its social consequences.
- Alternative viable solutions exist which require imagination, research and reorientation of investments (e.g., why maintain the same extremely expensive tradition of the Cloaca Maxima in cities of the Third World which still have no extensive sewerage systems, instead of searching for methods of eliminating residues through natural or organic techniques, for the house or neighbourhood units?).
- There are no good reasons to tie underdeveloped economies to forms of technological and economically exploitative dependence, based on trade-mark, know-how and other contracts. These could very well be transformed into assets of the national economies, provided the Third World countries organize themselves techno-scientifically and politically to control the activities of the transnational firms in this field and to compel them to share technical knowledge.
- The cultural revolution of the Third World countries should include among its goals the development of technically qualified cadres.

People in the Third World are convinced that alternative styles of development are possible—precisely because there is a crisis of confidence over the predatory-industrializing model among the élites of the industrialized countries, and because new paths for development and for international coexistence depend on the autonomous action of the men and women of the Third World. Belief in self-reliance is leading Third World people through their critical spokesmen and through some governments rather to look for mutual support than to trust in the now discredited aid from the centre (particularly that linked to military or corporation interests).

On the basis of such values, leaders of the international community at the United Nations and at specialized meetings (such as that resulting in the Cocoyoc Declaration)[4] and in special forums which are being created to discuss new strategies for development (such as the Third World Forum) have started to express the aims which should guide the new international order and give consistency to another development.

Inasmuch as the concept of self-reliance implicitly acknowledges the different historical experiences of the people and defends the real contribution which the impoverished masses have to offer towards the solution of their own problems, the movement of opinion which is at present under way is modest because it is totally honest. It does not propose formulas and "models" or "aid and assistance" plans. Another development requires that within the United Nations, in governments and among the élites, the vain pretension be done away with that the final objective is already known and that it is technically possible to define the programme of aid and planning that will show the way to the wonder world.

Therefore, the starting-point is completely opposite to that which inspired the unsuccessful "development decades." In that strategy the "gaps" between industrialized and Third World countries were computed; percentages of GNP which rich countries should offer as "contributions" to poor ones were defined; and specialized bodies appointed to give financial and technical support of the plans and programmes which would be applied in the Third World in order to bring it closer to the industrialized world.

It would be unfair and uncalled-for to say that the whole of the international cooperation apparatus failed. Some relevant experiences exist—in specific programmes which actually worked. And through these programmes and actions—especially through ventures such as the United Nations Regional Commissions—a rich exchange of opinions and experiences took place among Third World technicians and administrators and by these with institutions and individuals of the industrialized world, who were finally sensitized by the problems of the Third World countries. But as a system, international cooperation failed, inasmuch as it was carried out parallel to (and not even countering, when not favouring) international economic exploitation: reaffirming the existence of an asymmetric world order and of highly unequal national societies as well as propagating a deforming development model.

The reorganization of the world order should begin in the spirit of methodical humility which is now proposed to those wishing to cooperate in the field of international development, by some kind of collective criticism of the United Nations. This criticism should be based more on research and study of the variety of concrete experiences in dealing with critical situations faced by Third World countries than on the definition of mimetic development policies and the execution of such policies through the contemporary paraphernalia of "development plans."

An important institutional impediment in the United Nations system is to be found in the basically officious position assumed by all its bodies which, when operating in the field, are condemned to play a counterpoint to the national governments, marginalizing civil societies and giving non-governmental organizations an almost lip-service treatment. If new utopias, as we have seen, are conceived and acquire their force in social movements (feminism, anti-racial struggles, youth movements, urban protest organizations, forums for defending habitat and the environment, etc.) any international order intended to be legitimately representative within the emerging values, and any international organization wanting, in fact, to struggle shoulder to shoulder with the people (and not to act as an agency defending models to be imposed culturally on the people), should be more closely related to the roots of the national societies.

This requirement should result in a composite system at the level of the most active agencies of the international order which should provide a tribune, not only for governmental delegations, but for the voice of political minorities (they usually correspond to population majorities). Social categories such as consumers, workers (variously defined), women, ethnic and religious minorities, youth, poor peasants, shantytown dwellers, etc., should compose country delegations. This would offer greater authenticity to international forums and would enable countries to widen the style of representation based on the values of a participatory democracy.

At the level of formal equality among nations, the scope for reforms in the system based on the ideals of another development is endless. We need only refer to the veto power and the *de facto* situations which lead to the vetoing of minorities in the specialized financial bodies (the International Monetary Fund and the World Bank, for instance) as well as in political bodies. It would be unrealistic to propose abolishing economic and strategic inequalities among nations through declarations of ideals and intentions. But it would not be so illusory to propose a counter-

weight system, which would aim, for example, to organize Third World
delegation secretariats so as to set up and give consistency to informal
groups (such as that of the 77 or of the Non-aligned) or to regional
groups (such as the recently established Sistema Económico
Latinoamericano—SELA), or to specific groups in countries producing
raw materials—the first of which is OPEC. And it would be particularly
necessary—in order to be faithful to the principle of self-reliance—that
the Third World have access to organizational and financial resources, in
order to give a voice to the Third World countries in the discussion of
aims and experiences of development and in the easing of direct contacts
and exchange of experiences between leaders and practitioners of collective social movements.

Bringing about another development in Third World countries is even
harder. To begin with, it is necessary to circumscribe and demystify the
very notion of Third World: the historical experiences of these countries,
their relative degree of economic advance and the social and political systems existing in them are extremely varied. The language used is therefore
at times highly rhetorical when it alludes to the unity of the Third World.

The new approach to development problems starts with the recognition of the diversity of points of departure and of the present phase in the
historical process of the underdeveloped countries. Any pretence of im-
posing a unique framework on the aspirations and possibilities of these
countries would repeat the same mistake made in the past, when trying to
re-create in them the experience of industrialized countries. This warning
is necessary and valid, since no matter how fascinating the experience of
building socialist societies in countries of an agrarian-peasant economy
(as in Viet-Nam or Cambodia), or in countries limited in their historical
adventure owing to a relative lack of natural resources or to their colonial experience (e.g., Tanzania and Guinea now)—and also in countries
with cultural experience at least as ancient and diverse as in the west
(e.g., China, or Islamic countries in North Africa)—it would nevertheless be hasty and wrong to compare them, for example, to many countries in Latin America, some of which are highly urbanized, relatively industrialized and, though dependent, have almost completely assimilated
western culture (e.g., Argentina, Uruguay and Chile, and to a certain extent Brazil). The roads to equality, to participatory democracy and to
self-reliance in these countries follow completely different routes from
those of socialist agrarianism.

Conversely, the concretization of the axis and ideals of equality, of
participatory democracy, of the revitalization of regional space in
response to ecodevelopment, of activating basic forces in society, and of

self-reliance, in certain types of countries (for example, in rough terms, though with variations and qualifications specific to the Indian subcontinent, practically all the countries in southern Central Asia bordering the Indian Ocean down to the South-East Asian extremity) would seem to have elective similarities (which in fact are structural) with the model of egalitarian and frugal socialism which starts with agrarian expropriation and has its socio-political and economic basis in the commune—in the Chinese style. This characterization obviously does not commit these countries to agrarianism (China is industrializing), and the proletarian ideal of life is not excluded. But it colours the transition process with the hues of an almost direct democracy, of an anti-bureaucratic approach and of a puritan (in fact un-urban) renewal of life styles which separates them considerably from, for example, the political life style of the Maghreb, where agrarian feudalism is added to commercial colonialism. There the weight of an urbanization is based on craftsmanship and, in the strict sense, on the manufactures deriving from the strength of the bazaar— that inheritance of the Middle Ages—and all of it is organized through a cultural tradition based on hierarchies and exclusions much more differentiating than those to be found in Asian agrarian feudalism, itself already deteriorated by centuries of submission to multiple comprador bourgeoisies. Similarly, the richness of social situations derived from the coexistence of different forms of production, reorganized by neo-colonialism, succeeded in liquidating the traditional agrarian basis of many countries of black Africa, without substituting for it an urban-industrial or urban-mercantile economy able to survive without colonialist ties. In these countries the crisis of colonial domination and the passage to a style of free, self-sustaining, egalitarian and democratic development imposes the need to reinvent a society, thus giving the imagination of the Third World a large field for experimentation.

The opportunities open to Latin American countries in this sense are much more restricted. Many of them are going through a predetermined historical experience in the urban industrial destiny of their societies and there is no longer room (in some cases, there never was) to lay the groundwork of a communitarian mould for society. Others—especially those societies in which the weight of the Andean civilizations prior to colonization is still latent—have a bigger rural problem and any alternative development strategy should take into account what one of the most important social thinkers of the continent said about his country: a revolution is either made in terms of the Indian population or it is counterfeit. It goes without saying that even in these cases there is still a need to increase the technological efficiency of local economies, and we do not suggest that ruralization is all that is relevant to the historical experience of these countries. What is being considered is the definition and linking of strategic aims, which in order to be legitimate should always answer the question why and for whom and reflect the reality that the real subject of history is not individuals but social categories.

This brief outline of the varied alternatives and conditioning factors in the roads open to Third World countries in their struggle for autonomy and equality does not imply inaction or despair when confronted with such diversity. Though the roads are different the basic goals are the same. And indicators to measure performance should be devised, applied and criticized with at least as much enthusiasm as those invested in measuring economic growth. A little over two decades ago expressions such as gross national product, income per capita, import rates, etc., were unknown to most statesmen, journalists and students, in fact to people in general. With the development decades these measures of economic difference have become part of everyday language.

It is now time to reorient efforts to measure success in development by indicators centered on the *quality of life* and on *equality* in the distribution of goods and services. There has been progress in this field in the United Nations system (in the research efforts and systematizing of the United National Research Institute for Social Development [UNRISD], for instance), as well as in individual countries. But the point has not yet been reached at which, for example, international credits are tied to the objective advance of people's wellbeing and at which there are indicators on wellbeing as accurate as those at present measuring national solvency, the rate of inflation and the rate of growth.

Methodological instruments exist for measuring, for example, the rate of income concentration (such as the Gini coefficient), nutritional needs and minimum wage-level deficiencies. What does not yet exist—and this is an area in which the effort to attain another development should be invested—is the political will capable of transforming these indices into instruments of pressure to increase equality and improve the quality of life. It is therefore to be recommended that much effort be devoted to systematic measurement and wide publicity for the results of simple assessments to reveal, for example:

- the evolution of the rate of income concentration in each country
- the distribution of wealth and of salaries (including a comparative analysis at an international level of lowest and highest salaries by types of firms; average, median and modal salaries among types of firms in several countries; differences between salaries paid in

different countries for the same type of work, by the same transnational corporations, and so on)

- the ingredients of a basic rural and urban worker's shopping
  basket and the number of hours the worker uses in each country
  to acquire these common consumer goods
- a "time budget" in which the way different social classes spend
  their energies in leisure, work, transport, health care, etc., would
  be shown
- the coverage of social welfare systems, to identify in particular the
  relative degree of differentiation (or equality) in assistance services offered to different categories in each country
- the ways in which social welfare is financed, in order to evaluate
  its real effect as an instrument for income distribution and social
  equality, or to identify mechanisms — which are often to be found
  in underdeveloped countries — for transferring resources from the
  poor to the poorer without touching the overall distribution of
  wealth or the advantages of the higher income classes
- the mechanisms of tax systems, especially to expose such aspects
  as the proportion between direct and indirect taxes, etc.

The list of relevant social indicators is long and the selection strategy
should concentrate on those that are the most sensitive for the measurement of social equality. Nevertheless, the critical appraisal of present
development concepts does not end there: the concrete liberty of the people and participation in control over the decisions should also be included as parameters. In the search for methods to construct simple
indices that can be used systematically and have assured and universal
application everything remains to be done. The defence of basic liberties,
both individual and social, has been left to a few institutions and
organizations, generally private, and repeated denunciations made by
these organizations have lost their force from repetition and because they
stem from institutions which have themselves been accused many times
of defending private interests or of being ideologically dependent on one
particular party.

Is the time not ripe to begin through a movement springing from the
Third World to create a sort of Political Conscience Court, formed by
representatives of governments as well as of trade unions, universities,
churches and professions, in order to pass judgement annually — on the
basis of rules agreed to and previously established by the court — on the
degree of progress in political development of peoples and of governments? Instead of the models of liberty or of institutionalized oppression
which the centre proposes to the periphery, should we not look for in-

spiration to the participatory democracy arising in the Third World for the definition of codes of civil, social and political behaviour through which the effective advances of the people could be measured in the areas of expression of thought, organization of new fields of debate and decision, of rights assured to minorities and the opposition, of rejection of torture and violence?

The flaws of utopianism should not frighten those who not only wish to reform the economic and social orders, but the moral order as well. It was also utopian during the Cold War and during the McCarthy period to imagine that the sit-ins, the marches, the CIA accusations and telephone tappings and the pacific marches, would — in the United States itself — lead to a major break with high-handedness that ended in Watergate and the impossibility of continuing the war in Viet-Nam.

Is it impossible to propose, and start implementing standards for political conduct that will emerge from the dark depths of oppression in those very countries where violence and repression have been magnified into standards of national security? Such standards may finally reveal that the other development we are seeking, even if it is launched in the economic realm, opens up on the social plane, and acquires a political dimension through the equality it proposes and through the style of participation it advocates. But another development will only be fulfilled when it finds a means of transforming the utopia into daily reality, resorting to the human experience a dimension which although moral is not unreal. The strength of this character nevertheless does not derive from the individual's proud salvation, but from the humble recognition that the expression of existence and individual integrity depend on an agreement and an action which can only be collective. The self-reliance principle, in this sense, implies a hope and belief that it is already possible to inscribe in reality the goals we wish to attain.

It is with this conviction that the reconstruction of the international order and the establishment of more egalitarian, democratic and self-reliant national societies is proposed here. These new societies are not based on the underdevelopment of the periphery and the stagnation of the centre, but on a development style which has its *raison d'être* in the social calculation of costs and benefits.

Notes

1. See: Pierre Bourdieu and Yvette Delsant, "Le couturier et sa griffe: contribution à une théorie de la magie," *Paris Actes*, No. I, January 1975.
2. See: Patrick van Rensburg, *Report from Swaneng Hill. Education and*

Employment in an African Country, Uppsala, The Dag Hammarskjöld Foundation, 1974.

3. The best statement of this *problematique* is found in Ignacy Sachs, "Environment and Styles of Development," in: William H. Matthews (ed.), *Outer Limits and Human Needs*, Uppsala, The Dag Hammarskjöld Foundation, 1976.

4. See *Development Dialogue* (The Dag Hammarskjöld Foundation, Uppsala), No. 2, 1974.

Index